in memory of

CATHERINE

and R*FRED

ASHMAN

The Little Book of Bells

The Little Book of Bells

by

ERIC HATCH

With Sketches by

ERIC SLOANE

Duell, Sloan and Pearce
New York

First edition

Affiliate of
MEREDITH PRESS
Des Moines & New York

Library of Congress Catalogue Card Number: 64-13795

Manufactured in the United States of America for Meredith Press

VAN REES PRESS • NEW YORK

In appreciation of the wise counsel and friendship
Which made it possible
This book is dedicated to

DR. ALFRED F. RIZZOLO

Foreword

In the early afternoon of July 4 last year, I drove to Torrington, Connecticut. The short trip was made alone; I would have had it no other way. The downtown section of the city was deserted for the holiday except for an occasional car passing slowly along Main Street. I parked at an intersection in front of a department store whose window was devoted to a display of American flags, colonial documents, and bells.

I turned on the radio on the seat beside me, tuning in to a network station and toning the sound down to a whisper. Then I sat quietly and waited. The minutes passed. At 2 P.M., daylight-saving time, the almost complete silence of the city was broken. Church bells, first one and then another, sent their shimmering, silvery sounds echoing from the belfries. A moment before the radio had been broadcasting a ball game from Chicago, but this had been interrupted. In its place came the sound of bells from the state Capitol. I switched from station to station. From each came the peal of bells.

Feeling a little self-conscious and even a little foolish

though I was alone, I picked up the replica of the Williamsburgh Town Crier's Bell I had brought with me. I rang it. And I knew that in every state of the Union, in every major city, and in thousands of towns and villages across the land and around the world the bells of America were ringing a massive salute to the memory of the men who had given us freedom. I wanted to be a part of it. I rang my little bell and shamelessly wept with emotion.

This moment was the culmination of many months of effort. It all began when Eric Sloane and I joined in what was to become a project of patriotism. All our energies were to be devoted to a precisely timed national ringing of the bells. With the help of governors, state legislatures, individuals, and organizations of every kind, we had sown the wind. And the breezes of a summer day were to carry our message around the world.

When we set out on this mission, I realized that in the weeks and months ahead I should find myself in daily contact with bell-ringers and bell owners, and so I determined to learn something about their subject. I don't know what happened then. Perhaps some ancient temple bell whose vast vibrations still throb faintly on quiet winter nights cast a spell over me. I became enchanted with bells. And now I wish to share my small knowledge in the hope that others will also be touched by a little of the same magic.

E. H.

Contents

The Little Book of Bells

1. How the Bells Began

The bell was probably discovered by accident when primitive man began working with metals. The first resonance may have been caused by the striking of a metal dish. The edges of that dish were then gradually bent down to form skirts. And a crude version of the shape now so familiar was first fashioned.

True bell-making, however, did not come until man learned to make bronze by mixing copper and tin. An early bell of the bronze period was the quadrangular bell. Made from two bent plates of sheet iron and fastened together with iron rivets, this structure was then coated with bronze.

A bell of this type that remains intact today is the *Clog-an-eadhacta Phatraic* or "The Bell of the Will of St. Patrick." This little bell, 6 inches high, 4 3/4 inches wide at the shoulder, and 5 inches across at the base, is rung by hand. As its sound must be frightful, this may have been St. Patrick's secret weapon. No snake, if he were at all like the oriental snakes and addicted to sweet flute music, would have remained in Ireland and listened to the racket St. Patrick must have made when he rang his *Clog-an-eadhacta*. According to the *Annals of Ulster*, this bell was removed from St. Patrick's tomb by

St. Colomoille in A.D. 552 and is now preserved with its shrine in the National Museum of Ireland.

With the establishment of the Bronze Age, bells were taken seriously. (The actual business of making them has been traced back to 2697 B.C.) They were cast in molds, and though each bell had a resonance, once in a while, almost as if by accident, one emerged with a true tone of some beauty. But the arrival at anything approximating present bells was a long way off.

Much more rapid was the development of a totally different type of bell, whose contours and tone quality have remained the same throughout the ages. Known for millenniums as the Crotal, this bell is a little sphere with small holes in its sides and a tiny ball, originally of stone, now of metal, inside it. The sleigh bell is an example of this type; and today one may find these Crotal bells on Christmas trees, on children's rattles, or on the ankles of Pueblo Indian dancers.

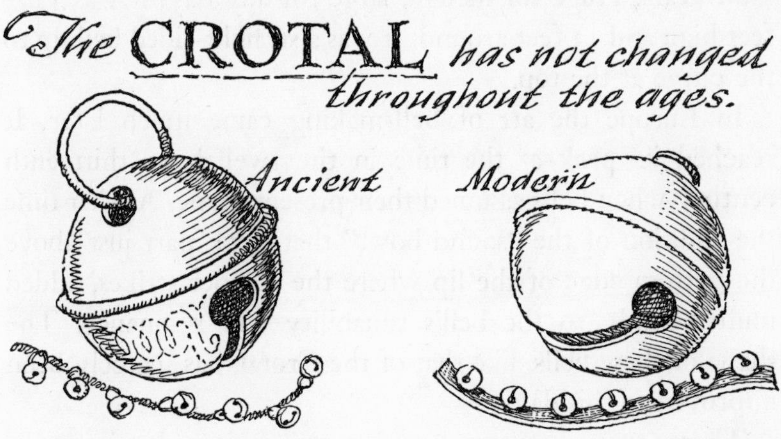
The CROTAL has not changed throughout the ages.
Ancient
Modern

Beyond any doubt these Crotals are the same little golden bells referred to in Exodus XXVIII: 33–34 as those commanded to be made for the adornment of Ephod of Aaron: "Upon the hem pomegranates of blue, and of purple, and of scarlet: . . . and bells of gold between them round about; a golden bell and a pomegranate, a golden bell and a pomegranate." The Crotal is a true bell form and is the most ancient of all forms. The marked resemblance between the ancient and modern Crotal is extraordinary. I cannot think of any other object that was created thousands of years ago in a form so perfect that no one since has been able to find a way of improving it.

The first bells to be foundry-cast in the western world did not appear until the late sixth or early seventh century. In the Orient the art of bell-making was much further advanced. The same emperor who built the Great Wall of China in 220 B.C. is mentioned by historians as having cast huge bells. And at one time in the dim mists of ancient history, the Great Bell of Pekin was cast. This bell may be as old as four thousand years. Huge for its day, large for any day, it was 14½ feet high and 13 feet around. It was a straight-sided bell up to the curve at the top.

In Europe the art of bell-making came much later. It reached its peak at the time in the twelfth or thirteenth century when bells assumed their present shape. At that time the addition of the "sound bow," that thick part just above the bottom edge of the lip where the clapper strikes, added immeasurably to the bell's tunability and resonance. The shape of these bells, like that of the Crotal, has scarcely been improved to this day.

There was, however, one more major development, although not in the bell itself. This came in the nineteenth century with the invention of a tuning machine, really no more than a vertical lathe. The process of bell-tuning then became scientific.

I never realized until I began visiting research libraries that bells were tuned. I thought they just rang. I knew that molds of some sort were made in the shape of a bell; metal was poured into them; and then, having had time to cool, the outside of these molds was removed; and there was the bell.

I thought some bells turned out treble and some bass, some dissonant and some true. I couldn't have been more mistaken. Even in the old days a bell-founder setting out to cast a "ring" or set of bells would try to shape them so that they would all have different notes, yet all emerge from the mold exactly in tune with each other, in harmony. Maybe once in a lifetime he'd be successful. When he was, it became a cause for wild celebration, and the peal he had cast was known as

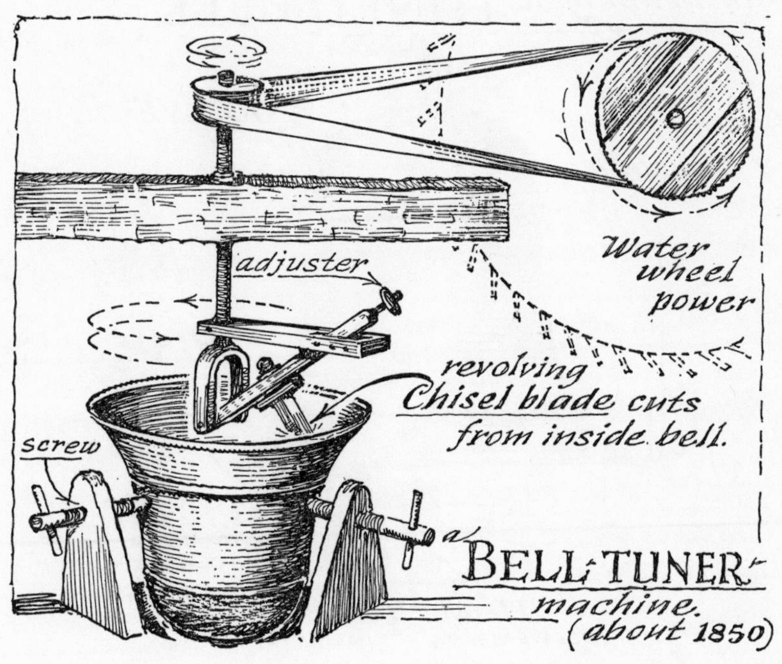

a "virgin ring." Such a bell-founder would not think highly of any tuned bell if the tuning were done by hacking away at the metal of the bell near the lip edge with a hammer and chisel. This process was laborious, slow, and noisy almost beyond endurance. However, one Englishman named Laurence Huddlestone, who was a bell-tuner by trade, spent his life going about with his hammer and chisel from church to church; and when he found bells whose sound was wrong, without asking anyone he simply went to work and tuned them.

At first glance this science of tuning bells might appear to

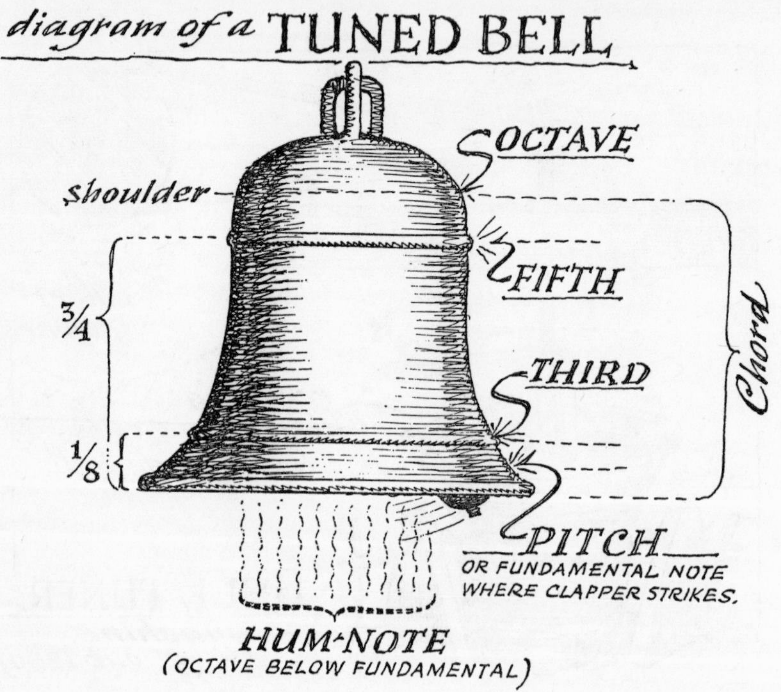

be of interest only to tintinnabulologists, campanologists, carillonneurs, change ringers, and sextons. This is far from true, particularly when you consider a carillon such as the one at Riverside Church in New York City. This carillon is composed of seventy-two separate bells and is probably the most public musical instrument in the world. Consider, too, that a tuned bell doesn't sound just one note. It sounds a chord of five notes. When you take into account the number of people who live within hearing distance of 490 Riverside Drive, thousands of people who don't even know they are interested in bell-tuning, you can see why any self-respecting carillonneur would feel just a little embarrassed if his bells were not in tune. After all, with five notes to a bell, the carillon totals 360 separate notes; and to make things tougher, the bourdon, or tenor bell, in the Riverside carillon has thirteen recognizable tones–recognizable to a carillonneur, that is.

To understand how one bell produces all these different notes, we must consider harmonics. An harmonic is described in Webster's dictionary as: "an overtone, esp. one produced by a vibration or frequency which is an integral multiple of the vibration rate producing the fundamental."

The Rev. George S. Tyack, of England wrote in 1898:

> A bell in perfect tune sounds a perfect chord. There is the note struck out directly by the clapper from the sound bow; this booms out most prominently and if the pitch of the bell be spoken of, it is this tone to which reference is made. But as the vibrations of the stroke set the whole mass of metal throbbing, the following notes are also sounded; at one eighth of the height of the bell from the brim, a third above the fundamental note is given; at three quarters of the height, a fifth; and at the shoulder the chord is completed by the octave. Besides these there is also developed from them the "hum note," as it is called, consisting of the note an octave below the fundamental.

This is the Simpson Principle of bell-tuning. The old system was to tune to the natural harmonics of the strike note with the hum note a seventh below. Here is the sheet music for tuning a bell:

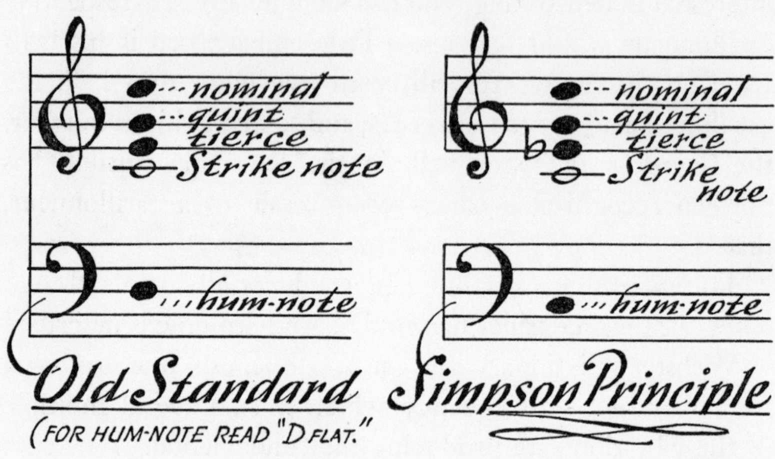

This seems thoroughly convincing, yet to my surprise it is a very controversial subject. Some carillonneurs angrily cry out, "Not so!" Others say, "You have to watch old Tyack—very frivolous chap!" But I'm going to stick to the Tyack version for the origin of noises, as the dissenters seem reluctant to make a flat statement as to just how, in their opinion, the chord is formed.

2.
the BIGGEST BELL *in the world.*

The biggest bell ever made never uttered a sound. However, if this book finds its way behind the iron curtain, I wouldn't be surprised if a few billion rubles weren't spent in a belated attempt to make it ring. But this would present a problem, not only because eleven tons of the bell are missing, but also because, even without that, it weighs roughly 423,000 pounds.

This behemoth of bells was cast by a founder named Michael Motorine in 1734, during the reign of Empress Anne of Russia. It was 19 feet high, 22½ feet in diameter and just under 2 feet thick. Its clapper, or tongue, was 14 feet long and 6 feet in circumference at its extreme width. As would seem necessary for ringing such a monster, instead of the bell itself being swung, the clapper was supposed to be swung. Noblemen and others who were enthusiastic about making the biggest bell in the world eagerly contributed seventy thousand pounds of gold and silver to the melting pot. Unfortunately, however, bronze is best for bells; and these precious metals served only to deaden any potential tone.

In 1737, this impressive mass of metal was somehow actually lifted into the air and supended from a frame built of tremendous wooden beams at one end of the Kremlin. But the god that governs bells must have decided it was never to ring. A fire broke out in the Kremlin, ate its way to the belfry, and before it could be brought under control chewed away the supporting timbers. The bell, which was called the great Tsar Kolokol and nicknamed Ivan Kiliki or Big John, fell so mightily that it dug 30 feet into the ground. And there it lay for exactly a hundred years, a monument to its own unheard voice. Then, by means of block and tackle and the united efforts of six hundred soldiers, Tsar Kolokol was hoisted out of the ground and slid onto a pedestal. As a bell it was a failure; but it does make a very nice chapel, for which purpose it is still used.

The Russians claim this was the biggest bell in the world; it did not ring, however, and so it does not really count. They *may*, however, have broken the record with Tsar Kolokol's predecessor. First cast in 1654, this bell was later melted down, recast with additional metal, and became Tsar Kolokol. It weighed 260,000 pounds and *did* ring, with fifty men hauling its giant clapper, twenty-five to a side. But there is still another giant bell, hanging in a pagoda at Mingoon, in Burma. Closer in shape to a bell of the West than most Eastern bells, its weight has been estimated at ninety tons and upward. A certain Dr. Chill writing in *Travel Magazine* in October, 1896, said of this bell, "[it] . . . is the largest in the world (not excepting the well-known Russian bell in

One way to ring a bell . . (Russian way)

Moscow), and can easily hold within it a picnic party of fifty people." Well, that's one way of measuring bells.

Although Russia probably has more big bells than any other country, China also has a good many. Aside from the difference in shape, you can always tell an Eastern bell from a Western one by the fact that the Eastern one doesn't have

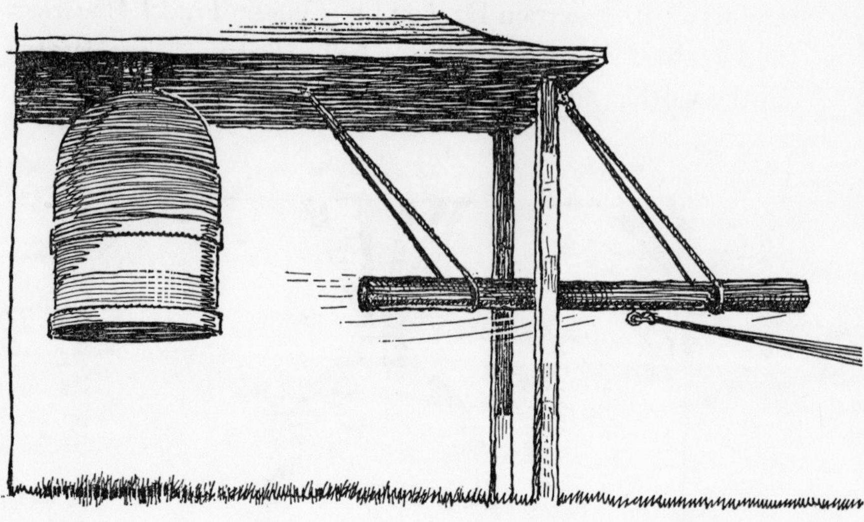

a clapper. Instead, mounted in the air beside it and suspended by ropes or chains in a horizontal position, is the trunk of a good-sized tree. To sound the bell, temple priests haul the trunk back as far as they can, then let her go. As the beam rebounds, they grab it. These big temple bells are called "the awakeners of Buddha," and their voices are deep, rich, mellow, and prolonged. The priests and the deeply religious believe implicitly that the sound of these chords and harmonics trembling on the air form the syllables, "*Na-ō-mi-to-fah*"—the soul of Asia calling out to the believers, "O Buddha, hail!"

Let us glance at some of the things Christians have believed about their bells. The following inscription appears on a medieval English bell:

FULGORA GRANGO, DISSIPITO VENTOS

or, in translation from the Latin:

Another way of ringing a bell . . .

(Oriental fashion)

"The lightning I shatter, the hurricane scatter."

And another, on a medieval bell at Otterham, Cornwall:

VOCE MEA VIVA DEPELLA CUNCTA NOCIVA

"With my living voice I drive away harmful things."

To show that this sort of inscription really was popular with the parishioners, here is a quotation from the *Golden Legend of Wynken de Worde*, an ancient printer:

> It is said, the evil spirytes, that ben in the regyon of thayre, doubte moche when they here the bells rongen: and this is the same why the bells rongen when it thondreth and when grete tempeste and outrages of wether happen, to the end that feinds and wycked spirytes should be abashed and flee, and cease the movynge of tempest.

Around 1562 the clergy were split on this matter of church bells abashing evil "spirytes" and causing them to quit blowing up a storm. The Most Reverend Pilkington, bishop of Durham, said ringing sacred bells for the above purpose was unlawful. As he put it:

> You know, when there was a storm or fearful weather, then we rang the holy bells; they were they that must make all things well; they must drive away the devil! But I tell you, if the holy bells would serve against the devil, or that he might be put away through their sound, no doubt we would soon banish him out of all England; for I think if all the bells of England should be rung together at a certain hour, there would be almost no place but some bells might be heard there, and so the devil should have no abiding place in England.

But the bishop of Malta did not agree and, as recently as 1852, in the midst of a howling gale ordered his church bells rung to drive the storm away. Also in the past century, the bishop of Chalons christened a peal of church bells and in the sermon that was part of the christening ritual said:

> The bells, placed like sentinels in the towers, watch over us, and turn away from us temptations of the enemy of our salvation, as well as storms and tempests.
>
> They speak and pray for us in our troubles, they inform Heaven of the necessity of earth.

The age of superstition in religion is partially past; and for the moment, at least, the imagined power of church bells over demons is forgotten. Church bells, however, still retain a very definite power over the minds and emotions of people, for their sounding has been a part of the ritual of most religions for fifteen hundred years. They have called man to worship, they have pealed at his marriage, and they have

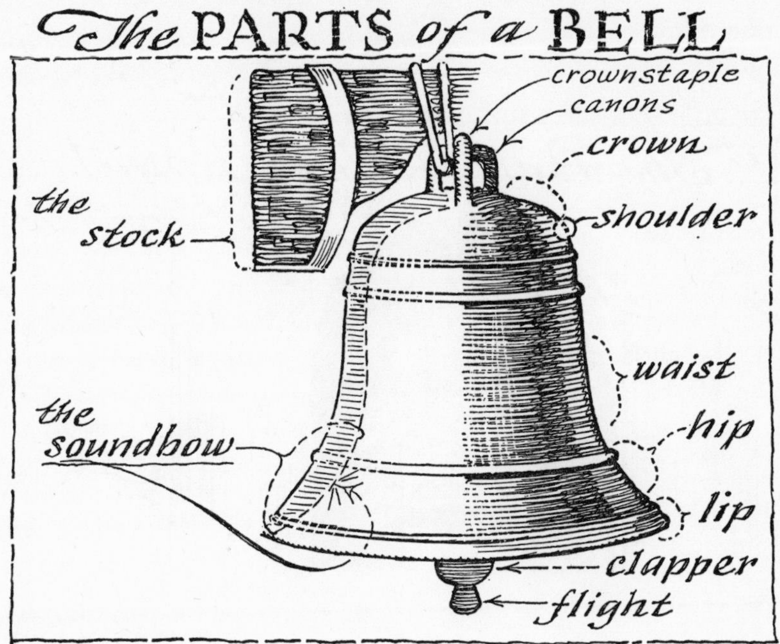

tolled his death, ringing thrice three times for the death of a man, thrice two for the death of a woman, and then in slow measured strokes the number of years of life on earth.* They have rung man's alarms for fire, flood, and hurricane; and they have signaled peace at the end of his wars. When they ring they cannot help but cause some emotional reaction. For even in the simple striking of the hour by a familiar town clock, the chord of the bell strikes a chord in the mind of its hearer.

* The possible origin of this is found quoted in an English publication called *Manners and Customs.* "The fourme of the Trinity was founden in manne, that was Adam our forefadir, of earth, oon personne, and Eve of Adam the secunde persone, and of them both was the third persone: at the death of a manne three bellis shulde be ronge, as his knyll, in worscheppe of the Trinetee, and for the womanne, who was the secunde persone of the Trinetee two bellis should be rungen."

3

The Bell of Port Royal

Today Jamaica is civilized and sophisticated. In the wintertime, Americans who want to switch from bourbon to rum or from sun lamps to sunshine, visit Kingston, Montego Bay, or several other Jamaican resorts. The island is now so cultivated that it is hard to remember that it was once one of the wildest spots in the world.

Kingston has a lovely, almost landlocked harbor. Yet Sir Henry Morgan, once admiral and governor of Jamaica, never heard of Kingston Harbor. It was Port Royal Harbor in the 1860's; and the town of Port Royal, on the tip of the curved point of land forming the sheltered harbor, was buccaneer capital of the Caribbean. It was bursting with wild men, loose women, captured Spanish silver and gold, and captive slaves, white as well as black. It was a prime town of sin; of pleasure for some, of deep anguish for others. These aspects of Port Royal have captured writers' imaginations and appear in their historical novels. That there was a church in Port Royal seems to have been entirely forgotten.

The church was a lovely one, with a bell tower made of well-fitted stones. It was a comfortable church to enter because there was always plenty of room for the congregation. The church bell had been cast in Spain; the parish priest who rang it maintained all the old traditions of the monastery where he had trained, religiously pulling away at the rope and ringing the hours. It gave him something to do and kept him from being lonely.

From time to time he used to go into the confessional and confess to himself of his angry thoughts and issue penances to himself. It was the only use the confessional got, for which in some ways he was thankful. His firm conviction was that if the whole population of Port Royal ever began confessing their sins, he would in short order get the notion he was dead and the Lord had committed him to hell. He prayed a great deal, mostly for strength, and often for the Lord to take violent vengeance on the sinners. After these prayers he would rush to the confessional. Praying for violence in a place that was already glutted with violence didn't seem Christian.

It was a long time before his prayers were answered, but they were. For on a very still and starshot night in the year sixteen hundred and ninety two, the bell in the stone tower of the Port Royal church began to ring. The sound was just a vibration at first, a soft tapping of the clapper against the bell as though someone were anxious to ring yet afraid of waking the town. Then the sound grew to a loud, measured stroke that awakened the priest in his nearby house. He hurried to the church. But the church and the bell tower were empty, though the bell itself was now ringing with a wild, unbridled clanging; the rope was writhing and snapping like a dancing snake.

Pausing only to dip his fingers in the holy water of the font, the priest crossed himself and ran on, stumbling through the darkness and out of the town toward the mainland. Twenty years after the buccaneers had quieted down and four years after their prince, Sir Henry Morgan, had himself died there in Jamaica, the great vengeance had come. The few who had regularly heeded the voice of the bell did so now and followed the priest through the darkness.

The next morning the streets of Port Royal were cleansed of sin, washed clean by the warm, green waves of the Caribbean. And they would stay cleansed, for the ruins of the whole town were tumbled about on the ocean floor. The bell tower of the church still stood, however, its bell once again quiet. But tropical fish now moved in and out of the belfry, and occasional swells swayed the giant bell clapper ever so slightly.

The bell was quiet, but not quite silenced. Once again, two centuries later, it spoke its warning. This time it was only faintly heard or perhaps just imagined by the people of Kingston, a thriving town across the lovely harbor. But to the native fishermen, descendants of slaves brought to Port Royal so long ago, who were making their way to sea in their fragile canoes for the night's work, the warning of the bell beneath the sea was loud and real. In the manner of all primitive peoples, the story of the "earthquake bell" had been handed down from generation to generation. They *knew*, and they put back to port. In a matter of hours, earthquake and tidal wave had once again all but destroyed Kingston.

The next morning . . .
. . . the bell was silent.

That was in 1909. I believe the story because I have seen the bell tower looming mistily through the clear water, some twenty feet below the surface. I was rowed out to it by a native one morning in 1922. He knew about the bell ringing for the earthquake; he had heard it himself. For he was one of the fishermen who had been putting to sea that night. As he told me the story he dipped his fingers in the sea and crossed himself.

4

Change Ringing.

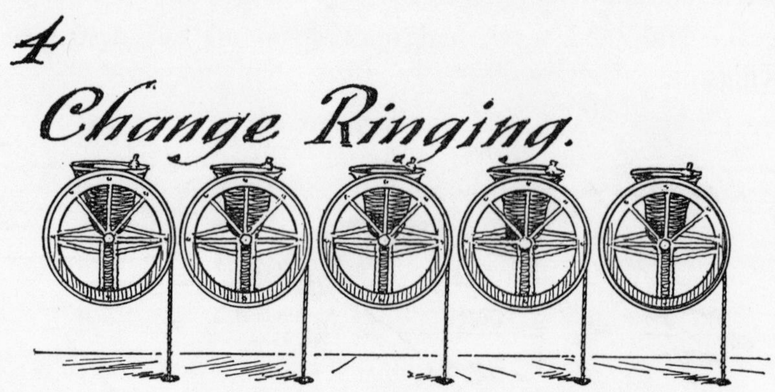

Change ringers and carillonneurs are the aristocrats of the bell world. Both groups are so ancient that their history is almost lost in antiquity. Of the two, the carillonneurs who play tunes, hymns, and fugues are the more musical. The change ringers, however, are the more colorful. And to explain change ringing I must introduce a few basic facts.

The church bell is usually hung in a frame on an axle. The bell is rung by pulling on a rope that goes around a wheel fastened securely to the axle. This wheel has a groove the bell rope fits into, and at one point the rope passes

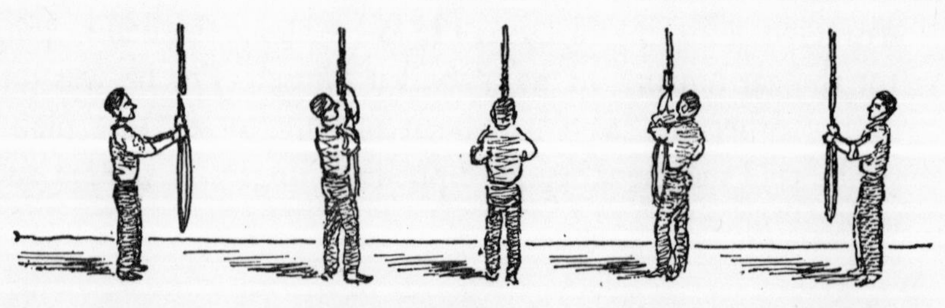

through to the inside of the wheel and is made fast to one of the spokes.

A *ring of bells*, often in change ringing called a *peal*, is a group of bells hung in the manner of an ordinary church bell except that they all rest upside down—they look like a nest of huge baby birds with their mouths open. A wooden device called a "stay," attached to the stock and resting against a "slider bar," keeps the bells from swinging over and maintains their balance in this upright position. The ringer pulls just hard enough so the bell will lose balance and swing down, strike, then rise up on the other side of its axle and remain there. The stay thus comes gently to rest against the opposite side of the slider. A very neat and acrobatic trick.

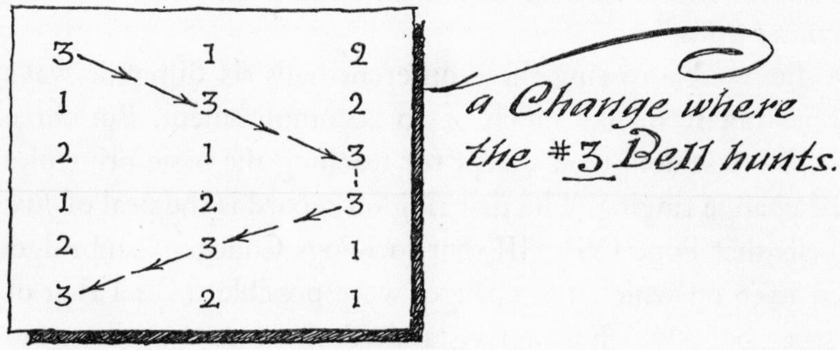

Change ringing is a trick of mathematics. If, for instance, you have a ring of three bells and you ring number one, then two, then three. you would not have rung a "change." But if you ring number two, then one, then three, you would have rung one change.

With a ring of three bells there are six possible changes.

You start ringing them in order, number one, number two, number three. This is called a "round."

In this example the number one bell is described as "hunting." * Switching places it goes from one end of the line to the other and then hunts its way back to where it began. This change, according to the language of the change ringers, is "true." You could of course do this in reverse and find the number three bell hunting. This pattern can also be repeated with the number two bell hunting, and at first glance it would appear that the mathematics quoted are incorrect and there are not six but eighteen possible changes from a set of three bells; but this is wrong. Change ringers for centuries have had their own laws and the second two sets are variations, not changes. In a contest the judge would throw these out as "false" since they contain repetitions, or "false course-ends."

Being able to ring three different bells six different ways does not seem like much of an accomplishment. But three bells are seldom used except for teaching the basic principles of change ringing. The first ring on record is the peal of *five* bells that Pope Calixt III sent to Kings College, Cambridge, in 1456 on which 120 changes were possible. (On a ring of seven bells, which is pretty standard, there are actually 5,040 potential changes. This is known as a triple.) At Kent School,

* The lingua obscura of change ringing is very difficult. The Reverend A. Gatty, M.A., as long ago as 1848 gave up trying to explain change-ringing terminology. Writing in *The Bell*, he said: " 'Great are the mysteries of bell ringing!' says Dr. Southey. 'The very terms are enough to frighten an amateur from any sort of explanation—*hunting*, *dodging*, *snapping*, and *place making*; *plain bobs*, *bob-triples*, *bob-majors*, and even up to *grandsire-bob-caters*. Heigho! Who can hope to translate all this gibberish to the uninitiated?' "

Connecticut, six bells out of a peal of ten are used; all six ring, each striking separately and distinctly, within only two seconds. The school's most impressive performance to date occurred during Easter, 1961, when it rang a "quarter peal"

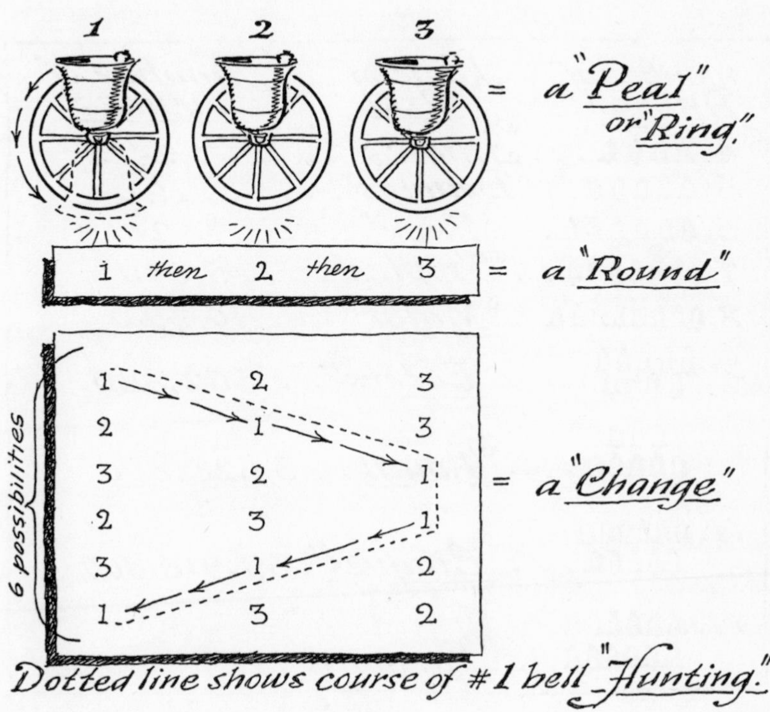

totaling 1,260 changes. This took forty-five minutes of steady ringing, for there are no pauses between changes. To appreciate fully the physical and mental effort that can be put into change ringing, take the all-time record. On Saturday, July 21, 1923, at the Church of St. Chad in Cheshire, England, the Chester Diocesan Guild, consisting of eight ringers, rang a peal of Kent Treble Bob Major, which totaled an appalling 17,280 changes. This took them exactly ten hours and is the official record. What is remarkable is not only that eight men could ring these huge bells steadily for ten hours but also that they could ring that number of changes

number of Bells	Name of Peal	Number of Changes
4	"Singles"	24
5	"Doubles"	120
6	"Minor"	720
7	"Triples"	5,040
8	"Major"	40,320
9	"Caters"	362,880
10	"Royal"	3,628,800
11	"Cinques"	39,916,800
12	"Maximus"	479,001,600!

surrounded by judges and timekeepers and not once ring a single bell at the wrong time or in the wrong order. There was one other ring of 18,240 changes completed by another group in eleven hours and thirteen minutes; but it didn't count, for somebody slipped and the composition was judged to be mathematically incorrect according to the rules of this ancient and weird ritual, because of false course-ends! On a maximus, or set of twelve bells, it would be mathematically possible to produce 479,001,600 changes. But this would take 137 years, and nobody's attention span is that long. But you are now able to see how change ringing can become a strange and fanatic pursuit.

At Kent School there is a change-ringing belfry patterned on the ancient belfries of England. It is a square room with bare walls and casement windows looking out over lovely, wooded hills. As one enters, by a flight of stone steps leading up from the chapel, he feels the dry coldness of an ancient castle tower. The ceiling is thirty feet high, and the room is quiet when the bells are not ringing.

The ropes hang in a somewhat circular pattern, with velvet handgrips nearly four feet long starting about five feet above the floor. The end of the rope is caught up in a loop rather suggestive of a hangman's noose. On my first visit I had no sooner gone into the ringing room than I was tempted by the handgrips. I walked to the nearest one and took hold. I just wanted to feel it, not pull it, but Mr. William Howard, my host, thought otherwise. I happened to glance at him as I reached up, and the horrified expression on his face made me freeze.

"*No!*" he cried in alarm. Then he explained that the bell at the other end of that rope weighed over a ton and was very delicately balanced. If I had given the rope a hard pull, the stay holding the bell in balance would have broken. The bell would have continued to ring; the wheel the rope was attached to would have spun around and gone right on spinning and, if I had not let go quickly, I should have been hoisted to the top of the belfry.

Considering this, I stepped well away from the rope.

Then I asked, "Mr. Howard, has this actually ever happened with the boys?"

He nodded. "Oh sure, but they're always warned about it when they start learning to ring. In spite of that, they still freeze to the grip occasionally and up they go."

"How high?"

"The thing at the other end of this rope weighs over a ton."

"Well," he said, "I've never seen one go up more than about eight feet. When the bells are hanging in the down position set for 'chiming,' the boys go up a ways just for fun." He smiled. "Like this."

He walked over to one of the ropes, seized the handgrip, and pulled down hard. As the rope went up Mr. Howard was lifted, perhaps six feet. Then as the rope descended, so did Mr. Howard, landing gracefully back on his feet.

A few Sundays later I returned to Kent and climbed up the belfry while the boys of the Bell Ringers Guild did change ringing on a peal of six bells. It's a little hard to describe the feeling you get; the boys in their Sunday suits minus jackets, looking exactly like photographs of English bell-ringers of the nineteenth century. The same rapt expressions on their faces; sweat pouring off them despite the open windows, freezing weather, and snow falling outside; the great bell booming and humming; the treble bells cascading notes out over the hills, dropping Christmas wreaths of sound over the Housatonic River and the school standing on its bank. And the ever changing sequences of the bells, sad one minute, gay the next.

There is an excitement about being in the midst of this, so close to the bells themselves, an elation that made me understand the mad, acrobatic bell-ringers of Seville, whom you will meet later.

When the change ringing was finished, the boys fought the bells, quite literally, so they would swing slower and slower and finally stop in the normal down position of a church bell. The boys wanted to practice Christmas carols, using the bells as chimes. This is done by pulling a different set of very thin ropes set in a panel on the wall; these are connected to hammers that strike the now stationary bells on the inside of the lip.

"Come on over," said Mr. Howard. "I'd like to have you get the feel of the tenor, the one I usually ring. She's down," he said. "You'll be all right."

I went over to the rope, seized the grip, and pulled. This was the big bell. There were 2,750 pounds of it over us, ready to spring to life. It moved. The grip went down a little as it began to swing, then up, down further, up fast, down still further, I felt a tingle all over me. I had made it do that! What a wonderful feeling! The grip started rushing up. I hung onto it with both hands as it rose, and up into the air I went with it.

"Hey!" yelled Mr. Howard.

When I came down, Mr. Howard and David Bailey, chairman of the Guild, put their arms around me to add their weight to mine so there would be no question of my taking off again.

I had read about bells having lives of their own in the minds of superstitious folk of other centuries. Of *course* they have! I know "my" bell seemed to come alive the moment I began to pull on the rope. Sheer weight and momentum give a bell an existence of its own. When the momentum is lost, it dies.

5
Change Ringers

Change ringers have remained the same throughout the ages, except for a greatly modified thirst. Present-day groups whose societies began in the 1400's have inherited a strange and rich remembrance.

Change ringers were colorful. Even the names of their groups, which were more like athletic clubs than intellectual societies, were colorful.

I have a picture of the Ancient Society of College Youths that was taken in 1907. There are twelve men in it. At a guess, only one of the College Youths is under forty, three of them must be at least fifty, and one is in his sixties. But this name was typical. There were also the Bromley Youths, the Croyden Youths, the Cumberland Youths, the Surrey Youths, and so on. The Western Green Caps sound sporty, but more realistic is the name of another group of ringers known simply as The Leatherhead.

At one period in England their competitions were as avidly followed as today's cricket and soccer matches. Quite

When I am filled with liquor strong.
Each man must drink & then ding-dong.
Drink not too much to Cloud your Knobbs
Lest you forget to make the bobbs!
... a Gift of
John Pattman, Beccles.

a few of the ancient societies are still in existence; their membership still maintains big-league status in the "sport," for that is exactly what they consider change ringing to be. Strangely enough, although their performances took place in a church, as a group they did not necessarily have a religious affiliation with any church. They were occasionally paid performers, and they were always given the run of the belfry for practice whenever they wished.

In the latter part of the eighteenth century and in the early decades of the nineteenth, the change ringers were a lively group. Frequently the prizes for their contests were liquid. In fact, it was traditional that a part of the ringers' pay was a gallon jug kept filled during working hours. The "ringers' jugs," or "jacks," as they are often called, have some antique value. A number of these jugs have been moved from churches to museums. Made of leather, metal, and earthenware, their inscriptions describe the bell-ringer of the day or at least indicate his thirst.

One pitcher preserved at Hinderclay, in Suffolk, bears the inscription:

From London I was sent,
As plainly doth appear
it was to this intent—
to be filled with strong beer.
Pray to remember the pitcher when empty.

Perhaps the prize indication of the ringers' chronic thirst is the inscription on a bell dated 1702 that hangs at Walsgrave in Warwickshire:

HARKEN DO YE HEARE OVR CLAPERES WANT BEERE

The fact that the spirited sportsmen of those days were not in the least slowed down by the amount of beer and ale they drank is borne out by a verse written by the parish clerk of St. Peter's Church in Norfolk. He lived near the church where the change ringers were in the habit of practicing at six on Sunday mornings. One day he reached the point where, so far as bells were concerned, he was finished. He wrote:

Ye rascally ringers, inveterate foes,
Disturbers of those who are fond of repose.
I wish, for the peace and the quiet of these lands
That ye had round your necks what ye pull with your hands.

Sadly for this man the time of "dumb practice" had not yet arrived when change ringers exercised on mute bells.

The rich days of the great change ringers have gone, but their independent attitude remains to this day one of their inherent characteristics. At Kent School we have a good example. The peal of ten bells was presented to that school in 1931 by Frank Humphreys and his wife. The bells were cast in England and were first rung in 1932. They belong to the school; but the students' Bell Ringers Guild of Kent, under the aegis of its faculty advisor, Mr. Howard, has full charge of their ringing.

On my first visit to the school I asked Mr. Howard when the guild would next be ringing. He said they usually rang from ten thirty until quarter of eleven Sunday mornings as well as sometimes in the late afternoon. I questioned him as to what afternoons. He answered that nobody knew, for it was entirely up to the boys; but that he might be able to find out a little ahead of time some day because he occasionally rang that big tenor bell in the peal band with them. I gather he was allowed to ring the bell by special permission, for he is one of the administrative executives of the school.

The most interesting thing he told me about this guild was that for one year after the bells were installed, there was a professional ringer at the school; but since then—for over thirty years now—the boys have handled the entire program themselves. The lore and the learning and the teaching has been handed down from class to class and from generation to generation. To me, this is fine and just how it should be, with anything so splendidly ancient.

There are very few active peals in this country. The most skillfully used is the new peal of ten bells at Groton School in Massachusetts. Change ringing is taken seriously at Groton. Russell Young, the ringing master, went to England to study the art before moving into the post; each year a group of Groton bell-ringers follow his path to the home of ringing. A second active peal is at Kent. At Ann Arbor, Michigan, there is a peal that I understand has not been used in years. (They favor hand-bell choirs at the university, and their "Spartan Bell Ringers" are regarded as just about the best.) There is also a peal at the Perkins Institute for the Blind in Boston, and sometimes it is rung by the "Grotties" and by the boys from Kent. Very recently a splendid new peal has been installed in the Episcopal Cathedral in Washington, D.C.

Our oldest change-ringing peal is as American as the thirteen colonies, yet so traveled as to be almost international. The bells hang now where they have hung always—well almost always—in the bell tower of St. Michael's Episcopal Church in Charleston, South Carolina. They are a change-ringing peal, no longer rung by hand but by the verdonic system.*

The bells of St. Michael's were hung in the mid-seventeen hundreds and were immediately called "the voice of

* The I. T. Verdin Company of Cincinnati, who imports cast bells from Petit and Fritzen, Founders, in Holland, coined the word *verdonic* in keeping with their competitor, Schulmerich, who had coined *carillonic*. The Verdin Company is what you might call "everyman's sexton," for they make electric timers and ringing mechanisms that can be placed on any existing bell to make it ring the hours or just about anything else you want.

Charleston." One black April night the signal lanterns were hung in the North Church in Boston and the countryside flamed into war.

In Charleston an English major stole the beautiful peal of bells from St. Michael's tower. The modern phrase would be "he liberated them," for he shipped them to England. There he sold them for private profit. It is doubtful whether he cared that by a small miracle he had actually sold the bells to a man who had formerly been a merchant in Charleston, who knew the bells and loved them so much he took care of them until the war's end and shipped them back to St. Michael's Church!

Once again the bells pealed the hours. Once again their notes were as much a part of the city of Charleston as the splashing of waves against the sea wall.

Then America was back at war with England, and this time the vestry of St. Michael's decided to move the bells to a remote church in Columbia, South Carolina. But alas this town, the church—and the bells—were burned by the British. What was to be done? Since the Revolution the British had proved themselves to be gentlemen and sportsmen, so the people of Charleston gathered the remains of their treasured bells and shipped them to England! There they were recast by the late enemy at the White Chapel Foundry, the same foundry that had cast the Liberty Bell.

Perhaps that's why the treble bells of that particular peal seem to have in them notes of laughter. Why not? They've crossed the ocean five times.

When Richard Fell, rector of St. Michael's, made a tape recording of his bells for a commemorative Independence Day record, he told me that the bells of St. Michael's had rung every Fourth of July since the first one (at least when they weren't in the hands of the British). He suggested that for the recording they might play the tunes and chimings they have always played on the Fourth. I said that was fine; then Mr. Fell, just a little hesitantly, added, "Perhaps I'd better explain to you that one of the tunes we play is not exactly what you might expect. You see, close to a century ago, the

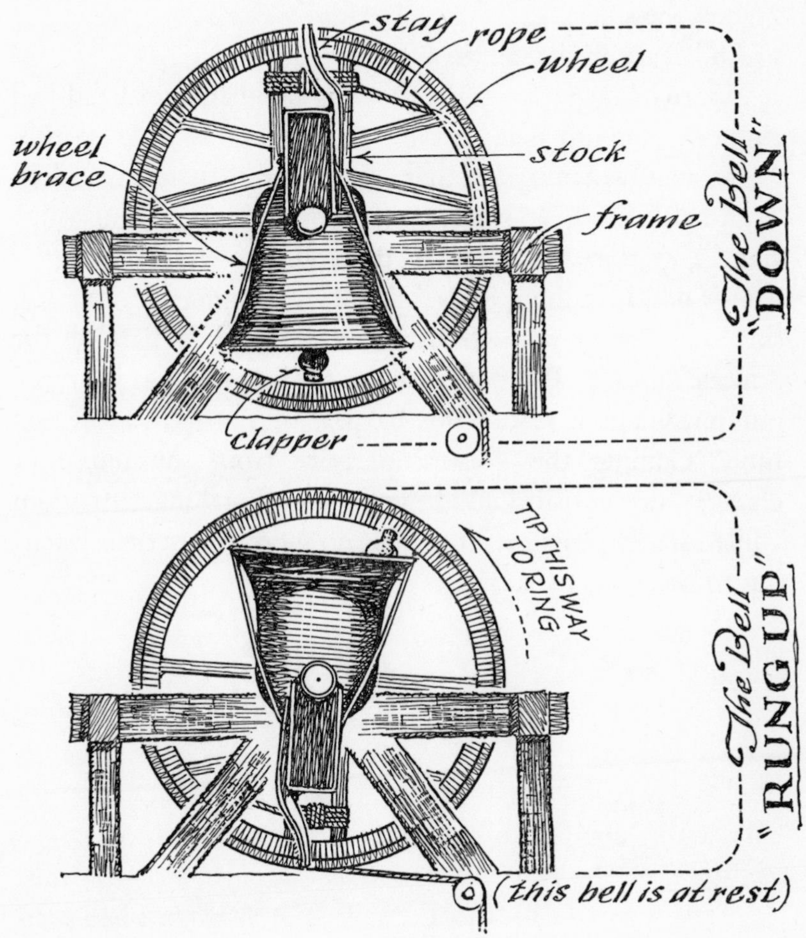

Fourth of July caught us with no bell-ringer except an ancient Negro who sometimes rang for the services. Well, of course he had to play a tune and this turned out to be the only one he knew."

I visualized a Negro spiritual, which I thought would sound wonderful on the bells. When I asked its name, Mr. Fell, who seemed to be stifling laughter, said, "I told you now, it is a little different. It's a tune called, 'Go Tell Aunt Nancy the Old Gray Goose Is Dead'!"

And that's how traditions are born.

Not to be neglected is the growing popularity of hand-bell ringing. Not too many years ago, there was little of this. Now, most fortunately, there are more than five hundred hand-bell choirs, composed of from eight to twenty-nine ringers, scattered throughout the country.

It is odd that there is so little change ringing in America, since the sound of bells has been so much a part of the American scene. But now it is the carillon that has captured our imagination. Could this be part of the laziness of our time? Gaining the greatest pleasure from the music of changes takes real knowledge and painstaking attention; while listening to a carillon takes no more effort than listening to the song of a lark.

6
Carillons and Carillonics

The carillon came into being long ago, but where and how it began is any carillonneur's guess. It might have started with an ancient Chinese musical instrument, the "Pien Ching," consisting of sixteen stones which when hammered give off metallic tones and cover two octaves of notes. In China, however, octaves are somewhat different, for they contain those curious little quarter and half tones.

I very briefly described a carillon some pages back as a set of bells tuned to the intervals of the chromatic scale. To be recognized technically as a carillon, however, its range must encompass at least three octaves. The bell with the deepest note is the heaviest, and it is sometimes very heavy indeed. The Bourdon Bell in the carillon of Riverside Church in New York weighs 20½ tons and is the biggest tuned bell in the world. (Incidentally, this and several of the other large bells at Riverside are not stationary but, despite their vast size, are swung like church bells, with a power assist.) The bell of the highest note weighs nine pounds. Between these two there are seventy others of varying weights.

Carillons are played by hand but they are also, and have been for hundreds of years, played by mechanisms attached to clocks. These, like the drums in old-fashioned music boxes, trip little hammers, causing them to strike the outside of the bells. Though the selections are changed from time to time, the music, like all mechanically produced music, lacks the touch and feeling of the master musician's heart and hands.

The cast bell carillon in the form we know it today, has been with us for over four hundred years. It arrived at this state of near perfection in Belgium and Holland, for the sober and stolid Flemish, Belgians, and Dutch adopted the carillon as their own. There was a carillon in Dunkerque in 1437, one in Alost in 1487, and a huge carillon of sixty bells in the cathredal at Antwerp by 1540.

Why should it have been in these unlikely lowlands that the carillon came into its own? The name itself comes from the Laten *quadrilionem* and the Italian *quadriglio*—both of which are related to four-beat dances—and becomes, in French, *carillon*. In each of these the name is based on the word for *four* and possibly was used because the very earliest carillons (the word refers to the music as well as the instrument) were played on four bells.

My research has found no definitive explanation as to why

the carillons flourished in the lowlands. So I have formed a theory of my own. As sound travels better over plains and water than over hilly terrain, the carillon was perfectly suited to the low countries' flat land and abundant water—

particularly abundant when the dykes broke and there didn't happen to be a small Dutch boy present to put his finger in the hole.

A carillonneur sits in a room below the bells or in a room in the center of the carillon. The tiers of smaller bells are above him and the big deeper ones beneath. He plays his bells by striking wooden levers with the sides of his hands while sounding the deeper throated bells with foot pedals.

There is a fascinating description by the Rev. H. R. Haweis, which appeared in the *Magazine of Art* in 1882, of Monsieur J. Denyn, of Mechlin, one of the great carillonneurs, at work. It sounds more like a description of an athletic event than an account of a man making sweet music:

> I stood first at a remote corner of the Market-place. . . . and after a short running prelude from the top bells weighing only a few pounds to the bottom one of several tons, M. Denyn settled to his work at a brisk gallop, and ably sustained at a good tearing pace without flagging for a single bar. Such an effort, involving the most violent muscular exercise, could not last long as I quickly perceived when I entered the belfry and watched the player.

Mr. Haweis himself must have been quite an athlete, for he speaks casually of entering the belfry while Denyn was still going at that gallop; yet Mr. Haweis fails to mention that to get from the street to the belfry at Mechlin, he had to climb four hundred steps!

> He [Denyn] was bathed in sweat and every muscle of his body seemed at full tension, as with feet he grappled with the huge pedal bells and manipulated with gloved hands and incredible rapidity his two rows of key pegs. After a brief breathing pause . . . [he] gave me an astonishing specimen of bravura playing, putting down the great nine-ton and six-ton bells for the melody with his feet, and carrying on a rattling accompaniment of demi-quavers and demi-semi-quavers on the treble bells, and, finally, after a few sweeping arpeggios he broke into a processional movement so stately it reminded me of Chopin's *Funeral March*. Just after this when he was in the middle of a grand fantasia on the *Dame*

> *Blanche* the clock barrel began working at the hour with a pretty French tune: "*Comme on aime a vingt ans.*"
>
> A lesser artist would have been taken aback! But M. Denyn seized his opportunity, and, waiting patiently until the barrel had done, plunged rapidly into an extempore continuation, which was so finely joined onto the mechanical tune that the people in the market-place must have thought that the barrel had suddenly become inspired.... then ... as a tribute to (me) his English guest, he wound up with "God Save the Queen!"

Today many carillonneurs insist on total privacy when they are at the clavier. This is not temperament, but rather modesty. The work is so very strenuous they strip to their shorts to play. I can understand this; I tried playing a twenty-five-bell carrillon recently and found that the force of the blows required to produce sounds from the bells was far greater than I had thought. I also found that after playing several bars of a hymn my hands ached, and I had had enough. In time, of course, carillonneurs develop protective calluses. But for hands too sensitive, it is possible to play with a glove.

Since the first quarter of this century the carillon of cast bells has become less a rarity in the United States. In 1930 there were only fifteen cast-bell carillons in this country while in Belgium and the Netherlands there were over a hundred. Now, though the wars have destroyed many of the bells in these countries, the number in North America has grown to more than a hundred.

Though the great carillon with its huge weight of bells will always be the true love of the carillonneur, during the past fifteen years there has been a good deal of electronic infidelity; and there is likely to be more of it. The infidelity runs from the North American College in Vatican City to St. Theresa Church in Fresno, California. This is not only understandable but forgivable, as cast-bell carillons cost over $100,000.

To describe just what constitutes a "carillonic bell," there is this explanation from a pamphlet by Schulmerich Carillon of Sellerseville, Pennsylvania, who coined the phrase.

> The "Arlington" Carillon uses precision-tuned, bell-metal *tone generators*, struck by metal hammers, as its tone sources.... Thus, because its action duplicates that of a metal clapper striking a cast bronze bell, the tones are produced in the traditional manner.
>
> Through the magic of modern electronics, the faint but perfect vibrations of the bells of the "Arlington" Carillon are amplified millions of times and projected from the tower or roof by special stentors. [Stentors are simply loud-speakers.]

Somewhere between the cast giants with their pure voices and the midgets with their amplified ones, we have a third modern carillon. This is the Van Bergen Maas-Rowe Carillon, part of whose trademark is: "They sound like bells because they are bells." Well, they are. The Van Bergen Bell Foundry in Holland has been casting huge, beautiful bells for a long time. One of their bells, weighing 12,980 pounds, is in the carillon given to the American people by the people of the Netherlands. This is a magnificent instrument. The same Van Bergen Foundry casts the bells for their electronic carillons, but these bells are small. In fact, they have shrunk to the point where an entire carillon of thirty-seven or more bronze bells, "... occupies about the space of an upright piano ..." The sound is then electronically amplified.

Some people say, and the companies of course agree, that it is almost impossible for even an expert carillonneur to notice the difference between a cast-bell, full-scale carillon and an electronic one. Other persons claim the difference is plainly noticeable. The actual difference would seem to rest in the fact that cast bells with their thousands of pounds of vibrating metal produce concussion and that electronic reproductions of bells do not. I believe the difference *is* noticeable, particularly in the deep-throated notes—the BONG rather than the dong. One tends almost to feel rather than to hear the difference.

To counter the claim that electronic carillons do not create concussion, John Dougherty, vice-president of Schulmerich, tells this story.

A few years ago a famous conductor came to him and explained that he was going to conduct the Boston Symphony in the *1812 Overture* and that the sound of the three bells called for in the score had never been properly used because the composer had written notes for the bells that were at least two octaves below the possible range of any bell that had ever been made. He wanted to know if Schulmeric with their little rods and hammers and amplifiers could possibly produce these sounds. Without hesitation John said they could.

The afternoon of the concert Dougherty arrived at the auditorium in Boston with a set of stentors and an enclosed console with three buttons on it. He set the console on the stage and hung the speakers so they faced the auditorium. The conductor looked at this box with disgust, shrugged his shoulders, and said, "Ah, well, I'll signal the musicians to play very softly so your little sounds can be heard."

"Perhaps," said John, "you'd like to hear them?"

The maestro shrugged, the muscians stared, and Dougherty pushed the buttons. The maestro and musicians jumped; it was immediately obvious that even if the symphony orchestra played its loudest, they were the ones who would not be heard. Furthermore, the stage hands had to spend the rest of the afternoon stuffing padding in all the auditorium windows that had been shaken loose by the deep vibrations.

Schulmerich, the Verdin Company, Van Bergen, and others, have installed between ten and fifteen thousand electronic carillons of various sizes all over the world. Considering these instruments cost only a fraction of the full-scale, cast-bell type, this means that the lovely, majestic music of beautiful bells has been brought to *millions* of people who might never have had their lives brightened by its enjoyment.

Can the carillonneurs be blamed for faithlessness to their first loves when they have had a part in doing this? Ah, no!

For the big bells will always be there, too, booming, throbbing, and sending chills of thrilled excitement out through their vibrant voices.

These voices, however, are not always as harmonious as they might be. In fact, at times they can be extremely raucous. The big bells in Spain are a good example, and the Giralda Tower in Seville is typical. The accepted ringing method is done by a rope attached to a tremendous timber lever. This is fastened to the center of the stock and, protruding upward, acts as a counterweight to the bell itself. As the bells are rung, they swing over and the rope winds around the stock. In "normal" ringing, this round-and-round business gradually retards the motion of the bell until it can be held up on end. These bells are generally hung in the wide-open arches of square towers, and first the bell and then the timber lever on top of it swing clear of the tower and out over the landscape. Now let Mr. Gadow, author of the book *Northern Spain,* describe what goes on in Seville's Giralda Tower:

> There are a dozen great bells which send forth the most discordant and unceasing peals, and the ringing of them is a strange exhibition. They are swung round and round; the rope is allowed to coil itself round the stock, or is jerked on the lip of the bell, and the ringer springs up by staunchions on the wall to get a purchase, then throws himself down; or he allows himself to be carried by the rope as it swings round outside. As I entered the gallery, I saw one of the ringers thrown out, as I imagined and expected, of course, that he would be dashed on the pavement below. I saw him the next moment perched on [top of] the bell, smiling at my terror.

At San Salvador young boys, for a fee, execute a similar performance. When the rope gets all wound up and the bell is ringing quite slowly, they leap onto the lever attached to the stock and ride over the bell and out through the arch. Then quickly moving in toward the stock, they stop the bell and by balancing hold it stationary at right angles to the ground far below them. When urged to start ringing again they step back toward the stock and, as the bell swings over itself bringing them back into the bell chamber, they hop off and just let her ring until the rope is unwound.

Thus from ancient China to twentieth-century Spain, carillons and carillonics have developed their own variations and their own methods of performance.

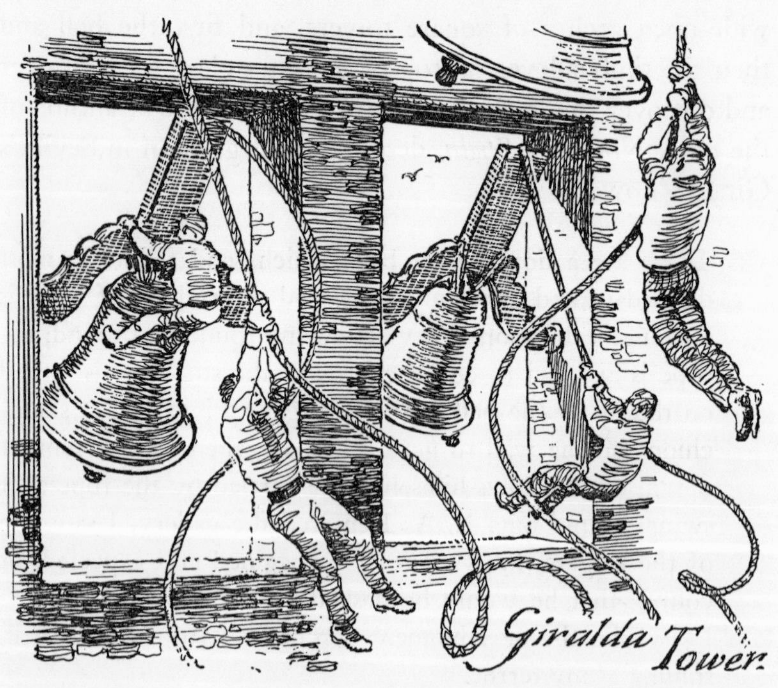

7 Sounds and Legends

In all my research I have found nothing definitive on how far the sound of bells will carry. Under different weather conditions the peal will transmit varying distances. Cold and still air is an effective carrier; warm and moving air is not.

I decided to get a bell and carry out a test. Borrowing a ship's bell from a friend, I stood outside my house one night and persuaded my wife to drive down the road, stopping periodically to see if she could still hear me ringing. She was able to hear me for a distance of exactly half a mile.

From this experiment I presumed to have learned that a bronze bell 7½ inches wide at the lip, 6 inches high, and weighing 4 pounds rung at an altitude of 1,200 feet above sea level can be heard for a distance of 2,640 feet. Here was a formula for figuring the distance any bell would carry if

I knew its size and weight. When I tried to apply this formula to the bell whose sound had carried from London to Windsor, a distance of twenty miles, my formula said it should have carried an additional 2,400 hundred miles. Hence, I gave up my formula and the idea of ever finding one.

While sound is temporal, legends endure. For a legend is simply a story that has passed down through the ages. Among legends relating to bells, some are macabre and some are humorous.

There was once an emperor who ordered a great bell to be cast and he entrusted the work to a mandarin named Kuan-yu. Over and over again Kuan-yu's castings failed; and finally the emperor sent word to him that if one more failure occurred, there would be a swishing sound followed by a swift crunch, then a plop, and that the plop would be the sound of Kuan-yu's head hitting the ground. Like all legendary mandarins, this one had a beautiful daughter. Her name was Ko-ai. As she was an unusually devoted daughter, she went to see a clairvoyant priest and asked, "How can I save my father?"

After several astrological observations, the priest told her that the only way to insure a perfect bell-casting was to see to it that the blood of a pure maiden was mixed with the molten metal.

Ko-ai went at once to the place where the bell was about to be cast, and crying, "For my father!" she flung herself into the huge, seething vat of liquid bronze. The casters tried to rescue her, but it was impossible. When the outer mold was stripped away and the bell was hung, the casting turned out to be perfect; but Kuan-yu had ceased to care. The great bell was rung. Its tone was perfection, but, to the horror of the thousands assembled to hear its voice, the deep resonance of its first sounding was followed by a strange high note, a very human wail.

To return to how far the sound of a bell will carry, there is this dubious but somewhat more cheerful legend. A long time ago in Toledo, Spain, a young man killed his opponent in a duel. Becaused this particular instance of polite murder was frowned on by the authorities, he fled to the cathedral for safety. His father, who was a rich count and famed bell fancier, went to the King to fix things up. The King did go so far in whimsicality as to say that if the count could make a bell in Toledo that could be heard all the way to the palace in Madrid, his son would be pardoned.

The count did this, and the son was quickly pardoned. The distance from Toledo to Madrid is sixty miles.

Another and very possibly true anecdote is about a bell, "Great Tom of Westminster," and a soldier on sentry duty at Windsor Castle during the reign of William III.

The sentry was accused of sleeping at his post. When formally charged with this most serious of offenses, he said to his superior, "I was not asleep, Sir, for I heard Great Tom strike at midnight."

"A likely story!" said the officer. "Westminster is full twenty miles from here."

"But, Sir, I did. I had special reason to remember it."

"And what reason?"

"Because, Sir, Great Tom struck thirteen times."

On occasion since then Great Tom actually has struck thirteen times, and it may well have done so on that particular night. After 1698, the bell was removed from its tower, recast, and hung in St. Paul's of London, where, shortly after that, it cracked and has since rung only to strike the hour and to toll at the funerals of royalty and other personages of great estate.

There is another legend of bell sounds that involves a valley in Nottinghamshire said to have been formed by a terrible earthquake many centuries ago. One Christmas morning, while the bells were tolling, a whole village was plunged beneath the earth. Every Christmas thereafter, so the story goes, if you put your ear to the ground you can hear the bells tolling again. What people have actually heard, however, are the bells from the church in a village a few miles away.

It's incredible but true that in 1793 the parishioners of Newington Church in England sold their church bells in order to raise the money to build a steeple in which to hang them!

In the fifteenth century a man, known only as Christian, was engaged to cast a bell to be hung in the south tower of the church of St. Mary Magdalene in Breslau. He was a gray-faced man better known for his quick temper than for his artistry as a bell-founder.

After weeks of work the core and cope were made, and the finest bell metal was procured and cast into the forge as the fires were brought to white heat. Just then a messenger arrived at Christian's house. Judging from the pounding at the door that it must be something important, the founder went into his house to answer the knock. Before he left, he told his young helper not to touch anything, mold or furnace, on pain of death, as the critical moment when he would pour was almost at hand.

Christian had hardly left when the boy, alone in the huge, dark room with the mold and the furnace, became possessed by an uncontrollable impulse to touch and see what would happen. He touched the metal catch that held the door of the forge closed, then leaped back in terror. With a roar and a hiss a river of glowing, molten metal poured from the furnace. The dark founding room became murky with steam. The boy ran screaming for his master just as Christian came back into the foundry and saw what to him was his own life's blood streaming wasted across the brick floor toward the pit where the mold of the bell lay. In a flash of blinding rage, he struck out with all his might. The boy fell dead.

What made his maddened action unbearable to Christian was that even as he killed the boy, the metal ran into the mold, filling it to the top. And days later, when the cope was removed and the bell lifted from the pit, it was smooth and beautiful in line, curve, and finish. With block, chain, and tackle he raised the bell clear of the cope. Its beauty enraged him and made the boy's death obscene. He seized a hammer, hoping to shatter the bell. Before the blow could land, a note sweeter and purer than any he had ever heard came from the swaying bell. Somehow he knew, though the tone came from the bell, it was not the bell he was hearing but instead was the voice of the boy whose soul had flowed with the metal.

He flung his hammer away and dropped to his knees in prayer, asking forgiveness and guidance. After a long while he rose, knowing what he must do. He left the foundry and marched to the house of the high sheriff to confess. Shortly thereafter he was hanged. The first time the new bell was rung from St. Mary's briefly, it tolled the funeral of the angry man who had created it. The bell was dedicated as "St. Mary's Bell." But it is still known, almost six hundred years later, as "The Bell of the Poor Sinner."

8

Inscriptions on Bells

Once you could tell who manufactured anything by just looking at it; as the saying goes, the maker's personality was "written all over it." And bells were no exception.

As soon as a craftsman was finished designing some piece of work he was proud of, he felt compelled to include upon it a date, his initials, and often just anything that popped into his head. Take the inscription on this old bell:

ARISE AND GO TO YOUR BUSINESS

which probably represents the absolute nadir of inscription writing. The level is raised only slightly in this one:

I RING AT SIX TO LET MEN KNOW WHEN TO
AND FROM THEIR WORK TO GO

And still in the pedantic vein, but again a little better, this one from a founder who believed in hedging his bets:

OUR VOICES SHALL IN CONCERT RING TO
HONOR BOTH OF GOD AND KING

One from a man who obviously had little faith in his craftsmanship:

IF YOU HAVE A JUDICIOUS EAR
YOU'LL OWN MY VOICE IS SWEET AND CLEAR

There is a strong tendency to use the first-person singular or plural in all bell inscriptions. This is the result of a curious psychotic reaction that runs through all literature about bells. Reference is made to them not as to so many hundreds of pounds of metal or even as musical instruments but as living, independent entities capable of expressing emotions of their own. Thus Tennyson speaks of them as "Wild bells" and Poe refers to wedding bells as "Ringing out their delight."

Bells, in other words, are taken seriously. Even when their inscriptions are tongue-in-cheek, like this:

ALL YE OF BATH WHO HEAR ME SOUND
THANK LADY HOPTON'S HUNDRED POUND

These inscriptions, despite their levity, apparently did not in the least daunt the strait-laced clergy of the day, for there is hardly an ancient church bell anywhere whose installation and hanging was not accompanied by a christening of the bells. In some cases, this was baptismal. In all cases, consecration ceremonies were conducted by the vicar, rector, or even the bishop, as the importance of the bells demanded.

Church bells sometimes announced "a sermon will be heard

at prayer services today." Such a bell hanging at Blakesley in Northants, England, was inscribed:

I RING TO SERMON WITH A LUSTY BOME,
THAT ALL MAY COME AND NONE MAY STOP AT HOME

The Puritans who enjoyed preaching so much they often stayed away from church unless there was to be a sermon, became a problem to one Bishop Wren. So in 1640 he ordered church bells to ring just the same whether there was to be a sermon or not.

People collect bell inscriptions as they do gravestone markings. The following are samples:

GIFTS FREE BOUGHT MEE
(Pilton, Somerset, 1726)

ONCE I'D A NOTE THAT NONE COULD BEAR
BUT BILBIE MADE ME SWEET AND CLEAR
(Bilbie Foundry, 1798)

I MEAN TO MAKE IT UNDERSTOOD
THAT THOUGH I'M LITTLE YET I'M GOOD
(Treble Bell at All-Saints)

THE GIFT OF JOS. PIZZIE AND WM. GWYNN
MUSIC & RINGING WE LIKE SO WELL
AND FOR THAT REASON WE GAVE THIS BELL
(Aldbourne, Wilts., 1787)

WHEN BACKWARDS RUNG WE TELL OF FIRE
THINK HOW THE WORLD SHALL THUS EXPIRE
(St. Ives, 1790)

IT IS REMARKABLE THAT THESE BELLS WERE
MOULDED DURING THE GREAT FROST
(York, 1783)

CURSED BE ALL CHURCH ROBBERS
(Norfolk, 1622)

THIS OLD BELL RUNG THE DOWNFALL OF
BUONAPARTE AND BROKE APRIL 1814
(Ashover, Derbyshire)

One founder evidentally at a loss for a suitable inscription, for a bell at Geddington, Northants, says:

ABCDEF GHIKLM NOPQRS

Very often the inscriptions on bells are just *there*, for no reason one can figure out. There is a case of this in East-hampton, Connecticut—"Jingletown"—where Bevins Broth-

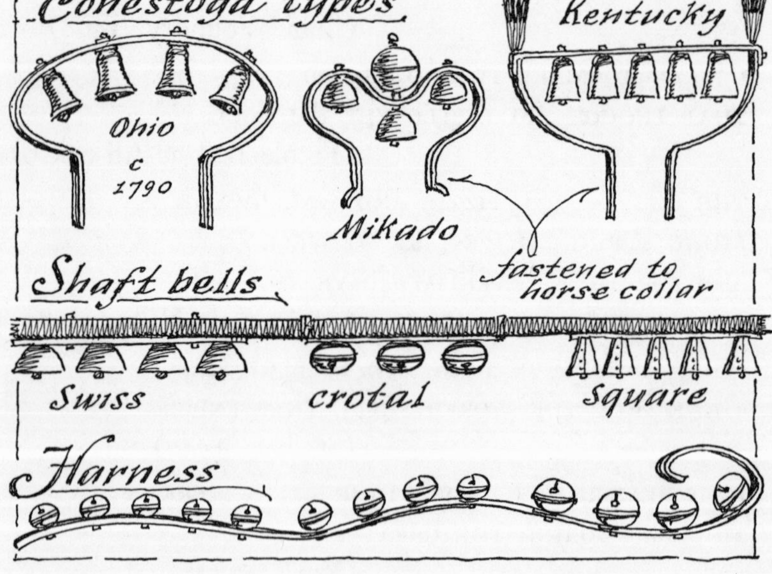

ers have for many years made bells by the ton and sold them by the pound, and still do. (A manufactured bell, incidentally, sells for about $2.50 a pound.) I drove up there one winter's day and talked with Chauncey Bevins and Avery West. Their catalogue had shown a set of cast cowbells ranging in size from a couple of inches in diameter for calflets

to 7½ inches for mammas. The bells were called Musical Swiss Cowbells, and they bore the inscription "Saignelegier," in script, and then above this in old-fashioned numerals, "1878." I was curious; I couldn't for the life of me figure out why they would put that particular date on bells cast in 1963.

The Bevins Brothers bell foundry was built in 1832. When I saw *that* inscription over the doorway in the old rose-brick office building, I was disappointed. *Why* couldn't it have said 1878?

Mr. West and Mr. Bevins greeted me at the door. After a brief hello, I immediately raised the question that had been on my mind: "Why do you have bells made in 1963 that say 1878 on them?"

Amused, Mr. Bevins replied: "I've seen some of our very old Swiss cowbells stamped 1865, 1866, and so on—right up to 1878. When the year 1879 came, the foundry probably got an unexpected rush order for sets of these bells, and they'd lost nine."

"Nine what?" I asked him.

"Not what," said Mr. Bevins. "Just plain nine. They'd lost the number nine. So they went on using eight."

Then we went for a tour of the factory, where they do everything from casting bells on exactly the same principle used four thousand years ago to turning out replicas of the Town Crier's bell similar to the one I rang on the Fourth of July. Bevins Brothers make about a million bells a year. The only other product they make is a brass knob that screws onto the horn of an ox!

9

Founders and Foundries

It is very strange that an nation like ours, which has done so much to advance and improve on the nature of almost anything that can be manufactured, has over the centuries done so little about making bigger and better bells. There never were a great many bell-founders in this country who cast bells of any great size.

Of nine notable American firms,* only the McShane Bell Foundry Company in Baltimore and Bevins Brothers in East-hampton, Connecticut are left. Though McShane will accept orders for bells of up to ten thousand pounds, Bevins will not cast a bell over ten inches in diameter. In addition to the nine original firms, there were two men whose names have become

* A complete list of the nine notable early American bell-founders appears in the Appendix.

famous, Pass and Stow of Philadelphia. These two recast the Liberty Bell when it cracked in 1753, though the official Independence Hall account of the incident does not refer to them as foundrymen, merely noting that the bell "... was recast by two workmen, Pass and Stow."

A great deal of the early bell-casting was done by individuals rather than by foundries. Probably, however, most of these individuals had much more experience in the art than the two famous Philadelphians. Furthermore, the habit of the times was not to cast big bells at one central place, but to set up temporary foundries in convenient places and there cast such bells as were ordered by churches in neighboring districts. A still more practical method frequently practiced in the fifteen and sixteen hundreds, when the English roads left a great deal to be desired, was casting big bells in the yards of the churches where they were to hang. Remains of furnaces discovered during excavations in such places as the open court of the church at Scalford in Leicestershire and at Epingham in Rutland attest to this practice. And it is well known that when in 1762 the great bell of Canterbury Cathedral was lowered to the ground for recasting, the founding was done in the cathedral yard.

Bell-casting in England became an established industry at an early age; so well established, in fact, that in 1483 importing foreign bells was declared illegal as it was reducing domestic profits. There were many bell-founders in England, and unlike our American bell foundries, many of them have survived. A letter I received recently from Douglas Hughes, a partner of the Whitechapel Bell Foundry in London, illustrates the longevity of British bell-founders. The letterhead contains the phrase "Established 1570." The letter itself speaks with interest about our American Fourth of July bell-ringing ceremonies and goes on to mention that this foundry, which cast the Liberty Bell in 1752, a number of years ago offered to recast it free of charge. They received indirect word from President Truman extending his deep appreciation for the offer but saying that the cracked Liberty Bell had become such an object of reverance to the American people that he wouldn't dare suggest its recasting.

I have the latest Whitechapel Foundry booklet at hand; it looks as though it might have been printed at any time within the last three hundred years. It includes a list of the twenty-eight chief founders since 1570, including the three Hughes men who are the partners today. This short statement from it I find appealing: "the eight bells at Westminster Abbey came from Whitechapel between 1583 and 1919, and we have recently rehung them; an unbroken connection [business] of over 350 years."

There is also a picture of an Ernest Oliver testing the pitch of a hand bell with a tuning fork and the modest sentence, "There have been members of the Oliver family at the Whitechapel Foundry for well over 200 years." Whitechapel still casts the majority of bells imported to this country today.

Among the most famous founders of all time is an American who is better known than any other bell-founder anywhere, though he is generally remembered for accomplishments other than bell-casting. As an express rider he once made the round trip to Philadelphia and back in nine days at a time when most riders took that long to ride it one way. As a colonel in the Continental Army he was a bit uninspired, regarding war as destructive rather than creative. But as a munitions-maker, a printer of currency, and a manufacturer of boilers, he was superb. He was a top American silversmith and designer, an artist, and an engineer. For all these remarkable abilities, his greatest fame comes from one ride on a horse.

The way Paul Revere got started in the bell-casting business is entirely typical of his, "Well, gentlemen, if I don't know how to do it I can sure as anything find out how pretty

quick" attitude toward everything in life. What happened was that the bell in Boston's Old North Church tower cracked in the year 1792. In almost any other year the logical thing would have been to ship the remains to England and have them recast. Understandably the directors of Paul Revere's church felt the English might feel just a little touchy about being asked to recast this particular bell.

The first American Churhes had no Belfries
and used ship's bells

It being a mechanical problem, the solution was simple. Get neighbor Paul to recast it. Paul went to work. He rode to Abington to talk with foundryman Aaron Hobart, and he came back with Hobart's foreman. He made his mold and cope and poured bell metal into the space between them. The long cooling period passed. Finally the bell emerged from the mold, and the great day came when the bell was hung and a clapper swung to produce the first silvery note.

It was a day still remembered in Boston, for the note that Paul Revere's first bell loosed into the world was beyond any doubt the worst note any bell-founder had yet achieved. It was conservatively described by a Bostonian of the time as "panny, harsh, and shrill." But to the Bostonians, it was beautiful. Their own Paul Revere had made it!

That was only the beginning. After he had sheathed the bottom of Old Ironsides with copper, Paul Revere really went at bell-casting. He studied and talked to people who knew bells.

Since copper represented such a large proportion of bell metal and American copper was far from plentiful and often of doubtful quality in America during the years of Revere's bell-casting, it is amazing that he achieved in his bells not only beauty but timelessness.

His masterpiece, his "great bell," was cast for Kings Chapel, Boston, in 1817. Today it still hangs in its belfry overlooking the heart of the city.

Not long ago I talked with Mr. Harold Haynes, verger of King's Chapel, to check on the condition of the bell and get the date on it, which I couldn't find in my research library. Mr. Haynes has a proper affection for things old and beautiful, and he spoke glowingly of the bell.

"The sweetest bell Paul Revere ever made. It says so right on the bell, 'The sweetest bell we ever made. Paul Revere & Son. 1817.' "

He told me the bell had originally been one of the Londonderry Chimes but that it had cracked in 1814 while tolling evening service. When Revere recast it, a lot of good Bostonians threw silver into the melting pot "to add more sweetness to the tone." I have an idea that Yankee frugality must

CHURCH BELLS.

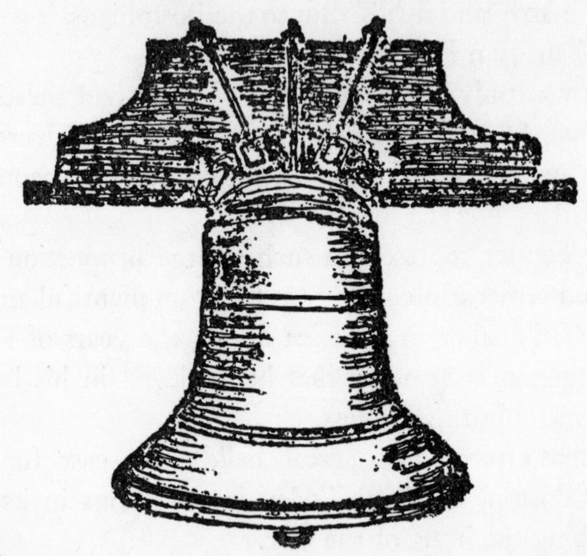

PAUL REVERE & SON,

No. 13, Lynn Street, North End, BOSTON,

HAVE conſtantly for ſale, CHURCH and ACADEMY BELLS, of all ſizes, which they will warrant *equal* to any made in Europe, or this *country.* From perſonal information obtained in Europe, and twenty years experience, they are aſſured they can give ſatisfaction, and will ſell, on as good terms, as they can be imported for, or obtained in this country.

have been at work in this situation, for with a high percentage of silver the bell would have soured long before now.

Mr. Haynes went on. "I ring out the old year on her and I ring in the new and I ring her for all regular services and for anything special, like Lindbergh's landing in Paris. I rang that out on her, too."

Then he thanked me for getting in touch with him, adding that somehow none of the other people who wrote about the bell in books managed to get its weight correct.

The Paul Revere Bell at King's Chapel, Boston, weighs exactly 2,475 pounds, without the clapper, which weighs an additional fifteen pounds.

Of the four hundred odd bells Paul Revere's firm made, forty-eight of them were cast during his lifetime. Thanks to Dr. Arthur Nichols and the study he made of Revere bells in 1911 and to the published work of Edward C. and Evelyn Stickney, specialists in Paul Revere bells (from which work they have most graciously permitted me to use material), it would appear that roughly three hundred have been either sent out of the country, burned in church fires, or (believe it or not), simply mislaid. About one hundred can be accounted for.

Of the bells Paul Revere himself cast, thirty-seven are still in existence.* Perhaps a dozen of these, unspoiled by mishanging, bad ringing, or other abuse, still ring out the sweet sounds he created so long ago.

* A list of the thirty-seven bells cast by Paul Revere that are still in existence appears in the Appendix.

Throughout history there have been bells that have rung, pealed, and tolled events of significance in the lives of many people. There is the Lutine Bell of Lloyds of London, at the Royal Exchange. This is a beautiful though small bell, mounted in an ornate filigree, with a most appropriate ship's anchor chain hung on it.

The bell first belonged to the *Lutine*, a French frigate. When the frigate was captured by an English ship, the bell changed homes. That English boat was wrecked at the entrance to the Zuider Zee in 1799, and Lloyds acquired the salvage rights to her; so the bell changed ownership again. It is still connected with the sea, for it is tolled with solemn majesty to announce the loss of any vessel insured by Lloyds.

A companion to this bell is the gong on the New York Stock Exchange. It is electric and roughly three feet in diameter. It clangs each morning at ten to announce the opening of the exchange and again at three to call the closing. But when this gong sounds just one stroke while the exchange is in session, a hush passed over the floor. It causes many a member to feel the chill of apprehension. For the sound of the one sonorous stroke means that a member firm has failed or has been expelled from membership, or that a member of the exchange has died. In the great depression of the thirties, the members became almost accustomed to the sound of the gong. An officer of the exchange told me a little diffidently that, for some reason he could not explain, the sound of the gong is different when it is rung to bespeak tragedy. I can understand.

Then there is the Liberty Bell in Philadelphia. It has its own mystique; for although the final casting took place in 1753, just short of a quarter of a century before the bell rang out the news of the proclamation of the Declaration of Independence in 1776, it bore the inscription:

> PROCLAIM LIBERTY THROUGHOUT ALL THE LAND . . . AND TO ALL THE INHABITANTS THEREOF.

The story is well known and only the bare facts need repeating. The bell cracked once and was recast, as mentioned earlier. Though it may have rung on the Fourth of July in '76, when the Continental Congress approved the Declaration of Independence, it *did* ring on July 8 to announce the proclamation of the Declaration.

The present crack in the bell occurred on the day in 1835 when it was being tolled in honor of John Marshall, chief justice of the United States Supreme Court, as his body passed through Philadelphia on the way to burial.

The bell presently stands in the entrance of Independence Hall in Philadelphia. It cannot be rung, and it would take a mighty cause to persuade its guardians even to tap it with a rubber hammer as was last done in World War II.

Strangely enough, the Liberty Bell has a "twin," cast by Whitechapel in London, of the same dimensions and within a few pounds of the same weight. This one was hung a year later in Christ Church at Second and Market Streets in Philadelphia, where it still hangs and still rings daily. It has never in all these long and turbulent decades shown the least sign of a crack.

I have wondered greatly about this and have at last come to believe that neither time, mishanging, nor misringing weakened the Liberty Bell, but rather the enormous importance of the message its voice cried out. It rang many strokes, loud and clear, but it rang only two words: "Liberty"—"FREEDOM!" And the ringing of them was to affect all mankind forevermore and to change the mighty course of history.

But let us remember what the Declaration of Independence meant to the men who signed it, what it has always meant to their countrymen. To quote from a contemporary account:

> On the Fourth of July in 1776, after a year of widely separated battles and skirmishes, in a desperate gesture to present a united effort in the struggle to win our freedom from the most blatant kind of tyranny and oppressions, a group of men met in the State House at Philadelphia [now Independence Hall]. There they, delegates from all

thirteen of the American colonies, officially known as the Continental Congress, signed and approved a document called the Declaration of Independence.

On that day we became a nation. On that day, too, we, a sparsely settled land of merchants, sailors, and farmers without adequate weapons, ammunition, or military supplies of any sort—including money; with our only weapons a few rifles and the enormous will and courage in our hearts, together with our faith in God, formally took on the whole and awesome might of the British Empire.

The men who signed Jefferson's document that long-ago summer in the State House in Philadelphia *knew* that if the war with England were lost this document they were signing would be of interest only because each would be signing his own death warrant. All would be hanged as traitors to the crown. It took extraordinary courage.

I have been thinking a lot about the Liberty Bell lately, and as a result of this I have come to a conclusion.

All my fierce calculating while I searched for a formula that would tell me the carrying range of a bell was time wasted. I was using the wrong kind of measurement. I have now learned that the voices of bells should not be measured in feet, yards, and miles, but should instead be measured in years, decades, and centuries. Here is my new and demonstrably correct equation:

> One peal of a bell 4 feet in diameter, 3 feet in height, and weighing 2,080 lbs., hanging in Philadelphia, can be heard for a minimum of 187 years.

Appendix

The nine notable early American bell-founders:

Hobart of Abington, Massachusetts
Fulton of Pittsburgh, Pennsylvania
Meneely Bros., of Troy, New York
Stukstede & Bros. of St. Louis, Missouri
William Blake & Co. of Troy, New York
Jones and Company of Troy, New York
The Buckeye Bell Foundry of Cincinnati, Ohio
Bevins Brothers of Easthampton, Connecticut
The McShane Bell Foundry Co., Inc. of Baltimore, Maryland

A list of the thirty-seven bells cast by Paul Revere that are still in existence:

1792, St. James Episcopal Church, N. Cambridge, Mass. Marked "The first church bell cast by P. Revere in Boston, 1792"

1795, Congregational Church, Groveland, Mass. Marked "Revere 1795, The living to the church I call, and to the grave I summon all"

1797, First Congregational Church, Essex, Mass. Marked "Revere & Sons Boston 1797"

1798, Historical Society, Dedham, Mass. Marked "Revere Boston 1798"

1801, First Parish Church, Weston, Mass. Marked "Paul Revere & Sons Boston 1801"

1801, Bentley School, Salem, Mass. Marked "Revere & Sons Boston 1801"

1802, New Old South Church, Worcester, Mass. Marked "Revere & Son Boston 1802"

1802, Congregational Church, Newington, N. H. Marked "Revere & Son Boston 1802"

1802, Town Hall, Milford, N. H. Marked "Revere & Son Boston 1802"

1803, Meetinghouse of the First Presbyterian Society, Old South, Newburyport, Mass. Marked "Revere & Son Boston 1803"

1804, M. T. Stevens & Sons Co., North Andover, Mass. Marked "Revere & Son Boston 1802"

1804, First Congregational Parish, Unitarian, Kennebunk, Me. Marked "Revere & Son Boston 1804"

1805, First Parish Church, Unitarian, East Bridgewater, Mass. Marked "Revere & Son Boston 1804"

1805, City Hall, Bath, Me. Marked "Revere & Son Boston 1802"

1806, The First Universalist Society in America, Gloucester, Mass. Marked "Revere & Son Boston 1806"

1807, Congregational Church, West Barnstable, Mass. Marked "Revere & Son Boston 1807"

1807, North Parish Church, North Andover, Mass. Marked "Revere & Son Boston 1806"

1807, Riverdale Methodist Church, Gloucester, Mass. Marked "Revere & Son Boston 1806"

1809, The Congregational Church, Northboro, Mass. Marked "Revere & Son Boston 1809"

1809, St. Paul's Church, Newburyport, Mass. Marked "Revere & Son Boston 1809"

1810, Congregational Parish, Unitarian, in Norton, Mass. Marked "Revere & Son Boston 1809"

1811, First Church, Congregational Meetinghouse, Hopkinton, N. H. Marked "Revere & Son Boston 1811"

1811, First Parish Church, Unitarian, Bridgewater, Mass. Marked "Revere & Son Boston 1811"

1811, First Parish Church, Needham, Mass. Marked "Revere & Son Boston 1811"

1814, The First Parish, Wayland, Mass. Marked "Revere & Son Boston 1814"

1815, First Congregational Church, Princeton, Mass. Marked "Revere & Son Boston 1815"

1815, Beebe Memorial Library, Wakefield, Mass. Marked "Revere & Son Boston 1815"

1816, Town Hall, North Hampton, N. H. Marked "Revere & Son Boston 1815"

1816, The First Church of Christ, Longmeadow, Mass. Marked "Revere & Son Boston 1815"

1816, King's Chapel, Boston, Mass. Marked "Revere & Son Boston 1816"

1816, First Congregational Church, Unitarian, Providence, R. I. Marked "For the Congregational Church, Providence, R. I., Revere & Son Boston 1816"

1816, First Methodist Church, Lynn, Mass. Marked "Revere & Son Boston 1816"

1816, Second Parish Church, Dorchester, Mass. Marked "Revere & Son Boston 1816"

1817, First Congregational Church, Norwich, Vt. Marked "Revere & Son Boston 1817"

1817, The Congregational Church of Topsfield, Mass. Marked "Revere & Son Boston 1817"

1818, St. Michael's Church, Marblehead, Mass. Marked "Revere & Son Boston 1818"

1818, The Congregational Church, Woodstock, Vt. Marked "Revere & Son Boston 1818"

SPOTLIGHT

OREGON'S SOUTHERN CASCADES CAMPING & HIKING

TOM STIENSTRA & SEAN PATRICK HILL

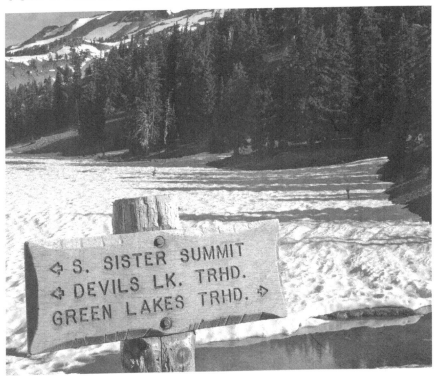

How to Use This Book

ABOUT THE CAMPGROUND PROFILES

The campgrounds are listed in a consistent, easy-to-read format to help you choose the ideal camping spot. If you already know the name of the specific campground you want to visit, or the name of the surrounding geological area or nearby feature (town, national or state park, forest, mountain, lake, river, etc.), look it up in the index and turn to the corresponding page. Here is a sample profile:

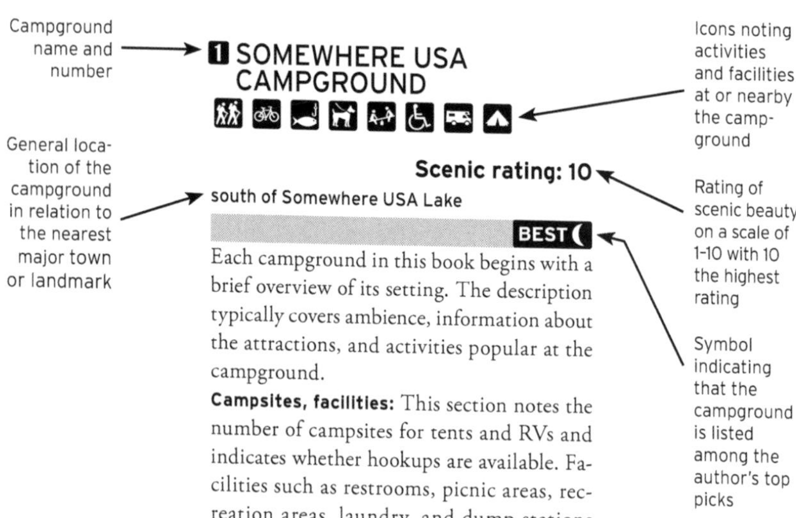

Each campground in this book begins with a brief overview of its setting. The description typically covers ambience, information about the attractions, and activities popular at the campground.

Campsites, facilities: This section notes the number of campsites for tents and RVs and indicates whether hookups are available. Facilities such as restrooms, picnic areas, recreation areas, laundry, and dump stations will be addressed, as well as the availability of piped water, showers, playgrounds, stores, and other amenities. The campground's pet policy and wheelchair accessibility is also mentioned here.

Reservations, fees: This section notes whether reservations are accepted, and provides rates for tent sites and RV sites. If there are additional fees for parking or pets, or discounted weekly or seasonal rates, they will also be noted here.

Directions: This section provides mile-by-mile driving directions to the campground from the nearest major town or highway.

Contact: This section provides an address, phone number, and website, if available, for the campground.

ABOUT THE ICONS

The icons in this book are designed to provide at-a-glance information on activities, facilities, and services available on-site or within walking distance of each campground.

Hiking trails	Hot springs
Biking trails	Pets permitted
Swimming	Playground
Fishing	Wheelchair accessible
Boating	RV sites
Canoeing and/or kayaking	Tent sites
Winter sports	

ABOUT THE SCENIC RATING

Each campground profile employs a scenic rating on a scale of 1 to 10, with 1 being the least scenic and 10 being the most scenic. A scenic rating measures only the overall beauty of the campground and environs; it does not take into account noise level, facilities, maintenance, recreation options, or campground management. The setting of a campground with a lower scenic rating may simply not be as picturesque that of as a higher rated campground, however other factors that can influence a trip, such as noise or recreation access, can still affect or enhance your camping trip. Consider both the scenic rating and the profile description before deciding which campground is perfect for you.

MAP SYMBOLS

Expressway	80 Interstate Freeway	Airfield
Primary Road	101 U.S. Highway	Airport
Secondary Road	21 State Highway	City/Town
Unpaved Road	66 County Highway	Mountain
Ferry	Lake	Park
National Border	Dry Lake	Pass
State Border	Seasonal Lake	State Capital

ABOUT THE TRAIL PROFILES

Each hike in this book is listed in a consistent, easy-to-read format to help you choose the ideal hike. From a general overview of the setting to detailed driving directions, the profile will provide all the information you need. Here is a sample profile:

Map number and hike number

1 SOMEWHERE USA HIKE

Round-trip mileage (unless otherwise noted) and the approximate amount of time needed to complete the hike (actual times can vary widely, especially on longer hikes)

9.0 mi/5.0 hrs 3 8

Difficulty and quality ratings

at the mouth of the Somewhere River

General location of the trail, named by its proximity to the nearest major town or landmark

BEST

Symbol indicating that the hike is listed among the author's top picks

Each hike in this book begins with a brief overview of its setting. The description typically covers what kind of terrain to expect, what might be seen, and any conditions that may make the hike difficult to navigate. Side trips, such as to waterfalls or panoramic vistas, in addition to ways to combine the trail with others nearby for a longer outing, are also noted here. In many cases, mile-by-mile trail directions are included.

User Groups: This section notes the types of users that are permitted on the trail, including hikers, mountain bikers, horseback riders, and dogs. Wheelchair access is also noted here.

Permits: This section notes whether a permit is required for hiking, or, if the hike spans more than one day, whether one is required for camping. Any fees, such as for parking, day use, or entrance, are also noted here.

Maps: This section provides information on how to obtain detailed trail maps of the hike and its environs. Whenever applicable, names of U.S. Geologic Survey (USGS) topographic maps and national forest maps are also included; contact information for these and other map sources are noted in the Resources section at the back of this book.

Directions: This section provides mile-by-mile driving directions to the trail head from the nearest major town.

Contact: This section provides an address and phone number for each hike. The contact is usually the agency maintaining the trail but may also be a trail club or other organization.

ABOUT THE ICONS

The icons in this book are designed to provide at-a-glance information on the difficulty and quality of each hike.

The **difficulty rating** (rated **1-5** with **1** being the lowest and **5** the highest) is based on the steepness of the trail and how difficult it is to traverse

The **quality rating** (rated **1-10** with **1** being the lowest and **10** the highest) is based largely on scenic beauty, but also takes into account how crowded the trail is and whether noise of nearby civilization is audible

ABOUT THE DIFFICULTY RATINGS

Trails rated 1 are very easy and suitable for hikers of all abilities, including young children.

Trails rated 2 are easy-to-moderate and suitable for most hikers, including families with active children 6 and older.

Trails rated 3 are moderately challenging and suitable for reasonably fit adults and older children who are very active.

Trails rated 4 are very challenging and suitable for physically fit hikers who are seeking a workout.

Trails rated 5 are extremely challenging and suitable only for experienced hikers who are in top physical condition.

MAP SYMBOLS

Expressway	80 Interstate Freeway	Airfield
Primary Road	101 U.S. Highway	Airport
Secondary Road	21 State Highway	City/Town
Unpaved Road	66 County Highway	Mountain
Ferry	Lake	Park
National Border	Dry Lake	Pass
State Border	Seasonal Lake	State Capital

ABOUT THE MAPS

This book is divided into chapters based on major regions in the state; an overview map of these regions precedes the table of contents. Each chapter begins with a map of the region, which is further broken down into detail maps. Sites are noted on the detail maps by number.

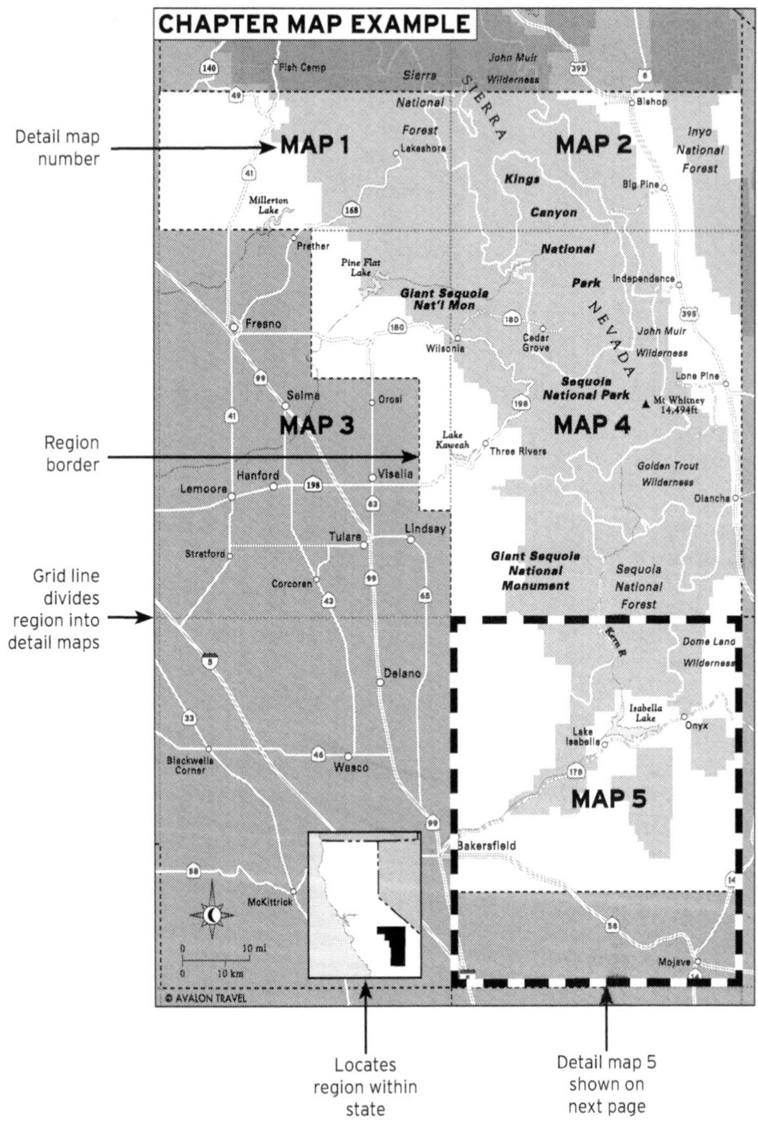

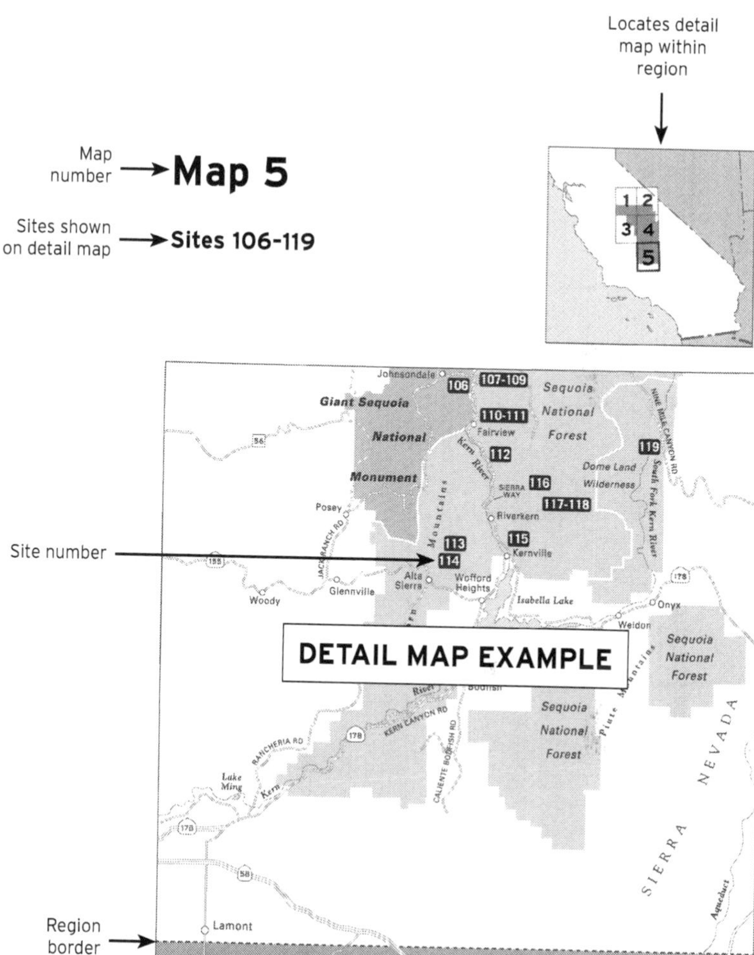
Locates detail map within region
Map number
Map 5
Sites shown on detail map
Sites 106-119
Site number
Region border
DETAIL MAP EXAMPLE
Giant Sequoia National Monument
Sequoia National Forest
Dome Land Wilderness
Johnsondale
Fairview
Posey
Riverkern
Kernville
Alta Sierra
Wofford Heights
Glennville
Woody
Isabella Lake
Onyx
Weldon
SIERRA NEVADA
Lamont
Arvin
Tehachapi
Brite Valley Aquatic Rec. Area
Mojave
© AVALON TRAVEL

Camping and Hiking Tips

HIKING ESSENTIALS

In Oregon, there are those days when you get off work and want to head out for a couple hours of hiking. A day hike is a day hike, and you certainly don't need to lug 30 pounds of tents, stoves, and sleeping bags on your back. But this is absolutely no excuse not to be prepared. The forests resound with stories of people who got lost wandering off the trail, getting hurt or worse. The number one Boy Scout rule for the mountains, shorelines, and deserts of Oregon is *be prepared.* Here's a standard list any good outdoors person should adhere to.

Food and Water

Be sure to carry enough food on even the shortest hike, the reason being you never know if you'll get caught in the woods longer than anticipated. Outdoor stores, even grocery stores, carry a great abundance of high-energy trail food that is lightweight and easy to pack. As far as food goes, suit your tastes but also consider what your body needs. Salty foods replenish much needed sodium lost in sweat. Sugary foods maintain, well, your sugar levels, and they also give good bursts of energy (there are all sorts of great sugar-syrups in little packets for the big burst you need to make it up that final hill). Carbohydrates and proteins are a necessity, as your body will need them for energy and a little muscle repair. In general, bring more food than you think you'll need.

Though food is important, not to mention a great thing to have while you're sitting beside that mountain lake you've been walking for hours to get to, it is water that is far and away the real necessity. What will get you in the woods, even kill you, is not starvation but dehydration. Heat sickness, which can quickly degenerate into hyperthermia, can be damaging if not deadly. On a shorter, easier hike, play it safe and bring at least two quarts of water in your pack. An easy and novel solution is the CamelBak and other such products—small backpacks perfect for day hiking, with plenty of room for food, water, and the rest of the essentials. I swear by it, as does everyone I know who uses one. When I'm properly equipped, I'm carrying upwards of six quarts of water.

If you plan on backpacking and need to carry less weight, be sure to invest in a water filter or some other method of purifying. Never drink straight from the creek! Backcountry water has, unfortunately, largely been infected with *Giardia lamblia* and *Cryptosporidium,* two microscopic organisms that cause a plethora of terrible gastrointestinal problems, the likes of which hardly need to be discussed here. Iodine is still a staple for many backpackers, and there are all sorts of newfangled ways to purify water, including ultraviolet light.

Trail Map and Compass

You'd be surprised how empowering a map can be, especially when you can read it well. Never go on a hike without a map. Despite trail signs, getting confused in the backcountry is more common an occurrence than you'd think. Signs can disappear or get blown down. Trails, too, have a way of sometimes getting lost in certain areas, especially in places with many so-called "user trails" (made by people walking off the designated trail). The best maps are topographic, which can be used in conjunction with a compass to easily pinpoint your position. Plus, they give a good sense of the lay of the land—the more detailed the better. You can find nearby trails and even start adventuring cross-country into areas without trails. But it is imperative to know what you're doing first; one wrong adjustment of the compass can land you miles off track.

You can easily obtain maps from outdoors stores and from the management agencies of the area you are visiting. See the *Resources* chapter for names and contact information for those agencies and for USGS topographical maps, National Forest maps, and maps from commercial services.

A compass is an essential tool for keeping you on track. Take a class from an outdoor group, or a store like REI, and learn to use it correctly and effectively. Many people use GPS devices, but they may not work in some areas. A dense forest canopy may run you the risk of losing a signal, so why depend on it? Knowledge is power, and the compass and map make use of that knowledge.

SOCKS

You cannot underestimate the value of good socks, your cushion against blisters, moisture, and soreness. Hiking socks should be thick enough to fit snugly and cushion your feet all around. Buy plenty, especially for extended backpacking trips, or plan to wash the ones you do have. Dirty, damp, and worn-out socks will not do what they are meant to do. Never wear cotton socks!

Wool blend socks help to wick away moisture from your skin. They run around $15 a pair. Believe me, they're worth it. They are also, I have found, wonderfully warm for when you finally get your boots off at camp.

Extra Clothing

Oregon has a classic saying: Don't like the weather? Wait five minutes, it'll change. Those who say this aren't lying. Conditions fluctuate rapidly, so the right clothing is essential. Being wet and cold is not only uncomfortable, but also downright dangerous. Cotton is the worst clothing to wear: When it gets wet, it stays wet. Wool, the old standby, gets wet and heavy. Today's hiking clothes are manufactured to be waterproof and quick-drying, and even to wick moisture away from the skin. Many clothes are also UV resistant. And they're lightweight, to boot.

You should always carry a lightweight jacket that is both waterproof and wind-resistant. Breathable jackets control your heat, as well. Think ahead if your hike will change in altitude: the higher you go, the colder it may get, so bring a hat and gloves, too. And an extra pair of socks can't hurt, either, particularly ones that keep your feet warm and dry.

Flashlight

You know how sometimes in winter you find yourself saying, "Wow, how'd it get so dark so early?" Well, the *last* place you want to say that is on the trail. It happens.

There is some great and lightweight gear you can use. Headlamps are all the rage, and can cast quite a powerful beam; plus, they keep your hands free. No matter what kind of light source you use, make sure you have extra batteries and an extra bulb. You'll find them very handy around the campsite, as well.

Sunglasses and Sunscreen

One of the trickiest things about hiking near or on a mountain peak is that the air is thinner and therefore—don't ask me how it works—the sun gets stronger. Thus, the mountains are a great place to get sunburned, even on a cold day. Bring both sunscreen with a high SPF and sunglasses with good UV resistance. Put on that sunscreen liberally, and at least 30 minutes before you hike. Later, put on more. Other good accessories to have on hand: a wide-brimmed hat and SPF lip balm.

Insect Repellent

Oregon is famous for its mosquitoes. I mean it. Some of the best destinations, like the mountain wildflower meadows or the lakes and rivers, are overrun with mosquitoes in late spring and early summer. There are many ways to avoid this. One, of course, is to just stay home and wait for fall. The other is to equip yourself with one of the many brands of "bug dope" available in any decent store. The most powerful ones contain a toxic chemical called DEET, which some people prefer to avoid. DEET should not be used on children, and adults should use safe levels. There are also handy mosquito nets that can be pulled over the face, and these are available in outdoors stores.

Long sleeves and long pants will help protect you from the other pest: ticks. Ticks are known to carry nasty diseases like Rocky Mountain Spotted Fever, so it's best to tuck those long pants into your socks and check yourself often. The high desert of Oregon, especially along rivers, is one place ticks frequent.

First-Aid Kit

You really only need a few things here, so frugality is okay when you're dealing with minor cuts, blisters, and sore muscles. A little antibiotic ointment, some bandages, and an anti-inflammatory medication like ibuprofen or acetaminophen can be invaluable. Also be aware of who in your party may be allergic to bee stings, as Oregon has a local ground wasp that can be nasty. Be sure to bring an epinephrine pen or other medication for those with allergies.

It never hurts to learn a little CPR, or even have some Wilderness First-Aid training. When you've gained experience hiking among the rocks, cliffs, and swift rivers, you will quickly see how many potential disasters lurk a little too close for comfort. Be prepared!

Swiss Army-Style Pocket Knife

In Oregon, say "Leatherman" and everyone will know what you're talking about. The Leatherman is a modern equivalent of the famous Swiss Army knife, and a good one has the essentials: a few blades, a can opener, scissors, and tweezers. Whether removing splinters or ticks, or cutting moleskin for that blister, this is a must-have tool.

Firestarter

At night, cold can come on quick in the Oregon mountains, and especially the desert. Starting a fire may be the ultimate necessity in an emergency, for warmth as well as a distress signal, and no hiker should be without either a butane lighter or waterproof matches—and in a state as rainy as Oregon, they should be carried in a waterproof container.

HIKING GEAR

Having the right clothing makes for a comfortable hike. Long gone are the days of climbing mountains in wool pants and hiking to the lake in a pair of cut-off jeans. Today's hiking clothes are made from largely synthetic materials designed to do breathe, meaning to release heat away from the body, and stay dry: that is, they both wick moisture away from the body and dry quickly.

Then, too, there are the feet, which are of course the most heavily used body part while hiking. Caring for your feet is the single most important thing you can do, since nothing makes for a more miserable walk than wet, cold feet or blisters. Take care when choosing footwear and don't worry about frugality: A good pair of hiking shoes or boots is one of the best investments you'll make.

Clothing

Synthetic material, as mentioned above, is what it's all about. So what to bring? With a visit to a good outdoors store, you should walk away with ten articles: synthetic T-shirts, both long sleeve and short sleeve; synthetic hiking shorts and pants (and many companies, like Columbia Sportswear, make those wonderful pants with removable leggings—instant shorts!); a fleece pullover, lightweight and medium-weight; lightweight thermal underwear; synthetic-blend socks that wick away moisture and stay dry; rain jacket and pants; lightweight fleece gloves; waterproof gloves; wide-brimmed sun hat; a warm pullover hat. Snug clothes are better than loose, so make sure they fit properly.

Footwear

In general, you should consider three things when looking for good hiking footwear. For one, there is **support:** a good shoe or boot needs to offer both the foot and ankle ideal support, so as to make those rocky crossings safer and less strenuous. The **weight** of footwear is as important; heavy footwear means tiresome walking, especially if you are considering a long-distance jaunt. Talk about dragging your feet! **Flexibility** will save you from that painful culprit: the blister. Flexibility must balance itself with overall boot fit, since slippage is what generally exacerbates the formation of blisters.

You should fit boots in relation to socks: the combination of the two, once mastered, will save you from sitting around the campfire at night, cutting moleskin for those welts.

There are many options for footwear, from trail running shoes and lightweight hiking boots to sturdier backpacking boots. Consider the tread on the boot, the ankle support, and whether the material is waterproof or water-resistant. Once you purchase new footwear, be sure to take a few test runs and break them in before that big backpacking trip. Your feet will applaud you.

CLIMATE AND WEATHER PROTECTION

Weather in Oregon is diverse and unpredictable. Wind, pouring rain, snow and ice, blazing sun, high and low humidity, all of these are part of the Oregon experience. It is essential to be prepared. Weather reports, especially those from the National Weather Service, help greatly, but be ready for sudden changes—especially along the coast, in the high desert, and in the mountains.

THE PACIFIC CREST TRAIL

The most famous long-distance trail through Oregon is the Pacific Crest Trail (PCT), part of the 2,650-mile trail that passes through three states between Canada and Mexico. The Beaver State has its fair share of this historic and well-used National Scenic Trail, and its 430-mile stretch is usually snow-free between July and September. There's a lot to see: the Siskiyou Mountains, Crater Lake National Park, the Oregon Cascades with its long line of volcanic peaks, and the Columbia Gorge National Scenic Area.

The PCT accounts for a number of popular day hikes, especially in Oregon's famed wilderness areas: Mount Hood, Three Sisters, and Sky Lakes to name a few. Along the way, the trail passes everything from errant graves to lava fields to the incredible Timberline Lodge.

Seasons

Oregon has roughly four seasons, and each region reflects those seasons differently. Everywhere in the state, summer, the peak season, tends to have higher temperatures (though the people of Bend, Oregon, still talk about the time it snowed on the Fourth of July). As late summer approaches, so does the occasional rain and sleet.

Autumn, too, makes for beautiful days, and is my favorite time to hike. The color displays are at a height, and days can be significantly cooler, thus making for a sweat-free ramble.

As winter approaches, so does the wind, rain, and snow. For the most part, a significant number of Oregon's mountains are snowed-in and inaccessible all winter long: check with local agencies before trying a hike in an unfamiliar place. Roads, too, tend to be snowed in, and access to trailheads can be nonexistent. Winter in Oregon, at least in the mountains (including the Cascades, the Blues, the Wallowas, and the high elevations of the Siskiyous), can stretch from November to July.

Spring brings mud and more rain, but also increasing wildflower shows.

Rain Gear

What more needs to be said? Oregonians aren't said to have webbed feet for nothing. Rain gear is crucial, and this is largely why Oregonians tend to not care if it's raining. It's not like hikers are the little kids in front of the window, glumly watching the rain, wishing they could go out. On the contrary, nothing stops hikers in Oregon.

Durable, breathable rain gear (along with waterproof or water-resistant footwear) is an investment that will allow access to many places in Oregon year-round. For the most part, the Oregon coast, the foothills of the Cascades, most of the Columbia River Gorge, and low-elevation valleys are open year-round. Take advantage of it! Much of Oregon's beauty is due to the rains. What else keeps Oregon so green?

SAFETY

Like many Western U.S. states, it is possible to run into rattlesnakes, mountain lions, and bears—not to mention poison oak and biting bugs. Here's a little information about the locals.

NON-TECHNICAL SUMMIT HIKES

Oregon is a mountain climber's dream. With numerous peaks exceeding the 10,000-foot elevation range, there are plenty of opportunities to get on top of the world and enjoy the stunning views that come with them. That being said, it is important to differentiate the kind of mountain climbs featured in this book as available to the common hiker.

A "technical" summit climb requires not just skill but equipment such as ropes, harnesses, protection gear, and other specialized tools like ice axes and crampons. Mount Hood is the most popular of all technical climbs in Oregon, and a summit climb of this kind should never be done without experienced partners and a great deal of training and conditioning. It is a sport unto itself.

Hikes recommended in this book are "non-technical" summits, meaning climbing gear is not required. The mountain hikes covered in this book are those that can be summited on trails recognized by management agencies and detailed on maps. They are generally a long, steep climb, but far safer than climbing extremely steep slopes and crossing glaciers. Think of a non-technical climb, also known as "scrambling," as a really tough hike, where the path may get arduous and you may have to cross some snow now and again.

No matter the climb – whether it be South Sister, Mount McLoughlin, or Eagle Cap – always be prepared as you would for any other hike, if not more so. Be sure to carry more than enough food, water, and clothing, and remember that any change in weather can prove disastrous. Also, pace yourself; any non-technical climb can be especially taxing if you are out-of-shape or tired. Practice on smaller climbs before attempting to bag the big peaks.

Wildlife

Rattlesnakes

Of the 15 species of snakes in Oregon, only *Crotalus viridis*, the Western Pacific Rattlesnake, is poisonous. They are most active in the spring, summer, and early fall and can be found in parts of the Willamette Valley, the Cascade Mountain foothills, the Siskiyou Mountains, and parts of Eastern Oregon. Their most easily identifiable characteristic, of course, is that heart-stopping rattle. And it's good to stop, because once it has warned you, a rattlesnake is going to try to retreat from you. Stand still; rattlers rarely attack a nonmoving object.

Although rattlesnake bites are certainly painful, they are rarely lethal. Not all rattlesnake bites contain venom, either. If you are bitten, the best thing you can do is call 911 and drive to a hospital. Remove any restrictive clothing and don't attempt to apply a tight tourniquet. Remain calm and avoid running, which can speed venom through the body.

Mountain Lions

Cougars, also known as mountain lions, are the largest of the big cats in Oregon. They range pretty much anywhere, and have even passed through towns and cities in the state, especially when following migrating prey such as elk. However, in all likelihood, you will never see one. Cougars will usually avoid humans at all cost. In fact, many people have been near one and never realized it.

In mountain lion country, keep children and pets close. Should you encounter a cougar, don't turn away and don't run. Instead, make yourself appear as large as possible by raising your arms, waving a stick, and opening your coat. Back away slowly, maintaining your pose and speaking loudly.

Black Bears

Like cougars, black bears range widely and try to steer clear of humans. Be alert and make a little noise in bear country to let them know you're coming. If you do see one—which is unlikely, but not impossible—you'll know what it is, since black bears are the only species of bear in Oregon.

If you do encounter a bear, don't run and don't look it in the eye: bears interpret this as a sign of aggression. Instead, back away slowly. If a bear does happen to charge you, stay calm and be prepared to fight back. You can make yourself look bigger by waving your arms and opening your coat. If you have a dog, keep it leashed; an over-protective dog can put a bear on the defensive. One of the worst-case scenarios is to come between a mother bear and her cubs.

A more common way to run into a bear is at camp. Bears are attracted by not only food, and sweet food at that, but by fragrances like toothpaste and perfume. Really. If bears know, or think, that there's something tasty in your tent or your bag, like that honey-almond granola you brought, they'll have at it. Though Oregon doesn't have the same issues with bears as, say, Yosemite National Park in California, it's still wise to hide your food. Backpackers should use a bear-proof canister for overnight trips. You can also make use of a food-hang, where you hang your food by rope from a tree limb, a minimum of 20 feet off the ground and 10 feet from the tree trunk. Tie your rope to a rock and throw it over a branch at least one inch in diameter and four inches at the trunk to accomplish this.

Insects and Plants

Aside from the large mammals and reptiles, it's the little things that get you: mosquitoes, ticks, poison oak, and stinging nettles. Here's how to avoid them.

Mosquitoes

Mosquitoes in Oregon are by far the peskiest pest of all. Come spring and summer, the valleys and mountains—even the deserts—bloom with the obnoxious buzzing and incessant biting. All this can make for a thoroughly annoying outdoor experience spent swatting and slapping.

Mosquitoes are not merely annoying; they may even be dangerous. As with other states, Oregon has had its first few experiences with West Nile Virus, though it has mostly been confined to a few infections in people, birds, and horses. Better safe than sorry. Know before you go: As snows melt in the mountains, mosquitoes are born, and this typically happens from June to August. Visiting a marshy wildlife refuge in spring? Expect skeeters. Even in deserts, you can expect hordes of them along rivers.

The worst of the worst is the Asian tiger mosquito, a non-native species thought to have been brought to America in automobile tires that contained stagnant water. You'll know them when you see them by their stripes. It's best to carry repellent and netting, or even to avoid certain areas in the peak hatching season.

Ticks

You'll want to corral a friend into a good old "tick check." Ticks find their way into the weirdest of places in an effort to lock in and draw from your blood. The frontline defense is long pants and long sleeves, and to check both your skin and your clothing after hiking. If you find a tick burrowed in, pull it straight out carefully with tweezers, grasping it firmly from the surface of the skin. It's important to get the body and head out, or you can risk infection.

Ticks are most active in spring and summer, in areas of tall grasses and shrubs. Of the four varieties of ticks in Oregon, only the Western black-legged tick is a carrier of Lyme disease. This little tick is mostly black; the larger brown ones are harmless. It's generally said that if you can save a removed tick and take it to a doctor for testing, that's a safe bet. If within a few days or a few weeks you begin to experience flu-like symptoms, see a doctor post-haste.

Dogs, too, are susceptible to ticks, so make sure to check them carefully when you've been hiking in susceptible areas.

Poison Oak

It's been said many times before, but let's say it again: "Leaves of three, let them be." Once you learn to recognize *Toxicodendron diversilobum,* it will become very familiar to you, especially in areas like southern Oregon, the Willamette Valley, and the Columbia Gorge. Otherwise, the brutal rash that can itch for weeks will teach you the hard way to remember. Even as the leaves dry, they still contain the chemical that affects us. Should you come into contact with poison oak, or think you may have, wash thoroughly with warm water and soap as soon as possible. There are several products and soap available that can deal with exposure to poison oak on the trail. As I've learned from experience, dogs pick it up on their fur. Rather than petting, offer your pooch a nice, hot bath.

Avoiding Poison Oak: Remember the old Boy Scout saying: "Leaves of three, let them be."

Stinging Nettles

This member of the nettle family likes to grow in clumps in the Coast Range and in the desert. Heart-shaped, coarse-toothed leaves on a stem bristling with little white hairs gives it away. If you come in contact with those hairs, the resulting sting will let you know immediately that your identification is successful. You'll have to ride out the sting for 24 hours, wondering all the while how it is possible—and delectable—to boil and eat nettles safely!

Safety on the Trail

Stories abound of unfortunate mishaps where people get lost in the wilderness for days on end, and every year seems to bring a new tale of woe. Most of these stories involve two kinds of hikers: the one who hikes alone, and the one who gets separated from a larger group. One wrong turn off a trail, or simply not paying attention in the midst of a huge mountain meadow, can have dire consequences. Weather, too, can have an impact on your safety—for example, getting caught on a ridgeline in a lightning storm (and this one comes from experience!) calls for quick thinking.

Should you find yourself lost, your first priority is to remain calm. Know that it's far better to stay put where you are than to try to keep moving; rescuers will be looking for where you were last known to be (this is why it's so important to fill out wilderness permits at trailheads). Emergency gear, especially a whistle and signaling device, will come in handy here, since rescuers will be listening and looking for signs.

What's the best way to avoid trouble? Simply this: Always tell someone where you'll be. Tell someone at home your travel plans and register with a local ranger station, especially if your plan is to hike into a remote wilderness area. Be specific and detail the area you're visiting, the times you intend to travel, and how long you think you'll be out. It's the responsible thing to do, and it saves searchers much time and effort should you become lost.

Driving Safely

If you think weather can wreak havoc on a trail, try a road. Many of the approaches to trailheads in Oregon require driving on dirt roads that can quickly turn to mud or, worse, can result in a washout. Always check road conditions before you go by calling the Oregon Department of Transportation at 511 or checking www.tripcheck.com. Detailed weather reports and forecasts are available through the National Weather Service online at www.nws.noaa.gov.

Make sure that your car is properly equipped. Fuel up often, check the oil and the brakes, and make sure you've got a spare tire. Have emergency road equipment like snow chains, flashers, and a cell phone.

Make sure your directions are accurate (even mine!). Carry a good atlas of Oregon, like the DeLorme or Benchmark, and don't rely exclusively on Internet maps or GPS devices. If all else fails, ask directions.

Check snow levels. Every year in recent memory has seen individuals or families getting trapped in the snow in the mountains. Just because it's raining in Portland doesn't mean it is at Mount Hood; most likely, it's piling up snow quick. Avoid roads closed in winter or otherwise impassable. Forest Service roads are not shortcuts; stick to main routes and get there safely.

HIKING ETHICS

Trail Etiquette

As wonderful as it is to think like Henry David Thoreau and head for the woods for a little soul-searching solitude, don't expect to find it all the time. Expect instead a lot of other intrepid hikers looking for their own Walden Pond, too. Here are some simple rules to follow to assure a good time for everyone.

WILDERNESS ETHICS

Congressionally designated Wilderness Areas are unique, and are preserved under certain criteria. It's important to maintain the wilderness experience for everyone by limiting human impact. Here are some basic guidelines:

Campfires: Gone are the days of singing around the campfire. For the most part, campfires are discouraged – if not outright prohibited – due to catastrophic forest fires rampant in the Western United States. Land management agencies have decreed that cooking is best done on a backpacking stove. Lighting can be provided by a variety of devices, from flashlights to headlamps.

Water sources: It is imperative to keep Oregon's waters clean. When camping near any lake, stream, or river, give yourself at least 100 feet distance from the waterline before pitching that tent. Likewise, wash all your cooking gear, socks, and hands by carrying water at least 100 feet away from the water source.

Campsites: When you pitch a tent, be aware of where you are plopping down. A misplaced tent can crush sensitive flowers and damage an area for years. You should always camp on a durable surface, such as rock, or even on sand or dead and dry organic matter – never on live vegetation. This helps maintain the environment for all and prevents area closures for rehabilitation.

Garbage: No one is impressed by a trashed campsite. Who wants to see another campfire ring filled with broken glass and blackened cans, or a campsite ringed by toilet paper wads? No matter what you bring, pack out your garbage. Neither burn nor bury it. That goes for human waste, too.

Maintain the silence. You and everyone else come to the wilderness to get away from the usual hustle and bustle of civilization. Be courteous to all the other hikers by refraining from undue noise. Avoid loud conversations, shouting, and above all, cell phones. This way, too, you're more likely to encounter wildlife and hear the falling water and wind in the trees.

Yield to other users accordingly. Standard rules on yielding apply for the three main user groups—hikers, horses, and bikers. In general, bikes must yield to everyone, and hikers should yield to horses.

Stay on maintained trails. Evidence of breaking this rule is everywhere. Degraded switchbacks and the ubiquitous "user trail" show for certain that people are taking shortcuts and wandering off-trail. Don't use closed trails or enter closed areas; often, they have been closed for restoration or because of overuse. Wandering off-trail tramples vegetation and in the end may force management agencies to limit access for everyone.

Hiking with Children

Always keep children close, especially in areas with cliffs and fast-moving water. Consider the trail carefully before taking children, as many routes are too difficult for them. By choosing appropriate trails, you'll make trips memorable and enjoyable for everyone.

Hiking with Dogs

It's possible that there's no more dog-friendly state than Oregon. That being so, you're sure to run into dogs on the trail or to want to bring your own. And what could be more charming than a dog carrying its own pack with little mitts on its paws?

Regardless, dogs open a whole new can of worms in the outdoors. For one thing, chasing wildlife is a leading reason why dogs get lost in the wilderness. A dog on a leash is a dog that goes home again.

Because of conflicts between hikers and pets, dogs are no longer allowed on many trails in Oregon, or are restricted to a leash on others. Some trails, like the Deschutes River Trail in Central Oregon, no longer allow dogs off-leash, but this may not be obvious at the trailhead. It's best to call the area's managing agency for up-to-date rules. If a posted sign says that dogs must be on a leash, follow it strictly. Otherwise, you could well end up with a ticket.

If a dog is allowed off-leash, as in many forest and wilderness areas, take care that your dog responds appropriately to verbal commands, for the dog's own safety. Why worry? Carry a leash or get good dog training and just enjoy the trip for you and your dog both.

Avoiding Crowds

On the one hand, you can hike into a place like Big Indian Gorge on a summer weekend and not see a soul but for a few deer. On the other hand, you can go to Multnomah Falls, trying to get to the top to hike on up to Larch Mountain and fight your way through throngs of tourists, day-trippers, kids with ice cream cones, and parents in flip-flops pushing strollers. What to do? With a little foresight, you can find a bit of solitude after all.

Avoid the weekends. Weekends are notorious for the so-called "weekend warrior" out for a Saturday afternoon. If you get the chance, take your hike when everyone else is at work. From Tuesday through Thursday seems to be the best, and quietest, time.

Be the first one at the trailhead. If you arrive at a trailhead at around 10 or 11 A.M. like most people do, you'll have trouble finding a parking spot and staying out of the parade. But get there at 6 A.M.? Now you're talking. More than likely, you'll be the only one there.

Hike more than just summer. For most of Oregon, the on-season is summer. Memorial Day (which can be horrendous) and Labor Day (even worse) and everything in between means everyone is out for that brief respite between rains. But once the kids are in school and everyone is secure in the usual routine, *now* is the time to get out.

Avoid the popular hikes. If you have a need for peace and quiet on an August weekend afternoon, then maybe Crater Lake is not your best bet. But then nearby Mount Bailey might be. Choose off-the-beaten-path journeys and you're less likely to see the casual tourist.

Hike in the rain. Any bad weather will do, and if you have good gear you can be out looking at wildflowers in the spring rain while the rest of the world is home keeping their feet warm. Oregon is a place of many moods: gale-force winds, fog, clouds, and rain. These make life more interesting—and memorable.

Leave No Trace

As Henry David Thoreau once said, "In wilderness is the preservation of the world." So how do we preserve our wilderness? The Center for Outdoor Ethics offers these simple dictums to "Leave only footprints and take only pictures":

Plan ahead and prepare. Know the special regulations of the area you are visiting. Be prepared. Schedule your trips to avoid high-use times. Visit in small groups. Repackage your food to minimize waste.

Travel and camp on durable surfaces. Use established trails and campsites. Keep campsites small. In pristine areas, disperse use to prevent the creation of camps or trails.

Dispose of waste properly. Pack it in, pack it out. Deposit human waste in a "cathole" dug 6–8 inches at least 200 feet from water, camp, and trails; cover and disguise when finished. Pack out toilet paper and hygiene products. To wash yourself or dishes, carry water 200 feet away from streams and lakes. If you must use soap, make sure it's biodegradable. Scatter the water when done.

Leave what you find. Examine, but do not touch or remove, cultural or historic structures and artifacts. Leave rocks, plants, and natural objects as you find them. Avoid introducing non-native species. Do not build structures or furniture or dig trenches.

Minimize campfire impacts. Use a stove for cooking, a candle for lighting. Where fires are permitted, use established fire rings, pans, or mounds. Keep fires small and use only ground material to burn. Burn wood and coals to ash, douse completely, and scatter the cool ashes.

Respect wildlife. Remember that you are only a visitor in the wilderness, but it is home to animals. Observe wildlife from a distance, and do not approach or follow. Never feed animals. Store your food securely and control your pets. Avoid wildlife during times of mating, nesting, and raising young.

Be considerate of other visitors. Respect others and protect the quality of their experience. Be courteous. Camp away from other people. Let nature's sounds prevail.

This copyrighted information has been reprinted with permission from the Leave No Trace Center for Outdoor Ethics. For more information or materials, please visit www.lnt.org or call 303/442-8222 or 800/332-4100.

Permits and Land Use

There are different permits you'll need for each of Oregon's 115 state parks, 13 national forest, and five state forests. Many trails on National Forest land, but not all, require the Northwest Forest Pass to park within a quarter-mile of a posted trailhead. These cost $5 a day or $30 for a yearly pass.

Most wilderness areas on National Forest land require a free wilderness permit (available at trailheads) to enter. There are exceptions, such as the Obsidian Trail or the Pamelia Lake area, which require a free special permit beforehand, secured simply by calling the ranger station.

Oregon State Parks vary widely. Some require a day-use fee, while others are free. Many of the more popular parks require a day-use fee, but the waysides—especially along beaches—tend to be free.

The Bureau of Land Management, National Forest Service, and National Park Service manage Oregon's national monuments, national recreation areas, Crater Lake National Park, and the Columbia Gorge National Scenic Area. In addition to the information provided in this book, be sure to contact the appropriate agency for up-to-date information on fees and permits.

OREGON'S SOUTHERN CASCADES CAMPING

BEST CAMPGROUNDS

Most Scenic
Scott Lake Walk-In, **page 49.**
North Waldo, **page 64.**
Lava Lake, **page 86.**
Squaw Lake Hike-In, **page 139.**

Families
Twin Lakes Resort, **page 92.**
Indian Mary Park, **page 110.**
Abbott Creek, **page 119.**
Lake of the Woods Resort, **page 129.**

Fishing
Belknap Hot Springs Resort, **page 38.**
Mallard Marsh, **page 86.**
Trapper Creek, **page 102.**

Hiking
Belknap Hot Springs Resort, **page 38.**
Boulder Flat, **page 73.**
Natural Bridge, **page 119.**
Aspen Point, **page 130.**

Waterfalls
Salmon Creek Falls, **page 64.**
Susan Creek, **page 70.**
Steamboat Falls, **page 71.**
Hemlock Lake, **page 78.**

Waterfront Campgrounds
Driftwood, **page 51.**
Hemlock Lake, **page 78.**
Gold Lake, **page 99.**
Bolan Lake, **page 118.**

Wildlife-Viewing
Crooked River Ranch RV Park, **page 48.**
Bolan Lake, **page 118.**
Mount Ashland, **page 140.**

This region of Oregon is famous for one of its lakes, but it holds many fantastic recreation secrets. The crown jewel is Crater Lake, of course, and visitors come from all over the world to see its vast cobalt-blue waters within cliff-like walls. The lake's Rim Drive is one of those trips that everybody should have on their life's to-do list.

Beyond the lake, though, you'll find stellar camping, fishing, and hiking spots. The best among them are neighboring Mount Washington Wilderness and Three Sisters Wilderness in Willamette National Forest, accessible via a beautiful drive on the McKenzie River Highway (Highway 126) east from Eugene and Springfield. Many ideal trailhead camps are detailed in this chapter for these areas.

But wait, there's more: Crane Prairie, Waldo Lake, and Wickiup Reservoir provide boating, camping, and good fishing. Wickiup, in turn, feeds into the headwaters of the Deschutes River, a prime steelhead locale. The Umpqua and Rogue National Forests offer some great water-sport destinations, including Diamond Lake, the headwaters of the Rogue River, and the headwaters of the North Umpqua, one of the prettiest rivers in North America. Upper Klamath Lake and the Klamath Basin are the number-one wintering areas in America for bald eagles. Klamath Lake also provides a chance to catch huge but elusive trout, as does the nearby Williamson River out of Chiloquin. All of this is but a small sampling of one of Oregon's best regions for adventure.

This region is all the more special for me because it evokes powerful personal memories. One of these is of a time at Hills Creek Reservoir southeast of Eugene. My canoe flipped on a cold winter day and I almost drowned after 20 minutes in the icy water. After I'd gone down for the count twice, my brother Bob jumped in, swam out, grabbed the front of the flipped canoe, and towed me to shore. Then, once ashore, he kept me awake, preventing me from lapsing into a coma from hypothermia.

Thanks, Bob.

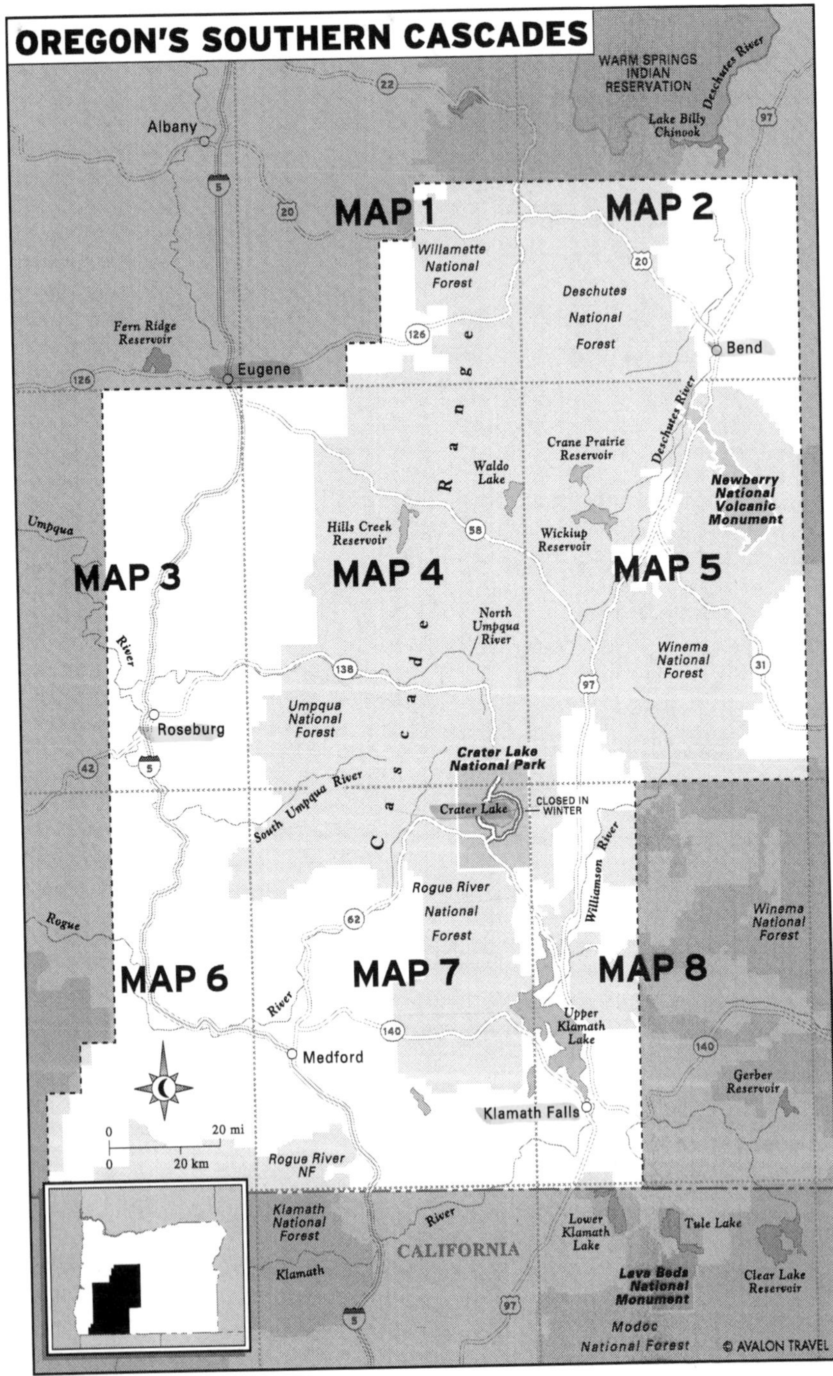
OREGON'S SOUTHERN CASCADES
WARM SPRINGS INDIAN RESERVATION
Deschutes River
Lake Billy Chinook
Albany
MAP 1
MAP 2
Willamette National Forest
Deschutes National Forest
Bend
Fern Ridge Reservoir
Eugene
Cascade Range
Crane Prairie Reservoir
Waldo Lake
Deschutes River
Newberry National Volcanic Monument
Umpqua
Hills Creek Reservoir
Wickiup Reservoir
MAP 3
MAP 4
MAP 5
North Umpqua River
River
Winema National Forest
Umpqua National Forest
Roseburg
Crater Lake National Park
Crater Lake
CLOSED IN WINTER
South Umpqua River
Williamson River
Rogue River National Forest
Rogue
Winema National Forest
MAP 6
MAP 7
MAP 8
River
Upper Klamath Lake
Medford
Gerber Reservoir
Klamath Falls
0 20 mi
0 20 km
Rogue River NF
Klamath National Forest
River
CALIFORNIA
Lower Klamath Lake
Tule Lake
Klamath
Lava Beds National Monument
Clear Lake Reservoir
Modoc National Forest
© AVALON TRAVEL

Map 1

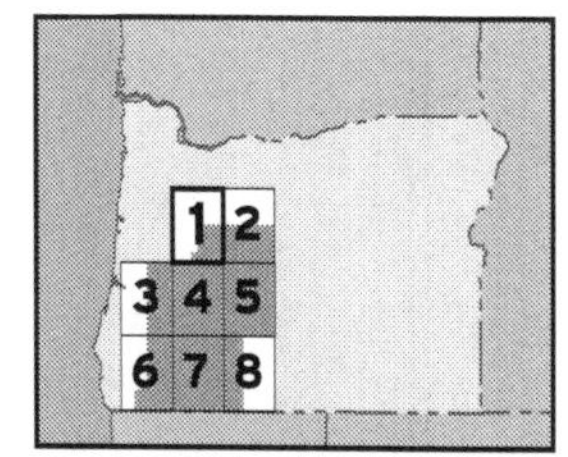

Campgrounds 1-17

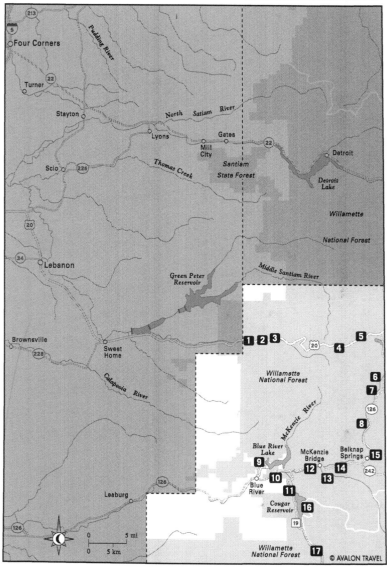

Four Corners
Pudding River
Turner
Stayton
North Satiam River
Lyons
Gates
Mill City
Detroit
Scio
Thomas Creek
Santiam State Forest
Detroit Lake
Willamette National Forest
Lebanon
Middle Santiam River
Green Peter Reservoir
Brownsville
Sweet Home
1 2 3 4 5
Calapooia River
Willamette National Forest
6
7
8
McKenzie River
Blue River Lake
McKenzie Bridge
Belknap Springs
15
9
12 14
10 13
Blue River
Leaburg
11
Cougar Reservoir
16
0 5 mi
0 5 km
Willamette National Forest
17

CAMPING

Map 2

Campgrounds 18–51

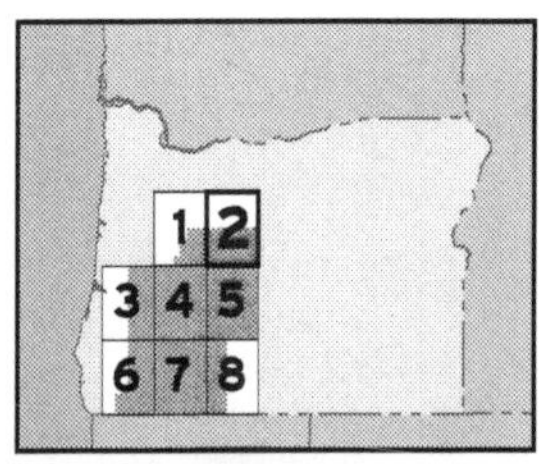

Mutton Mountains
WARM
SPRINGS
INDIAN
RESERVATION
Warm Springs River
Boulder Creek
26
Warm Springs
97
Mount Jefferson Wilderness
Mt Jefferson 10,497ft
22
Lake Simtustus
Lake Billy Chinook
Madras
Metolius
Deschutes National Forest
Cove Palisades SP
Culver
Mount Jefferson Wilderness
29
26
18-27
28
97
Crooked
Creek
126
FR 14
39
34-36
32-33
37
30
Squaw
38
Terrebonne
31
Mt Washington 7,794ft
River
Mount Washington Wilderness
20
126
Sisters
40
Redmond
41
Three Sisters Wilderness
242
42
Deschutes River
43
44
45
46
47-48
Deschutes National Forest
49
0 5 mi
0 5 km
Bend
50
20
CASCADE LAKES HWY
46
46
97
51

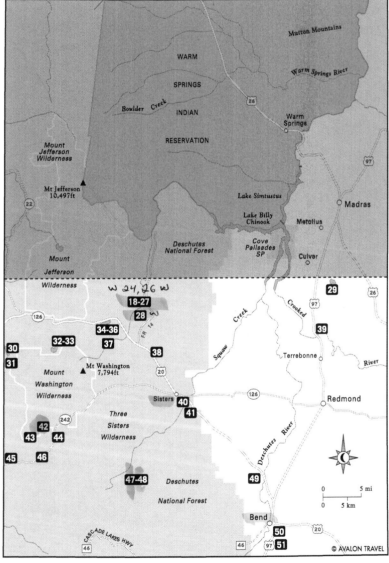

Map 3

Campgrounds 52-61

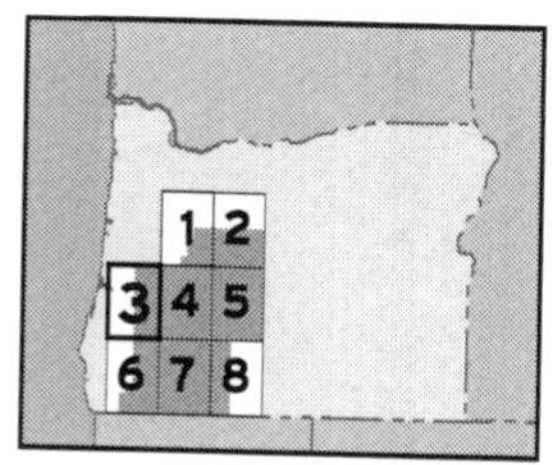

Siuslaw National Forest
Creswell
Siuslaw River
52
53
Smith River
Cottage Grove
5
54
55-56
Cottage Grove Lake
38
Elkton
99
Yoncalla
Umpqua River
138
Oakland
Sutherlin
North Umpqua River
57
S Fork Coos River
58
Roseburg
59
60
61
East Fork Coquille River
Green
42
0 5 mi
0 5 km
Myrtle Creek
South Myrtle Creek

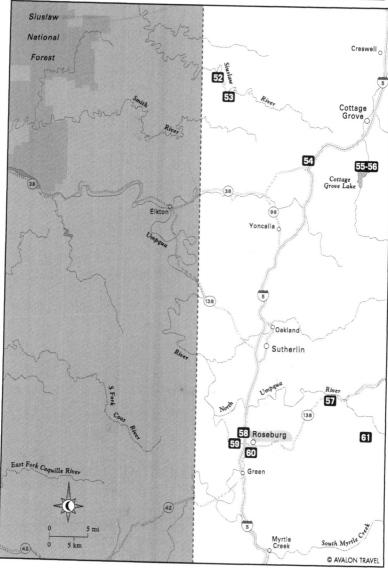

Map 4

Campgrounds 62-121

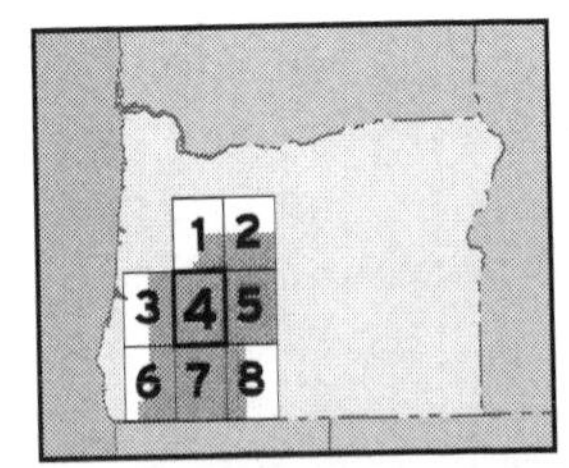

58
63
64-65
66-67
68
62
Lowell
Lookout Point Lake
Willamette National Forest
72
69
70
71
19
73
77
Dorena Lake
58
76
78
79
Westfir
Oakridge
74-75
Waldo Lake
80
Hills Creek Reservoir
81
84
58
82
83
Diamond Pk 8,744ft
85
Diamond Peak Wilderness
Calapooya Mountains
Middle Fork
86
Willamette River
87-89
Umpqua National Forest
90
91
93
106
94
Steamboat
95
96
101-105
138
92
98-99
North Umpqua River
97
100
138
112
113
107
108
110
109
111
114-116
Diamond Lake
Umpqua National Forest
Mount Thielsen Wilderness
230
0 5 mi
0 5 km
South Umpqua River
117
118
138
Rogue River
Crater Lake National Park
120
121
119

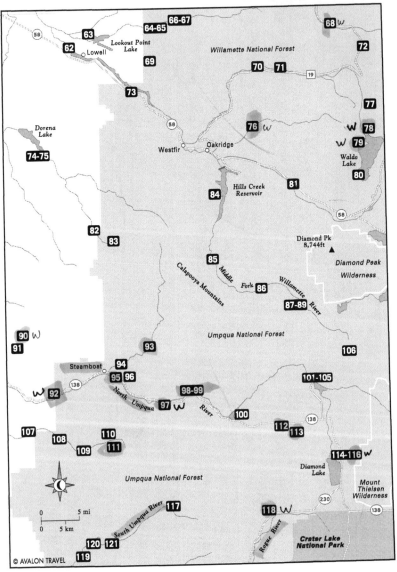

Map 5

Campgrounds 122-188

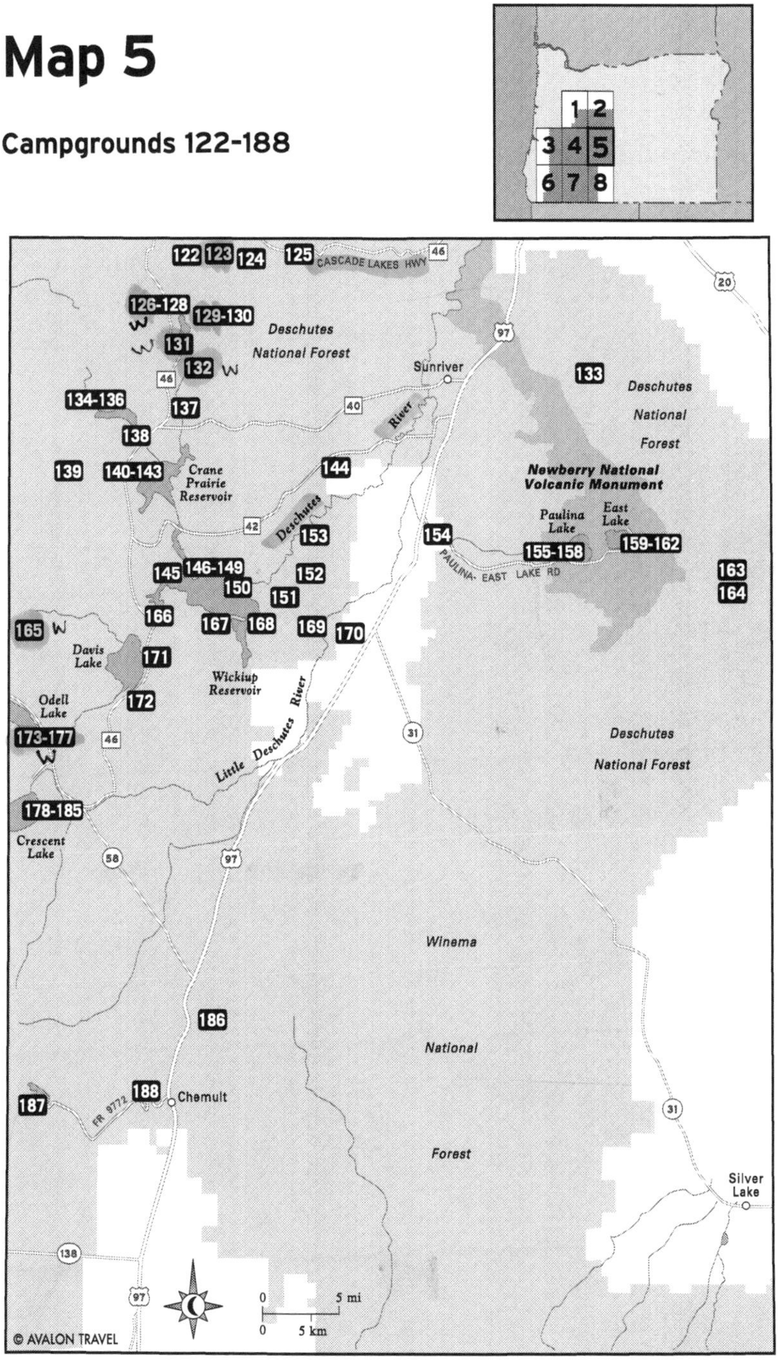

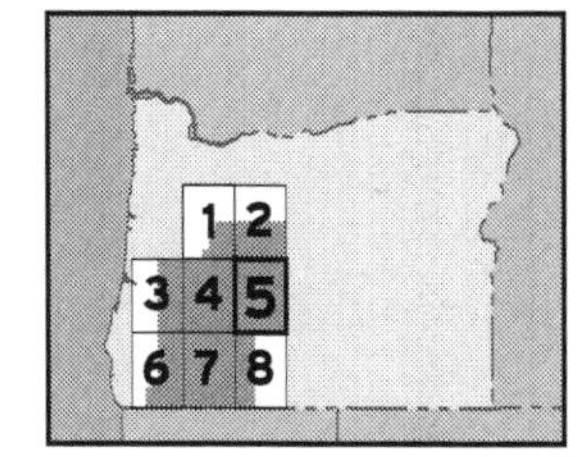

122 123 124 125
CASCADE LAKES HWY
46
20
126-128
129-130
Deschutes
National Forest
131
132
97
Sunriver
133
Deschutes
National
Forest
134-136
137
40
River
138
139
140-143
Crane
Prairie
Reservoir
144
Newberry National
Volcanic Monument
Paulina
Lake
East
Lake
42
Deschutes
153
154
155-158
159-162
PAULINA-EAST LAKE RD
163
164
145
146-149
150
152
151
166
167
168
169
170
165
Davis
Lake
171
Wickiup
Reservoir
River
172
Odell
Lake
173-177
46
Little Deschutes
31
Deschutes
National Forest
178-185
Crescent
Lake
58
97
Winema
National
Forest
186
187
FR 9772
188
Chemult
31
Silver
Lake
138
97
0 5 mi
0 5 km

Map 6

Campgrounds 189-210

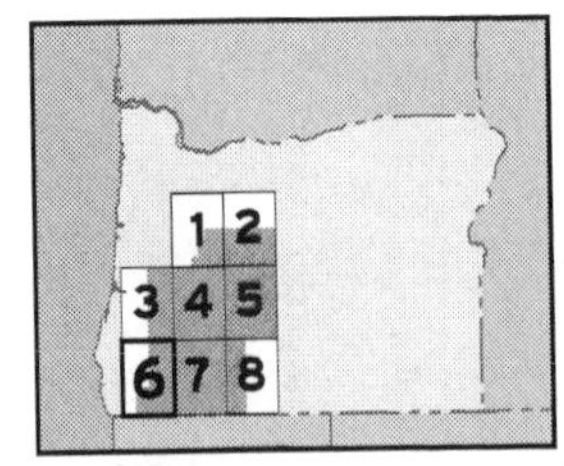

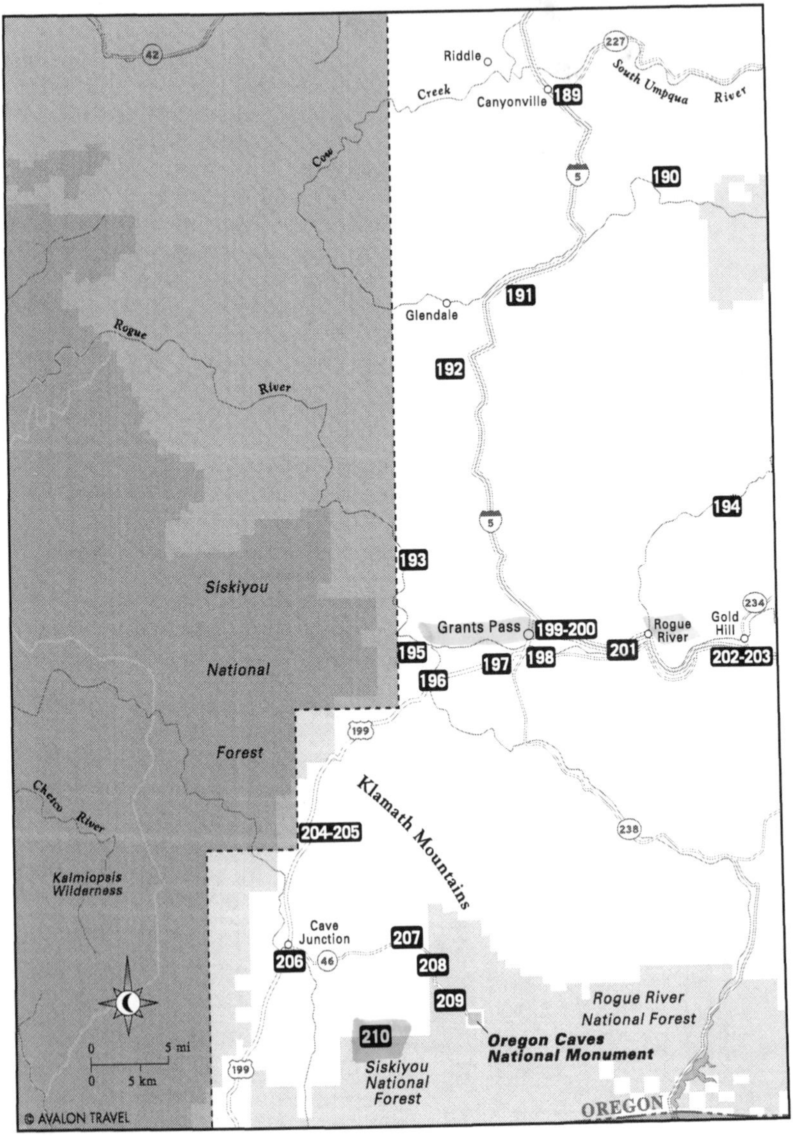

42
Riddle
227
South Umpqua River
Creek
Canyonville
189
Cow
5
190
191
Glendale
Rogue River
192
5
194
193
Siskiyou National Forest
234
Grants Pass
199-200
Rogue River
Gold Hill
195
197
198
201
202-203
196
199
Klamath Mountains
Chetco River
204-205
238
Kalmiopsis Wilderness
Cave Junction
207
206
46
208
209
Rogue River National Forest
0 5 mi
0 5 km
210
Oregon Caves National Monument
199
Siskiyou National Forest
OREGON

Map 7

Campgrounds 211-262

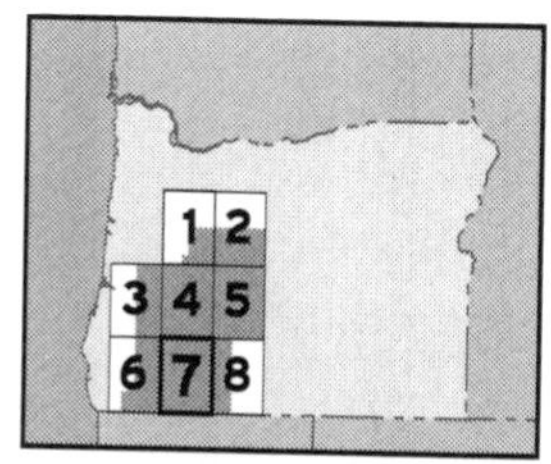

Crater Lake National Park
Crater Lake
Rogue River National Forest
230
211-213
214-215
62
216
217
218
219
227
62
Lost Creek Reservoir
223
222
221
Trail
220
Shady Cove
224
Rogue River National Forest
225
226
Sky Lakes Wilderness
62
Butte Falls
Upper Klamath NWR
231
228
230
229
234
Eagle Point
227
White City
140
232
Upper Klamath Lake
233
5
140
234
236-238
235
Fish Lake
140
239-241
Lake of the Woods
Mountain Lakes Wilderness
Central Point
Medford
Jacksonville
Phoenix
Howard Prairie Lake
245-246
Aspen Lake
242
Talent
247-251
243-244
Ashland
Hyatt Res
253
Emigrant Lake
252
66
Pinehurst
66
254
5
255
256
Mt. Ashland 7,533ft
Rogue River National Forest
261
262
257-259
260
0 5 mi
0 5 km
OREGON
© AVALON TRAVEL

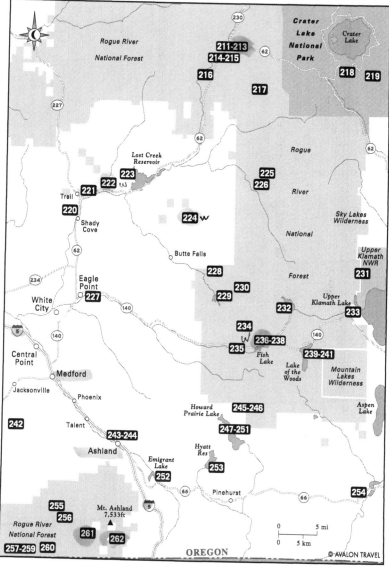

Map 8

Campgrounds 263-269

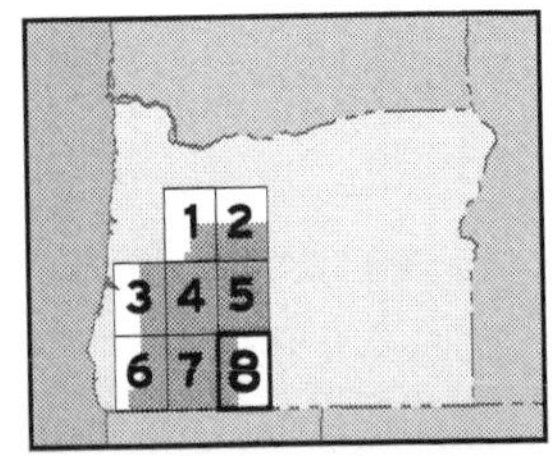

Crater Lake National Park
97
SUN MTN RD
Winema National Forest
River
Winema
263
264
62
62
Williamson
265
266
National
Chiloquin
267
Agency Lake
268
269
Forest
Modoc Point
Upper Klamath Lake
97
140
Klamath Falls
Altamont
Round Lake
66
39
97
© AVALON TRAVEL
OREGON
Thompson Reservoir
Fremont
National
Winema
National
Forest
Forest
Williamson River
Sprague River
140
140
Fremont National Forest
140
Bonanza
Gerber Reservoir
0 5 mi
0 5 km
Merrill
Malin

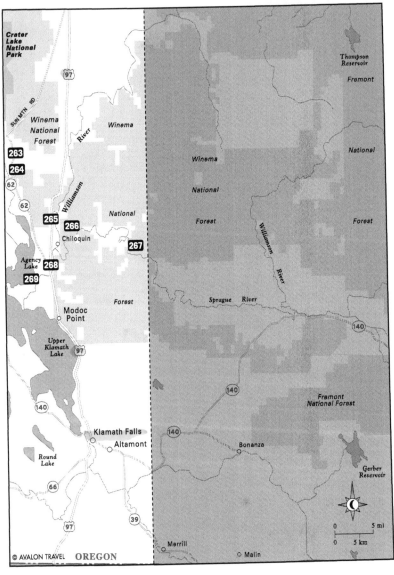

1 TROUT CREEK

Scenic rating: 8

on the South Santiam River in Willamette National Forest

Trout Creek campground is set along the banks of the South Santiam River at 1,200 feet in elevation, about seven miles east of Cascadia. Fishing and swimming are some of the recreation possibilities here. There is a historic shelter and the remains of stonework from the era of the Civilian Conservation Corps. The Trout Creek Trail, just across the highway, leads into the Menagerie Wilderness. The Long Ranch Elk Viewing Area is immediately west of the campground, and, at the Trout Creek Trailhead, you'll also find a short trail leading to an elk-viewing platform. Nearby is the Old Santiam Wagon Road.

Campsites, facilities: There are 24 sites for tents or RVs up to 32 feet long. Picnic tables, garbage bins, and fire rings are provided. Drinking water and vault toilets are available. Some facilities are wheelchair accessible. Leashed pets are permitted.

Reservations, fees: Reservations are not accepted. Sites are $12 per night, $5 per night per additional vehicle. Open May–October, weather permitting.

Directions: From Albany, drive east on U.S. 20 for 45 miles (19 miles past Sweet Home) to the campground entrance on the right.

Contact: Willamette National Forest, Sweet Home Ranger District, 541/367-5168, fax 541/367-2367, www.fs.fed.us.

2 YUKWAH

Scenic rating: 7

on the Santiam River in Willamette National Forest

Yukwah campground is nestled in a second-growth Douglas fir forest on the banks of the Santiam River. The camp is 0.25 mile east of Trout Creek Campground and offers the same recreation possibilities, including a 0.5-mile, compacted-surface interpretive trail that's barrier-free.

Campsites, facilities: There are 20 sites for tents or RVs up to 32 feet long, including a deluxe group site for up to 20 people. Picnic tables, garbage bins, and fire grills are provided. Drinking water, vault toilets, a picnic area, and a fishing platform are available. Some facilities, including the fishing platform, are wheelchair accessible. Leashed pets are permitted.

Reservations, fees: Reservations are not accepted. Sites are $12 per night, $5 per night per additional vehicle. The deluxe site is $24 per night. Open May–October, weather permitting.

Directions: From Albany, drive east on U.S. 20 for 45 miles (19 miles past Sweet Home) to the campground.

Contact: Willamette National Forest, Sweet Home Ranger District, 541/367-5168, fax 541/367-2367, www.fs.fed.us.

3 FERNVIEW

Scenic rating: 7

on the Santiam River in Willamette National Forest

This campground is perched high above the confluence of Boulder Creek and the Santiam River, just south of the Menagerie Wilderness. A stepped walkway leads down to the river. Just across U.S. 20 lies the Rooster Rock Trail, which leads to—where else?—Rooster Rock, the site of an old lookout tower. The Old Santiam Wagon Road runs through the back of the campground. The camp is best suited for tent and small RV camping: The sites are small. The elevation is 1,400 feet.

Campsites, facilities: There are nine sites for tents or RVs up to 22 feet long and two tent-

only sites. Picnic tables, garbage bins, and fire grills are provided. Drinking water and vault toilets are available. Some facilities are wheelchair accessible. Leashed pets are permitted.
Reservations, fees: Reservations are not accepted. Sites are $12 per night, $5 per night per additional vehicle. Open mid-May–mid-September, weather permitting.
Directions: From Albany drive east on U.S. 20 for 49 miles (23 miles past Sweet Home) to the campground entrance on the right.
Contact: Willamette National Forest, Sweet Home Ranger District, 541/367-5168, fax 541/367-2367, www.fs.fed.us.

4 HOUSE ROCK

Scenic rating: 8

on the Santiam River in Willamette National Forest

House Rock campground is situated at the confluence of Sheep Creek and the South Santiam River. The camp is set in the midst of an old-growth forest and is surrounded by huge, majestic Douglas fir. Trout fishing can be good, particularly during summer evenings. Botany students come here from long distances to see firsthand many uncommon and spectacular specimens of plantlife. History buffs should explore the short loop trail out of camp, which passes by House Rock, a historic rock shelter for Native Americans, and continues to the historic Old Santiam Wagon Road.
Campsites, facilities: There are 12 sites for tents or RVs up to 22 feet long and five tent-only sites. Picnic tables, garbage bins, and fire grills are provided. Vault toilets and drinking water are available. Some facilities are wheelchair accessible. Leashed pets are permitted.
Reservations, fees: Reservations are not accepted. Sites are $12 per night, $5 per night per additional vehicle. Open May–October, weather permitting.
Directions: From Albany drive east on U.S. 20 for 52.5 miles (26 miles past Sweet Home) to Latiwi Road (Forest Road 2044). Turn right and drive a short distance to the campground.
Contact: Willamette National Forest, Sweet Home Ranger District, 541/367-5168, fax 541/367-2367, www.fs.fed.us.

5 LOST PRAIRIE

Scenic rating: 7

on Hackleman Creek in Willamette National Forest

Lost Prairie campground hugs the banks of Hackleman Creek at 3,200 feet elevation in an area of Douglas fir and spruce. Three excellent hiking trails can be found within five miles of the camp: Hackleman Old-Growth Grove, Cone Peak, and Iron Mountain. The last two offer spectacular wildflower-viewing in the late spring and early summer. This camp provides an alternative to nearby Fish Lake.
Campsites, facilities: There are 10 sites for tents or RVs up to 28 feet long (eight are walk-in sites). Picnic tables, garbage bins, and fire grills are provided. Drinking water and vault toilets are available. Some facilities are wheelchair accessible. Leashed pets are permitted.
Reservations, fees: Reservations are not accepted. Sites are $14 per night, $7 per night per additional vehicle. Open May–October, weather permitting.
Directions: From Albany, drive east on U.S. 20 for 63 miles (approximately 38 miles past Sweet Home) to the camp on the right.
Contact: Willamette National Forest, Sweet Home Ranger District, 541/367-5168, fax 541/367-2367, www.fs.fed.us; Hoodoo Recreation, 541/822-3799.

6 LAKES END BOAT-IN

Scenic rating: 9

on Smith Reservoir in
Willamette National Forest

This secluded boat-in campground is set along the shore of the headwaters of Smith Reservoir, a long narrow lake. You'll find no cars and no traffic. The trout fishing in this reservoir can be exceptional; note the 10-mph speed limit. The campground is split into two areas, providing camping opportunities on Smith Creek and on the reservoir.

Campsites, facilities: There are 17 boat-in tent sites. Picnic tables and fire grills are provided. Pit toilets are available. There is no drinking water, and garbage must be packed out. Boat docks are nearby. Leashed pets are permitted.

Reservations, fees: Reservations are not accepted. There is no fee for camping. Open May–September, weather permitting.

Directions: From Eugene, drive east on Highway 126 for 47 miles to the town of McKenzie Bridge. Continue on Highway 126 for 13 miles to the signed turnoff for Lakes End at the north end of Trail Bridge Reservoir. Turn left on Forest Road 1477 and drive a short distance; then bear left and continue (past Trail Bridge Campground) for 0.5 mile to Forest Road 730 (Smith Reservoir Road). Continue three miles to the boat launch.

Contact: Willamette National Forest, McKenzie River Ranger District, 541/822-3381, fax 541/822-7254, www.fs.fed.us.

7 TRAIL BRIDGE

Scenic rating: 6

on Trail Bridge Reservoir in
Willamette National Forest

Set along the shore of Trail Bridge Reservoir (2,000 feet elevation), this campground offers boating, fishing, and hiking among its recreation options. From the camp, there is access to the McKenzie River National Recreation Trail. Highway 126 east of McKenzie Bridge is a designated scenic route, providing a pleasant trip to the camp and making Trail Bridge an exceptional spot for car campers. For a good side trip, take the beautiful 40-minute drive east to the little town of Sisters.

Campsites, facilities: There are 46 sites for tents or RVs up to 45 feet long and a large camping area at Trail Bridge Flats. Picnic tables, garbage service, and fire grills are provided. Drinking water and vault and flush toilets are available. Boat ramps are nearby. Some facilities are wheelchair accessible. Leashed pets are permitted.

Reservations, fees: Reservations are not accepted. Sites are $10 per night, $5 per night per additional vehicle. Open late April–September, weather permitting.

Directions: From Eugene, drive east on Highway 126 for 47 miles to the town of McKenzie Bridge. Continue on Highway 126 for 13 miles to Forest Road 1477. Turn left on Forest Road 1477 and drive a short distance; then bear left and continue 0.25 mile to the campground on the left.

Contact: Willamette National Forest, McKenzie River Ranger District, 541/822-3381, fax 541/822-7254, www.fs.fed.us.

8 OLALLIE

Scenic rating: 7

on the McKenzie River in
Willamette National Forest

Olallie campground sits at an elevation of 2,000 feet elevation along the banks of the McKenzie River. Boating, fishing, and hiking are among its recreational opportunities, and fishing for rainbow trout usually is good. Other bonuses include easy access from Highway 126. The campground is two miles southwest of Trail Bridge Reservoir off Highway 126.

Campsites, facilities: There are 16 sites for tents or RVs up to 35 feet long. Picnic tables and fire grills are provided. Vault toilets, drinking water, and garbage service are available. A boat launch is nearby (non-motorized boats only). Leashed pets are permitted.

Reservations, fees: Reservations are accepted at 877/444-6777 or www.recreation.gov ($10 reservation fee). Sites are $12–14 per night, $7 per night per additional vehicle. Open late April–October, weather permitting.

Directions: From Eugene, drive east on Highway 126 for 47 miles to the town of McKenzie Bridge. Continue on Highway 126 for 11 miles to the campground on the left.

Contact: Willamette National Forest, McKenzie River Ranger District, 541/822-3381, fax 541/822-7254, www.fs.fed.us; Hoodoo Recreation, 541/822-3799.

9 MONA

Scenic rating: 8

near Blue River Reservoir in Willamette National Forest

This forested campground (1,360 feet elevation) is set along the shore of Blue River Reservoir, close to where the Blue River joins it. A boat ramp is located across the river from the campground (at Lookout Campground); another boat ramp is situated at the south end of the reservoir. After launching a boat, campers can ground it near their campsite. Note that this camp is extremely popular when the reservoir is full.

Campsites, facilities: There are 23 sites for tents or RVs up to 36 feet long. Picnic tables, garbage bins, and fire grills are provided. Drinking water and flush toilets are available. Some facilities are wheelchair accessible. Leashed pets are permitted.

Reservations, fees: Reservations are not accepted. Single sites are $16 per night, $30 per night for double sites, $8 per night per additional vehicle. Open May–mid-September, weather permitting.

Directions: From Eugene, drive east on Highway 126 for 41 miles to Blue River. Continue east on Highway 126 for three miles to Forest Road 15. Turn left (north) and drive three miles to the campground on the left.

Contact: Willamette National Forest, McKenzie River Ranger District, 541/822-3381, fax 541/822-7254, www.fs.fed.us; Hoodoo Recreation, 541/822-3799.

10 PATIO RV PARK

Scenic rating: 7

near the South Fork of the McKenzie River

This RV park is situated near the banks of the South Fork of the McKenzie River, not far from Cougar Lake, which offers opportunities for fishing, swimming, and waterskiing. Nearby recreation options include a golf course, hiking trails, and bike paths. The Hoodoo Ski Area is approximately 30 miles away.

Campsites, facilities: There are 60 sites with full hookups for RVs of any length and a grassy area for tents. Picnic tables are provided. Restrooms with flush toilets and coin showers, ice, firewood, a recreation hall, video rentals, group kitchen facilities, cable TV, modem access, a community fire pit, horseshoe pits, and a coin laundry are available. A store, gasoline, propane, and a café are within two miles. Leashed pets are permitted.

Reservations, fees: Reservations are accepted at 800/650-0290 or via email at reservations@patiorv.com. RV sites are $26–31 per night, tent sites are $20 per night, $2 per person per night for more than two people, and $8 per night per additional vehicle. Some credit cards are accepted. Open year-round, weather permitting.

Directions: From Eugene, drive east on Highway 126 for 37 miles to the town of Blue River.

Continue east on Highway 126 for six miles to McKenzie River Drive. Turn right and drive two miles to the park on the right.
Contact: Patio RV Park, 541/822-3596, fax 541/822-8392, www.patiorv.com.

11 DELTA

Scenic rating: 8

on the McKenzie River in Willamette National Forest

This popular campground sits along the banks of the McKenzie River in a spot heavily forested primarily with old-growth Douglas fir. The Delta Old Growth Nature Trail, a 0.5-mile wheelchair-accessible interpretive trail, is adjacent to the campground. The camp also features an amphitheater. Nearby are Blue River and Cougar Reservoirs (seven and five miles away, respectively), both of which offer swimming, trout fishing, and waterskiing.
Campsites, facilities: There are 38 sites for tents or RVs up to 36 feet long. Picnic tables, garbage bins, and fire grills are provided. Drinking water and vault toilets are available. Some facilities are wheelchair accessible. Leashed pets are permitted.
Reservations, fees: Reservations are not accepted. Single sites are $14 per night, $26 per night for double sites, and $7 per night per additional vehicle. Open late April–October, weather permitting.
Directions: From Eugene, drive east on Highway 126 for 37 miles to the town of Blue River. Continue east on Highway 126 for five miles to Forest Road 19 (Aufderheide Scenic Byway). Turn right (south) and drive 0.25 mile to Forest Road 400. Turn right and drive one mile to the campground.
Contact: Willamette National Forest, McKenzie River Ranger District, 541/822-3381, fax 541/822-7254, www.fs.fed.us; Hoodoo Recreation, 541/822-3799.

12 McKENZIE BRIDGE

Scenic rating: 8

on the McKenzie River in Willamette National Forest

McKenzie campground is set at 1,400 feet elevation along the banks of the McKenzie River, one mile from the town of McKenzie Bridge. During the summer, this stretch of river provides good evening fly-fishing for trout; only non-motorized boats are permitted on the river.
Campsites, facilities: There are 20 sites for tents or RVs up to 40 feet long. Picnic tables, garbage service, and fire rings are provided. Flush toilets and drinking water are available. A grocery store and restaurants are available within one mile. Some facilities are wheelchair accessible. Leashed pets are permitted.
Reservations, fees: Reservations are accepted at 877/444-6777 or www.recreation.gov ($10 reservation fee). Sites are $14 per night, $7 per night per additional vehicle. Open April–September, weather permitting.
Directions: From Eugene, drive east on Highway 126 for 46 miles to the campground entrance on the right (one mile west of the town of McKenzie Bridge).
Contact: Willamette National Forest, McKenzie River Ranger District, 541/822-3381, fax 541/822-7254, www.fs.fed.us; Hoodoo Recreation, 541/822-3799.

13 HORSE CREEK GROUP CAMP

Scenic rating: 9

on Horse Creek in Willamette National Forest

This campground reserved for groups borders Horse Creek near the town of McKenzie Bridge. In spite of the name, no horse camping is permitted. Fishing is catch-and-release only;

check current regulations. The camp sits at 1,400 feet elevation.

Campsites, facilities: This is a group camp with 21 sites for tents or RVs up to 27 feet long. Picnic tables and fire grills are provided. Vault toilets, drinking water, and garbage service are available. Leashed pets are permitted.

Reservations, fees: Reservations are accepted at 877/444-6777 or www.recreation.gov ($10 reservation fee). The fees are $40 per night for up to 49 people and $60 per night for 50–100 people. Open May–September, weather permitting.

Directions: From Eugene, drive east on Highway 126 for 47 miles to the town of McKenzie Bridge and Horse Creek Road. Turn right (south) on Horse Creek Road and drive one mile to the campground on the left.

Contact: Willamette National Forest, McKenzie River Ranger District, 541/822-3381, fax 541/822-7254, www.fs.fed.us.

14 PARADISE

Scenic rating: 9

on the McKenzie River in Willamette National Forest

Paradise campground (1,600 feet elevation), along the banks of the McKenzie River, may be right off the highway, but it offers a rustic, streamside setting with access to the McKenzie River National Recreation Trail. Trout fishing can be good here.

Campsites, facilities: There are 64 sites for tents or RVs of any length. Picnic tables, garbage service, and fire rings are provided. Flush and vault toilets, drinking water, a boat ramp, and firewood are available. Some facilities are wheelchair accessible. Leashed pets are permitted.

Reservations, fees: Reservations are accepted at 877/444-6777 or www.recreation.gov ($10 reservation fee). Single sites are $18 per night, double sites are $32 per night, $9 per night per additional vehicle. Open May–September, weather permitting.

Directions: From Eugene, drive east on Highway 126 for 47 miles to the town of McKenzie Bridge. Continue east on Highway 126 for 3.5 miles to the campground on the left.

Contact: Willamette National Forest, McKenzie River Ranger District, 541/822-3381, fax 541/822-7254, www.fs.fed.us; Hoodoo Recreation, 541/822-3799.

15 BELKNAP HOT SPRINGS RESORT

Scenic rating: 9

on the McKenzie River

BEST

This beautiful park, with 60 acres of developed and landscaped gardens, has been featured on at least one magazine cover. It's in a wooded, mountainous area on the McKenzie River. Trout fishing can be excellent here. If you're looking for hiking opportunities, the McKenzie River Trail can be accessed from camp. Other hiking opportunities include the Three Sisters and Mount Washington Wilderness Areas, both accessible by driving west of Sisters on Highway 242. Exceptionally scenic and pristine expanses of forest, they are well worth exploring. The Pacific Crest Trail runs north and south through both wilderness areas.

Campsites, facilities: There are 62 sites with full or partial hookups for RVs of any length, 15 sites for tents, a lodge with 18 rooms, and six cabins. Picnic tables and fire pits are provided. Drinking water, restrooms with showers, and a dump station are available. Recreational facilities include two hot-spring fed swimming pools, massage therapy on weekends, and a recreation field. Some facilities are wheelchair accessible. Leashed pets are permitted at the campground and in some of the cabins; pets are not permitted in the other cabins and lodge rooms.

Reservations, fees: Reservations are accepted

at 541/822-3512. Tent sites are $25–30 per night, RV sites are $35 per night, cabins are $65–400, $10 pet fee, lodge rooms are $100–185, $8 per person per night for more than two people. All fees include access to the hot springs. Some credit cards are accepted. Open year-round.

Directions: From Eugene, drive east on Highway 126 for 56 miles to Belknap Springs Road. Turn left and drive 0.5 mile until the road dead-ends at the lodge.

Contact: Belknap Hot Springs Resort, 541/822-3512, fax 541/822-3327, www.belknaphotsprings.com.

16 SLIDE CREEK

Scenic rating: 6

on Cougar Reservoir in Willamette National Forest

Slide Creek campground sits on a hillside overlooking Cougar Reservoir, which covers about 1,300 acres, has a paved boat landing and offers opportunities for fishing, swimming, and waterskiing. This pretty lakeside camp at 1,700 feet in elevation is quite popular, so plan to arrive early on weekends. If the camp is full, Cougar Crossing (off Road 19) and Sunnyside (off Road 500) are nearby alternatives.

Campsites, facilities: There are 16 sites for tents or RVs up to 50 feet long. Picnic tables and fire grills are provided. Drinking water, garbage bins, and vault toilets are available. A boat ramp is also available. Leashed pets are permitted.

Reservations, fees: Reservations are not accepted. Single sites are $16 per night, $30 per night for double sites, $8 per night per additional vehicle. Open May–September, weather permitting.

Directions: From Eugene, drive east on Highway 126 for 41 miles to the town of Blue River. Continue east on Highway 126 for five miles to Aufderheide Scenic Byway. Turn right (south) and drive 11 miles (along the west shore of Cougar Reservoir, crossing the reservoir bridge) to Eastside Road (Forest Road 500). Turn left and drive 1.5 miles northeast to the campground set on the southeast shore of the lake.

Contact: Willamette National Forest, McKenzie River Ranger District, 541/822-3381, fax 541/822-7254, www.fs.fed.us; Hoodoo Recreation, 541/822-3799.

17 FRENCH PETE

Scenic rating: 8

on the South Fork of the McKenzie River in Willamette National Forest

This quiet, wooded campground is set on the banks of the south fork of the McKenzie River and French Pete Creek at 1,800 feet in elevation. Fishing is catch-and-release only. A trail across the road from the campground provides access to the Three Sisters Wilderness (permit required; contact district office). French Pete is only two miles from Cougar Reservoir, and the camp attracts campers wanting to use Cougar Reservoir facilities. Two more primitive camps (Homestead and Frissell Crossing) are located a few miles southeast on the same road.

Campsites, facilities: There are 17 sites for tents or RVs up to 40 feet long. Picnic tables, garbage containers, and fire grills are provided. Drinking water and vault toilets are available. Leashed pets are permitted.

Reservations, fees: Reservations are not accepted. Sites are $14 per night, $5 per night per additional vehicle. Open May–September, weather permitting.

Directions: From Eugene, drive east on Highway 126 for 41 miles to the town of Blue River. Continue east on Highway 126 for five miles to Forest Road 19 (Aufderheide Scenic Byway). Turn right (south) and drive 12 miles to the campground on the right.

Contact: Willamette National Forest, McKenzie River Ranger District, 541/822-3381, fax 541/822-7254, www.fs.fed.us.

18 CAMP SHERMAN

Scenic rating: 6

on the Metolius River in Deschutes National Forest

Camp Sherman is set at an elevation of 2,950 feet along the banks of the Metolius River, where you can fish for wild trout. This place is for expert fly anglers seeking a quality fishing experience. Camp Sherman is one of five camps in the immediate area. It's advisable to obtain a map of the Deschutes National Forest that details back roads, streams, and trails.

A personal note: My late pal, John Korb, named his dog Sherman after this camp.

Campsites, facilities: There are 14 sites for tents or RVs up to 40 feet long. Picnic tables and fire grills are provided. Drinking water and garbage service is available mid-April–mid-October. Vault toilets and a picnic shelter are available. Leashed pets are permitted.

Reservations, fees: Reservations are accepted at 877/444-6777 or www.recreation.gov ($10 reservation fee). Sites are $12–16 per night, $6–8 per night per additional vehicle. Open year-round, weather permitting.

Directions: From Albany, drive east on U.S. 20 for 87 miles (near Black Butte) to the sign for Camp Sherman and Forest Road 14. Turn left on Forest Road 14 and drive five miles to Camp Sherman, the store, and Forest Road 900. Turn left on Forest Road 900 and drive 0.5 mile to the campground on the left.

Contact: Deschutes National Forest, Sisters Ranger District, 541/549-7700, fax 541/549-7746, www.fs.fed.us.

19 ALLINGHAM

Scenic rating: 5

on the Metolius River in Deschutes National Forest

One of five camps in the immediate area, Allingham sits along the banks of the Metolius River. The river is perfect for trout fishing, and fly anglers will find a quality fishing experience.

Campsites, facilities: There are 10 sites for tents or RVs up to 40 feet long. Picnic tables and fire grills are provided. Vault toilets, drinking water, and garbage service are available. A dump station is nearby. Leashed pets are permitted.

Reservations, fees: Reservations are not accepted. Sites are $16 per night, $8 per night per additional vehicle. Open May–September, weather permitting.

Directions: From Albany, drive east on U.S. 20 for 87 miles (near Black Butte) to the sign for Camp Sherman and Forest Road 14. Turn left on Forest Road 14 and drive five miles to Camp Sherman, the store, and Forest Road 900. Turn left on Forest Road 900 and drive one mile to the campground on the left.

Contact: Deschutes National Forest, Sisters Ranger District, 541/549-7700, fax 541/549-7746, www.fs.fed.us.

20 BLACK BUTTE RESORT

Scenic rating: 6

near the Metolius River

Black Butte offers a choice of graveled or grassy sites in a clean, scenic environment. Located near the Camp Sherman area, this is a nice spot for bird-watching, fishing, and hiking.

Campsites, facilities: There are 30 sites with

full or partial hookups for RVs of any length and six motel rooms. Picnic tables and barbecues are provided. Restrooms with flush toilets and showers, a dump station, recreation room, firewood, and a coin laundry are available. Propane gas, an additional dump station, a store, café, and ice are within one block. Leashed pets are permitted.

Reservations, fees: Reservations are accepted. Sites are $26–28 per night, $3 per person per night for more than two people, $7 per additional vehicle (unless towed). Some credit cards are accepted. Open year-round.

Directions: From Albany, drive east on U.S. 20 for 87 miles (near Black Butte) to the sign for Camp Sherman. Turn left (north) on Forest Road 1419 and drive four miles to a stop sign and the resort access road. Turn right and drive 0.25 mile to the park on the right.

Contact: Black Butte Resort, 541/595-6514, fax 541/595-5971, http://blackbutterv.com.

21 PINE REST

Scenic rating: 5

on the Metolius River in Deschutes National Forest

Pine Rest campground is set at an elevation of 2,900 feet along the banks of the Metolius River. Fly-fishing and hiking are recreation options.

Campsites, facilities: There are eight tent sites. Picnic tables and fire grills are provided. Vault toilets, a picnic shelter, and drinking water are available. Garbage service is available in season. Leashed pets are permitted.

Reservations, fees: Reservations are not accepted. Sites are $16–30 per night, $6–8 per night per additional vehicle. Open year-round, weather permitting.

Directions: From Albany, drive east on U.S. 20 for 87 miles (near Black Butte) to the sign for Camp Sherman and Forest Road 14. Turn left on Forest Road 14 and drive five miles to Camp Sherman, the store, and Forest Road 900. Turn left on Forest Road 900 and drive two miles to the campground on the left.

Contact: Deschutes National Forest, Sisters Ranger District, 541/549-7700, fax 541/549-7746, www.fs.fed.us.

22 GORGE

Scenic rating: 5

on the Metolius River in Deschutes National Forest

Here is another of the camps set along the banks of the Metolius River near Camp Sherman. Gorge campground is located at an elevation of 2,900 feet and is more open, with less vegetation than many of the others. Fly-fishing and hiking trails provide recreation opportunities.

Campsites, facilities: There are 18 sites for tents or RVs up to 40 feet long. Picnic tables and fire grills are provided. Vault toilets, drinking water, and garbage service are available. Leashed pets are permitted.

Reservations, fees: Reservations are not accepted. Sites are $16 per night, $8 per night per additional vehicle. Open May–September, weather permitting.

Directions: From Albany, drive east on U.S. 20 for 87 miles (near Black Butte) to the sign for Camp Sherman and Forest Road 14. Turn left on Forest Road 14 and drive five miles to Camp Sherman, the store, and Forest Road 900. Turn left on Forest Road 900 and drive 2.5 miles to the campground on the left.

Contact: Deschutes National Forest, Sisters Ranger District, 541/549-7700, fax 541/549-7746, www.fs.fed.us.

23 SMILING RIVER

Scenic rating: 5

on the Metolius River in Deschutes National Forest

Smiling River sits along the banks of the Metolius River at an elevation of 2,900 feet. Another campground in the popular Camp Sherman area, Smiling River has access to fly-fishing and nearby hiking trails.

Campsites, facilities: There are 35 sites for tents or RVs up to 50 feet long. Picnic tables and fire grills are provided. Vault toilets, drinking water, and garbage service are available. Leashed pets are permitted.

Reservations, fees: Reservations are accepted at 877/444-6777 or www.recreation.gov ($10 reservation fee). Sites are $16 per night, $8 per night per additional vehicle. Open May–October, weather permitting.

Directions: From Albany, drive east on U.S. 20 for 87 miles (near Black Butte) to the sign for Camp Sherman and Forest Road 14. Turn left on Forest Road 14 and drive five miles to Camp Sherman, the store, and Forest Road 900. Turn left on Forest Road 900 and drive one mile to the campground on the left.

Contact: Deschutes National Forest, Sisters Ranger District, 541/549-7700, fax 541/549-7746, www.fs.fed.us.

24 ALLEN SPRINGS

Scenic rating: 7

on the Metolius River in Deschutes National Forest

Shady Allen Springs campground is nestled in a conifer forest along the banks of the Metolius River, where fishing and hiking can be good. For an interesting side trip, head to the Wizard Falls Fish Hatchery about a mile away.

Campsites, facilities: There are 16 sites for tents or RVs up to 36 feet long. Picnic tables and fire grills are provided. Vault toilets, drinking water, and garbage service are available. A store, café, and ice are within five miles. Leashed pets are permitted.

Reservations, fees: Reservations are not accepted. Single sites are $14 per night, double sites are $30 per night, $7 per night per additional vehicle. Open April–October, weather permitting.

Directions: From Albany, drive east on U.S. 20 for 87 miles (near Black Butte) to the sign for Camp Sherman and Forest Road 14. Turn left on Forest Road 14 and drive about nine miles to the campground on the left.

Contact: Deschutes National Forest, Sisters Ranger District, 541/549-7700, fax 541/549-7746, www.fs.fed.us.

25 LOWER BRIDGE

Scenic rating: 6

on the Metolius River in Deschutes National Forest

Lower Bridge campground is set along the banks of the Metolius River at an elevation of 2,700 feet. The setting is similar to Pioneer Ford, but with less vegetation. A picnic area is located across the bridge.

Campsites, facilities: There are 12 sites for tents or RVs up to 30 feet long. Picnic tables and fire grills are provided. Vault toilets, drinking water, and garbage service are available. Leashed pets are permitted.

Reservations, fees: Reservations are not accepted. Sites are $16 per night, $8 per night per additional vehicle. Open May–October, weather permitting.

Directions: From Albany, drive east on U.S. 20 for 87 miles (near Black Butte) to the sign for Camp Sherman and Forest Road 14. Turn left on Forest Road 14 and drive 12 miles to the campground on the right.

Contact: Deschutes National Forest, Sisters

Ranger District, 541/549-7700, fax 541/549-7746, www.fs.fed.us.

26 PIONEER FORD

Scenic rating: 7

on the Metolius River in Deschutes National Forest

Quiet and serene Pioneer Ford campground is set along the banks of the Metolius River at an elevation of 2,750 feet. The wooded campground features grassy sites north of the Camp Sherman area. Hiking and fly-fishing are activities here.

Campsites, facilities: There are 20 sites for tents or RVs up to 50 feet long. Picnic tables and fire grills are provided. Drinking water and garbage service are provided. Vault toilets are available. Some facilities are wheelchair accessible. Leashed pets are permitted.

Reservations, fees: Reservations are not accepted. Sites are $16 per night, $8 per night per additional vehicle. Open May–September, weather permitting.

Directions: From Albany, drive east on U.S. 20 for 87 miles (near Black Butte) to the sign for Camp Sherman and Forest Road 14. Turn left on Forest Road 14 and drive 11 miles to the campground on the left.

Contact: Deschutes National Forest, Sisters Ranger District, 541/549-7700, fax 541/549-7746, www.fs.fed.us.

27 COLD SPRINGS RESORT & RV PARK

Scenic rating: 7

on the Metolius River

This pretty, wooded RV park on the Metolius River is world-famous for its fly-fishing and features an acre of riverfront lawn. Bird-watching is also popular. Recreation options in the area include boating, swimming, waterskiing, and windsurfing. In addition, nearby facilities include a golf course, hiking and biking trails, a riding stable, and tennis courts. Winter activities vary from alpine and Nordic skiing to sledding, snowmobiling, and winter camping. A private footbridge leads from the resort to Camp Sherman; the towns of Sisters and Bend are nearby (15 miles and 35 miles, respectively).

Campsites, facilities: There are 45 sites with full hookups for RVs of any length, a grassy area for tents, and five cabins on the river. Fire pits, picnic tables, and patios are provided. Restrooms with showers, coin laundry, wireless Internet service, firewood, and a riverfront picnic facility are available. Propane gas, a convenience store, fishing and sport supplies, a café, a post office, and ice are within 0.25 mile. Leashed pets are permitted.

Reservations, fees: Reservations are accepted. Sites are $30 per night, $2 per person per night for more than two people, and $2 per pet per night. Some credit cards are accepted. Open year-round.

Directions: From Albany, drive east on U.S. 20 for 87 miles (near Black Butte) to the sign for Camp Sherman/Metolius River. Turn left (north) on Forest Road 14 and drive 4.5 miles to a stop sign. Turn right (still Forest Road 14) and drive about 300 feet to Cold Springs Resort Lane. Turn right and drive through the forest and the meadow, crossing Cold Springs Creek, to the resort.

Contact: Cold Springs Resort & RV Park, 541/595-6271, fax 541/595-1400, www.coldsprings-resort.com.

28 RIVERSIDE WALK-IN

Scenic rating: 7

on the Metolius River in Deschutes National Forest

Riverside Walk-In is set 100 yards back from the banks of the Metolius River, less than a mile from Metolius Springs at the base of Black Butte. Because this is a tent-only campground, and just far enough off the highway to be missed by most other people, it stays very quiet. You'll find plenty of solitude here. After parking along the road, you must walk to the campsites, carrying any gear in the process.

Campsites, facilities: There are 16 tent sites. Picnic tables and fire grills are provided. Vault toilets, garbage service, and drinking water are available. Leashed pets are permitted.

Reservations, fees: Reservations are not accepted. Sites are $12 per night, $6 per night per additional vehicle. Open May–September, weather permitting.

Directions: From Albany, drive east on U.S. 20 for 87 miles to the sign for Camp Sherman and Forest Road 14. Turn left and drive five miles to Forest Road 800. Turn left and drive a short distance to the campground.

Contact: Deschutes National Forest, Sisters Ranger District, 541/549-7700, fax 541/549-7746, www.fs.fed.us.

29 HAYSTACK RESERVOIR

Scenic rating: 5

on Haystack Reservoir in Crooked River National Grassland

This campground can be found in the high desert along the shore of Haystack Reservoir, a bright spot in an expansive desert landscape. The camps feature a moderate amount of privacy, as well as views of nearby Mount Jefferson. Haystack Reservoir receives moderate numbers of people who boat, camp, fish, swim, and water ski.

Campsites, facilities: There are 24 sites for tents or RVs up to 32 feet long; some sites are pull-through. Picnic tables and fire grills are provided. Flush toilets, drinking water, and covered picnic shelters are available. A store, café, and ice are within five miles. Boat docks and launching facilities are nearby. Leashed pets are permitted.

Reservations, fees: Reservations are not accepted. Sites are $8 per night, $3 per night per additional vehicle. Open mid-May–mid-September.

Directions: From Madras, drive south on U.S. 97 for nine miles to Jericho Lane. Turn left and drive one mile to County Road 100. Turn right and drive two miles to Forest Road 96. Turn left (north) and drive 0.5 mile to the campground.

Contact: Crooked River National Grassland, 541/475-9272 or 541/416-6640, www.fs.fed.us.

30 COLD WATER COVE

Scenic rating: 10

on Clear Lake in Willamette National Forest

Cold Water campground sits at 3,000 feet elevation on the south shore of Clear Lake, a spring-fed lake formed by a natural lava dam and the source of the McKenzie River. No motors are permitted on the lake, making it ideal for anglers in rowboats or canoes. The northern section of the McKenzie River National Recreation Trail passes by the camp.

Campsites, facilities: There are 35 sites for tents or RVs up to 40 feet long. Picnic tables and fire grills are provided. Vault toilets, drinking water, and garbage service are available. Boat docks, launching facilities, rowboats, a store, a café, and cabin rentals are available nearby at Clear Lake Resort. Some facilities are wheelchair accessible. Leashed pets are permitted.

Reservations, fees: Reservations are accepted at 877/444-6777 or www.recreation.gov ($10 reservation fee). Sites are $16 per night, $30 per night for double sites, $8 per night per additional vehicle. Open mid-May–mid-October, weather permitting.

Directions: From Eugene, drive east on

Highway 126 for 47 miles to the town of McKenzie Bridge. Continue on Highway 126 for 14 miles to Forest Road 770. Turn right (east) and drive to the campground.

Contact: Willamette National Forest, McKenzie River Ranger District, 541/822-3381, fax 541/822-7254, www.fs.fed.us; Hoodoo Recreation, 541/822-3799.

31 ICE CAP

Scenic rating: 9

on Carmen Reservoir in Willamette National Forest

Ice Cap campground is perched at 3,000 feet elevation on a hill above Carmen Reservoir, created by a dam on the McKenzie River. The McKenzie River National Recreation Trail passes by the camp, and Koosah Falls and Sahalie Falls are nearby. Clear Lake, a popular local vacation destination, is two miles away.

Campsites, facilities: There are 13 sites for tents or RVs up to 50 feet long, and nine walk-in sites. Picnic tables and fire grills are provided. Vault toilets, drinking water, and garbage service are available. Boat-launching facilities and boat rentals are about two miles away at Clear Lake Resort (541/967-5030). Only non-motorized boats are allowed on Carmen Reservoir. Leashed pets are permitted.

Reservations, fees: Reservations are not accepted. Sites are $16 per night, $8 per night per additional vehicle. Open mid-May–September, weather permitting.

Directions: From Eugene, drive east on Highway 126 for 47 miles to the town of McKenzie Bridge. Continue on Highway 126 for 19 miles to the campground entrance road on the left. Turn left and drive 200 yards to the campground.

Contact: Willamette National Forest, McKenzie River Ranger District, 541/822-3381, fax 541/822-7254, www.fs.fed.us; Hoodoo Recreation, 541/822-3799.

32 BIG LAKE

Scenic rating: 9

on Big Lake in Willamette National Forest

This jewel of a spot on the north shore of Big Lake at 4,650 feet elevation offers a host of activities, including fishing, hiking, swimming, and waterskiing. Big Lake has heavy motorized boat use. One of the better hikes is the five-mile wilderness loop trail (Patjens Lakes Trail) that heads out from the south shore of the lake and cuts past a few small lakes before returning. There's a great view of Mount Washington from the lake. The Pacific Crest Trail is only 0.5 mile away.

Campsites, facilities: There are 49 sites for tents or RVs up to 35 feet long. Picnic tables and fire grills are provided. Drinking water, vault and flush toilets, and garbage service are available. Boat ramps are nearby. Some facilities are wheelchair accessible. Leashed pets are permitted.

Reservations, fees: Reservations are accepted at 877/444-6777 or www.recreation.gov ($10 reservation fee). Single sites are $18 per night, $32 for double sites, $9 per night per additional vehicle. Open late May–mid-October, weather permitting.

Directions: From Eugene, drive east on Highway 126 for 47 miles to the town of McKenzie Bridge. Continue northeast on Highway 126 for 40 miles to Big Lake Road (Forest Road 2690). Turn right and drive three miles to the campground on the left.

Contact: Willamette National Forest, McKenzie River Ranger District, 541/822-3381, fax 541/822-7254, www.fs.fed.us; Hoodoo Recreation, 541/822-3799.

33 BIG LAKE WEST WALK-IN

Scenic rating: 9

on Big Lake in Willamette National Forest

This spot, located west of the Big Lake Campground at an elevation of 4,650 feet, has many of the same attractions, but the walk-in sites offer some seclusion and quiet. The Mount Washington Wilderness and Patjens Lake access trails can be reached from here.

Campsites, facilities: There are 11 walk-in sites (only 200 feet from the road). Fire pits and picnic tables are provided. Vault toilets and garbage service are available. There is no drinking water. Leashed pets are permitted.

Reservations, fees: Reservations are not accepted. Single sites are $22 per night, $35 per night for double sites, $10 per night per additional vehicle. Open late May–early October, weather permitting.

Directions: From Eugene, drive east on Highway 126 for 47 miles to the town of McKenzie Bridge. Continue northeast on Highway 126 for 40 miles to Big Lake Road (Forest Road 2690). Turn right and drive four miles to the campground entrance on the left.

Contact: Willamette National Forest, McKenzie River Ranger District, 541/822-3381, fax 541/822-7254, www.fs.fed.us; Hoodoo Recreation, 541/822-3799.

34 SOUTH SHORE

Scenic rating: 6

on Suttle Lake in Deschutes National Forest

This campground is at 3,500 feet elevation on the south shore of Suttle Lake, where waterskiing is permitted. A hiking trail winds around the lake and other popular activities include fishing and windsurfing. The camp often fills up on weekends and holidays, so reserve early.

Campsites, facilities: There are 38 sites for tents or RVs up to 40 feet long. Picnic tables and fire grills are provided. Vault toilets, drinking water, and garbage service are available. A fish-cleaning station, boat docks, launching facilities, and rentals are nearby. Leashed pets are permitted.

Reservations, fees: Reservations are accepted at 877/444-6777 or www.recreation.gov ($10 reservation fee). Sites are $16 per night, $8 per night per additional vehicle. Open May–September, weather permitting.

Directions: From Albany, drive east on U.S. 20 to the junction with Highway 126. Continue east on Highway 126 for 12 miles to Forest Road 2070 (Suttle Lake). Turn right and proceed a short distance to the campground.

Contact: Deschutes National Forest, Sisters Ranger District, 541/549-7700, fax 541/549-7746, www.fs.fed.us.

35 LINK CREEK

Scenic rating: 6

on Suttle Lake in Deschutes National Forest

Link Creek campground is set at the west end of Suttle Lake at an elevation of 3,450 feet. The high-speed boating area is located on this end of the lake, making it a popular spot with water-skiers. Other activities include fishing, swimming, and windsurfing.

Campsites, facilities: There are 33 sites for tents or RVs up to 50 feet long. Picnic tables and fire grills are provided. Vault toilets, drinking water, and garbage service are available. Boat docks, launching facilities, and rentals are nearby. Leashed pets are permitted.

Reservations, fees: Reservations are accepted at 877/444-6777 or www.recreation.gov ($10 reservation fee). Sites are $16–30 per night, $8 per night per additional vehicle. Open April–mid-October, weather permitting.

Directions: From Albany, drive east on U.S. 20 for 74 miles to the junction of U.S. 20 and

Highway 126. Continue east on Highway 126 for 12 miles to Forest Road 2070 (Suttle Lake). Turn right and drive a short distance to the campground.
Contact: Deschutes National Forest, Sisters Ranger District, 541/549-7700, fax 541/549-7746, www.fs.fed.us.

36 BLUE BAY

Scenic rating: 7

on Suttle Lake in Deschutes National Forest

Blue Bay campground is situated along the south shore of Suttle Lake at an elevation of 3,450 feet. It's a quieter campground at the low-speed end of the lake, and with more tree cover than South Shore or Link Creek. Recreation activities include fishing, boating, and hiking.
Campsites, facilities: There are 21 single sites and three double sites for tents or RVs up to 50 feet long. Picnic tables and fire grills are provided. Vault toilets, drinking water, and garbage service are available. A fish-cleaning station, boat docks, launching facilities, and rentals are nearby. Leashed pets are permitted.
Reservations, fees: Reservations are accepted at 877/444-6777 or www.recreation.gov ($10 reservation fee). Sites are $16–30 per night, $8 per night per additional vehicle. Open May–mid-September, weather permitting.
Directions: From Albany, drive east on U.S. 20 for 74 miles to the junction of U.S. 20 and Highway 126. Continue east on Highway 126 for 12 miles to Forest Road 2070 (Suttle Lake). Turn right and drive a short distance to the campground.
Contact: Deschutes National Forest, Sisters Ranger District, 541/549-7700, fax 541/549-7746, www.fs.fed.us.

37 SCOUT LAKE GROUP

Scenic rating: 5

on Scout Lake in Deschutes National Forest

Scout Lake is a group campground, with a mix of sunny and shady sites, at an elevation of 3,700 feet. The camp lies about 0.5 mile from Suttle Lake and is a good spot for swimming and hiking.
Campsites, facilities: There are nine sites—singles, doubles and triple sites—for tents or RVs up to 40 feet long. The triple group site can accommodate up to 100 people. Picnic tables and fire grills are provided. Vault toilets, drinking water, garbage service, a picnic shelter, a volleyball court, and horseshoe pits are available. Leashed pets are permitted in the campground only (not in the day-use area).
Reservations, fees: Reservations are accepted at 877/444-6777 or www.recreation.gov ($10 reservation fee). Single sites are $16 per night, double sites are $30 per night, triple group site is $40 per night, $8 per night per additional vehicle. Open May–September, weather permitting.
Directions: From Eugene, drive east on Highway 126 for 74 miles to the junction of U.S. 20 and Highway 126. Continue east on Highway 126 for 12 miles to Forest Road 2070 (Suttle Lake). Turn right and drive to Forest Road 2066. Turn left and drive less than one mile to the campground.
Contact: Deschutes National Forest, Sisters Ranger District, 541/549-7700, fax 541/549-7746, www.fs.fed.us.

38 KOA SISTERS/BEND

Scenic rating: 7

on Branchwater Lake

This park is located amid wooded mountains outside of Sisters at an elevation of 3,200 feet.

Branchwater Lake, a three-acre lake at the campground, offers good trout fishing. (For hiking opportunities, explore the McKenzie River Trail or the Three Sisters and Mount Washington Wilderness Areas (west of Sisters on Hwy. 242). The Pacific Crest Trail runs north and south through both wilderness areas.

Campsites, facilities: There are 100 sites for tents or RVs of any length (full hookups); many sites are pull-through. There are also three cabins. Picnic tables and fire pits are provided. Drinking water, air-conditioning, cable TV, modem access, restrooms with showers, a dump station, coin laundry, convenience store, ice, RV supplies, and propane gas are available. Recreational facilities include a playground, game room, horseshoes, table tennis, a spa, and a seasonal heated swimming pool. Leashed pets are permitted.

Reservations, fees: Reservations are accepted at 800/562-0363. Sites are $48–65 per night, $2–9 per person per night for more than two people, and $2 per night per additional vehicle. Some credit cards are accepted. Open late March–November, weather permitting.

Directions: From Eugene, drive east on Highway 126 to its junction with U.S. 20. Turn east on U.S. 20 and drive 26 miles to Sisters. Continue southeast on U.S. 20 for three miles to the park on the right side of the highway.

Contact: KOA Sisters/Bend, 541/549-3021, fax 541/549-8144, www.koa.com.

39 CROOKED RIVER RANCH RV PARK

Scenic rating: 6

near Smith Rock State Park

BEST

Crooked River Ranch is a short distance from Smith Rock State Park, which contains unusual, colorful volcanic formations overlooking the Crooked River Canyon. Spectacular wildlife abounds in this area. Lake Billy Chinook to the north is a good spot for waterskiing and fishing for bass and panfish. The park has a basketball court and a softball field, and seasonal horseback riding is available. Nearby recreation options include fishing, golf, and tennis; one of Oregon's nicest golf courses is nearby.

Campsites, facilities: There are 90 sites with full or partial hookups for RVs of any length (some pull-through) and 20 tent sites. Picnic tables are provided. No open fires are allowed; propane is permitted. Restrooms with flush toilets and coin showers, a dump station, cable TV, Wi-Fi, a convenience store, coin laundry, ice, a covered picnic shelter, playground, horseshoe pits, a tennis court, and a seasonal swimming pool are available. A café is nearby. Leashed pets are permitted, with certain restrictions.

Reservations, fees: Reservations are accepted at 800/841-0563. RV sites are $25–34 per night; tent sites are $20–24 per night. Some credit cards are accepted. Open mid-March–October, weather permitting.

Directions: From Redmond, drive north on U.S. 97 for six miles to Terrebonne and Lower Bridge Road. Turn left (west) on Lower Bridge Road and drive approximately two miles to 43rd Street. Turn right and drive two miles to a T-intersection with Chinook. Turn left on Chinook and drive approximately 4.5 miles (becomes Clubhouse Road, then Hays Road) to the ranch on the right.

Contact: Crooked River Ranch RV Park, 541/923-1441 or 800/841-0563, www.crookedriverranch.com.

40 INDIAN FORD

Scenic rating: 4

on Indian Ford Creek in Deschutes National Forest

This campground sits on the banks of Indian Ford Creek at an elevation of 3,250 feet. Used

primarily by overnighters on their way to the town of Sisters, the camp is subject to a lot of traffic noise from U.S. 20. The grounds are sprinkled with aspen trees and great bird-watching opportunities are available.
Campsites, facilities: There are 25 sites for tents or RVs up to 50 feet long. Picnic tables, garbage service, and fire grills are provided. Vault toilets are available. There is no drinking water. Leashed pets are permitted.
Reservations, fees: Reservations are not accepted. Sites are $12 per night, $6 per night per additional vehicle. Open May–mid-October, weather permitting.
Directions: From Albany, drive east on U.S. 20 to the junction with Highway 126. Continue east on Highway 126 and drive 21 miles to the campground on the left.
Contact: Deschutes National Forest, Sisters Ranger District, 541/549-7700, fax 541/549-7746, www.fs.fed.us.

41 COLD SPRINGS

Scenic rating: 7

in Deschutes National Forest

Wooded Cold Springs campground is set at 3,400 feet elevation at the source of a small seasonal creek. It's just far enough off the main drag to be missed by many campers. Spring and early summer are the times to come for great bird-watching in the area's abundant aspen trees.
Campsites, facilities: There are 22 sites for tents or RVs up to 50 feet long. Picnic tables, fire grills, and garbage service are provided. Vault toilets and drinking water are available. Leashed pets are permitted.
Reservations, fees: Reservations are not accepted. Sites are $14 per night, $7 per night per additional vehicle. Open May–October, weather permitting.
Directions: From Albany, drive east on U.S. 20 to the junction with Highway 126. Continue east on Highway 126 and drive 26 miles to Sisters and Highway 242. Turn right and drive 4.2 miles to the campground on the right.
Contact: Deschutes National Forest, Sisters Ranger District, 541/549-7700, fax 541/549-7746, www.fs.fed.us.

42 SCOTT LAKE WALK-IN

ATLAS p. 50
C2

Scenic rating: 10

on Scott Lake in Willamette National Forest

BEST

Scott Lake Walk-In offers hike-in sites just over 0.1 mile from the road. The campground borders Scott Lake at an elevation of 4,680 feet; only non-motorized boats are allowed on the lake. Trails leading out of the camp provide access to several small lakes in the Mount Washington Wilderness, and there are great views of the Three Sisters Mountains. Be forewarned: Mosquitoes are heavy during the spring and early summer.
Campsites, facilities: There are 20 walk-in tent sites. Picnic tables and fire rings are provided. Vault toilets are available. There is no drinking water, and garbage must be packed out. Leashed pets are permitted.
Reservations, fees: Reservations are not accepted. Sites are $5 per night. Open July–October, weather permitting.
Directions: From Eugene, drive east on Highway 126 for 54 miles to the junction with Highway 242 (part of the Santiam Scenic Byway). Turn right (east) on Highway 242 and drive 14.5 miles to Forest Road 260. Turn left and drive to the campground.

Note: Highway 242 is spectacularly scenic, but it's also very narrow, winding, and steep; it is not recommended for RVs or trailers. The maximum vehicle length is 35 feet.
Contact: Willamette National Forest, McKenzie River Ranger District, 541/822-3381, fax 541/822-7254, www.fs.fed.us.

43 LAVA CAMP LAKE

Scenic rating: 4

near the Pacific Crest Trail in Deschutes National Forest

Lava campground sits at an elevation of 5,300 feet among subalpine fir in the McKenzie Pass. It's not far from the Pacific Crest Trail, and a number of other trails provide additional hiking possibilities. Fishing is allowed, but don't expect to catch anything—perhaps that is why this campground gets such light use!

Campsites, facilities: There are 10 sites for tents or RVs up to 20 feet long. Picnic tables and fire grills are provided. Vault toilets are available. There is no drinking water, and garbage must be packed out. Leashed pets are permitted.

Reservations, fees: Reservations are not accepted. There is no fee for camping. Open June–October, weather permitting.

Directions: From Eugene, drive east on Highway 126 for 47 miles to the town of McKenzie Bridge. Continue east on Highway 126 for five miles to Highway 242. Turn right (east) and drive 14.6 miles on Highway 242 to the campground entrance on the right. Note: Highway 242 is spectacularly scenic, but also very narrow, winding, and steep. RVs and trailers are strictly held to a 35-foot length limit.

Contact: Deschutes National Forest, Sisters Ranger District, 541/549-7700, fax 541/549-7746, www.fs.fed.us.

44 WHISPERING PINE HORSE CAMP

Scenic rating: 5

near the Trout Creek Swamp in Deschutes National Forest

This wooded campground (elevation 4,400 feet) near Trout Creek Swamp is pretty, isolated, and private. Although generally not crowded, it's set up as a horse camp with corrals and is gaining in popularity; groups of horse users occasionally fill it up. Hikers, beware: You'll be sharing the trails with horses.

Campsites, facilities: There are nine primitive sites for tents or RVs up to 30 feet long. Picnic tables and fire grills are provided. Vault toilets and garbage service are available. There is no drinking water. Leashed pets are permitted.

Reservations, fees: Reservations are not accepted. Sites are $16 per night, $8 per night per additional vehicle. Open May–October, weather permitting.

Directions: From Albany, drive east on U.S. 20 to the junction with U.S. 126. Turn east on U.S. 126 and drive for 26 miles to Sisters and Highway 142. Turn right (east) and drive six miles on Highway 242 to Forest Road 1018. Turn left and drive four miles to the campground entrance. Note: Highway 242 is spectacularly scenic, but also very narrow, winding, and steep. RVs and trailers are discouraged (a 35-foot length limit is in effect).

Contact: Deschutes National Forest, Sisters Ranger District, 541/549-7700, fax 541/549-7746, www.fs.fed.us or www.hoodoo.com.

45 LIMBERLOST

Scenic rating: 9

on Lost Creek in Willamette National Forest

Limberlost is a secluded campground set at 1,800 feet elevation along Lost Creek, about two miles from where it empties into the McKenzie River. Relatively unknown, the camp gets light use; it makes a good base camp for a trout-fishing trip.

Campsites, facilities: There are 12 sites for tents or RVs up to 16 feet long. Picnic tables, garbage service, and fire grills are provided. Vault toilets are available, but there is no drinking water. Some facilities are wheelchair accessible. Leashed pets are permitted.

Reservations, fees: Reservations are not accepted. Sites are $12 per night, $6 per night per additional vehicle. Open May–September, weather permitting.
Directions: From Eugene, drive east on Highway 126 for 47 miles to the town of McKenzie Bridge. Continue east on Highway 126 for five miles to Highway 242. Turn right (east) and drive 1.5 miles on Highway 242 to the camp. Note: Highway 242 is spectacularly scenic, but also very narrow, winding, and steep. RVs and trailers are discouraged (a 35-foot length limit is in effect).
Contact: Willamette National Forest, McKenzie River Ranger District, 541/822-3381, fax 541/822-7254, www.fs.fed.us.

46 ALDER SPRINGS

Scenic rating: 7

in Willamette National Forest

Remote Alder Springs campground sits at 3,600 feet elevation in the Willamette Forest. The camp features good hiking possibilities, including access to the Linton Lake Trail, a three-mile hike that leads to Linton Lake... and fishing. The Three Sisters Wilderness is just south of the highway.
Campsites, facilities: There are six tent sites. Picnic tables and fire grills are provided. Vault toilets are available. No drinking water is available, and garbage must be packed out. Some facilities are wheelchair accessible. Leashed pets are permitted.
Reservations, fees: Reservations are not accepted. There is no fee for camping. Open June–September, weather permitting.
Directions: From Eugene, drive east on Highway 126 for 47 miles to the town of McKenzie Bridge. Continue east on Highway 126 for five miles to Highway 242. Turn right (east) and drive 10 miles on Highway 242 to the campground on the left. Note: Highway 242 is spectacularly scenic, but also very narrow, winding, and steep. RVs and trailers are discouraged (a 35-foot length limit is in effect).
Contact: Willamette National Forest, McKenzie River Ranger District, 541/822-3381, fax 541/822-7254, www.fs.fed.us.

47 DRIFTWOOD

ATLAS 50 D3

Scenic rating: 9

on Three Creek Lake in Deschutes National Forest

BEST

This wooded campground, at 6,600 feet elevation, is often blocked by snowdrifts until early July. At this high elevation, the views of Tam McArthur Rim are spectacular. Although located on the lakeshore and hidden from outsiders, the area can get very crowded, and the campground is full most weekends from the Fourth of July through Labor Day. Some recreation options include boating (non-motorized only), fishing, hiking, and swimming.
Campsites, facilities: There are 18 sites for tents or RVs up to 40 feet long. Picnic tables and fire grills are provided. Vault toilets and garbage service are available. There is no drinking water. Boats with motors are not allowed. Leashed pets are permitted.
Reservations, fees: Reservations are not accepted. Sites are $14 per night, $7 per night per additional vehicle. Open June–October, weather permitting.
Directions: From Eugene, drive east on Highway 126 to its junction with U.S. 20. Turn east and drive 26 miles to Sisters and Forest Road 16. Turn right and drive 16.4 miles to the campground.
Contact: Deschutes National Forest, Sisters Ranger District, 541/549-7700, fax 541/549-7746, www.fs.fed.us.

From Bend, take 20 to Sisters then south on 16 (38 mi 1.5 hrs)

48 THREE CREEK LAKE

Scenic rating: 8

on Three Creek Lake in Deschutes National Forest

Three Creek Lake is in a pretty spot at 6,600 feet elevation; this forested campground lies along the south shore of its namesake lake. Boating (non-motorized only), fishing, hiking, and swimming are the highlights.

Campsites, facilities: There are 11 sites for tents or RVs up to 40 feet long. Picnic tables and fire grills are provided. Vault toilets and garbage service are available. There is no drinking water. Boats with motors are not allowed. Leashed pets are permitted.

Reservations, fees: Reservations are not accepted. Sites are $14 per night, $7 per night per additional vehicle. Open June–October, weather permitting.

Directions: From Eugene, drive east on Highway 126 to its junction with Highway 20. Turn east and drive 26 miles to Sisters and Forest Road 16. Turn right and drive 17 miles to the campground.

Contact: Deschutes National Forest, Sisters Ranger District, 541/549-7700, fax 541/549-7746, www.fs.fed.us.

49 TUMALO STATE PARK

Scenic rating: 7

on the Deschutes River

Tumalo State Park sits along the banks of the Deschutes River, just four miles from Bend. Trout fishing can be good, and bird-watching is popular. The swimming area is generally safe and a good spot for children. Rafting is also an option here. Mount Bachelor is just up the road and provides plenty of winter recreation opportunities.

Campsites, facilities: There are 54 sites for tents or self-contained RVs, 23 sites with full hookups for RVs up to 44 feet long, a hiker/bicyclist area, seven yurts, and two group tent areas for up to 25 people each. Drinking water, fire grills, and picnic tables are provided. Restrooms with flush toilets and showers, firewood, and a playground are available. A store, café, and ice are within one mile. Some facilities are wheelchair accessible. Leashed pets are permitted.

Reservations, fees: Reservations are accepted at 800/452-5687 or www.reserveamerica.com ($8 reservation fee). RV sites are $17–26 per night, tent sites are $13–21, $4–5 per person per night for hikers/bikers, $29–39 per night for yurts, $43–76 per night for the group areas, and $5 per night per additional vehicle. Some credit cards are accepted. Open year-round.

Directions: From Bend, drive north on U.S. 97 for two miles to U.S. 20 West. Turn west and drive five miles to Tumalo Junction. Turn left at Tumalo Junction onto Cook Avenue (the road becomes O. B. Riley), and drive one mile to the campground.

Contact: High Desert Management Unit, Oregon State Parks, 541/388-6055 or 800/551-6949, www.oregonstateparks.org.

50 SCANDIA RV AND MOBILE PARK

Scenic rating: 5

near the Deschutes River

This in-town park near the Deschutes River is close to bike paths, a golf course, a stable, and tennis courts.

Campsites, facilities: There are 97 sites for tents or RVs of any length (full hookups); some are pull-through sites. Picnic tables and cable TV are provided. Restrooms with flush toilets and showers, modem access, a picnic area, and a coin laundry are available. Propane gas, a dump station, store, café, and ice are within one mile. Leashed pets are permitted.

Reservations, fees: Reservations are accepted. Sites are $28–32 per night, plus $2.50 per person per night for more than two people. Some credit cards are accepted. Open year-round.
Directions: In Bend, drive south on Business U.S. 97 (3rd Street) for 0.5 mile to the park entrance on the right.
Contact: Scandia RV and Mobile Park, 541/382-6206, fax 541/382-4087.

51 CROWN VILLA RV RESORT

Scenic rating: 6

near Bend

This RV park offers large and landscaped grassy sites. Nearby recreation options include horseback riding and golf.
Campsites, facilities: There are 116 sites with full or partial hookups for RVs of any length; some sites are pull-through. Picnic tables are provided. Restrooms with flush toilets and showers, cable TV, wireless Internet service, a coin laundry, a bistro, propane gas, and ice are available. A store and a café are within one mile. Some facilities are wheelchair accessible. Leashed pets are permitted.
Reservations, fees: Reservations are accepted. Sites are $35–70 per night, $3 per person per night for more than four people. Some credit cards are accepted. Open year-round.
Directions: From Bend, drive south on Business U.S. 97 (3rd Street) for two miles to Brosterhous Road. Turn left (east) and drive approximately one mile to a T intersection. Bear right to stay on Brosterhous Road. Continue about one mile to the park on the right.
Contact: Crown Villa RV Resort, 541/388-1131, www.crownvillarvresort.com.

52 WHITTAKER CREEK

Scenic rating: 7

near the Siuslaw River

Whittaker Creek campground is home to one of the area's premier salmon spawning grounds, where annual runs of chinook, coho salmon, and steelhead can be viewed. The (Whitaker Creek) Old Growth Ridge Trail, a national recreation trail, is accessible from the campground. This moderately difficult trail ascends 1,000 feet above the Siuslaw River through a stand of old-growth Douglas fir.
Campsites, facilities: There are 31 sites for tents or RVs up to 35 feet long. Picnic tables and fire pits are provided. Drinking water, vault toilets, garbage bins, a boat ramp, swimming beach, playground, and picnic shelter are available. A camp host is on-site. Some facilities are wheelchair accessible. Leashed pets are permitted.
Reservations, fees: Reservations are not accepted. Sites are $10 per night, $5 per night for each additional vehicle. Open mid-May–September, weather permitting.
Directions: From Eugene, drive west on Highway 126 for 33 miles to Siuslaw River Road. Turn left (south) and drive two miles to the first junction. Turn right and drive a short distance across Siuslaw River to the campground on the right.
Contact: Bureau of Land Management, Eugene District Office, 541/683-6600 or 888/442-3061, fax 541/683-6981, www.blm.gov.

53 CLAY CREEK

Scenic rating: 7

near the Siuslaw River

This campground gets a medium amount of use. Sites are situated in a forest of cedar, Douglas fir, and maple trees. Clay Creek Trail, a two-mile loop, takes you to a ridge overlooking the river valley and is well worth the walk. Fishing for trout and crayfish is popular.

Campsites, facilities: There are 21 sites for tents or RVs up to 35 feet long. Picnic tables and fire pits are provided. Drinking water, vault toilets, garbage bins, a swimming beach with changing rooms, a softball field, horseshoe pits, and two group picnic shelters with fireplaces are available. There is a camp host. Some facilities are wheelchair accessible. Leashed pets are permitted.

Reservations, fees: Reservations are not accepted. Sites are $10 per night, $5 per night for each additional vehicle. Open mid-May–September, weather permitting.

Directions: From Eugene, drive west on Highway 126 for 33 miles to Siuslaw River Road. Turn left (south) and drive 16 miles to BLM Road 19-7-2001 (signed for Clay Creek). Turn right and drive a short distance to the campground on the right.

Contact: Bureau of Land Management, Eugene District Office, 541/683-6600 or 888/442-3061, fax 541/683-6981, www.blm.gov.

54 PASS CREEK COUNTY PARK

Scenic rating: 7

near Cottage Grove

Pass Creek provides a decent layover spot for travelers on I-5. Situated in a wooded, hilly area, the camp features many shaded sites, and mountain views give the park scenic value. There is a covered pavilion and gazebo with barbecue grills for get-togethers. A bonus is the fishing pond with bluegill, crappie, and largemouth bass. There are no other campgrounds in the immediate area, so if it's late and you need a place to stay, grab this one.

Campsites, facilities: There is a grassy area for tents and 30 sites with full hookups (50-amp) for RVs up to 45 feet long. Picnic tables and fire rings or barbecues are provided. Drinking water, restrooms with flush toilets and showers, a coin laundry, and a playground are available. A store and ice are within one mile. Some facilities are wheelchair accessible. Leashed pets are permitted.

Reservations, fees: Reservations are not accepted. Sites are $15–20 per night, $3 per night for an additional vehicle unless towed. Open year-round.

Directions: On I-5, drive to Exit 163 (between Roseburg and Eugene). Take Exit 163 and turn west on Curtin Park Road. Drive west (under the freeway) for a very short distance to the park entrance.

Contact: Pass Creek County Park, 541/942-3281, www.co.douglas.or.us.

55 PINE MEADOWS

Scenic rating: 6

on Cottage Grove Reservoir

Pine Meadows campground is surrounded by a varied landscape of forest, grassland, and marsh near the banks of Cottage Grove Reservoir. Campsites are within 200 feet of the water. Boating, fishing, swimming, and waterskiing are among the recreation options. It's an easy hop from I-5.

Campsites, facilities: There are 93 sites for tents or RVs of any length, with some pull-through sites. Drinking water, picnic tables, garbage bins, and fire rings are provided. Restrooms with flush toilets and showers, a dump station, a children's play area, an amphitheater, interpretive displays, and a swimming area are available. A boat dock, launching facilities, and a small store are nearby. Leashed pets are permitted.

Reservations, fees: Reservations are accepted at 877/444-6777 or www.recreation.gov ($10 reservation fee). Sites are $15 per night, $5 per night for an additional vehicle. Open mid-May–mid-September.

Directions: From Eugene, drive south on I-5 past Cottage Grove to Exit 172. Take that exit to London Road and drive south for 4.5 miles to Reservoir Road. Turn left and drive three miles to the camp entrance on the right.

Contact: U.S. Army Corps of Engineers, Recreation Information, Cottage Grove, 541/942-8657 or 541/942-5631, fax 541/942-1305, www.nwp.usace.army.mil.

56 PINE MEADOWS PRIMITIVE SITES

Scenic rating: 6

on Cottage Grove Reservoir

Located adjacent to Pine Meadows, this primitive campground offers the same boating, fishing, swimming, and waterskiing activities on Cottage Grove Reservoir.

Campsites, facilities: There are 15 primitive sites for tents or small, self-contained RVs. Picnic tables, vault toilets, drinking water, garbage bins, and fire rings are provided. Boat docks, launching facilities, and a mini-market are nearby. Leashed pets are permitted.

Reservations, fees: Reservations are accepted at 877/444-6777 or www.recreation.gov ($10 reservation fee). Sites are $10 per night, $5 per night for an additional vehicle. Campers must have a permit, obtained at the entrance booth. Open late May–early September.

Directions: From Eugene, drive south on I-5 past Cottage Grove to Exit 172. Take that exit to London Road and drive south for 4.5 miles to Reservoir Road. Turn left and drive three miles to the camp entrance.

Contact: U.S. Army Corps of Engineers, Recreation Information, Cottage Grove, 541/942-8657 or 541/942-5631, fax 541/942-1305, www.nwp.usace.army.mil.

57 WHISTLER'S BEND PARK

Scenic rating: 7

on the North Umpqua River

This 175-acre county park along the banks of the North Umpqua River is an idyllic spot because it gets little pressure from outsiders, yet it is just a 20-minute drive from I-5. Two boat ramps accommodate boaters, and fishing is a plus. A wildlife reserve provides habitat for deer.

Campsites, facilities: There are 23 sites for tents or RVs up to 35 feet long (no hookups) and two yurts. Two group camps are available. Picnic tables and fire grills are provided. Drinking water, restrooms with flush toilets and showers, a playground, disc golf, and launching facilities are available. Some facilities are wheelchair accessible. Leashed pets are permitted.

Reservations, fees: Reservations are accepted for yurts and group camps at 541/957-7001 ($10 reservation fee) but not for tent or RV sites. Single sites are $15 per night, $3 per night per additional vehicle, $32 per night for yurts, $50 per night for the group camp for up to 50 people, $100 per night for the group camp for up to 100 people. Some credit cards are accepted. Individual sites are open April–November; group sites are open year-round.

Directions: From Roseburg, drive east on Highway 138 for 12 miles to Whistler's Bend Park Road (well signed). Turn left and drive two miles to the end of the road and the park entrance.

Contact: Whistler's Bend Park, 541/673-4863, www.co.douglas.or.us.

58 AMACHER PARK

Scenic rating: 5

on the Umpqua River

A wooded Douglas County park set along the banks of the North Umpqua River, Amacher is a prime layover spot for I-5 RV cruisers. This park has one of the few Myrtlewood groves in the country. Tent sites are located underneath the freeway next to the railroad tracks; trains come by intermittently. An 18-hole golf course and tennis courts are close by, riding stables are within a 20-minute drive, and Winchester Dam is within 0.25 mile.

Campsites, facilities: There are 10 sites for tents or self-contained RVs and 20 sites with full or partial hookups (20-amp service only) for RVs up to 30 feet long. Picnic tables are provided; some sites have fire rings. Drinking water, restrooms with flush toilets and showers, a gazebo, and picnic area are available. Propane gas, a store, café, coin laundry, and ice are within one mile. Boat-launching facilities are available. Some facilities are wheelchair accessible. Leashed pets are permitted.

Reservations, fees: Reservations are not accepted. Sites are $15–20 per night, $3 per night per additional vehicle. Cash only. Open March–October (closed in winter).

Directions: From Roseburg, drive five miles north on I-5 to Exit 129. Take that exit and drive south on Old Highway 99 for 0.25 mile to the park on the right (just across Winchester Bridge).

Contact: Amacher Park, 541/672-4901; Douglas County, 541/672-4901, www.co.douglas.or.us.

59 TWIN RIVERS VACATION PARK

Scenic rating: 6

near the Umpqua River

This wooded campground is near the Umpqua River. It features large shaded pull-through sites and more than 100 kinds of trees on the property. Groups are welcome and clubhouses are available for group use. Nearby recreation options include bike paths, a county park, and a golf course.

Campsites, facilities: There are 82 sites with full or partial hookups for RVs of any length; many are pull-through sites. Cable TV, fire pits, and picnic tables are provided. Restrooms with flush toilets and showers, modem access, propane gas, firewood, a convenience store, a coin laundry, ice, and a playground are available. Boat-launching facilities are nearby. Leashed pets are permitted.

Reservations, fees: Reservations are accepted. Sites are $22–33 per night, $3 per person per night for more than two people. Some credit cards are accepted. Open year-round.

Directions: In Roseburg on I-5, take Exit 125 to Garden Valley Road. Drive west for five miles (over the river) to Old Garden Valley Road. Turn left and drive 1.5 miles to River Forks Road. Turn left and drive a short distance to the park entrance on the left.

Contact: Twin Rivers Vacation Park, 541/673-3811, www.twinriversrvpark.com.

60 DOUGLAS COUNTY FAIRGROUNDS RV PARK

Scenic rating: 8

on the South Umpqua River

This 74-acre county park is very easily accessible off the highway. Nearby Umpqua River, one of Oregon's prettiest rivers, often has good fishing in season. Bike paths, a golf course, and tennis courts are nearby. Horse stalls and a boat ramp are available at the nearby fairgrounds. The campground fills up the third weekend in March, during the annual fiddlers' convention.

Campsites, facilities: There are 50 sites with partial hookups for tents or RVs of any length. Drinking water and picnic tables are provided. Restrooms with flush toilets and showers and a dump station are available. A store, café, coin laundry, and ice are within one mile. Some facilities are wheelchair accessible. Leashed pets are permitted.

Reservations, fees: Reservations are not accepted. Sites are $15–20 per night, with a 14-day stay limit. Tent camping is limited to two nights. Open year-round, except one week in August during the county fair. Phone ahead to confirm current status.

Directions: Heading south on I-5 in Roseburg, take Exit 123 and drive south under the freeway to Frear Street. Turn right and enter the park.

Contact: Douglas County Fairgrounds & Speedway, 541/957-7010, fax 541/440-6023, www.co.douglas.or.us/dcfair.

61 CAVITT CREEK FALLS

Scenic rating: 8

west of Roseburg

The locals might try to hunt me down for revealing this spot, but here it is. This campground is located near a sensational swimming hole at the base of a 10-foot waterfall on Cavitt Creek. The elevation is 1,040 feet, and an abundant forest of fir, maple, and oak trees surrounds the campground. It is overlooked because it is set on land run by the Bureau of Land Management, not the Park Service or Forest Service. Fishing is closed on Cavitt Creek by the Oregon Department of Fish and Wildlife.

Campsites, facilities: There are 10 sites for tents or RVs up to 20 feet long. Picnic tables, garbage bins, and fire rings are provided. Drinking water and vault toilets are available. A camp host is on-site. Some facilities are wheelchair accessible. Leashed pets are permitted.

Reservations, fees: Reservations are not accepted. Sites are $8 per night, $4 per night for an additional vehicle. Open mid-May–mid-October, weather permitting.

Directions: From Roseburg, drive east on Highway 138 for 16.5 miles to Little River Road. Turn right (south) on Little River Road and drive 6.7 miles to the covered bridge. Turn right onto Cavitt Creek Road and drive 3.2 miles to Cavitt Creek Falls Recreation Site.

Contact: Bureau of Land Management, Roseburg District, 541/440-4930, fax 541/440-4948, www.or.blm.gov/or/resources/recreation.

62 DEXTER SHORES RV PARK

Scenic rating: 7

near Dexter Reservoir

If you're traveling on I-5, this RV park is well worth the 15-minute drive out of Springfield. It's across the street from Dexter Reservoir, where fishing and boating are permitted year-round. Speedboat races are held at Dexter in the summer. There is seasonal fishing for salmon and steelhead below Dexter dam. The local area is good for bird-watching. Nearby Lookout and Fall Creek Lakes offer sailing, swimming, waterskiing, and windsurfing. There are three authentic Sioux tepees on the property in the summer and two cabins. Many of the campsites have a lake view.

Campsites, facilities: There are 56 sites with full or partial hookups for RVs up to 40 feet long; 12 sites are pull-through. There are also eight tent sites, three tepees, and two one-bedroom cabins. Drinking water, cable TV and telephone hookups, picnic tables, and fire pits are provided. Restrooms with flush toilets and showers, a dump station, modem access, a clubhouse, lending library, video rentals, firewood, horseshoe pits, and a coin laundry are available. Propane gas, a café, restaurant, and ice are within one mile. Boat docks and launching facilities are nearby. Leashed pets are permitted in the campground, but not in the cabins or tepees.

Reservations, fees: Reservations are accepted at 866/558-9777. RV sites are $30–45 per night, tent sites are $20 per night, tepees are $25–35 per night, $3 per person per night for more than four people, and $1 per pet per night. Some credit cards are accepted. Open year-round.

Directions: From south Eugene on I-5, drive to Exit 188A and Highway 58. Take Highway 58 east and drive 11.5 miles to Lost Creek Road. Turn right (south) and drive several hundred feet to Dexter Road. Turn left (in front of the café) and drive east for half a block to the park on the right.

Contact: Dexter Shores RV Park, 866/558-9777 or 541/937-3711, fax 541/937-1724, www.dextershoresrv.com.

63 FALL CREEK STATE RECREATION AREA

Scenic rating: 7

in Fall Creek State Recreation Area

There are two campgrounds here: Cascara and the group camp area, Fisherman's Park. Most of these spacious sites have Douglas fir and white fir tree cover. Water recreation is the primary activity here; boating and water skis are allowed. The lake level drops in August, and water temperatures are ideal for summer swimming.

Campsites, facilities: There are 42 primitive sites for tents or RVs up to 45 feet, five walk-in sites for tents, and a group area for RVs of any length up to 16 vehicles; there are no pull-through sites. Picnic tables and fire rings are provided. Drinking water, vault toilets, garbage service, and firewood are available. A camp host is on-site. A boat launch, dock, and swimming area are also available. Leashed pets are permitted.

Reservations, fees: Reservations are accepted for the RV group area only at 800/452-5687. Sites are $19 per night, $10 per night for primitive sites, $5 per night for an additional vehicle. The group RV area is $109 per night for up to 10 RVs. Some credit cards are accepted. Open May–September.

Directions: From south Eugene on I-5, take Exit 188 to Highway 58. Drive 11 miles south to Lowell and Pioneer Street (at the covered bridge). Turn left on Pioneer Street and drive less than 0.25 mile to West Boundary Road. Turn left and drive one block to Lowell Jasper Road. Turn right and drive 1.5 miles to Unity and Place Road. Turn right and drive about one mile to a fork with North Shore Road (Big Fall Creek Road). Bear left onto Big Fall Creek Road and drive about eight miles to the head of Fall Creek Reservoir and Peninsula Road (Forest Road 6250). Turn right and drive 0.5 mile to the campground. The park is approximately 27 miles southeast of Eugene.

Contact: Fall Creek State Recreation Area, 541/937-1173 or 800/551-6949, www.oregonstateparks.org.

64 DOLLY VARDEN

Scenic rating: 6

on Fall Creek in Willamette National Forest

This pretty campground is adjacent to Fall Creek and is at the lower trailhead for the scenic, 13.7-mile Fall Creek National Recreation Trail, which follows the creek and varies between 960 and 1,385 feet in elevation. This small campground gets moderate-heavy use. It is set on the inlet stream for Fall Creek Reservoir.

Campsites, facilities: There are five sites for tents or RVs up to 30 feet. Picnic tables and fire grills are provided. Vault toilets and garbage service are available. There is no drinking water. Leashed pets are permitted.

Reservations, fees: Reservations are not accepted. Sites are $12 per night, $6 per night per additional vehicle. Open May–September, weather permitting.

Directions: From south Eugene on I-5, take Exit 188 to Highway 58. Drive 11 miles south to Lowell and Pioneer Street (at the covered bridge). Turn left and drive 0.2 mile to West Boundary Road. Turn left and drive one block to Lowell Jasper Road. Turn right and drive 1.5 miles to Unity and Place Road. Turn right and drive about one mile to a fork with North Shore Road. Bear left onto North Shore Road (Big Fall Creek Road) and drive about 10 miles (the road becomes Forest Road 18) to the campground on the left.

Contact: Willamette National Forest, Middle Fork Ranger District, 541/782-2283, fax 541/782-5306, www.fs.fed.us; Hoodoo Recreation, 541/822-3799.

65 BIG POOL

Scenic rating: 6

on Fall Creek in Willamette National Forest

Big Pool campground is quiet, secluded, and primitive. The camp sits along Fall Creek at about 1,000 feet elevation, and the scenic Fall Creek National Recreation Trail passes the camp on the other side of the creek, providing hiking opportunities.

Campsites, facilities: There are three tent sites and two sites for tents or RVs up to 24 feet long. Picnic tables, garbage containers, and fire grills are provided. Vault toilets and drinking water are available. Leashed pets are permitted.

Reservations, fees: Reservations are not accepted. Sites are $12 per night, $6 per night per additional vehicle. Open late May–September, weather permitting.

Directions: From south Eugene on I-5, take Exit 188 to Highway 58. Drive 11 miles south to Lowell and Pioneer Street (at the covered bridge). Turn left and drive 0.2 mile to West Boundary Road. Turn left and drive one block to Lowell Jasper Road. Turn right and drive 1.5 miles to Unity and Place Road. Turn right and drive about one mile to a fork with North Shore Road. Bear left onto North Shore Road (Big Fall Creek Road) and drive about 12 miles (the road becomes Forest Road 18) to the campground on the right.

Contact: Willamette National Forest, Middle Fork Ranger District, 541/782-2283, fax 541/782-5306, www.fs.fed.us; Hoodoo Recreation, 541/822-3799.

66 BEDROCK

Scenic rating: 6

on Fall Creek in Willamette National Forest

Bedrock lies along the banks of Fall Creek amid Douglas firs and cedars. This is one of the access points for the scenic Fall Creek National Recreation Trail, which in turn offers access to Jones Trail, a six-mile uphill climb. Swimming holes offer relief in summer. Note that the campground suffered previous fire damage, but it is recovering.

Campsites, facilities: There are 18 single sites and one multiple site for tents or RVs up to 36 feet long. Picnic tables and fire grills are provided. Vault toilets and garbage service are available. There is no drinking water. Some facilities are wheelchair accessible. Leashed pets are permitted.

Reservations, fees: Reservations are not accepted. Single sites are $14 per night, $22 per night for double sites, and $7 per night per additional vehicle. Open May–mid-September, weather permitting.

Directions: From south Eugene on I-5, take

Exit 188 to Highway 58. Drive 11 miles south to Lowell and Pioneer Street (at the covered bridge). Turn left and drive 0.2 mile to West Boundary Road. Turn left and drive one block to Lowell Jasper Road. Turn right and drive 1.5 miles to Unity and Place Road. Turn right and drive about one mile to a fork with North Shore Road. Bear left onto North Shore Road (Big Fall Creek Road) and drive about 14 miles (the road becomes Forest Road 18) to the campground on the left.

Contact: Willamette National Forest, Middle Fork Ranger District, 541/782-2283, fax 541/782-5306, www.fs.fed.us; Hoodoo Recreation, 541/822-3799.

67 PUMA

Scenic rating: 6

on Fall Creek in Willamette National Forest

Puma campground hugs the banks of Fall Creek at an elevation of 1,100 feet. This is one of four camps in the immediate area, located across from the popular Fall Creek National Recreation Trail. The trail offers hiking opportunities, while Fall Creek provides a nice spot to cool off in summer.

Campsites, facilities: There are 11 sites for tents or RVs up to 36 feet long. Picnic tables and fire grills are provided. Vault toilets, drinking water, and garbage bins are available. Leashed pets are permitted.

Reservations, fees: Reservations are not accepted. Sites are $14 per night, $7 per night per additional vehicle. Open late May–September, weather permitting.

Directions: From I-5 south of Eugene, take Exit 188 to Highway 58. Drive about 11 miles to Lowell. Turn left at Pioneer Street (at the covered bridge), drive 0.2 mile, and turn left on West Boundary Road. Drive one block and turn right at Lowell Jasper Road. Drive 1.5 miles to Place Road and turn right. Drive about one mile to a fork and bear left onto North Shore Road (Big Fall Creek Road). Drive about 16 miles (the road becomes Forest Road 18) to the campground on the left.

Contact: Willamette National Forest, Middle Fork Ranger District, 541/782-2283, fax 541/782-5306, www.fs.fed.us.

68 FRISSELL CROSSING

Scenic rating: 8

near the Three Sisters Wilderness in Willamette National Forest

If you're looking for solitude, this place should be heaven to you. Frissell campground (elevation 2,600 feet) sits on the banks of the South Fork of the McKenzie River, adjacent to a trailhead that provides access to the backcountry of the Three Sisters Wilderness. Note that Frissell Crossing is the only camp in the immediate area that has drinking water.

Campsites, facilities: There are 12 sites for tents or RVs up to 36 feet long. Picnic tables, garbage bins, and fire grills are provided. Drinking water and vault toilets are available. Leashed pets are permitted.

Reservations, fees: Reservations are not accepted. Sites are $12 per night, $6 per night per additional vehicle. Open mid-May–mid-September, weather permitting.

Directions: From Eugene, drive east on Highway 126 for 37 miles to Blue River. Continue east on Highway 126 for five miles to Forest Road 19 (Aufderheide Scenic Byway). Turn right (south) and drive 21.5 miles to the camp on the left.

Contact: Willamette National Forest, McKenzie River Ranger District, 541/822-3381, fax 541/822-7254, www.fs.fed.us; Hoodoo Recreation, 541/822-3799.

69 WINBERRY

Scenic rating: 6

on Winberry Creek in Willamette National Forest

This campground is on Winberry Creek in a tree-shaded area at 1,900 feet elevation. The closest hiking option is Station Butte Trail, just downstream from the campground on Forest Road 1802-150. Be cautious: Poison oak grows at the top of the butte.

Campsites, facilities: There are six sites for tents or RVs up to 14 feet long. Picnic tables and fire grills are provided. Drinking water, vault toilets, garbage service, and two A-frame shelters are available. Some facilities are wheelchair accessible. Leashed pets are permitted.

Reservations, fees: Reservations are not accepted. Sites are $5 per night, $2 per night per additional vehicle. Open late May–early September, weather permitting.

Directions: From south Eugene on I-5, take Exit 188 to Highway 58. Drive 11 miles south to Lowell and Pioneer Street (at the covered bridge). Turn left and drive 0.2 mile to West Boundary Road. Turn left and drive one block to Lowell Jasper Road. Turn right and drive 1.5 miles to Unity and Place Road. Turn right and drive about one mile to a fork with Winberry Road. Bear right and drive six miles (the road becomes Forest Road 1802). Continue 3.5 miles to the campground.

Contact: Willamette National Forest, Middle Fork Ranger District, 541/782-2283, fax 541/782-5306, www.fs.fed.us.

70 BLAIR LAKE WALK-IN

Scenic rating: 6

on Blair Lake in Willamette National Forest

If you're looking for a pristine, alpine lakeside setting, you'll find it here. The lake, set at 4,800 feet elevation, is small (only 35 acres) and shallow (20 feet). It supports a population of brook and rainbow trout and is stocked in the summer. The surrounding meadows and woods are well known for their wide range of wildflowers and huckleberries.

Campsites, facilities: There are seven walk-in tent sites. Picnic tables and fire rings are provided. Drinking water, a vault toilet, and garbage bins are available. Some facilities are wheelchair accessible. Leashed pets are permitted.

Reservations, fees: Reservations are not accepted. Sites are $8 per night, $4 per night per additional vehicle. Open mid-June–October, weather permitting.

Directions: From south Eugene on I-5, take Exit 188 to Highway 58. Drive 35 miles southeast on Highway 58 to Oakridge. Turn left at the signal to downtown and Salmon Creek Road. Turn east and drive nine miles (it becomes Forest Road 24) to Forest Road 1934. Turn left and drive eight miles to Forest Road 733. Turn right and continue for 1.25 miles to the campground.

Contact: Willamette National Forest, Middle Fork Ranger District, 541/782-2283, fax 541/782-5306, www.fs.fed.us.

71 KIAHANIE

Scenic rating: 5

on the North Fork of the Willamette River in Willamette National Forest

This is one heck of a spot for fly-fishing (and the only kind of fishing allowed). Kiahanie is a remote campground that sits at 2,200 feet elevation along the North Fork of the Willamette River, a designated Wild and Scenic River. If you want beauty and quiet among enormous Douglas fir trees, you came to the right place. An even more remote campground, Box Canyon Horse Camp, is farther north on Forest Road 19.

Campsites, facilities: There are 19 sites for tents or RVs up to 24 feet long. Picnic tables and fire rings are provided. Drinking water, vault toilets, garbage bins, and a recycling center are available. Some facilities are wheelchair accessible. Leashed pets are permitted.
Reservations, fees: Reservations are not accepted. Sites are $10 per night, $5 per night per additional vehicle. Open late May–late October, weather permitting.
Directions: From south Eugene on I-5, take Exit 188 to Highway 58. Drive 31 miles southeast on Highway 58 to Westfir. Take the Westfir exit and drive two miles to Westfir and the junction with Aufderheide Scenic Byway (Forest Road 19). Bear left (northeast) and drive 19 miles to the campground.
Contact: Willamette National Forest, Middle Fork Ranger District, 541/782-2283, fax 541/782-5306, www.fs.fed.us.

72 BOX CANYON HORSE CAMP

Scenic rating: 4

near Chucksney Mountain in Willamette National Forest

Only 80 miles from Eugene, this secluded campground with sparse tree cover offers wilderness trails, including the Chucksney Mountain Trail, Crossing-Way Trail, and Grasshopper Trail. It's a good base camp for a backpacking trip and is at 3,600 feet in elevation.
Campsites, facilities: There are 13 sites for tents or RVs up to 30 feet long that allow horse and rider to camp close together. Picnic tables, fire grills, stock water, and corrals are provided. Vault toilets are available. There is no drinking water, and garbage must be packed out. Leashed pets are permitted.
Reservations, fees: Reservations are not accepted. There is no fee for camping. Open June–November, weather permitting.
Directions: From Eugene, drive east on Highway 126 for 41 miles to Blue River. Continue east on Highway 126 for five miles to Forest Road 19 (Aufderheide Scenic Byway). Turn right (south) and drive 33 miles to the camp on the right.
Contact: Willamette National Forest, McKenzie River Ranger District, 541/822-3381, fax 541/822-7254, www.fs.fed.us.

73 BLACK CANYON

Scenic rating: 7

on the Middle Fork of the Willamette River in Willamette National Forest

Black Canyon campground is set along the banks of the Middle Fork of the Willamette River, not far above Lookout Point Reservoir, where fishing and boating are available. The elevation is 1,000 feet. The camp is pretty and wooded and has comfortable sites. Within the camp is a one-mile-long nature trail with interpretive signs. You will hear train noise from the other side of the river.
Campsites, facilities: There are 70 sites for tents or RVs up to 40 feet long, and one group site is available. Picnic tables, garbage service, and fire grills are provided. Drinking water, vault toilets, and firewood are available. A dump station, café, and coin laundry are within six miles. Launching facilities are nearby at the south end of Lookout Point Reservoir. Some facilities are wheelchair accessible. Leashed pets are permitted.
Reservations, fees: Reservations are accepted at 877/444-6777 or www.recreation.gov ($10 reservation fee). Single sites are $16 per night, $30 per night for double site, $8 per night per additional vehicle, $75 for the group site. Open late April–early October, weather permitting.
Directions: From south Eugene on I-5, take Exit 188 to Highway 58. Drive southeast on Highway 58 for 27 miles to the camp on the left (six miles west of Oakridge).

Contact: Willamette National Forest, Middle Fork Ranger District, 541/782-2283, fax 541/782-5306, www.fs.fed.us.

74 BAKER BAY COUNTY PARK

Scenic rating: 6

on Dorena Lake

Baker Bay is set along the shore of Dorena Lake, where boating, canoeing, fishing, sailing, swimming, and waterskiing are among the recreation options. Row River Trail follows part of the lake for a hike or bike ride, and there are covered bridges in the area. For golf, head to Cottage Grove.

Campsites, facilities: There are 49 sites for tents or self-contained RVs up to 35 feet, plus two group sites for up to 25 people each. Picnic tables and fire grills are provided. Drinking water, restrooms with flush toilets and coin showers, firewood, garbage bins, and a dump station are available. A concession stand with ice is in the park, and a store is within two miles. Boat docks, launching, and rentals are nearby, with seasonal onshore facilities for catamarans. Some facilities are wheelchair accessible. Leashed pets are permitted.

Reservations, fees: Reservations are accepted for group sites only at 541/682-2000 ($10 reservation fee). Single sites are $16 per night, $6.50 for an additional vehicle. Group sites are $50 per night. Open April–October.

Directions: From Eugene, drive south on I-5 for 22 miles to Cottage Grove and Exit 174 (Dorena Lake exit). Take that exit to Row River Road and drive east for 4.4 miles (the road becomes Shore View Drive). Bear right on Shore View Drive and continue 2.8 miles to the campground entrance on the left.

Contact: Baker Bay Park, 541/942-7669, www.co.lane.or.us/parks.

75 SCHWARZ PARK

Scenic rating: 7

on Dorena Lake

This large campground sits below Dorena Lake on the Row River, where boating, fishing, swimming, and waterskiing are among the recreation options at the lake. Note that chances of rain are high May to mid-June and that there is a posted warning against consumption of fish from Dorena Lake. The Row River Trail, a paved trail for biking, walking, and shoreline access, parallels Dorena Lake's north shoreline and then extends 12 miles.

Campsites, facilities: There are 69 sites for tents or RVs of any length and six group sites for up to 15–50 people. Drinking water, garbage bins, picnic tables, and fire rings are provided. Restrooms with flush toilets and showers and a dump station are available. Boat-launching facilities are on the lake about two miles upstream. Some facilities are wheelchair accessible. Leashed pets are permitted.

Reservations, fees: Reservations are accepted at 877/444-6777 or www.recreation.gov ($10 reservation fee). Sites are $13 per night, group sites are $130 per night, and an additional vehicle is $5 per night. Open late April–late September.

Directions: From Eugene, drive south on I-5 for 22 miles to Cottage Grove and Exit 174. Take that exit to Shoreview Drive and drive one mile to Row River Road. Turn left and drive four miles east to the campground entrance.

Contact: U.S. Army Corps of Engineers, Recreation Information, Cottage Grove, 541/942-1418 or 541/942-5631, fax 541/942-1305, http://corpslakes.usace.army.mil.

76 SALMON CREEK FALLS

Scenic rating: 8

on Salmon Creek in Willamette National Forest

BEST

This pretty campground sits in a lush, old-growth forest, right along Salmon Creek at 1,500 feet in elevation. The rocky gorge area creates two small but beautiful waterfalls and several deep pools in the clear, blue-green waters. Springtime brings a full range of wildflowers and wild thimbleberries; hazelnuts abound in the summer. This area is a popular recreation spot.

Campsites, facilities: There are 14 sites for tents or RVs up to 40 feet long. Picnic tables, garbage bins, and fire grills are provided. Drinking water and vault toilets are available. A store, café, coin laundry, and ice are available within five miles. Leashed pets are permitted.

Reservations, fees: Reservations are not accepted. Sites are $14 per night, $7 per night per additional vehicle. Open late April–mid-September, weather permitting.

Directions: From south Eugene on I-5, take Exit 188 to Highway 58. Drive southeast on Highway 58 for 35 miles to Oakridge and the signal light for downtown. Turn left on Crestview Street and drive 0.25 mile to 1st Street. Turn right and drive five miles (the road becomes Forest Road 24, then Salmon Creek Road) to the campground entrance on the right.

Contact: Willamette National Forest, Middle Fork Ranger District, 541/782-2283, fax 541/782-5306, www.fs.fed.us; Hoodoo Recreation, 541/822-3799.

77 SKOOKUM CREEK

Scenic rating: 7

near the Three Sisters Wilderness in Willamette National Forest

Skookum Creek, at 4,500 feet elevation, is a popular starting point for backcountry fishing, hiking, and horseback riding. The Erma Bell Lakes Trail, a portal into the Three Sisters Wilderness, begins here. This trail is maintained for wheelchair accessibility, though it is challenging.

Campsites, facilities: There are nine walk-in tent sites. Picnic tables and fire rings are provided. Drinking water, hitching rails, garbage service, and vault toilets are available. Some facilities are wheelchair accessible. Leashed pets are permitted.

Reservations, fees: Reservations are not accepted. Sites are $8 per night, $4 per night per additional vehicle. Open mid-June–mid-October, weather permitting.

Directions: From Eugene, drive east on Highway 126 for 37 miles to Blue River. Continue east for five miles to Forest Road 19 (Aufderheide Scenic Byway). Turn right and drive 35 miles south to Forest Road 1957. Turn right (south) and drive four miles to the campground.

Contact: Willamette National Forest, Middle Fork Ranger District, 541/782-2283, fax 541/782-5306.

78 NORTH WALDO

ATLAS 43 B8

Scenic rating: 10

on Waldo Lake in Willamette National Forest

BEST

North Waldo is the most popular of the Waldo Lake campgrounds. Set at an elevation of 5,400 feet, Waldo Lake has the special distinction of being one of the three purest lakes in the world. The boat launch here is deeper than the others on the lake, which makes it more accommodating for large sailboats (gas motors are not allowed on the lake). Amphitheater programs are presented here on weekends late July–Labor Day. North Waldo is also a popular starting point to many wilderness trails and lakes, most notably Rigdon, Torrey, and Wahanna lakes. The drier environment supports fewer mosquitoes, but they can still be plentiful in season.

Campsites, facilities: There are 56 sites for tents or RVs up to 40 feet long. Picnic tables and fire rings are provided. Drinking water, composting toilets, garbage bins, recycling center, swimming area, and amphitheater are available. Boat-launching facilities are available. Leashed pets are permitted.

Reservations, fees: Reservations are not accepted. Single sites are $18 per night, double sites $20 per night, $9 per night per additional vehicle. A Northwest Forest Pass ($5 daily fee or $30 annual fee per vehicle) is required at the nearby boat launch and trailheads. Open early June–early October, weather permitting.

Directions: From Eugene, drive south on I-5 for four miles to Exit 188 and Highway 58. Turn southeast and drive about 60 miles to Waldo Lake Road (Forest Road 5897). Turn left and drive north on Waldo Lake Road for 14 miles to Forest Road 5898. Turn left and drive about two miles to the campground at the northeast end of Waldo Lake.

Contact: Willamette National Forest, Middle Fork Ranger District, 541/782-2283, fax 541/782-5306, www.fs.fed.us; Hoodoo Recreation, 541/822-3799.

79 ISLET

Scenic rating: 10

on Waldo Lake in Willamette National Forest

You'll find sandy beaches and an interpretive sign at this campground at the north end of Waldo Lake. The winds blow consistently every afternoon, great for sailing. A picnic table placed strategically on the rock jetty provides a great spot to enjoy a sunset. A one-mile shoreline trail stretches between Islet and North Waldo Campground. Bring your mosquito repellent June–August—you'll need it.

Campsites, facilities: There are 55 sites, including four multiple sites, for tents or RVs up to 40 feet long. Picnic tables, garbage bins, a recycling center, and fire rings are provided. Drinking water and composting toilets are available. Boat-launching facilities are available nearby. Leashed pets are permitted.

Reservations, fees: Reservations are not accepted. Single sites are $18 per night, $9 per night per additional vehicle. Double sites are $25 per night. A Northwest Forest Pass ($5 daily fee or $30 annual fee per parked vehicle) is required at the nearby boat launch and trailheads. Open July–October, weather permitting.

Directions: From Eugene, drive south on I-5 for four miles to Exit 188 and Highway 58. Turn southeast and drive about 60 miles to Waldo Lake Road (Forest Road 5897). Turn left and drive north on Waldo Lake Road for 14 miles to Forest Road 5898. Turn left and continue 1.5 miles to the campground at the northeast end of Waldo Lake.

Contact: Willamette National Forest, Middle Fork Ranger District, 541/782-2283, fax 541/782-5306, www.fs.fed.us; Hoodoo Recreation, 541/822-3799.

80 SHADOW BAY

Scenic rating: 10

on Waldo Lake in Willamette National Forest

Shadow Bay campground, at 5,400 in elevation, is situated on a large bay at the south end of Waldo Lake. It has a considerably wetter environment than either North Waldo or Islet, supporting a more diverse and prolific ground cover—as well as more mosquitoes. The camp receives considerably lighter use than North Waldo. You have access to the Shore Line Trail and then the Waldo Lake Trail from here. Note that gas motors are not permitted on Waldo Lake.

Campsites, facilities: There are 92 sites, including several multiple sites, for tents or RVs up to 44 feet long. Picnic tables, garbage bins, a recycling center, and fire grills are provided. Drinking water and vault and composting toilets are available. A camp host is on-site in season. Boat-launching facilities and a swimming area are nearby. Leashed pets are permitted.

Reservations, fees: Reservations are accepted at 877/444-6777 or www.recreation.gov ($10 reservation fee). Single sites are $18 per night, $32 per night for double sites, $9 per night per additional vehicle. A Northwest Forest Pass ($5 daily fee or $30 annual fee per vehicle) is required at the nearby boat launch and trailheads. Open July–October, weather permitting.

Directions: From Eugene, drive south on I-5 for four miles to Exit 188 and Highway 58. Turn southeast and drive about 60 miles to Waldo Lake Road (Forest Road 5897). Turn left on Waldo Lake Road and drive north for 6.5 miles to the Shadow Bay turnoff. Turn left and drive on Forest Road 5896 to the campground at the south end of Waldo Lake.

Contact: Willamette National Forest, Middle Fork Ranger District, 541/782-2283, fax 541/782-5306, www.fs.fed.us; Hoodoo Recreation, 541/822-3799.

81 BLUE POOL

Scenic rating: 4

on Salt Creek in Willamette National Forest

This campground is situated in an old-growth forest alongside Salt Creek at 1,900 feet elevation. The camp features a large picnic area along the creek with picnic tables, a large grassy area, and fire stoves built in the 1930s by the Civilian Conservation Corps. One-half mile east of the campground on Highway 58 is McCredie Hot Springs. This spot is undeveloped, without any facilities. Exercise caution when using the hot springs; they can be very hot.

Campsites, facilities: There are 24 sites for tents or RVs up to 36 feet long. Picnic tables, garbage bins, a recycling center, and fire rings are provided. Drinking water and vault and flush toilets are available. Leashed pets are permitted.

Reservations, fees: Reservations are not accepted. Sites are $14 per night, $7 per night per additional vehicle. Open mid-May–September, weather permitting.

Directions: From Eugene, drive south on I-5 for four miles to Exit 188 and Highway 58. Turn southeast and drive 35 miles to Oakridge. Continue east on Highway 58 for eight miles to the campground on the right.

Contact: Willamette National Forest, Middle Fork Ranger District, 541/782-2283, fax 541/782-5306, www.fs.fed.us; Hoodoo Recreation, 541/822-3799.

82 SHARPS CREEK

Scenic rating: 5

on Sharps Creek

Like nearby Rujada, this camp on the banks of Sharps Creek is just far enough off the beaten path to be missed by most campers. It's quiet, primitive, and remote, and fishing, gold-panning, and swimming are popular activities in the day-use area.

Campsites, facilities: There are 10 sites for tents or RVs up to 30 feet long. Picnic tables and fire pits are provided. Drinking water and vault toilets are available. A camp host is here in summer. Some facilities are wheelchair accessible. Leashed pets are permitted.

Reservations, fees: Reservations are not accepted. Sites are $8 per night, with a 14-day stay limit, and $3 per night per additional vehicle. Open mid-May–September, weather permitting.

Directions: From Eugene, drive south on I-5 to Cottage Grove and Exit 174. Take that exit and drive east on Row River Road for 18 miles to Sharps Creek Road. Turn right (south) and drive four miles to the campground.

Contact: Bureau of Land Management, Eugene District, 541/683-6600 or 888/442-3061, fax 541/683-6981, www.blm.gov.

83 RUJADA

Scenic rating: 7

on Layng Creek in Umpqua National Forest

Rujada campground is nestled on a river terrace on the banks of Layng Creek, right at the national forest border. The Swordfern Trail follows Layng Creek through a beautiful forest within a lush fern grotto. There is a fair swimming hole near the campground. Those with patience and persistence can fish in the creek. By continuing east on Forest Road 17, you reach a trailhead that leads 0.5 mile to beautiful Spirit Falls, a spectacular 60-foot waterfall. A bit farther east is another easy trail, which leads to Moon Falls, even more awe-inspiring at 125 feet. Another campground option is Cedar Creek, about six miles southeast on Brice Creek Road (County Road 2470).

Campsites, facilities: There are 15 sites for tents or RVs up to 22 feet long. Picnic tables, garbage bins, and fire pits are provided. Flush and vault toilets, drinking water, and a softball field are available. Some facilities are wheelchair accessible. Leashed pets are permitted.

Reservations, fees: Reservations are not accepted. Sites are $8 per night, $3 per night per additional vehicle. Open late May–late September, weather permitting.

Directions: From Eugene, drive south on I-5 to Cottage Grove and Exit 174. Take that exit and drive east on Row River Road for 19 miles to Layng Creek Road (Forest Road 17). Turn left and drive two miles to the campground on the right.

Contact: Umpqua National Forest, Cottage Grove Ranger District, 541/767-5000, fax 541/767-5075, www.fs.fed.us.

84 PACKARD CREEK

Scenic rating: 6

on Hills Creek Reservoir in Willamette National Forest

Packard Creek campground is located on a large flat beside Hills Creek Reservoir. This camp is extremely popular with families and fills up on weekends and holidays. The mix of vegetation in the campground unfortunately includes an abundance of poison oak. The speed limit around the swimming area and boat ramp is 5 mph. The elevation is 1,600 feet.

Campsites, facilities: There are 37 sites, including two multiple sites, for tents or RVs up to 40 feet long, and a group area for up to 75 people. Picnic tables and fire rings are provided. Drinking water, vault toilets, garbage bins, a recycling center, and firewood are available. Fishing and boat docks, boat-launching facilities, a roped swimming area, picnic shelter, and an amphitheater are available. Some sites have their own docks. Some facilities are wheelchair accessible. Leashed pets are permitted.

Reservations, fees: Reservations are accepted at 877/444-6777 or www.recreation.gov ($10 reservation fee). Single sites are $16 per night, $30 per night for double sites, $8 per night per additional vehicle, $125 for the group site. Open mid-April–mid-September, weather permitting.

Directions: From Eugene, drive south on I-5 for four miles to Exit 188 and Highway 58. Turn southeast and drive 35 miles to Oakridge. Continue east on Highway 58 for two miles to Kitson Springs Road. Turn right and drive 0.5 mile to Forest Road 21. Turn right and continue six miles to the campground on the left.

Contact: Willamette National Forest, Middle Fork Ranger District, 541/782-2283, fax 541/782-5306, www.fs.fed.us; Hoodoo Recreation, 541/822-3799.

85 SAND PRAIRIE

Scenic rating: 6

on the Willamette River in Willamette National Forest

Situated at 1,600 feet elevation in a mixed stand of cedar, dogwood, Douglas fir, hazelnut, and western hemlock, this campground provides easy access to the Middle Fork of the Willamette River. An access road leads to the south (upstream) end of the Hills Creek Reservoir. The 27-mile Middle Fork Trail begins at the south end of the campground. Fishing is good here; you can expect to catch large cutthroat trout, rainbow trout, and suckers in the Middle Fork.

Campsites, facilities: There are 21 sites for tents or RVs up to 40 feet long. Picnic tables, garbage bins, and fire rings are provided. Vault and flush toilets, a group picnic area, and drinking water are available. A camp host is on-site. A boat launch is nearby on Hills Creek Reservoir. Some facilities are wheelchair accessible. Leashed pets are permitted.

Reservations, fees: Reservations are not accepted. Sites are $12 per night, $6 per night per additional vehicle. Open late May–early September, weather permitting.

Directions: From Eugene, drive south on I-5 for four miles to Exit 188 and Highway 58. Turn southeast and drive 35 miles to Oakridge. Continue east on Highway 58 for two miles to Kitson Springs Road. Turn right and drive 0.5 mile to Forest Road 21. Turn right and continue 11 miles to the campground on the right.

Contact: Willamette National Forest, Middle Fork Ranger District, 541/782-2283, fax 541/782-5306, www.fs.fed.us.

86 SACANDAGA

Scenic rating: 5

on the Willamette River in Willamette National Forest

Sacandaga campground sits along the middle fork of the Willamette River, where a segment of the historic Oregon Central Military Wagon Road is visible. Two trails from the campground access the Willamette River, and the Middle Fork Trail is in close proximity. Also, a short trail leads to a viewpoint with a bench, great for a short break. This campground gets low use, and the sites are well separated by vegetation. Count on solitude here. The elevation is 2,400 feet.

Campsites, facilities: There are 17 sites for tents or RVs up to 24 feet long. Picnic tables and fire rings are provided. Drinking water, vault toilets, and firewood are available. Leashed pets are permitted.

Reservations, fees: Reservations are not accepted. Sites are $8 per night, $4 per night per additional vehicle. Open mid-May–mid-November, weather permitting.

Directions: From Eugene, drive south on I-5 for four miles to Exit 188 and Highway 58. Turn southeast and drive 35 miles to Oakridge. Continue east on Highway 58 for two miles to Kitson Springs Road. Turn right and drive 0.5 mile to Forest Road 21. Turn right and drive 24 miles to the campground on the right.

Contact: Willamette National Forest, Middle Fork Ranger District, 541/782-2283, fax 541/782-5306, www.fs.fed.us.

87 CAMPERS FLAT

Scenic rating: 5

on the Willamette River in Willamette National Forest

Small, pretty Campers Flat campground sits adjacent to the Middle Fork Willamette River, near Deadhorse Creek. Though the camp is right next to Forest Road 21, you're likely to hear more river than road. Fishing is a popular activity here, with good river access. For mountain bikers, the Young's Rock Trailhead awaits on the other side of the road. While at camp, be sure to check out the interpretive sign detailing the history of the Oregon Central Military Wagon Road.

Campsites, facilities: There are five sites for tents or RVs up to 40 feet long. Picnic tables, garbage bins, and fire grills are provided. Vault toilets and firewood are available. Well water may be available for drinking, but bring your own just in case. Leashed pets are permitted.

Reservations, fees: Reservations are not accepted. Sites are $12 per night, $6 per night per additional vehicle. Open late May–September.

Directions: From Eugene, drive south on I-5 for five miles to Exit 188 and Highway 58. Turn east and drive 35 miles to the town of Oakridge. From Oakridge, continue east on Highway 58 about two miles to Kitson Springs Road. Turn right and drive 0.5 mile to Forest Road 21. Turn right and drive 19 miles to the campground on the right.

Contact: Willamette National Forest, Middle Fork Ranger District, 541/782-2283, fax 541/782-5306, www.fs.fed.us.

88 SECRET

Scenic rating: 5

on the Willamette River in Willamette National Forest

This small campground, set on the middle fork of the Willamette River, gets regular use from locals in the know. The tree cover is scant, but there is adequate vegetation to buffer the campsites from the nearby road noise. Fishing the Middle Fork Willamette is generally fair.

Campsites, facilities: There are six sites for tents or RVs up to 36 feet long. Picnic tables, garbage bins, and fire rings are provided. Pit toilets are available, but there is no drinking water. Leashed pets are permitted.

Reservations, fees: Reservations are not accepted. Sites are $12 per night, $6 per night per additional vehicle. Open May–late September, weather permitting.

Directions: From Eugene, drive south on I-5 for five miles to Exit 188 and Highway 58. Turn east and drive 35 miles to the town of Oakridge. From Oakridge, continue east on Highway 58 about two miles to Kitson Springs Road. Turn right and drive 0.5 mile to Forest Road 21. Turn right and drive 18 miles to the campground.

Contact: Willamette National Forest, Middle Fork Ranger District, 541/782-2283, fax 541/782-5306, www.fs.fed.us; Hoodoo Recreation, 541/822-3799.

89 INDIGO SPRINGS

Scenic rating: 5

near the Willamette River in Willamette National Forest

This small, semi-open tent campground sits at 2,800 feet elevation in a stand of old-growth Douglas fir. A nearby 250-foot walk leads to the origin of this cold-water spring. A remnant of the historic Oregon Central Military Wagon Road passes near the campground, with an interpretive sign explaining it.

Campsites, facilities: There are three sites for tents. Picnic tables and fire grills are provided. Vault toilets and firewood are available. There is no drinking water. Leashed pets are permitted.

Reservations, fees: Reservations are not accepted. There is no fee for camping. Open May–October, weather permitting.

Directions: From Eugene, drive south on I-5 for five miles to Exit 188 and Highway 58. Turn east and drive 35 miles to the town of Oakridge. From Oakridge, continue east on Highway 58 about two miles to Kitson Springs

Road. Turn right and drive 0.5 mile to Forest Road 21. Turn right and drive 27 miles to the campground on the left.

Contact: Willamette National Forest, Middle Fork Ranger District, 541/782-2283, fax 541/782-5306, www.fs.fed.us.

90 ROCK CREEK

Scenic rating: 8

on Rock Creek

Since I started roaming around the state 20 years ago, this campground on the banks of Rock Creek in a relatively obscure spot has been considerably improved by the BLM. It's not well known, either, so you're likely to have privacy as a bonus. No fishing is allowed in Rock Creek.

Campsites, facilities: There are 17 sites for tents or RVs up to 40 feet long. Picnic tables and fire grills are provided. A camp host is on-site, and vault toilets, drinking water, a pavilion, and firewood are available. Some facilities are wheelchair accessible. Leashed pets are permitted.

Reservations, fees: Reservations are not accepted. Sites are $10 per night, with a 14-day stay limit, and $4 per night per additional vehicle. Open mid-May–mid-September.

Directions: From Roseburg, drive east on Highway 138 for 22 miles to Rock Creek Road. Turn right (north) and drive seven miles to the campground on the right.

Contact: Bureau of Land Management, Roseburg District, 541/440-4930, fax 541/440-4948, www.blm.gov.

91 MILLPOND

Scenic rating: 8

on Rock Creek

Rock Creek flows past Millpond and empties into the North Umpqua River five miles downstream. Just above this confluence is the Rock Creek Fish Hatchery, which is open year-round to visitors, with free access. This campground along the banks of Rock Creek is the first camp you'll see along Rock Creek Road, which accounts for its relative popularity in the area. Like Rock Creek Campground, it's primitive and remote. No fishing is allowed in Rock Creek.

Campsites, facilities: There are 12 sites for tents or RVs up to 45 feet long. Picnic tables, garbage service, and fire grills are provided. A camp host is on-site, and flush and vault toilets, drinking water, firewood, a ball field, playground, and pavilion are available. Some facilities are wheelchair accessible. Leashed pets are permitted.

Reservations, fees: Reservations are not accepted. Sites are $10 per night, with a 14-day stay limit, and $4 per night per additional vehicle. Open early May–early November.

Directions: From Roseburg, drive east on Highway 138 for 22 miles to Rock Creek Road. Turn right (north) and drive five miles to the campground on the right.

Contact: Bureau of Land Management, Roseburg District, 541/440-4930, fax 541/440-4948, www.blm.gov.

92 SUSAN CREEK

Scenic rating: 9

on the North Umpqua River

BEST

This popular and pretty campground borders the North Umpqua Wild and Scenic River. This lush setting features plenty of trees and river access. Highlights include two barrier-free trails, one traveling 0.5 mile to the day-use area. From there, a hike of about 0.75 mile leads to the 50-foot Susan Creek Falls. Another 0.4 mile up the trail are the Susan Creek Indian Mounds. These moss-covered rocks are believed to be a spiritual site and are visited by Native Americans in search of guardian spirit visions. This area also boasts an excellent osprey interpretive site with a viewing platform along the river.

Campsites, facilities: There are 29 sites for RVs up to 65 feet long. Picnic tables, garbage service, and fire grills are provided. Restrooms with flush toilets and showers, drinking water, and firewood are available, and there is a camp host. Some facilities and trails are wheelchair accessible. Leashed pets are permitted.

Reservations, fees: Reservations are not accepted. Sites are $14 per night, with a 14-day stay limit, and $4 per night per additional vehicle. Open late April–mid-November.

Directions: From Roseburg, drive east on Highway 138 for 29.5 miles to the campground (turnoff well signed).

Contact: Bureau of Land Management, Roseburg District, 541/440-4930, fax 541/440-4948, www.blm.gov.

93 STEAMBOAT FALLS

Scenic rating: 8

on Steamboat Creek in Umpqua National Forest

BEST

This Steamboat Creek campground boasts some excellent scenery. Beautiful Steamboat Falls features a fish ladder that provides passage for steelhead and salmon on their upstream migration. No fishing is permitted in Steamboat Creek. Other nearby camping options are Island and Canton Creek.

Campsites, facilities: There are 10 sites for tents or RVs up to 24 feet long. Picnic tables, garbage bins, vault toilets, and fire grills are provided. There is no drinking water. Leashed pets are permitted.

Reservations, fees: Reservations are not accepted. Sites are $7 per night, $4 per night per additional vehicle. Open year-round, weather permitting.

Directions: From Roseburg on I-5, take Exit 120 to Highway 138. Drive east on Highway 138 to Steamboat and Forest Road 38. Turn left on Forest Road 38 (Steamboat Creek Road) and drive six miles to a fork with Forest Road 3810. Turn right and drive one mile on a paved road to the campground.

Contact: Umpqua National Forest, North Umpqua Ranger District, 541/496-3532, fax 541/496-3534, www.fs.fed.us.

94 SCAREDMAN

Scenic rating: 6

on Canton Creek

Scaredman is a small campground along the banks of Canton Creek, virtually unknown to out-of-towners. Set in an old-growth forest, this private and secluded camp offers a chance to swim in the creek. Scaredman gets its name from an old legend that says some early settlers camped here, heard a pack of hungry wolves, and then ran off, scared to death. This is one of the few free camps left in the region. Although fishing is closed on Canton Creek and all Steamboat drainages, the North Umpqua River 3.5 miles downstream offers fly-fishing for steelhead or salmon.

Campsites, facilities: There are nine sites for tents or RVs up to 25 feet long. Picnic tables, garbage service, and fire grills are provided. Vault toilets and drinking water are available. A camp host is on-site in season. Leashed pets are permitted.

Reservations, fees: Reservations are not accepted. There is no fee for camping. The stay limit is 14 days. Open year-round.

Directions: From Roseburg, drive east on Highway 138 for 40 miles to Steamboat Creek Road. Turn left (north) and drive 0.5 mile to Canton Creek Road. Turn left (north) and drive three miles to the campground.

Contact: Bureau of Land Management, Roseburg District, 541/440-4930, fax 541/440-4948, www.blm.gov.

95 ISLAND

ATLAS 36 B3

Scenic rating: 8

on the Umpqua River in Umpqua National Forest

The North Umpqua is one of Oregon's most beautiful rivers, and this scenic campground borders its banks at a spot popular for both rafting and steelhead fishing. Note: Only fly-fishing is allowed here. A hiking trail that leads east and west along the river is accessible a short drive to the west.

Campsites, facilities: There are seven sites for tents or RVs up to 24 feet long. Picnic tables, garbage bins, and fire grills are provided. There is no drinking water. Some facilities are wheelchair accessible. Leashed pets are permitted.

Reservations, fees: Reservations are not accepted. Sites are $8 per night, $4 per night per additional vehicle. Open year-round, weather permitting.

Directions: From Roseburg, drive east on Highway 138 for 40 miles (just past Steamboat) to the camp on the right. The campground is along the highway.

Contact: Umpqua National Forest, North Umpqua Ranger District, 541/496-3532, fax 541/496-3534, www.fs.fed.us.

96 CANTON CREEK

ATLAS 36B3

Scenic rating: 8

near the North Umpqua River in Umpqua National Forest

Set at an elevation of 1,195 feet at the confluence of Canton and Steamboat Creeks, this camp is less than a mile from the North Umpqua River and gets little overnight use—but lots of day swimmers come here in July and August. No fishing is permitted on Steamboat or Canton Creeks because they are spawning areas for steelhead and salmon. Steamboat Falls is six miles north on Forest Road 38.

Campsites, facilities: There are five sites for tents or RVs up to 22 feet long. Picnic tables, garbage bins, and fire grills are provided. Drinking water, a covered picnic gazebo, and flush toilets are available. Leashed pets are permitted.

Reservations, fees: Reservations are not accepted. Sites are $8 per night, $4 per night per additional vehicle. Open mid-May–mid-October, weather permitting.

Directions: From Roseburg, drive east on Highway 138 for 39 miles to Steamboat and Forest Road 38 (Steamboat Creek Road). Turn left and drive 0.25 mile to the campground on the right.

Contact: Umpqua National Forest, North Umpqua Ranger District, 541/496-3532, fax 541/496-3534, www.fs.fed.us.

97 HORSESHOE BEND/ DEER FLAT GROUP

ATLAS 36 B4

Scenic rating: 8

on the Umpqua River in Umpqua National Forest

This campground, set at an elevation of 1,300 feet, is in the middle of a big bend in the North Umpqua River. This spot is a major launching point for white-water rafting. Fly-fishing is popular here.

Campsites, facilities: There are 24 sites for tents or RVs up to 35 feet long and one group site, Deer Flat, for up to 70 people. Picnic tables, fire grills, garbage bins, drinking water, and flush toilets are provided. A store, gas, and propane are available one mile east. Raft-launching facilities are nearby. Some facilities are wheelchair accessible. Leashed pets are permitted.

Reservations, fees: Reservations are accepted for the group site (Deer Flat, not Horseshoe Bend) at 877/444-6777 or www.recreation.

gov ($10 reservation fee) but are not accepted for family sites. Sites are $12 per night, $4 per night per additional vehicle, and $85 per night for group sites. Open mid-May–late September, weather permitting.

Directions: From Roseburg on I-5, take Exit 120. Drive east on Highway 138 for 47 miles to Forest Road 4750. Turn right and drive south a short distance to the campground entrance road on the right.

Contact: Umpqua National Forest, North Umpqua Ranger District, 541/496-3532, fax 541/496-3534, www.fs.fed.us.

98 EAGLE ROCK

Scenic rating: 9

on the North Umpqua River in Umpqua National Forest

Eagle Rock camp sits next to the North Umpqua River and adjacent to the Boulder Creek Wilderness. It is named after Eagle Rock, which, along with Rattlesnake Rock, towers above the campground. The camp offers outstanding views of these unusual rock formations. It gets moderate use, heavy on weekends. The camp sits at 1,676 feet elevation near Boulder Flat, a major launch point for rafting. Fishing here is restricted to the use of artificial lures with a single barbless hook.

Campsites, facilities: There are 25 sites for tents or RVs up to 30 feet long. Picnic tables and fire grills are provided. Vault toilets and garbage bins are available. There is no drinking water. A store, propane, and ice are within five miles. Some facilities are wheelchair accessible. Leashed pets are permitted.

Reservations, fees: Reservations are not accepted. Sites are $10 per night, $4 per night per additional vehicle. Open mid-May–October, weather permitting.

Directions: From Roseburg, drive east on Highway 138 for 53 miles to the campground on the left.

Contact: Umpqua National Forest, North Umpqua Ranger District, 541/496-3532, fax 541/496-3534, www.fs.fed.us.

99 BOULDER FLAT

Scenic rating: 8

on the North Umpqua River in Umpqua National Forest

BEST

Boulder Flat campground is nestled along the banks of the North Umpqua River at the confluence with Boulder Creek. There's good trout fishing here (fly-fishing only) and outstanding scenery. The camp sits at a major launching point for white-water rafting. Across the river from the campground, a trail follows Boulder Creek north for 10.5 miles through the Boulder Creek Wilderness, a climb in elevation from 2,000 to 5,400 feet. It's a good thumper for backpackers. Access to the trail is at Soda Springs Dam, two miles east of the camp. A little over a mile to the east you can see some huge, dramatic pillars of volcanic rock, colored with lichen.

Campsites, facilities: There are nine sites for tents or RVs up to 24 feet long. Picnic tables, garbage bins, and fire grills are provided. Vault toilets are available. There is no drinking water. A store, propane, and ice are within five miles. A raft launch is on-site. Leashed pets are permitted.

Reservations, fees: Reservations are not accepted. Sites are $8 per night, $4 per night per additional vehicle. Open year-round.

Directions: From Roseburg, drive east on Highway 138 for 54 miles to the campground on the left.

Contact: Umpqua National Forest, North Umpqua Ranger District, 541/496-3532, fax 541/496-3534, www.fs.fed.us.

100 TOKETEE LAKE

Scenic rating: 7

on Toketee Lake in Umpqua National Forest

Located just north of Toketee Lake, this campground sits at an elevation of 2,200 feet. The North Umpqua River Trail passes near camp and continues east along the river for many miles. Die-hard hikers can also take the trail west toward the Boulder Creek Wilderness. Toketee Lake, a 97-acre reservoir, offers a good population of brown and rainbow trout and many recreation options. A worthwhile point of interest is Toketee Falls, just west of the lake turnoff. Another is Umpqua Hot Springs, a few miles northeast of the camp. The area sustains a wide variety of wildlife; you might see bald eagles, beavers, a variety of ducks and geese, great blue herons, kingfishers, and otters in fall and winter.

Campsites, facilities: There are 33 sites for tents or RVs up to 22 feet long and one group site for up to 30 people. Picnic tables, garbage bins, and fire grills are provided. Vault toilets are available, but there is no drinking water. Boat docks and launching facilities are nearby. Leashed pets are permitted.

Reservations, fees: Reservations are accepted only for the group site at 541/498-2531. Sites are $7 per night, $3 per night per additional vehicle, and $25 per night for the group site. Open year-round.

Directions: From Roseburg, drive east on Highway 138 for 59 miles to Forest Road 34. Turn left (north) and drive 1.5 miles to the campground on the right.

Contact: Umpqua National Forest, Diamond Lake Ranger District, 541/498-2531, fax 541/498-2515, www.fs.fed.us.

101 EAST LEMOLO

Scenic rating: 8

on Lemolo Lake in Umpqua National Forest

This campground is on the southeastern shore of Lemolo Lake, where boating and fishing are some of the recreation possibilities. Boats with motors and personal watercraft are allowed. The North Umpqua River and its adjacent trail lie just beyond the north shore of the lake. If you hike for two miles northwest of the lake, you can reach spectacular Lemolo Falls. Large German brown trout, a wild, native fish, can be taken on troll and fly. Lemolo Lake also provides fishing for brook trout, kokanee, and a sprinkling of rainbow trout.

Campsites, facilities: There are 14 sites for tents or small RVs up to 22 feet long. No drinking water is available. Picnic tables, garbage bins, and fire rings are provided. Vault toilets are available. Boat docks, launching facilities, boat rentals, dump station, restaurants, a store, coin laundry, and showers are nearby. Leashed pets are permitted.

Reservations, fees: Reservations are not accepted. Sites are $7 per night, $3 per night per additional vehicle. Open mid-May–late October, weather permitting.

Directions: From Roseburg, drive east on Highway 138 for 73 miles to Forest Road 2610 (three miles east of Clearwater Falls). Turn left (north) and drive three miles to Forest Road 2614. Turn right and drive two miles to Forest Road 2614-430. Turn left and drive a short distance to the campground at the end of the road.

Contact: Umpqua National Forest, Diamond Lake Ranger District, 541/498-2531, fax 541/498-2515, www.fs.fed.us.

102 POOLE CREEK

Scenic rating: 8

on Lemolo Lake in Umpqua National Forest

Poole Creek campground on the western shore of Lemolo Lake isn't far from Lemolo Lake Resort, which is open for recreation year-round. The camp is just south of the mouth of Poole Creek in a lodgepole pine, mountain hemlock, and Shasta red fir forest. This is by far the most popular U.S. Forest Service camp at the lake, especially with water-skiers, who are allowed to ski in designated areas of the lake.

Campsites, facilities: There are 60 sites for tents or RVs up to 35 feet long and a group site for up to 60 people. Picnic tables and fire grills are provided. Drinking water and vault toilets are available. A grocery store, a restaurant, boat docks, launching facilities, and rentals are nearby. Leashed pets are permitted.

Reservations, fees: Reservations are not accepted for single sites but are required for the group camp at 877/444-6777 or www.recreation.gov ($10 reservation fee). Single sites are $11–14 per night, $4 per night per additional vehicle, and $72 per night for the group camp. Open late April–late October, weather permitting.

Directions: From Roseburg, drive east on Highway 138 for 73 miles to Forest Road 2610 (Bird's Point Road). Turn left (north) and drive four miles to the signed turnoff for the campground entrance on the right.

Contact: Umpqua National Forest, Diamond Lake Ranger District, 541/498-2531, fax 541/498-2515, www.fs.fed.us.

103 INLET

Scenic rating: 5

on Lemolo Lake in Umpqua National Forest

Inlet campground sits on the eastern inlet of Lemolo Lake, hidden in the deep, green, and quiet forest where the North Umpqua River rushes into Lemolo Reservoir. The camp is just across the road from the North Umpqua River Trail, which is routed east into the Oregon Cascades Recreation Area and the Mount Thielsen Wilderness. Lemolo Lake exceeds 100 feet in depth in some spots; boating and fishing for brook trout, kokanee, and rainbow trout are some recreation possibilities. (Boats with motors and personal watercraft are allowed.) Two miles northwest of the lake lies spectacular Lemolo Falls, a good hike.

Campsites, facilities: There are 14 sites for tents or RVs up to 22 feet long. Vault toilets are available, but there is no drinking water. Picnic tables, garbage bins, and fire grills are provided. Boat docks, launching facilities, rentals, a restaurant, groceries, and a gas station are available nearby. Leashed pets are permitted.

Reservations, fees: Reservations are not accepted. Sites are $7 per night, $3 per night per additional vehicle. Open mid-May–late October, weather permitting.

Directions: From Roseburg, drive east on Highway 138 for 73 miles to Forest Road 2610. Turn left (north) and drive three miles to Forest Road 2614. Turn right (east) and drive three miles to the campground.

Contact: Umpqua National Forest, Diamond Lake Ranger District, 541/498-2531, fax 541/498-2515, www.fs.fed.us.

104 BUNKER HILL

Scenic rating: 7

on Crescent Lake in Umpaqua National Forest

Bunker Hill campground, on the northwest shore of Lemolo Reservoir, is in a heavily wooded area of lodgepole pine. Fishing is excellent for kokanee as well as brook, rainbow, and large native brown trout. Nearby hiking trails lead to Lemolo Falls, the North Umpqua River, and the Pacific Crest Trail.

Campsites, facilities: There are five sites for

tents or RVs up to 22 feet long. Picnic tables and fire rings are provided. Vault toilets and garbage bins are available. There is no drinking water. A boat ramp, boat rentals, a dump station, a restaurant, coin laundry, and coin showers are available 1.5 miles away at Lemolo Lake Resort (541/643-0750). Leashed pets are permitted.

Reservations, fees: Reservations are not accepted. Sites are $7 per night, $3 per night per additional vehicle. Open May–October, weather permitting.

Directions: From Roseburg, drive east on Highway 138 for 73 miles to Bird's Point Road/Forest Road 2610. Turn left and drive 5.5 miles (crossing the dam) to Forest Road 2612. Turn right and drive to the camp at the north end of the lake.

Contact: Umpqua National Forest, Diamond Lake Ranger District, 541/498-2531, fax 541/498-2515, www.fs.fed.us.

105 LEMOLO LAKE RV PARK

Scenic rating: 7

in Umpqua National Forest

Lemolo Lake is situated high in the Cascade Mountains at just over 4,000 feet elevation. This RV park is set up for folks to bring their own boats and enjoy the lake. Boating, waterskiing, wakeboarding, and Jet Skis are all popular, along, of course, with fishing and swimming, on the lake (40-mph speed limit). Each campground reservation includes free boat launch. There are also miles of hiking trails in the vicinity, plus Crater Lake National Park and Diamond Lake are a quick drive away. In winter, cross-country skiing is popular, and an extensive snowmobile loop runs through the property.

Campsites, facilities: There are 26 sites for tents or RVs; full hookups are available. Picnic tables and fire rings are provided. Drinking water, flush toilets, coin showers, and coin laundry are available. A restaurant and store are on the premises. Boat and ATV rentals are available.

Reservations, fees: Reservations are accepted at 541/643-0750. RV sites with full hookups are $25, tent sites are $12–16. Open year-round.

Directions: From Roseburg, drive east on Highway 138 (Diamond Lake Highway) for about 73 miles to Birds Point Road. Turn left on Birds Point Road and drive five miles to the resort.

Contact: Lemolo Lake RV Park, 541/643-0750, www.lemololakeresort.com.

106 TIMPANOGAS

Scenic rating: 8

on Timpanogas Lake in Willamette National Forest

Timpanogas Lake is the headwaters of the Middle Fork Willamette River. This campground, at 5,200 feet elevation, is situated in a stand of grand, noble, and silver fir. Fishing for brook trout and cutthroat is good; only non-motorized boating is permitted. Nearby activities include 23 miles of hiking trails in the Timpanogas Basin trails, with views of the Cowhorn Mountains, Diamond Peak, and Sawtooth. Warning: Time it wrong (July–Aug.) and the mosquitoes will eat you alive if you forget insect repellent.

Campsites, facilities: There are 10 sites for tents or RVs up to 24 feet long. Picnic tables, garbage bins, and fire rings are provided. Drinking water, vault toilets, and firewood are available. A primitive boat ramp is nearby, but no boats with motors are allowed. Some facilities are wheelchair accessible. Leashed pets are permitted.

Reservations, fees: Reservations are not accepted. Sites are $8 per night, $4 per night per additional vehicle. Open June–October, weather permitting.

Directions: From Eugene, drive south on I-5 for five miles to Exit 188 and Highway 58. Turn east and drive 35 miles to the town of Oakridge. Continue east on Highway 58 for two miles to Kitson Springs Road. Turn right and drive 0.5 mile to Forest Road 21. Turn right and drive 32 miles to Forest Road 2154. Turn left and drive about 10 miles to the campground on the left.
Contact: Willamette National Forest, Middle Fork Ranger District, 541/782-2283, fax 541/782-5306, www.fs.fed.us.

107 WOLF CREEK

Scenic rating: 6

on the Little River in Umpqua National Forest

This pretty Little River camp is located at the entrance to the national forest, near the Wolf Creek Civilian Conservation Center. It is set at an elevation of 1,100 feet, with easy access to civilization. The campground has abundant wildflowers in the spring. If you want to get deeper into the Cascades, Hemlock Lake and Lake of the Woods are about 21 and 15 miles east, respectively.
Campsites, facilities: There are eight sites for tents or RVs up to 30 feet long and one group site for up to 130 people. Picnic tables and fire grills are provided. Flush toilets, drinking water, a covered pavilion for groups, garbage bins, horseshoe pits, a softball field, and a volleyball court are available. Note that if the group site is taken, some recreation facilities may not be available to single-site campers. Some facilities are wheelchair accessible. Leashed pets are permitted.
Reservations, fees: Reservations are accepted only for the group site at 877/444-6777 or www.recreation.gov ($10 reservation fee). Sites are $10 per night, $4 per night per additional vehicle, and $95 per night for the group site. Open mid-May–September, weather permitting.
Directions: From Roseburg on I-5, take Exit 120. Drive east on Highway 138 for 18 miles to Glide and County Road 17. Turn right (southeast) and drive 12 miles (the road becomes Little River Road) to the campground on the right.
Contact: Umpqua National Forest, North Umpqua Ranger District, 541/496-3532, fax 541/496-3534, www.fs.fed.us.

108 COOLWATER

Scenic rating: 6

on the Little River in Umpqua National Forest

Coolwater campground (1,300 feet elevation) along the banks of the Little River gets moderate use. It features a pretty forest setting with some scenic hiking trails nearby. Overhang Trail is within 0.5 mile of the campground. Fishing and swimming are also options here. Scenic Grotto Falls can be reached by traveling north on Forest Road 2703 (across the road from the camp). Near the falls, you'll find Emile Grove, home of a thicket of old-growth Douglas firs and the huge "Bill Taft Tree," named after the former president.
Campsites, facilities: There are seven sites for tents or RVs up to 24 feet long. Picnic tables and fire grills are provided. Vault toilets are available. There is no drinking water. Leashed pets are permitted.
Reservations, fees: Reservations are not accepted. Sites are $6 per night, $4 per night per additional vehicle. Open year-round, weather permitting.
Directions: From Roseburg on I-5, take Exit 120. Drive east on Highway 138 for 18 miles to Glide and County Road 17. Turn right (southeast) and drive 17 miles (the road becomes Little River Road) to the campground on the right.
Contact: Umpqua National Forest, North Umpqua Ranger District, 541/496-3532, fax 541/496-3534, www.fs.fed.us.

109 WHITE CREEK

Scenic rating: 6

on the Little River in Umpqua National Forest

Hiking and fishing are two of the recreation options at this campground set at the confluence of White Creek and the Little River. There is a sandy beach on shallow Little River, and waterfalls are in the area.

Campsites, facilities: There is an open parking area for tents or RVs up to 16 feet long. Picnic tables, fire grills, and garbage bins are provided. Vault toilets are available. There is no drinking water. Leashed pets are permitted.

Reservations, fees: Reservations are not accepted. Sites are $6 per night, $4 per night per additional vehicle. Open year-round, weather permitting.

Directions: From Roseburg on I-5, take Exit 120. Drive east on Highway 138 for 18 miles to Glide and County Road 17. Turn right (southeast) and drive 18 miles (the road becomes Little River Road) to Forest Road 2792 (Red Butte Road). Bear right and drive 0.25 mile to the campground on the left.

Contact: Umpqua National Forest, North Umpqua Ranger District, 541/496-3532, fax 541/496-3534, www.fs.fed.us.

110 LAKE IN THE WOODS

Scenic rating: 7

on Lake in the Woods in Umpqua National Forest

The shore of little Lake in the Woods is the setting of this camp, which makes a nice home base for several good hikes. One of them leaves the camp and heads south for about three miles to the Hemlock Lake Campground. Two other nearby trails provide short, scenic hikes to either Hemlock Falls or Yakso Falls. The campground sits at 3,200 feet elevation. This is a man-made, four-acre lake, eight feet at its deepest point. Boats without motors are allowed.

Campsites, facilities: There are 11 sites for tents or RVs up to 35 feet long. Picnic tables, fire grills, and garbage bins are provided. Vault toilets are available. There is no drinking water. Leashed pets are permitted.

Reservations, fees: Reservations are not accepted. Sites are $10 per night, $4 per night per additional vehicle. Open late May–late October, weather permitting.

Directions: From Roseburg on I-5, take Exit 120. Drive east on Highway 138 for 18 miles to Glide and County Road 17. Turn right (southeast) and drive 18 miles (the road becomes Little River Road) to Forest Road 27. Continue 11 miles to the campground. The last seven miles are gravel.

Contact: Umpqua National Forest, North Umpqua Ranger District, 541/496-3532, fax 541/496-3534, www.fs.fed.us.

111 HEMLOCK LAKE

ATLAS 36 C3 **Scenic rating: 8**

on Hemlock Lake in Umpqua National Forest

BEST

This is a little-known jewel of a spot. For starters, it's set along the shore of Hemlock Lake at 4,400 feet elevation. This is a 28-acre, manufactured reservoir that is 33 feet at its deepest point. An eight-mile loop trail called the Yellow Jacket Loop is just south of the campground. Another trail leaves camp and heads north for about three miles to the Lake in the Woods campground. From there, it's just a short hike to either Hemlock Falls or Yakso Falls, both spectacularly scenic.

Campsites, facilities: There are 13 sites for tents or RVs up to 35 feet long. Picnic tables, fire grills, and garbage bins are provided. Vault toilets are available, but there is no drinking water. Boat docks and launching facilities are nearby. No motors are allowed on the lake. Leashed pets are permitted.

Reservations, fees: Reservations are not accepted. Sites are $8 per night, $4 per night per additional vehicle. Open year-round, weather permitting.
Directions: From Roseburg on I-5, take Exit 120. Drive east on Highway 138 for 18 miles to Glide and County Road 17. Turn right (southeast) and drive 32 miles to the campground on the right.
Contact: Umpqua National Forest, North Umpqua Ranger District, 541/496-3532, fax 541/496-3534, www.fs.fed.us.

112 WHITEHORSE FALLS

Scenic rating: 8

on the Clearwater River in Umpqua National Forest

Whitehorse Falls campground sits along the Clearwater River, one of the coldest streams in Umpqua National Forest. Even though the camp is adjacent to the highway, the setting is primitive. It is shaded by old-growth Douglas fir and is located at an elevation of 3,790 feet. Pretty Clearwater Falls, a few miles east, makes for a good side trip. Other recreation options include fishing and hiking.
Campsites, facilities: There are five sites for tents or RVs up to 22 feet long. Picnic tables, fire grills, and garbage bins are provided. Vault toilets are available, but there is no drinking water. Leashed pets are permitted.
Reservations, fees: Reservations are not accepted. Sites are $7 per night, $3 per night per additional vehicle. Open June–late October, weather permitting.
Directions: From Roseburg, drive east on Highway 138 for 66 miles to the campground on the left.
Contact: Umpqua National Forest, Diamond Lake Ranger District, 541/498-2531, fax 541/498-2515, www.fs.fed.us.

113 CLEARWATER FALLS

Scenic rating: 8

on the Clearwater River in Umpqua National Forest

The main attraction at this campground along the banks of the Clearwater River is the nearby cascading section of stream called Clearwater Falls. Hiking and fishing opportunities abound. The camp sits at an elevation of 4,100 feet.
Campsites, facilities: There are nine sites for tents or RVs up to 30 feet long. Picnic tables, fire grills, and garbage bins are provided. Vault toilets are available. There is no drinking water. Leashed pets are permitted.
Reservations, fees: Reservations are not accepted. Sites are $7 per night, $3 per night per additional vehicle. Open mid-May–October, weather permitting.
Directions: From Roseburg, drive east on Highway 138 for 70 miles to a signed turn for Clearwater Falls. Turn right and drive to the campground.
Contact: Umpqua National Forest, Diamond Lake Ranger District, 541/498-2531, fax 541/498-2515, www.fs.fed.us.

114 BROKEN ARROW

Scenic rating: 6

on Diamond Lake in Umpqua National Forest

Broken Arrow campground sits at 5,190 feet elevation near the south shore of Diamond Lake, the largest natural lake in Umpqua National Forest. Set back from the lake, it is surrounded by lodgepole pine and features views of Mount Bailey and Mount Thielsen. Bicycling, boating, fishing, hiking, and swimming keep visitors busy here. Diamond Lake is adjacent to Crater Lake National Park, Mount Bailey, and the Mount Thielsen Wilderness, all of which offer a variety of recreation opportunities year-round. Diamond Lake is quite popular with anglers because of its good trout trolling, particularly in early summer.

Campsites, facilities: There are 117 sites for tents or RVs up to 40 feet long and group sites for 40–104 people. Picnic tables, fire grills, and garbage bins are provided. Restrooms with flush toilets and showers, a dump station, and drinking water are available. Boat docks, launching facilities, and rentals are nearby. Some facilities are wheelchair accessible. Leashed pets are permitted.

Reservations, fees: Reservations are accepted only for group sites at 877/444-6777 or www.recreation.gov ($10 reservation fee). Sites are $11–14 per night, $4 per night per additional vehicle, and $54–132 per night for group sites. Open June–mid-September.

Directions: From Roseburg, drive east on Highway 138 for 78.5 miles to Diamond Lake Loop (Forest Road 4795). Turn right (south) and drive four miles (along the east shore) to the campground turnoff road. Turn right and continue one mile to the camp on the left at the southern end of the lake.

Contact: Umpqua National Forest, Diamond Lake Ranger District, 541/498-2531, fax 541/498-2515, www.fs.fed.us.

115 THIELSEN VIEW

Scenic rating: 7

on Diamond Lake in Umpqua National Forest

This campground sits along the west shore of Diamond Lake in the shadow of majestic Mount Bailey. There is a beautiful view of Mount Thielsen from here.

Diamond Lake is popular with anglers, and bicycling, boating, fishing, hiking, and swimming keep everyone else busy. Nearby Crater Lake National Park, Mount Bailey, and the Mount Thielsen Wilderness offer recreation opportunities year-round.

Campsites, facilities: There are 60 sites for tents or RVs up to 30 feet long. Picnic tables, fire grills, and garbage bins are provided. Drinking water and vault toilets are available. Boat docks and launching facilities are located adjacent to the campground, and boats can be rented at a resort five miles away. Some facilities are wheelchair accessible. Leashed pets are permitted.

Reservations, fees: Reservations are not accepted. Sites are $11–14 per night, $4 per night per additional vehicle. Open mid-May–mid-September, weather permitting.

Directions: From Roseburg, drive east on Highway 138 for 78.5 miles to Diamond Lake Loop (Forest Road 4795). Turn right and drive a short distance to the junction with the loop road. Continue on the loop road and drive four miles to the campground on the left.

Contact: Umpqua National Forest, Diamond Lake Ranger District, 541/498-2531, fax 541/498-2515, www.fs.fed.us.

116 DIAMOND LAKE

Scenic rating: 9

on Diamond Lake in Umpqua National Forest

Diamond Lake is a true gem of the Cascades, and there's finally hope the trout fishing will return to its once famous status. This extremely popular camp along the east shore of Diamond Lake has all the luxuries: flush toilets, showers, and drinking water. There are campfire programs every Friday and Saturday night in the summer. Jet Skis and other motorized watercraft are not allowed.

Campsites, facilities: There are 238 sites for tents or RVs up to 45 feet long. Picnic tables, garbage bins, and fire grills are provided. Restrooms with flush toilets and showers, drinking water, a dump station, and an amphitheater are available. Boat docks, launching facilities, and a fish-cleaning station are available. Boat rentals are nearby. Leashed pets are permitted.

Reservations, fees: Reservations are accepted at 877/444-6777 or www.recreation.gov ($10 reservation fee). Sites are $12–24 per night, $6 per night per additional vehicle. Open late April–late October, weather permitting.
Directions: From Roseburg, drive east on Highway 138 for 78.5 miles to Diamond Lake Loop (Forest Road 4795). Turn right and drive a short distance to the junction with a loop road. Turn right (south) and drive two miles (along the east shore) to the campground on the right.
Contact: Umpqua National Forest, Diamond Lake Ranger District, 541/498-2531, fax 541/498-2515, www.fs.fed.us.

117 CAMP COMFORT

Scenic rating: 6

on the South Umpqua River in Umpqua National Forest

Camp Comfort is located near the upper South Umpqua River, deep in the Umpqua National Forest, at an elevation of 2,000 feet. Large old-growth cedars shade the campsites. No fishing is permitted. South Umpqua Falls (you will pass the access point while driving to this camp) makes a good side trip. Nearby trailheads provide access to Rogue-Umpqua Divide Wilderness (a map of Umpqua National Forest will be helpful in locating them).
Campsites, facilities: There are five sites for tents or RVs up to 22 feet long. Picnic tables and fire grills are provided. A vault toilet and garbage bins are available. There is no drinking water. Some facilities are wheelchair accessible. Leashed pets are permitted.
Reservations, fees: Reservations are not accepted. Sites are $6 per night, $3 per night per additional vehicle. Open May–October.
Directions: At Canyonville on I-5, take Exit 99 to County Road 1. Drive east on County Road 1 for 25 miles to Tiller and County Road 46. Turn left and drive six miles northeast (County Road 46 turns into South Umpqua Road/Forest Road 28). Continue northeast and drive 22 miles to the camp on the right.
Contact: Umpqua National Forest, Tiller Ranger District, 541/825-3100, fax 541/825-3110, www.fs.fed.us.

118 HAMAKER

Scenic rating: 8

near the Upper Rogue River in Rogue River National Forest

Set at 4,000 feet elevation near the Upper Rogue River, Hamaker is a beautiful little spot high in a mountain meadow. Wildflowers and wildlife abound in the spring and early summer. One of the least-used camps in the area, it's a prime camp for Crater Lake visitors.
Campsites, facilities: There are 10 sites for tents or RVs up to 30 feet long. Picnic tables, fire grills, garbage service, and stoves are provided. Drinking water and vault toilets are available. Firewood is available for purchase. Leashed pets are permitted.
Reservations, fees: Reservations are not accepted. Sites are $10 per night, $5 per night per additional vehicle. Open late May–late October, weather permitting.
Directions: From Medford, drive northeast on Highway 62 for 57 miles (just past Union Creek) to Highway 230. Turn left (north) and drive 11 miles to a junction with Forest Road 6530. Continue on Forest Road 6530 for 0.5 mile to Forest Road 6530-900. Turn right and drive 0.5 mile to the campground.
Contact: Rogue River National Forest, Prospect Ranger District, 541/560-3400, fax 541/560-3444; Rogue Recreation, 541/560-3900, www.fs.fed.us.

119 BOULDER CREEK

Scenic rating: 4

on the South Umpqua River in Umpqua National Forest

Set at 1,400 feet elevation, this campground hugs the banks of the South Umpqua River near Boulder Creek. Unfortunately, no fishing is allowed here, but pleasant side trips include the fishing ladder and waterfall at nearby South Umpqua Falls.

Campsites, facilities: There are seven sites for tents or RVs up to 22 feet long. Picnic tables, fire grills, and garbage bins are provided. Vault toilets and drinking water are available. Some facilities are wheelchair accessible. Leashed pets are permitted.

Reservations, fees: Reservations are not accepted. Sites are $6 per night, $3 per night per additional vehicle. Open May–October, weather permitting.

Directions: At Canyonville on I-5, take Exit 99 to County Road 1. Drive east on County Road 1 for 25 miles to Tiller and County Road 46. Turn left, then drive six miles northeast (County Road 46 turns into South Umpqua Road/Forest Road 28). Continue northeast and drive seven miles to the camp.

Contact: Umpqua National Forest, Tiller Ranger District, 541/825-3100, fax 541/825-3110, www.fs.fed.us.

120 DUMONT CREEK

Scenic rating: 4

on the South Umpqua River in Umpqua National Forest

Dumont Creek is set at 1,300 feet elevation along the banks of the South Umpqua River, just above the mouth of Dumont Creek. Quiet, primitive, and remote, it gets moderate to heavy use. A short trail leads to a small beach on the river. No fishing is allowed at this camp, and there is no trailer turnaround here. Boulder Creek, just a few miles east, provides a camping alternative. A good side trip is nearby South Umpqua Falls, a beautiful, wide waterfall featuring a fish ladder and a platform so you can watch the fish struggle upstream.

Campsites, facilities: There are three sites for tents. Picnic tables, fire grills, and garbage bins are provided. Vault toilets are available, but there is no drinking water. Some facilities are wheelchair accessible. Leashed pets are permitted.

Reservations, fees: Reservations are not accepted. Sites are $6 per night, $3 per night per additional vehicle. Open May–October, weather permitting.

Directions: At Canyonville on I-5, take Exit 99 to County Road 1. Drive east on County Road 1 for 25 miles to Tiller and County Road 46. Turn left and drive six miles northeast (County Road 46 turns into South Umpqua Road/Forest Road 28). Continue northeast and drive 5.5 miles to the camp.

Contact: Umpqua National Forest, Tiller Ranger District, 541/825-3100, fax 541/825-3110, www.fs.fed.us.

121 COVER

Scenic rating: 4

on Jackson Creek in Umpqua National Forest

If you want quiet, this camp set at 1,700 feet elevation along the banks of Jackson Creek is the right place, since hardly anyone knows about it. Cover gets light use during the summer. During the fall hunting season, however, it is known to fill. If you head east to Forest Road 68 and follow the road south, you'll have access to a major trail into the Rogue-Umpqua Divide Wilderness. Be sure not to miss the world's largest sugar pine tree, a few miles west of camp. No fishing is allowed here.

Campsites, facilities: There are seven sites for tents or RVs up to 22 feet long. Picnic tables, fire grills, and garbage bins are provided. Drinking water and vault toilets are available. Some facilities are wheelchair accessible. Leashed pets are permitted.
Reservations, fees: Reservations are not accepted. Sites are $6 per night, $2 per night per additional vehicle. Open May–October, weather permitting.
Directions: At Canyonville on I-5, take Exit 99 to County Road 1. Drive east on County Road 1 for 25 miles to Tiller and County Road 46. Turn left and drive five miles to Forest Road 29 (Jackson Creek Road). Turn right and drive east for 12 miles to the campground on the right.
Contact: Umpqua National Forest, Tiller Ranger District, 541/825-3100, fax 541/825-3110, www.fs.fed.us.

122 QUINN MEADOW HORSE CAMP

Scenic rating: 8

near Quinn Creek in Deschutes National Forest

This scenic campground (elevation 5,100 feet) is open only to horse camping and gets high use. The Elk-Devil's Trail and Wickiup Plains Trail offer access to the Three Sisters Wilderness. There's also a horse route to Devil's Lake via Katsuk Trail.
Campsites, facilities: There are 26 sites for tents or RVs up to 40 feet long. Picnic tables and fire rings are provided. Horse corrals, stalls, and a manure disposal site are available. Drinking water, vault toilets, and garbage bins are also available. Some facilities are wheelchair accessible. Leashed pets are permitted.
Reservations, fees: Reservations are accepted at 877/444-6777 or www.recreation.gov ($10 reservation fee). Two-horse corral sites are $14 and four-horse sites are $18; it's $7 per night per additional vehicle. Open late June–September, weather permitting.
Directions: From Bend, drive southwest on Cascades Lakes Highway (also called Century Drive Highway and County Road 46) for 31.2 miles to the campground entrance on the left.
Contact: Deschutes National Forest, Bend-Fort Rock Ranger District, 541/383-4000, fax 541/383-4700, www.fs.fed.us.

123 DEVIL'S LAKE WALK-IN

Scenic rating: 8

on Devil's Lake in Deschutes National Forest

This walk-in campground borders the shore of a scenic alpine lake with aqua-jade water and fishing access. Devil's Lake, set at 5,500 feet, is a popular rafting and canoeing spot, and several trailheads lead from the lake into the wilderness. The Elk-Devil's Trail and Wickiup Plains Trail offer access to the Three Sisters Wilderness. There's also a horse route to Quinn Meadow Horse Camp via Katsuk Trail.
Campsites, facilities: There are nine walk-in tent sites. Picnic tables and fire grills are provided. Vault toilets are available. There is no drinking water, and garbage must be packed out. Leashed pets are permitted.
Reservations, fees: Reservations are not accepted. There is no fee, but a Northwest Forest Pass ($5 daily fee or $30 annual fee per parked vehicle) is required. Open June–October, weather permitting.
Directions: From Bend, drive southwest on Cascades Lakes Highway (Century Drive Highway, which becomes County Road 46) for 28.7 miles to the parking area. Walk 200 yards to the campground.
Contact: Deschutes National Forest, Bend-Fort Rock Ranger District, 541/383-4000, fax 541/383-4700, www.fs.fed.us.

124 SODA CREEK

Scenic rating: 5

near Sparks Lake in Deschutes National Forest

This campground, nestled between two meadows in a pastoral setting, is on the road to Sparks Lake. Boating—particularly canoeing—is ideal at Sparks Lake, about a two-mile drive away. Also at the lake, a loop trail hugs the shore; about 0.5 mile of it is paved and barrier-free. Only fly-fishing is permitted. The camp sits at 5,450 feet elevation.

Campsites, facilities: There are six sites for tents or RVs up to 30 feet long and one multiple site. Picnic tables and fire grills are provided. Vault toilets are available. There is no drinking water, and garbage must be packed out. Leashed pets are permitted.

Reservations, fees: Reservations are not accepted. Single sites are $10 per night, multiple sites are $20 per night, $5 per night per extra vehicle. Open June–October, weather permitting.

Directions: From Bend, drive southwest on Cascades Lakes Highway (also called Century Drive Highway and County Road 46) for 26.2 miles to Forest Road 400 (at sign for Sparks Lake). Turn left (east) and drive 25 yards to the campground.

Contact: Deschutes National Forest, Bend-Fort Rock Ranger District, 541/383-4000, fax 541/383-4700, www.fs.fed.us.

125 TODD LAKE HIKE-IN

Scenic rating: 8

near Todd Lake in Deschutes National Forest

Todd Lake is a trailhead camp, with a trail access point here for hikers and horses to the Three Sisters Wilderness. One of numerous camps in the area that offer a pristine mountain experience yet can be reached by car, small Todd Lake campground sits 0.5 mile from the shore of an alpine lake at 6,200 feet elevation. It's popular for canoeing and offers great views. No bikes or horses are allowed on the trail around the lake.

Campsites, facilities: There are 11 hike-in tent sites. Picnic tables and fire grills are provided. Vault toilets are available. There is no drinking water, and garbage must be packed out. Leashed pets are permitted.

Reservations, fees: Reservations are not accepted. There no fee, but a Northwest Forest Pass ($5 daily fee or $30 annual fee per parked vehicle) is required. Open July–October, weather permitting.

Directions: From Bend, drive southwest on Cascades Lakes Highway (also called Century Drive Highway and County Road 46) for 24 miles to Forest Road 370. Turn right (north) and drive 0.5 mile to the parking area. Hike 0.5 mile to the campground.

Contact: Deschutes National Forest, Bend-Fort Rock Ranger District, 541/383-4000, fax 541/383-4700, www.fs.fed.us.

126 POINT

Scenic rating: 8

on Elk Lake in Deschutes National Forest

Point campground is situated along the shore of Elk Lake at an elevation of 4,900 feet. Fishing for kokanee salmon and brook trout can be good; hiking is another option. Swimming and water sports are popular during warm weather.

Campsites, facilities: There are eight sites for tents or RVs up to 26 feet long, and one group site. Picnic tables and fire grills are provided. Vault toilets, drinking water, and garbage service are available. Boat docks and launching facilities are on-site. A store, restaurant, and propane are at Elk Lake Resort, one mile away. Leashed pets are permitted.

Reservations, fees: Reservations are not

accepted. Sites are $12 per night, $6 per night per additional vehicle; the group site is $22 for up to 15 people and four vehicles. Open late May–late September, weather permitting.

Directions: From Bend, drive southwest on Cascades Lakes Highway (Century Drive Highway, which becomes County Road 46) for 34 miles to the campground on the left.

Contact: Deschutes National Forest, Bend-Fort Rock Ranger District, 541/383-4000, fax 541/383-4700, www.fs.fed.us.

127 ELK LAKE

Scenic rating: 8

on Elk Lake in Deschutes National Forest

This campground hugs the shore of Elk Lake at 4,900 feet elevation. It is adjacent to Elk Lake Resort, which has a store, a restaurant, and propane. Elk Lake is popular for windsurfing and sailing.

Campsites, facilities: There are 22 sites for tents or RVs up to 30 feet long. Picnic tables and fire grills are provided. Vault toilets, drinking water, and garbage service are available. Boat-launching facilities are on-site. Boat rentals can be obtained nearby. Leashed pets are permitted.

Reservations, fees: Reservations are not accepted. Sites are $14 per night, $7 per night per additional vehicle. Open mid-May–mid-September, weather permitting.

Directions: From Bend, drive southwest on Cascades Lakes Highway (Century Drive Highway, which becomes County Road 46) and drive 33.1 miles to the campground at the north end of Elk Lake.

Contact: Deschutes National Forest, Bend-Fort Rock Ranger District, 541/383-4000, fax 541/383-4700, www.fs.fed.us.

128 LITTLE FAWN

Scenic rating: 5

on Elk Lake in Deschutes National Forest

Choose between sites on the water's edge or nestled in the forest at this campground along the eastern shore of Elk Lake. Afternoon winds are common here, making this a popular spot for sailing and windsurfing. Fishing for kokanee salmon and brook trout can be good; hiking is another option. Swimming and water sports are popular during warm weather. A play area for children can be found at one of the lake's inlets. The camp sits at 4,900 feet elevation, with Little Fawn Group Camp located just beyond Little Fawn campground.

Campsites, facilities: There are 20 sites for tents or RVs up to 36 feet long and one group site for up to 75 campers. Picnic tables and fire grills are provided. Vault toilets, drinking water, and garbage service are available. Boat-launching facilities and rentals are on-site. Leashed pets are permitted.

Reservations, fees: Reservations are accepted only for the group site at 877/444-6777 or www.recreation.gov ($10 reservation fee). Sites are $12 per night, $6 per night per additional vehicle, and $75 per night for the group site. Open late May–September, weather permitting.

Directions: From Bend, drive southwest on Cascades Lakes Highway (Century Drive Highway, which becomes County Road 46) and drive 35.5 miles to Forest Road 4625. Turn left (east) and drive 1.7 miles to the campground.

Contact: Deschutes National Forest, Bend-Fort Rock Ranger District, 541/383-4000, fax 541/383-4700, www.fs.fed.us.

129 MALLARD MARSH

Scenic rating: 8

on Hosmer Lake in Deschutes National Forest

BEST

Quiet Mallard Marsh campground is located on the shore of Hosmer Lake, at an elevation of 5,000 feet. The lake is stocked with brook trout and Atlantic salmon and reserved for catch-and-release fly-fishing only. You'll get a pristine, quality fishing experience here. The lake is ideal for canoeing. Only non-motorized boats are allowed.

Campsites, facilities: There are 15 sites for tents or RVs up to 40 feet long. Picnic tables, garbage service, and vault toilets are provided. No drinking water is available. Boat-launching facilities are nearby. Leashed pets are permitted.

Reservations, fees: Reservations are not accepted. Sites are $10 per night, $5 per night per additional vehicle. Open May–October, weather permitting.

Directions: From Bend, drive southwest on Cascades Lakes Highway (Century Drive Highway, which becomes County Road 46) and drive 35.5 miles to Forest Road 4625. Turn left (southeast) and drive 1.3 miles to the camp.

Contact: Deschutes National Forest, Bend-Fort Rock Ranger District, 541/383-4000, fax 541/383-4700, www.fs.fed.us.

130 SOUTH

Scenic rating: 8

on Hosmer Lake in Deschutes National Forest

South campground is located along the shore of Hosmer Lake, adjacent to Mallard Marsh, and enjoys the same fishing experience. It's a good option if Mallard Marsh is full.

Campsites, facilities: There are 23 sites for tents or RVs up to 40 feet long. Picnic tables, garbage service, and fire grills are provided. Vault toilets and boat-launching facilities are available. No drinking water is provided. Leashed pets are permitted.

Reservations, fees: Reservations are not accepted. Sites are $10 per night, $5 per night per additional vehicle. Open late May–early October, weather permitting.

Directions: From Bend, drive southwest on Cascades Lakes Highway (Century Drive Highway, which becomes County Road 46) and drive 35.5 miles to Forest Road 4625. Turn left (east) and drive 1.2 miles to the campground on the right.

Contact: Deschutes National Forest, Bend-Fort Rock Ranger District, 541/383-4000, fax 541/383-4700, www.fs.fed.us.

131 LAVA LAKE

Scenic rating: 10

on Lava Lake in Deschutes National Forest

BEST

This well-designed campground sits on the shore of pretty Lava Lake at 4,750 feet elevation. Mount Bachelor and the Three Sisters are in the background, making a classic picture. Boating and fishing are popular here. A bonus is nearby Lava Lake Resort, which has showers, laundry facilities, an RV dump station, store, gasoline, and propane.

Campsites, facilities: There are 44 sites for tents or RVs up to 40 feet long. Picnic tables, garbage service, and fire grills are provided. Vault toilets, drinking water, and a fish-cleaning station are available. Boat docks and launching facilities are on-site. Boat rentals are nearby. Some facilities are wheelchair accessible. Leashed pets are permitted.

Reservations, fees: Reservations are not accepted. Sites are $14 per night, $7 per night per additional vehicle. Open mid-April–October, weather permitting.

Directions: From Bend, drive southwest on Cascades Lakes Highway (Century Drive

Highway, which becomes County Road 46) and drive 38.4 miles to Forest Road 4600-500. Turn left (east) and drive one mile to the campground.

Contact: Deschutes National Forest, Bend-Fort Rock Ranger District, 541/383-4000, fax 541/383-4700, www.fs.fed.us.

132 LITTLE LAVA LAKE

Scenic rating: 8

on Little Lava Lake in Deschutes National Forest

Little Lake feeds into the Deschutes River; boating, fishing, hiking, and swimming are some of the recreation options here. Choose from lakeside or riverside sites set at an elevation of 4,750 feet.

Campsites, facilities: There are 15 sites for tents or RVs up to 40 feet long and a group site for up to 30 people. Picnic tables and fire grills are provided. Vault toilets, drinking water, and garbage service are available. A boat launch, docks, and rentals are nearby. There are also launching facilities on-site. Leashed pets are permitted.

Reservations, fees: Reservations are not accepted for the single sites. The group site can be reserved at 877/444-6777 or www.recreation.gov ($10 reservation fee). Sites are $12 per night, $6 per night per additional vehicle. Open early May–late October, weather permitting.

Directions: From Bend, drive southwest on Cascades Lakes Highway (Century Drive Highway, which becomes County Road 46) and drive 38.4 miles to Forest Road 4600-500. Turn left (east) and drive 0.7 mile to Forest Road 4600-520. Continue east for 0.4 mile to the campground.

Contact: Deschutes National Forest, Bend-Fort Rock Ranger District, 541/383-4000, fax 541/383-4700, www.fs.fed.us.

133 SWAMP WELLS HORSE CAMP

Scenic rating: 3

near the Arnold Ice Caves in Deschutes National Forest

If you look at the map, this campground may appear to be quite remote, but it's actually in an area less than 30 minutes from Bend. Set at an elevation of 5,450 feet, this camp is a good place for horseback riding, but you don't need a horse to enjoy this spot. Trails heading south re-enter the forested areas. The system of lava tubes at the nearby Arnold Ice Caves is fun to explore; bring a bicycle helmet, a flashlight, and knee pads.

Campsites, facilities: There are five primitive sites for tents or RVs up to 16 feet long. Picnic tables and fire grills are provided. There are vault toilets, but no drinking water, and garbage must be packed out. Manure bins are available for horses. Leashed pets are permitted.

Reservations, fees: Reservations are not accepted. There is no fee for camping. Open April–late November, weather permitting.

Directions: From Bend, drive south on U.S. 97 for four miles to Forest Road 18/China Hat Road. Turn left (southeast) and drive 5.4 miles to Forest Road 1810. Turn right (south) and drive 5.8 miles to Forest Road 1816. Turn left (east) and drive three miles to the campground. The last mile is rough and primitive.

Contact: Deschutes National Forest, Bend-Fort Rock Ranger District, 541/383-4000, fax 541/383-4700, www.fs.fed.us.

134 WEST CULTUS LAKE

Scenic rating: 5

on Cultus Lake in Deschutes National Forest

This campground, set at 4,700 feet elevation along the west shore of Cultus Lake, is accessible by boat or trail only. It's about three miles by trail from the parking area to the campground. The lake is a good spot for fishing, swimming, and waterskiing. Trails branch out from the campground and provide access to numerous small backcountry lakes. Drinking water and boat-launching facilities are available at Cultus Lake.

Campsites, facilities: There are 12 boat-in or hike-in tent sites. Picnic tables and fire pits are provided. Vault toilets are available. There is no drinking water, and garbage must be packed out. Boat docks are available on-site; boat rentals are at Cultus Lake Resort. Leashed pets are permitted.

Reservations, fees: Reservations are not accepted. Sites are $15 per night. A Northwest Forest Pass ($5 daily fee or $30 annual fee per parked vehicle) is required. Open May–late September, weather permitting.

Directions: From Bend, drive southwest on Cascades Lakes Highway (Century Drive Highway, which becomes County Road 46) and drive 46 miles to Forest Road 4635. Turn right (west) and drive two miles to the parking area. Boat or hike in about three miles to the west end of the lake.

Contact: Deschutes National Forest, Bend-Fort Rock Ranger District, 541/383-4000, fax 541/383-4700, www.fs.fed.us.

135 CULTUS LAKE

Scenic rating: 7

on Cultus Lake in Deschutes National Forest

Located along the east shore of Cultus Lake at 4,700 feet elevation, this camp is a popular spot for fishing, hiking, swimming, waterskiing, and windsurfing. The sites fill up early on weekends and holidays.

Campsites, facilities: There are 55 sites for tents or RVs up to 36 feet long. Picnic tables and fire grills are provided. Vault toilets, drinking water, and garbage service are available. Boat docks and launching facilities are on-site. Boat rentals are nearby. A restaurant, gasoline, and cabins are available nearby at Cultus Lake Resort. Leashed pets are permitted.

Reservations, fees: Reservations are not accepted. Sites are $16 per night, $8 per night per additional vehicle. Open mid-April–late September, weather permitting.

Directions: From Bend, drive southwest on Cascades Lakes Highway (Century Drive Highway, which becomes County Road 46) and drive 46 miles to Forest Road 4635. Turn right (west) and drive two miles to the campground.

Contact: Deschutes National Forest, Bend-Fort Rock Ranger District, 541/383-4000, fax 541/383-4700, www.fs.fed.us.

136 CULTUS CORRAL HORSE CAMP

Scenic rating: 3

near Cultus Lake in Deschutes National Forest

Located at 4,450 feet elevation, about one mile from Cultus Lake, this camp sits in a stand of lodgepole pine. Several nearby trails provide access to backcountry lakes. This is a good overflow campground for Quinn Meadow Horse Camp.

Campsites, facilities: There are 11 sites for tents or RVs up to 40 feet long. Picnic tables, garbage service, fire grills, and four-horse corrals are provided. Drinking water and vault toilets are available. Leashed pets are permitted.

Reservations, fees: Reservations accepted at 877/444-6777 or www.recreation.gov ($10 reservation fee). Sites are $14 per night, $7 per night per additional vehicle. Open May–late September, weather permitting.

Directions: From Bend, drive southwest on Cascades Lakes Highway (Century Drive Highway, which becomes County Road 46) and drive 46 miles to Forest Road 4635. Turn right (west) and drive one mile to Forest Road

4630. Turn right and drive 0.75 mile to the campground on the right.
Contact: Deschutes National Forest, Bend-Fort Rock Ranger District, 541/383-4000, fax 541/383-4700, www.fs.fed.us.

137 DESCHUTES BRIDGE

Scenic rating: 5

on the Upper Deschutes River in Deschutes National Forest

Wooded Deschutes campground is set on the banks of the Deschutes River in a beautiful, green spot at 4,650 feet elevation. Fishing—the main activity—is often difficult and is restricted to artificial lures with a single barbless hook.
Campsites, facilities: There are 12 sites for tents or RVs up to 30 feet long. Picnic tables and fire grills are provided. Vault toilets, drinking water, and garbage service are available. Leashed pets are permitted.
Reservations, fees: Reservations are not accepted. Sites are $6 per night per vehicle. Open August–October.
Directions: From Bend, drive southwest on Cascades Lakes Highway (Century Drive Highway, which becomes County Road 46) and drive 41.1 miles to the campground on the left (just past the Deschutes River Bridge).
Contact: Deschutes National Forest, Bend-Fort Rock Ranger District, 541/383-4000, fax 541/383-4700, www.fs.fed.us.

138 LITTLE CULTUS LAKE

Scenic rating: 7

on Little Cultus Lake in Deschutes National Forest

This campground is set near the shore of Little Cultus Lake at an elevation of 4,800 feet. It's a popular spot for boating (10-mph speed limit), fishing, hiking, and swimming. Nearby trails offer access to numerous backcountry lakes, and the Pacific Crest Trail passes about six miles west of the camp.
Campsites, facilities: There are 31 sites for tents or RVs up to 40 feet long. Picnic tables, garbage service, and fire grills are provided. Drinking water, vault toilets, and a boat launch are available. Leashed pets are permitted.
Reservations, fees: Reservations are not accepted. Sites are $14 per night, $7 per night per additional vehicle. Open May–September, weather permitting.
Directions: From Bend, drive southwest on Cascades Lakes Highway (Century Drive Highway, which becomes County Road 46) and drive 46 miles to Forest Road 4635. Turn right (west) and drive two miles to Forest Road 4630. Turn left (south) and drive 1.7 miles to Forest Road 4636. Turn left (west) and drive one mile to the campground.
Contact: Deschutes National Forest, Bend-Fort Rock Ranger District, 541/383-4000, fax 541/383-4700, www.fs.fed.us.

139 IRISH AND TAYLOR

Scenic rating: 7

near Irish and Taylor Lakes in Deschutes National Forest

Little known and beautiful, this remote campground is situated between two small lakes about a mile from the Pacific Crest Trail. Other nearby trails provide access into the Three Sisters Wilderness. A four-wheel-drive vehicle with high clearance is recommended for access. The camp sits at 5,550 feet elevation.
Campsites, facilities: There are six tent sites. Picnic tables and fire grills are provided. Vault toilets are available. There is no drinking water. Leashed pets are permitted.
Reservations, fees: Reservations are not

accepted. There is no fee. Open June–early October, weather permitting.

Directions: From Bend, drive southwest on Cascades Lakes Highway (Century Drive Highway, which becomes County Road 46) and drive 46 miles to Forest Road 4635. Turn right (west) on Forest Road 4635 and drive a short distance to Forest Road 4630. Turn right (south) and drive 1.7 miles to Forest Road 4636. Turn left (west) and drive 6.4 miles to the campground. A high-clearance vehicle is needed for the last four miles.

Contact: Deschutes National Forest, Bend-Fort Rock Ranger District, 541/383-4000, fax 541/383-4700, www.fs.fed.us.

140 COW MEADOW

Scenic rating: 6

on Crane Prairie Reservoir in Deschutes National Forest

Cow Meadow campground is located near the north end of Crane Prairie Reservoir and near the Deschutes River. It's a pretty spot (elevation is 4,450 feet), great for fly-fishing and bird-watching.

Campsites, facilities: There are 18 sites for tents or RVs up to 30 feet long. Picnic tables, garbage service, and fire grills are provided. Vault toilets are available. There is no drinking water. A boat launch for small boats is nearby. Leashed pets are permitted.

Reservations, fees: Reservations are not accepted. Sites are $10 per night, $5 per night per additional vehicle. Open May–mid-October, weather permitting.

Directions: From Bend, drive southwest on Cascades Lakes Highway (Century Drive Highway, which becomes County Road 46) for 44.7 miles to Forest Road 40. Turn left (east) on Forest Road 40 and drive 0.4 mile to Forest Road 4000-970. Turn right (south) and drive two miles to the campground on the right.

Contact: Deschutes National Forest, Bend-Fort Rock Ranger District, 541/383-4000, fax 541/383-4700, www.fs.fed.us.

141 CRANE PRAIRIE

Scenic rating: 6

on Crane Prairie Reservoir in Deschutes National Forest

This campground along the north shore of Crane Prairie Reservoir is a good spot for anglers and boaters. World-renowned for rainbow trout fishing, this reservoir is also popular for bass fishing.

Campsites, facilities: There are 146 sites for tents or RVs of any length. There are also four group sites for up to 150 people each, depending on the site. Picnic tables and fire grills are provided. Vault toilets, drinking water, and garbage service are available. Boat docks, launching facilities, and a fish-cleaning station are available on-site. Boat rentals, showers, gas, and a coin laundry are nearby. Some facilities are wheelchair accessible. Leashed pets are permitted.

Reservations, fees: Reservations are accepted for group sites only at 877/444-6777 or www.recreation.gov ($10 reservation fee). Single sites are $16 per night, multiple sites are $30 per night, group sites are $200 per night, $8 per night per additional vehicle. Open April–October, weather permitting.

Directions: From Bend, drive south on U.S. 97 for 26.8 miles to Wickiup Junction and County Road 43. Turn right (west) on County Road 43 and drive 11 miles to Forest Road 42. Continue west on Forest Road 42 for 5.4 miles to Forest Road 4270. Turn right (north) and drive 4.2 miles to the campground on the left.

Contact: Deschutes National Forest, Bend-Fort Rock Ranger District, 541/383-4000, fax 541/383-4700, www.fs.fed.us.

142 QUINN RIVER

Scenic rating: 5

on Crane Prairie Reservoir in Deschutes National Forest

Set along the western shore of Crane Prairie Reservoir, this campground is a popular spot for anglers and a great spot for bird-watching. A separate, large parking lot is available for boats and trailers. Boat speed is limited to 10 mph here. The elevation is 4,450 feet.

Campsites, facilities: There are 41 sites for tents or RVs up to 45 feet long. Picnic tables and fire grills are provided. Vault toilets, drinking water, and garbage service are available. Boat-launching facilities are available. Some facilities are wheelchair accessible. Leashed pets are permitted.

Reservations, fees: Reservations are not accepted. Sites are $14 per night, $7 per night per additional vehicle. Open late April–September, weather permitting.

Directions: From Bend, drive southwest on Cascade Lakes Highway (Century Drive Highway, which becomes County Road 46) for 48 miles to the campground.

Contact: Deschutes National Forest, Bend-Fort Rock Ranger District, 541/383-4000, fax 541/383-4700, www.fs.fed.us.

143 ROCK CREEK

Scenic rating: 5

on Crane Prairie Reservoir in Deschutes National Forest

Rock Creek campground is set along the west shore of Crane Prairie Reservoir at an elevation of 4,450 feet. The setting is similar to Quinn River campground, and provides another good spot for anglers when that camp is full.

Campsites, facilities: There are 31 sites for tents or RVs up to 40 feet long. Picnic tables, garbage service, and fire grills are provided. Drinking water, a fish-cleaning station, and vault toilets are available. Boat docks and launching facilities are on-site. Some facilities are wheelchair accessible. Leashed pets are permitted.

Reservations, fees: Reservations are not accepted. Sites are $14 per night, $7 per night per additional vehicle. Open April–September, weather permitting.

Directions: From Bend, drive southwest on Cascade Lakes Highway (Century Drive Highway, which becomes County Road 46) for 48.8 miles to the campground.

Contact: Deschutes National Forest, Bend-Fort Rock Ranger District, 541/383-4000, fax 541/383-4700, www.fs.fed.us.

144 FALL RIVER

Scenic rating: 5

on the Fall River in Deschutes National Forest

Fall River is beautiful, crystal clear, and cold, and this campground is right on it at an elevation of 4,300 feet. Fishing is restricted to fly-fishing only, and it's wise to check the regulations for other restrictions. The Fall River Trail meanders along the river for 3.5 miles and is open for bicycling.

Campsites, facilities: There are 12 sites for tents or RVs up to 40 feet long. Picnic tables, garbage service, and fire grills are provided. Vault toilets are available. There is no drinking water. Leashed pets are permitted.

Reservations, fees: Reservations are not accepted. Sites are $10 per night, $5 per night per additional vehicle. Open early May–late October, weather permitting.

Directions: From Bend, drive south on U.S. 97 for 17.3 miles to the Vandevert Road exit. Take that exit and turn right on Vandevert Road. Drive 1.5 miles to Forest Road 42. Turn left and drive 12.2 miles to the campground.

Contact: Deschutes National Forest, Bend-Fort Rock Ranger District, 541/383-4000, fax 541/383-4700, www.fs.fed.us.

145 SHEEP BRIDGE

Scenic rating: 3

near Wickiup Reservoir in Deschutes National Forest

This campground is set along the north Deschutes River Channel of Wickiup Reservoir in an open, treeless area that has minimal privacy and is dusty in summer. Dispersed sites here are popular with group campers. The elevation is 4,350 feet.

Campsites, facilities: There are 20 sites and three group sites for tents or RVs up to 40 feet long. Picnic tables, garbage service, and fire grills are provided. Drinking water, vault toilets, boat-launching facilities, and a picnic area are available. Leashed pets are permitted.

Reservations, fees: Reservations are not accepted for single sites; group sites can be reserved at 877/444-6777 or www.recreation.gov ($10 reservation fee). Single sites are $12 per night, $22 for multiple sites, $6 per night per additional vehicle. Open early May–October, weather permitting.

Directions: From Bend, drive south on U.S. 97 for 26.8 miles to Wickiup Junction. Turn right (west) on County Road 43 and drive 11 miles to Forest Road 42. Continue 4.6 miles west on Forest Road 42 to Forest Road 4260. Turn left (south) and drive 0.75 mile to the campground on the right.

Contact: Deschutes National Forest, Bend-Fort Rock Ranger District, 541/383-4000, fax 541/383-4700, www.fs.fed.us.

146 NORTH TWIN LAKE

Scenic rating: 6

on North Twin Lake in Deschutes National Forest

Although small and fairly primitive, North Twin Lake has lake access and a pretty setting. The campground is located on the shore of North Twin Lake and is a popular weekend spot for families. Only non-motorized boats are permitted. The elevation is 4,350 feet.

Campsites, facilities: There are 20 sites for tents or RVs up to 40 feet long. Picnic tables and fire grills are provided. Vault toilets are available. There is no drinking water. Boat-launching facilities are on-site. Leashed pets are permitted.

Reservations, fees: Reservations are not accepted. Sites are $12 per night, $6 per night per additional vehicle. Open April–October, weather permitting.

Directions: From Bend, drive southwest on Cascade Lakes Highway (Century Drive Highway, which becomes County Road 46) for 52 miles and drive past Crane Prairie Reservoir to Forest Road 42. Turn east and drive four miles to Forest Road 4260. Turn right (south) and drive 0.25 mile to the campground.

Contact: Deschutes National Forest, Bend-Fort Rock Ranger District, 541/383-4000, fax 541/383-4700, www.fs.fed.us.

147 TWIN LAKES RESORT

Scenic rating: 8

on Twin Lakes

BEST

Twin Lakes Resort is a popular family vacation destination with a full-service marina and all the amenities, including beach areas. Recreational activities vary from hiking to boating, fishing, and swimming on Wickiup Reservoir. Nearby South Twin Lake is popular with paddleboaters and kayakers; it's stocked with rainbow trout.

Campsites, facilities: There are 22 full-hookup sites for RVs of any length. There are also 14 cabins. Picnic tables and fire rings are provided. Restrooms with flush toilets and coin showers, a dump station, coin laundry, convenience store, restaurant, ice, snacks, some RV supplies, propane gas, and gasoline are available. A boat ramp, rentals, and a dock are provided; no motors are permitted on South Twin Lake. Leashed pets are permitted.

Reservations, fees: Reservations are recommended. Sites are $30 per night, $10 per tent in addition to RV. There are no tent-only sites. Some credit cards are accepted. Open late April–mid-October, weather permitting.

Directions: From Bend, drive south on U.S. 97 for 26.8 miles to Wickiup Junction. Turn right (west) on County Road 43 and drive 11 miles to Forest Road 42. Turn left and continue 4.6 miles west on Forest Road 42 to Forest Road 4260. Turn left (south) and drive two miles to the resort.

Contact: Twin Lakes Resort, 541/382-6432, fax 541/410-4688, www.twinlakesresort oregon.com.

148 SOUTH TWIN LAKE

Scenic rating: 6

on South Twin Lake in
Deschutes National Forest

This campground is on the shore of South Twin Lake, a popular spot for boating (nonmotorized only), fishing, and swimming. The elevation is 4,350 feet.

Campsites, facilities: There are 21 sites for tents or RVs up to 40 feet long. Picnic tables, garbage service, and fire grills are provided. Drinking water, vault and flush toilets, and dump station are available. Boat-launching facilities (small boats only), boat rentals, showers, and laundry facilities are nearby. Some facilities are wheelchair accessible. Leashed pets are permitted.

Reservations, fees: Reservations are not accepted. Sites are $16 per night, $8 per night per additional vehicle. Open April–October, weather permitting.

Directions: From Bend, drive south on U.S. 97 for 26.8 miles to Wickiup Junction. Turn right (west) on County Road 43 and drive 11 miles to Forest Road 42. Continue west on Forest Road 42 for 4.6 miles to Forest Road 4260. Turn left (south) and drive two miles to the campground on the left.

Contact: Deschutes National Forest, Bend-Fort Rock Ranger District, 541/383-4000, fax 541/383-4700, www.fs.fed.us.

149 WEST SOUTH TWIN

Scenic rating: 4

on South Twin Lake in
Deschutes National Forest

A major access point to the Wickiup Reservoir, this camp is situated on South Twin Lake adjacent to the reservoir. It's a popular angling spot with very good kokanee salmon fishing. Twin Lakes Resort is adjacent to West South Twin. The elevation is 4,350 feet.

Campsites, facilities: There are 24 sites for RVs up to 40 feet long. Picnic tables and fire grills are provided. Vault toilets, drinking water, garbage service, and a dump station are available. Boat-launching facilities are on-site, and boat rentals, a restaurant, showers, coin laundry, gas, propane, cabins, and a store are nearby. Leashed pets are permitted.

Reservations, fees: Reservations are not accepted. Sites are $14 per night, $7 per night per additional vehicle. Open April–mid-October, weather permitting.

Directions: From Bend, drive southwest on Cascade Lakes Highway (Century Drive Highway, which becomes County Road 46) for 40 miles (past Crane Prairie Reservoir) to Forest Road 42. Turn left (east) and drive four miles to Forest Road 4260. Turn right (south) and drive 0.25 mile to the campground.

Contact: Deschutes National Forest, Bend-Fort Rock Ranger District, 541/383-4000, fax 541/383-4700, www.fs.fed.us.

150 GULL POINT

Scenic rating: 5

on Wickiup Reservoir in Deschutes National Forest

Gull Point campground sits in an open ponderosa stand on the north shore of Wickiup Reservoir. You'll find good fishing for kokanee salmon here. About two miles from West South Twin Campground, Gull Point is the most popular campground on Wickiup Reservoir.

Campsites, facilities: There are 73 sites for tents or RVs up to 40 feet long and two group sites for up to 30 people each. Picnic tables, garbage service, and fire grills are provided. Drinking water, a dump station, and flush and vault toilets are available. Boat-launching facilities and fish-cleaning stations are on-site. Coin showers and a small store are nearby. Some facilities are wheelchair accessible. Leashed pets are permitted.

Reservations, fees: Reservations are not accepted for single sites but can be made for the group sites at 877/444-6777 or www.recreation.gov ($10 reservation fee). Sites are $16 per night, $8 per night per additional vehicle, and $75 per night for group sites. Open mid-April–October, weather permitting.

Directions: From Bend, drive south on U.S. 97 for about 26.8 miles to County Road 43 (three miles north of LaPine). Turn right (west) on County Road 43 and drive 11 miles to Forest Road 42. Turn west on Forest Road 42 and drive 4.6 miles to Forest Road 4260. Turn left (south) and drive three miles to the campground on the right.

Contact: Deschutes National Forest, Bend-Fort Rock Ranger District, 541/383-4000, fax 541/383-4700, www.fs.fed.us.

151 BULL BEND

Scenic rating: 5

on the Deschutes River in Deschutes National Forest

Bull Bend campground is located on the inside of a major bend in the Deschutes River at 4,300 feet elevation. For a mini-float trip, start at the upstream end of camp, float around the bend, and then take out at the downstream end of camp. This is a low-use getaway spot.

Campsites, facilities: There are 12 sites for tents or RVs up to 40 feet long. Picnic tables, garbage service, fire grills, vault toilets, and boat-launching facilities are available. There is no drinking water. Leashed pets are permitted.

Reservations, fees: Reservations are not accepted. Sites are $10 per night, $5 per night per additional vehicle. Open early May–late October, weather permitting.

Directions: From Bend, drive south on U.S. 97 for 26.8 miles to Wickiup Junction. Turn right (west) on County Road 43 and drive eight miles to Forest Road 4370. Turn left (south) and drive 1.5 miles to the campground.

Contact: Deschutes National Forest, Bend-Fort Rock Ranger District, 541/383-4000, fax 541/383-4700, www.fs.fed.us.

152 PRINGLE FALLS

Scenic rating: 4

on the Deschutes River in Deschutes National Forest

This campground fringing the Deschutes River is less than a mile from Pringle Falls. The camp gets light use and is pretty and serene.

Campsites, facilities: There are seven sites for tents or RVs up to 30 feet long. Picnic tables, garbage service, and fire grills are provided. Vault toilets are available. There is no drinking water. Leashed pets are permitted.

Reservations, fees: Reservations are not accepted. Sites are $10 per night, $5 per night per additional vehicle. Open May–October, weather permitting.
Directions: From Bend, drive south on U.S. 97 for 26.8 miles to Wickiup Junction. Turn right (west) on County Road 43 and drive 7.4 miles to Forest Road 4330-500. Turn north (right) and drive one mile to the campground.
Contact: Deschutes National Forest, Bend-Fort Rock Ranger District, 541/383-4000, fax 541/383-4700, www.fs.fed.us.

153 BIG RIVER

Scenic rating: 4

on the Deschutes River in Deschutes National Forest

Big River is a good spot. Located between the banks of the Deschutes River and the road, it has easy access and is popular as an overnight camp. Fishing, motorized boating, and rafting are permitted.
Campsites, facilities: There are 10 sites for tents or RVs up to 40 feet long, and one group site for up to 40 people. Picnic tables, garbage service, and fire grills are provided. Vault toilets are available. There is no drinking water. Boat-launching facilities are on-site. Some facilities are wheelchair accessible. Leashed pets are permitted.
Reservations, fees: Reservations are not accepted. Sites are $10 per night, $5 per night per additional vehicle, and the group site is $30 per night. Open early May–late October, weather permitting.
Directions: From Bend, drive south on U.S. 97 for 17.3 miles to the Vandevert Road exit. Take that exit and turn right on Vandevert Road. Drive 1.5 miles to Forest Road 42. Turn left and drive 7.9 miles to the campground.
Contact: Deschutes National Forest, Bend-Fort Rock Ranger District, 541/383-4000, fax 541/383-4700, www.fs.fed.us.

154 PRAIRIE

Scenic rating: 4

on Paulina Creek in Deschutes National Forest

Here's another good overnight campground that is quiet and private. Set along the banks of Paulina Creek, Prairie is located about 0.5 mile from the trailhead for the Peter Skene Ogden National Recreation Trail. The elevation is 4,300 feet.
Campsites, facilities: There are 16 sites for tents or RVs up to 40 feet long. Picnic tables, garbage service, and fire grills are provided. Drinking water, firewood, and vault toilets are available. Leashed pets are permitted.
Reservations, fees: Reservations are not accepted. Sites are $14 per night, $7 per night per additional vehicle. Open mid-May–late September, weather permitting.
Directions: From Bend, drive south on U.S. 97 for 23.5 miles to County Road 21 (Paulina/East Lake Road). Turn left (east) and drive 3.1 miles to the campground.
Contact: Deschutes National Forest, Bend-Fort Rock Ranger District, 541/383-4000, fax 541/383-4700, www.fs.fed.us.

155 PAULINA LAKE

Scenic rating: 8

on Paulina Lake in Deschutes National Forest

This campground (6,350 feet elevation) is located along the south shore of Paulina Lake and within the Newberry National Volcanic Monument. The camp is adjacent to Paulina Lake Resort. The lake itself sits in a volcanic crater. Nearby trails provide access to the remains of volcanic activity, including craters and obsidian flows. My longtime friend, Guy Carl, caught the state's record brown trout here, right after I'd written a story about his unique method of using giant Rapala and

Rebel bass lures for giant browns. The recreation options here include boating, fishing, hiking, mountain biking, and sailing. The boat speed limit is 10 mph. Note that food-raiding bears are common at all the campgrounds in the Newberry Caldera area and that all food must be kept out of reach. Do not store food in vehicles.

Campsites, facilities: There are 69 sites for RVs up to 30 feet long. Picnic tables, garbage service, and fire grills are provided. Drinking water and flush and vault toilets are available. Boat docks, launching facilities, boat rentals, coin showers, coin laundry, a small store, restaurant, cabins, gas, and propane are within five miles. The Newberry RV dump station is nearby. Some facilities are wheelchair accessible. Leashed pets are permitted.

Reservations, fees: Reservations are accepted at 877/444-6777 or www.recreation.gov ($10 reservation fee). Sites are $16–18 per night, $8 per night per additional vehicle. Open May–late October, weather permitting.

Directions: From Bend, drive south on U.S. 97 for 23.5 miles to County Road 21 (Paulina/East Lake Road). Turn left (east) and drive 12.9 miles to the campground on the left.

Contact: Deschutes National Forest, Bend-Fort Rock Ranger District, 541/383-4000, fax 541/383-4700, www.fs.fed.us.

156 CHIEF PAULINA HORSE CAMP

Scenic rating: 4

on Paulina Lake in Deschutes National Forest

Chief Paulina campground sits at an elevation of 6,400 feet, about 0.25 mile from the south shore of Paulina Lake, where fishing is good. Horse trails and a vista point are close by. Horse campers must use only certified weed-seed-free hay.

Campsites, facilities: There are 14 sites for tents or RVs up to 40 feet long. Picnic tables and fire grills are provided. A vault toilet, garbage service, and corrals are available. There is no drinking water. Boat docks and rentals are nearby. Leashed pets are permitted.

Reservations, fees: Reservations are accepted at 877/444-6777 or www.recreation.gov ($10 reservation fee). Sites are $14–18 per night, $7 per night per additional vehicle. Open May–late October, weather permitting.

Directions: From Bend, drive south on U.S. 97 for 23.5 miles to County Road 21 (Paulina/East Lake Road). Turn left (east) and drive 14 miles to the campground.

Contact: Deschutes National Forest, Bend-Fort Rock Ranger District, 541/383-4000, fax 541/383-4700, www.fs.fed.us.

157 LITTLE CRATER

Scenic rating: 8

near Paulina Lake in Deschutes National Forest

Little Crater is a very popular campground (6,350 feet elevation) near the east shore of Paulina Lake in Newberry National Volcanic Monument, a caldera. Sites are situated on the scenic lake edge, perfect for fishing, and there are great hiking opportunities in the area. The place fills up most summer weekends.

Campsites, facilities: There are 50 sites for tents or RVs up to 40 feet long. Picnic tables and fire grills are provided. Vault toilets, drinking water, and garbage service are available. Boat docks and launching facilities are on-site, and boat rentals are nearby. Some facilities are wheelchair accessible. Leashed pets are permitted.

Reservations, fees: Reservations are not accepted. Sites are $16 per night, $8 per night for each additional vehicle. Parking at the nearby trailhead requires a Northwest Forest Pass ($5 daily fee or $30 annual fee per parked vehicle). Open early May–late October, weather permitting.

Directions: From Bend, drive south on U.S.

97 for 23.5 miles to County Road 21 (Paulina/East Lake Road). Turn left (east) and drive 14.5 miles to Forest Road 2100. Turn left (north) and drive 0.5 mile to the campground on the left.

Contact: Deschutes National Forest, 541/383-4000, fax 541/383-4700.

158 NEWBERRY GROUP CAMP

Scenic rating: 7

west of Roseburg

Newberry Group has a great location on Paulina Lake and is the only area on Newberry Monument designed exclusively for group camping. The parking area and roads are paved, and the group sites are separated from one another, although group sites B and C can be joined to accommodate large groups. One site accommodates groups of up to 35 people, while the other two accommodate up to 50. The entire campground can be reserved as well. Cabins were renovated in 2009 for use starting 2010.

Campsites, facilities: There are three group sites for tents or RVs to 40 feet. Picnic tables and fire rings are provided. Drinking water and vault toilets are available. Leashed pets are permitted.

Reservations, fees: Reservations are accepted at 877/444-6777 or www.recreation.gov ($10 reservation fee). Sites are $75 per night for the smaller camp, $100 per night for the larger two camps. Open June–September, weather permitting.

Directions: From Bend, drive south on U.S. 97 for 23.5 miles to County Road 21 (Paulina/East Lake Road). Turn left (east) and drive 1.5 miles to the campground.

Contact: Deschutes National Forest, 541/383-4000, fax 541/383-4700.

159 CINDER HILL

Scenic rating: 7

on East Lake in Deschutes National Forest

This campground hugs the northeast shore of East Lake at an elevation of 6,400 feet. Located within the Newberry National Volcanic Monument, Cinder Hill makes a good base camp for area activities. Boating, fishing, and hiking are among the recreation options here. Boat speed is limited to 10 mph.

Campsites, facilities: There are 110 sites, including pull-through sites, for tents or RVs of any length. Picnic tables and fire grills are provided. Drinking water, flush and vault toilets, and garbage service are available. A camp host is on-site. Boat docks and launching facilities are on-site, and boat rentals, a store, restaurant, coin showers, coin laundry, and cabins are nearby at East Lake Resort. Some facilities are wheelchair accessible. Leashed pets are permitted.

Reservations, fees: Reservations are accepted at 877/444-6777 or www.recreation.gov ($10 reservation fee). Sites are $16 per night, $8 per night per additional vehicle. Parking at the nearby trailhead requires a Northwest Forest Pass ($5 daily fee or $30 annual fee per parked vehicle). Open mid-May–September, weather permitting.

Directions: From Bend, drive south on U.S. 97 for 23.5 miles to County Road 21 (Paulina/East Lake Road). Turn left (east) and drive 17.6 miles to Forest Road 2100-700. Turn left (north) and drive 0.5 mile to the campground.

Contact: Deschutes National Forest, Bend-Fort Rock Ranger District, 541/383-4000, fax 541/383-4700, www.fs.fed.us.

160 EAST LAKE

Scenic rating: 8

on East Lake in Deschutes National Forest

This campground is set along the south shore of East Lake at an elevation of 6,400 feet. Boating and fishing are popular here, and hiking trails provide access to signs of former volcanic activity in the area. East Lake Campground is similar to Cinder Hill, but smaller. Boat speed is limited to 10 mph.

Campsites, facilities: There are 29 sites for tents or RVs up to 40 feet long. Picnic tables and fire grills are provided. Drinking water, flush and vault toilets, and garbage service are available. A camp host is on-site. Boat docks, launching facilities, and rentals are nearby. Some facilities are wheelchair accessible. Leashed pets are permitted.

Reservations, fees: Reservations are not accepted. Sites are $16 per night, $8 per night per additional vehicle. Open early May–late October, weather permitting.

Directions: From Bend, drive south on U.S. 97 for 23.5 miles to County Road 21 (Paulina/East Lake Road). Turn left (east) and drive 16.6 miles to the campground on the left.

Contact: Deschutes National Forest, Bend-Fort Rock Ranger District, 541/383-4000, fax 541/383-4700, www.fs.fed.us.

161 HOT SPRINGS

Scenic rating: 5

near East Lake in Deschutes National Forest

Don't be fooled by the name: there are no hot springs at this campsite. It lies across the road from East Lake at 6,400 feet elevation, making it a good tent camping spot if you want to be near East Lake but farther away from RVs.

Campsites, facilities: There are 52 sites for tents or RVs up to 26 feet long. Picnic tables and fire grills are provided. Vault toilets, drinking water, and garbage service are available. Boat docks, launching facilities, and rentals are nearby. Leashed pets are permitted.

Reservations, fees: Reservations are not accepted. Sites are $10 per night and $5–7 per night per additional vehicle. Open July–late September, weather permitting.

Directions: From Bend, drive south on U.S. 97 for 23.5 miles to County Road 21 (Paulina/East Lake Road). Turn left (east) and drive 17.2 miles to the campground on the right.

Contact: Deschutes National Forest, Bend-Fort Rock Ranger District, 541/383-4000, fax 541/383-4700, www.fs.fed.us.

162 EAST LAKE RESORT AND RV PARK

Scenic rating: 7

on East Lake

This resort offers shaded sites in a wooded, mountainous setting on the east shore of East Lake. Opportunities for boating, fishing, and swimming abound.

Campsites, facilities: There are 40 sites with partial hookups for tents or RVs up to 40 feet long and 16 cabins. Some sites are pull-through. Drinking water, barbecues, and picnic tables are provided. Restrooms with flush toilets and coin showers, propane gas, firewood, a dump station, convenience store, café, coin laundry, ice, boat-launching facilities, boat rentals, moorage, and a playground are available. Leashed pets are permitted.

Reservations, fees: Reservations are accepted. Sites are $27 per night. Some credit cards are accepted. Open mid-May–September, weather permitting.

Directions: From Bend, drive south on U.S. 97 for 23.5 miles to County Road 21 (Paulina/East Lake Road). Turn left (east) and drive 18 miles to the park at the end of the road.

Contact: East Lake Resort and RV Park, 541/536-2230, www.eastlakeresort.com.

163 CHINA HAT

Scenic rating: 3

in Deschutes National Forest

Remote China Hat campground is located at 5,100 feet elevation in a rugged, primitive area. There is direct trail access here to the East Fort Rock OHV Trail System. Hunters use China Hat as a base camp in the fall, but in summer it is a base camp for off-road motorcyclists.

Campsites, facilities: There are 14 sites for tents or RVs up to 30 feet long. Picnic tables and fire grills are provided. Vault toilets are available. There is no drinking water, and garbage must be packed out. Leashed pets are permitted.

Reservations, fees: Reservations are not accepted. There is no fee for camping. Open April–early November, weather permitting.

Directions: From Bend, drive south on U.S. 97 for 29.6 miles to Forest Road 22. Turn left (east) and drive 26.4 miles to Forest Road 18. Turn left (north) and drive 5.9 miles to the campground on the left.

Contact: Deschutes National Forest, Bend-Fort Rock Ranger District, 541/383-4000, fax 541/383-4700, www.fs.fed.us.

164 CABIN LAKE

Scenic rating: 3

in Deschutes National Forest

This remote campground (4,550 feet elevation) is adjacent to a bird blind that's more than 80 years old—it's a great place to watch birds. Primitive and secluded with sparse tree cover, this spot receives little use even in the busy summer months.

Campsites, facilities: There are 14 sites for tents or RVs up to 30 feet long. Picnic tables and fire grills are available, but not at each site. There are no toilets or drinking water, and garbage must be packed out. Leashed pets are permitted.

Reservations, fees: Reservations are not accepted. There is no fee for camping. Open April–late October, weather permitting.

Directions: From Bend, drive south on U.S. 97 for 29.6 miles to Forest Road 22. Turn left (east) and drive 26.4 miles to Forest Road 18. Turn left (north) and drive six miles to the campground on the left.

Contact: Deschutes National Forest, Bend-Fort Rock Ranger District, 541/383-4000, fax 541/383-4700, www.fs.fed.us.

165 GOLD LAKE

ATLAS 43C8

Scenic rating: 8

on Gold Lake in Willamette National Forest

BEST

Gold Lake campground wins the popularity contest for high use. Although motors are not allowed on this small lake (100 acres, 25 feet deep), rafts and rowboats provide excellent fishing access. A primitive log shelter built in the early 1940s provides a dry picnic area. In the spring and summer, this area abounds with wildflowers and huckleberries. The Gold Lake Bog is another special attraction where one can often see deer, elk, and smaller wildlife.

Campsites, facilities: There are 21 sites for tents or RVs up to 32 feet long. Picnic tables, garbage bins, and fire grills are provided. Drinking water and vault toilets are available. Boat docks and launching facilities are nearby. Some facilities are wheelchair accessible. Leashed pets are permitted.

Reservations, fees: Reservations are not accepted. Sites are $16 per night, $8 per night per additional vehicle. Open mid-May–October, weather permitting.

Directions: From Eugene, drive south on I-5 for five miles to Exit 188 and Highway 58. Turn east and drive 35 miles to the town of Oakridge. From Oakridge, continue east on Highway 58 for 28 miles to Gold Lake Road (Forest Road 500). Turn left (north) and drive two miles to the campground on the right.

Contact: Willamette National Forest, Middle Fork Ranger District, 541/782-2283, fax 541/782-5306, www.fs.fed.us.

166 NORTH DAVIS CREEK

Scenic rating: 4

on North Davis Creek in Deschutes National Forest

Set at an elevation of 4,350 feet, this remote, secluded campground is located along a western channel that feeds into Wickiup Reservoir. Fishing for brown and rainbow trout as well as kokanee salmon is good here. In late summer, the reservoir level tends to drop. The camp receives little use and makes a good overflow camp if campsites are filled at Wickiup.

Campsites, facilities: There are 14 sites for tents or RVs up to 40 feet long. Picnic tables and fire grills are provided. Vault toilets and garbage service are available. There is no drinking water. Boat-launching facilities are on-site. Leashed pets are permitted.

Reservations, fees: Reservations are not accepted. Sites are $10 per night, $5 per night per additional vehicle. Open April–early September.

Directions: From Bend, drive southwest on Cascade Lake Highway (Highway 46/Forest Road 46) for 56.2 miles to the campground on the left.

Contact: Deschutes National Forest, Bend-Fort Rock Ranger District, 541/383-4000, fax 541/383-4700, www.fs.fed.us.

167 RESERVOIR

Scenic rating: 4

on Wickiup Reservoir in Deschutes National Forest

You'll find this campground along the south shore of Wickiup Reservoir, where the kokanee salmon fishing is good. The camp is best in early summer, before the lake level drops. This camp gets little use, so you won't find crowds here. The elevation is 4,350 feet.

Campsites, facilities: There are 28 sites for tents or RVs up to 24 feet long. Picnic tables, garbage service, and fire grills are provided. Boat-launching facilities and vault toilets are available, but there is no drinking water. Leashed pets are permitted.

Reservations, fees: Reservations are not accepted. Sites are $6 per night. Open April–September, weather permitting.

Directions: From Bend, drive southwest on Cascade Lakes Highway (Century Drive Highway, which becomes County Road 46) for 57.8 miles to Forest Road 44. Turn left (east) and drive 1.7 miles to the campground.

Contact: Deschutes National Forest, Bend-Fort Rock Ranger District, 541/383-4000, fax 541/383-4700, www.fs.fed.us.

168 WICKIUP BUTTE

Scenic rating: 4

on Wickiup Reservoir in Deschutes National Forest

Wickiup Butte is more remote than the other campgrounds on Wickiup Reservoir, set at an elevation of 4,350 feet. This campground borders the southeast shore of Wickiup Reservoir, where kokanee salmon fishing is good during the early summer.

Campsites, facilities: There are eight sites for tents or RVs up to 22 feet long. Picnic tables, garbage service, and fire grills are provided. Vault toilets are available. There is no drinking water. Boat-launching facilities are nearby. Leashed pets are permitted.

Reservations, fees: Reservations are not accepted. Sites are $5 per night per vehicle. Open April–late September, weather permitting.

Directions: From Bend, drive south on U.S. 97 for 26.8 miles to Wickiup Junction. Turn right (west) on County Road 43 and drive 10.4 miles to Forest Road 4380. Turn left (south) and drive 3.6 miles to Forest Road 4260. Turn left (east) and drive three miles to the campground.

Contact: Deschutes National Forest, Bend-Fort Rock Ranger District, 541/383-4000, fax 541/383-4700, www.fs.fed.us.

169 LAPINE STATE PARK

Scenic rating: 7

on the Deschutes River

This peaceful and clean campground sits next to the trout-filled Deschutes River (a legendary fly-fishing spot) with many more high-mountain lakes in proximity. The camp is set in a subalpine pine forest populated by eagles or red-tailed hawks. Trails surround the campground; be sure to check out Oregon's "Big Tree." Skiing is a popular wintertime option in the area.

Campsites, facilities: There are 128 sites with full or partial hookups for tents or RVs of any length; only 20-amp service is available. There are also 10 cabins. Picnic tables and fire grills are provided. Drinking water, restrooms with flush toilets and showers, garbage bins, a dump station, a seasonal store, a day-use area with a sandy beach, a meeting hall that can be reserved, ice, and firewood are available. A boat launch is nearby. Some facilities are wheelchair accessible. Leashed pets are permitted.

Reservations, fees: Reservations are accepted at 800/452-5687 or www.oregonstateparks.org ($8 reservation fee). Sites are $13–22 per night, $5 per night per additional vehicle. Cabins are $38–81 per night. Some credit cards are accepted. Open year-round, weather permitting.

Directions: From Bend, turn south on U.S. 97 and drive 23 miles to State Recreation Road. Turn right and drive four miles to the park.

Contact: LaPine State Park, 541/536-2071 or 800/551-6949, www.oregonstateparks.org.

170 HIDDEN PINES RV PARK

Scenic rating: 7

near the Little Deschutes River

So you think you've come far enough, eh? If you want a spot in a privately run RV park two miles from the bank of the Little Deschutes River, you've found it. Within a 30-minute drive are two reservoirs, four lakes, and a golf course. The nearby town of LaPine is the gateway to the Newberry National Volcanic Monument.

Campsites, facilities: There is an area for tents, plus 25 sites with full or partial hookups for RVs of any length; most are pull-through sites. Drinking water, cable TV, and picnic tables are provided. Restrooms with flush toilets and showers, a dump station, coin laundry, RV supplies, propane gas, a community fire ring with firewood, and ice are available. The full-service community of LaPine is about five miles away. Leashed pets are allowed.

Reservations, fees: Reservations are accepted. Sites are $19.44–25.92 per night, plus $2.50 per person per night for more than two people. Some credit cards are accepted. Open year-round.

Directions: From Bend, drive south on U.S. 97 for 24 miles to Wickiup Junction, Milepost 165, and County Road 43/Burgess Road. Turn right (west) on Burgess Road and drive 2.4 miles to Pine Forest Road. Turn left and drive 0.7 mile to Wright Avenue. Turn left and drive one block to the park on the left.

Contact: Hidden Pines RV Park, 541/536-2265.

171 NORTH LAVA FLOW

Scenic rating: 8

on Davis Lake in Deschutes National Forest

North Lava Flow campground is surrounded by old-growth forest along the northeast shore of Davis Lake, a very shallow lake formed by lava flow. The water level fluctuates here, and this campground can sometimes be closed in summer. There's good duck hunting during the fall. Fishing can be decent, but only fly-fishing is allowed. Boat speed is limited to 10 mph.

Campsites, facilities: There are 25 sites for tents or RVs up to 30 feet long. Picnic tables and fire grills are provided. Vault toilets and firewood (which can be gathered from the surrounding area) are available. There is no drinking water, and garbage must be packed out. A primitive boat ramp is nearby. Leashed pets are permitted.

Reservations, fees: Reservations are not accepted. Sites are $9–11 per night, $5 per night per additional vehicle. Open April–December, weather permitting.

Directions: From Eugene, drive south on I-5 for five miles to Exit 188 and Highway 58. Turn east on Highway 58 and drive 86 miles to County Road 61. Turn left and drive three miles to Forest Road 46. Turn left and drive 7.7 miles to Forest Road 850. Turn left and drive 1.8 miles to the campground.

Contact: Deschutes National Forest, Crescent Ranger District, 541/433-3200, fax 541/433-3224, www.fs.fed.us.

172 EAST DAVIS LAKE

Scenic rating: 9

on Davis Lake in Deschutes National Forest

This campground is nestled in the lodgepole pines along the south shore of Davis Lake. Recreation options include boating (speed limit 10 mph), fly-fishing, and hiking. Leeches prevent swimming here. Bald eagles and sandhill cranes are frequently seen.

Campsites, facilities: There are 29 sites for tents or RVs up to 40 feet long. Picnic tables, garbage service, fire grills, drinking water, and vault toilets are provided. Firewood may be gathered from the surrounding area. Primitive boat-launching facilities are available onsite. Some facilities are wheelchair accessible. Leashed pets are permitted.

Reservations, fees: Reservations are not accepted. Sites are $12 per night, $6 per night per additional vehicle. Open mid-April–late September, weather permitting.

Directions: From Eugene, drive south on I-5 for five miles to Exit 188 and Highway 58. Turn east and drive 73 miles to County Road 61. Turn left (east) and drive three miles to Forest Road 46. Turn left and drive 7.7 miles to Forest Road 850. Turn left and drive 0.25 mile to the campground entrance road on the right.

Contact: Deschutes National Forest, Crescent Ranger District, 541/433-3200, fax 541/433-3224, www.fs.fed.us.

173 TRAPPER CREEK

Scenic rating: 8

on Odell Lake in Deschutes National Forest

BEST

The west end of Odell Lake is the setting for this camp. Boat docks and rentals are available nearby at the Shelter Cove Resort. One of Oregon's prime fisheries for kokanee salmon and mackinaw (lake trout), this lake also has some huge brown trout.

Campsites, facilities: There are 26 sites for tents or RVs up to 40 feet long and three group sites. Picnic tables and fire grills are provided. Drinking water, vault toilets, garbage service and a boat launch are available. Firewood may be gathered from the surrounding area.

A store, coin laundry, and ice are within one mile. Leashed pets are permitted.

Reservations, fees: Reservations are accepted at 877/444-6777 or www.recreation.gov ($10 reservation fee). Sites are $16–18 per night, $5 per night per additional vehicle; group sites are $30–34, $8 per night per additional vehicle. Open mid-May–October, weather permitting.

Directions: From Eugene, drive south on I-5 for five miles to Exit 188 and Highway 58. Turn east and drive 61 miles to the turnoff for Odell Lake and Forest Road 5810. Turn right on Forest Road 5810 and drive 1.9 miles to the campground on the left.

Contact: Deschutes National Forest, Crescent Ranger District, 541/433-3200, fax 541/433-3224, www.fs.fed.us.

174 SHELTER COVE RESORT

Scenic rating: 9

on Odell Lake

Shelter Cove is a private resort along the north shore of Odell Lake, set at the base of the Diamond Peak Wilderness. The area offers opportunities for fishing, hiking, and swimming. The cabins sit right on the lakefront, and a general store and tackle shop are available.

Campsites, facilities: There are 64 sites with partial or full hookups for RVs up to 40 feet long; some sites are pull-through. There are also 13 cabins. Picnic tables and fire rings are provided. Drinking water, restrooms with flush toilets and showers, a dump station, wireless Internet service, an ATM, convenience store, coin laundry, and ice are available. Boat docks, launching facilities, and boat rentals are on-site. Leashed pets are permitted.

Reservations, fees: Reservations are accepted at 800/647-2729. Sites are $16–27 per night. Some credit cards are accepted. Open year-round.

Directions: From Eugene, drive south on I-5 for five miles to Exit 188 and Highway 58. Turn east and drive 61 miles to the turnoff for Odell Lake and West Odell Lake Road. Turn right and drive south for 1.8 miles to the resort at the end of the road.

Contact: Shelter Cove Resort, 541/433-2548, www.sheltercoveresort.com.

175 ODELL CREEK

ATLAS 43 8D

Scenic rating: 9

on Odell Lake in Deschutes National Forest

You can fish, hike, and swim at this campground (4,800 feet elevation) along the east shore of Odell Lake. A trail from the nearby Crater Buttes trailhead leads southwest into the Diamond Peak Wilderness and provides access to several small lakes in the backcountry. Another trail follows the north shore of the lake. Boat docks, launching facilities, and rentals are available at the Odell Lake Lodge and Resort, adjacent to the campground. Windy afternoons are common here.

Campsites, facilities: There are 26 sites for tents or RVs up to 50 feet long. Picnic tables and fire grills are provided. Vault toilets, drinking water, and garbage service are available. Firewood may be gathered from the surrounding area. Leashed pets are permitted.

Reservations, fees: Reservations are accepted at 541/433-2540. Sites are $13–15 per night, $5 per night per additional vehicle. Open May–late September, weather permitting.

Directions: From Eugene, drive south on I-5 for five miles to Exit 188 and Highway 58. Turn east and drive 68 miles to Odell Lake and Forest Road 680 (at the east end of the lake). Turn right on Forest Road 680 and drive 400 yards to the campground on the right.

Contact: Deschutes National Forest, Crescent Ranger District, 541/433-3200, fax 541/433-3224, www.fs.fed.us; Odell Lake Lodge, 541/433-2540.

176 SUNSET COVE

Scenic rating: 8

on Odell Lake in Deschutes National Forest

Sunset Cove campground borders the northeast shore of Odell Lake. Boat docks and rentals are available nearby at Odell Lake Lodge and Resort. Campsites are surrounded by large Douglas fir and some white pine trees. The camp backs up to the highway; expect to hear the noise.

Campsites, facilities: There are 20 sites for tents or RVs up to 22 feet long. Picnic tables and fire grills are provided. Drinking water, vault toilets, garbage service, a boat launch and day-use area, and fish-cleaning facilities are available. Firewood may be gathered from the surrounding area. Some facilities are wheelchair accessible. Leashed pets are permitted.

Reservations, fees: Reservations are not accepted. Sites are $13 per night, $5 per night per additional vehicle. Open mid-May–mid-October, weather permitting.

Directions: From Eugene, drive south on I-5 for five miles to Exit 188 and Highway 58. Turn east and drive 67 miles to the campground on the right.

Contact: Deschutes National Forest, Crescent Ranger District, 541/433-3200, fax 541/433-3224, www.fs.fed.us.

177 PRINCESS CREEK

Scenic rating: 9

on Odell Lake in Deschutes National Forest

This wooded campground is on the northeast shore of Odell Lake, but it backs up to the highway so expect traffic noise. Boat docks and rentals are available nearby at the Shelter Cove Resort. Fishing, hiking, and swimming are popular activities at the lake. A trail from the nearby Crater Buttes trailhead leads southwest into the Diamond Peak Wilderness and provides access to several small lakes in the backcountry.

Campsites, facilities: There are 44 sites for tents or RVs up to 30 feet long. Picnic tables and fire grills are provided. Vault toilets, garbage service, and boat-launching facilities are available. Drinking water is available at times, but not guaranteed. Firewood may be gathered from the surrounding area. Showers, a store, coin laundry, and ice are within five miles. Leashed pets are permitted.

Reservations, fees: Reservations are not accepted. Sites are $14 per night, $7 per night per additional vehicle. Open April–September, weather permitting.

Directions: From Eugene, drive south on I-5 for five miles to Exit 188 and Highway 58. Turn east and drive 64 miles to the campground on the right.

Contact: Deschutes National Forest, Crescent Ranger District, 541/433-3200, fax 541/433-3224, www.fs.fed.us.

178 CONTORTA FLAT

Scenic rating: 8

on Crescent Lake in Deschutes National Forest

This campground on Crescent Lake was named for the particular species of lodgepole pine *(pinus contorta)* that grows here. The elevation is 4,850 feet.

Campsites, facilities: There are 19 sites for tents or RVs up to 40 feet long. Picnic tables and fire grills are provided. Vault toilets and garbage bins are available. There is no drinking water. Some facilities are wheelchair accessible. Leashed pets are permitted.

Reservations, fees: Reservations are not accepted. Sites are $12 per night, $6 per night per additional vehicle. Open June–October, weather permitting.

Directions: From Eugene, drive south on I-5 for five miles to Exit 188 and Highway 58. Turn east and drive 69 miles to County Road

60. Turn right (west) and drive 10 miles to the camp on the left.

Contact: Deschutes National Forest, Crescent Ranger District, 541/433-3200, fax 541/433-3224, www.fs.fed.us.

179 WINDY GROUP

Scenic rating: 8

on Crescent Lake in Deschutes National Forest

Windy Group is located near the beaches on Crescent Lake. The lake warms up more easily than many high-mountain lakes, making swimming and waterskiing two popular options. Mountain biking and hiking are also available.

Campsites, facilities: There is one group site for tents or RVs up to 60 feet long and up to 40 people. Picnic tables and fire rings are provided. Vault toilets and garbage bins are available. There is no drinking water. Some facilities are wheelchair accessible. Leashed pets are permitted.

Reservations, fees: Reservations are accepted at 877/444-6777 or www.recreation.gov ($10 reservation fee). The site is $65 per night. Open May–September, weather permitting.

Directions: From Eugene, drive south on I-5 for five miles to Exit 188 and Highway 58. Turn east and drive 69 miles to County Road 60. Turn right (west) and drive 7.5 miles to the camp.

Contact: Deschutes National Forest, Crescent Ranger District, 541/433-3200, fax 541/433-3224, www.fs.fed.us.

180 SIMAX GROUP CAMP

Scenic rating: 8

on Crescent Lake in Deschutes National Forest

This camp is set at an elevation of 4,850 feet on Crescent Lake and provides trails to day-use beaches. Fishing is variable year to year and is usually better earlier in the season. A boat launch is available at neighboring Crescent Lake, about two miles away. Nearby Diamond Peak Wilderness (free permit required) provides hiking options.

Campsites, facilities: There are three group campsites for 30–50 campers each. Drinking water, tent pads, restrooms with flush toilets and showers, picnic tables, garbage service, fireplaces, and a group shelter are available. Tents must be placed on tent pads. Some facilities are wheelchair accessible. Leashed pets are permitted.

Reservations, fees: Reservations are accepted at 877/444-6777 or www.recreation.gov ($10 reservation fee). Site A is $80–100 per night and Sites B and C are $100–120 per night. (Note that Site C is best for RVs.) The group shelter is $50 per day. Open mid-May–October, weather permitting.

Directions: From Eugene, drive south on I-5 for five miles to Exit 188 and Highway 58. Turn east and drive 70 miles to Crescent Lake Highway (Forest Road 60). Turn right and drive two miles to Forest Road 6005. Turn left and drive one mile to the campground on the right.

Contact: Deschutes National Forest, Crescent Ranger District, 541/433-3200, fax 541/433-3224, www.fs.fed.us.

181 CRESCENT LAKE

Scenic rating: 8

on Crescent Lake in Deschutes National Forest

This campground is set along the north shore of Crescent Lake, and it is often windy here in the afternoon. Boat docks, launching facilities, and rentals are available at Crescent Lake Resort, adjacent to the campground. A trail from camp heads into the Diamond Peak Wilderness (free permit required; available on-site) and also branches north to Odell Lake.

Campsites, facilities: There are 46 sites for tents or RVs up to 36 feet long. Picnic tables and fire grills are provided. Drinking water, vault toilets, garbage service, and boat-launching facilities are available. Firewood may be gathered from the surrounding area. Leashed pets are permitted.
Reservations, fees: Reservations are not accepted. Sites are $16 per night, $8 per night per additional vehicle. Open April–late October, weather permitting.
Directions: From Eugene, drive south on I-5 for five miles to Exit 188 and Highway 58. Turn east and drive 70 miles to Crescent Lake Highway (Forest Road 60). Turn right (west) and drive 2.2 miles southwest. Bear right to remain on Forest Road 60, and drive another 0.25 mile to the campground on the left.
Contact: Deschutes National Forest, Crescent Ranger District, 541/433-3200, fax 541/433-3224, www.fs.fed.us.

182 SPRING

Scenic rating: 8

on Crescent Lake in Deschutes National Forest

Spring campground is nestled in a lodgepole pine forest on the southern shore of Crescent Lake. Sites are open, with some on the lake offering Diamond Peak views. Boating, swimming, and waterskiing are popular activities, and the Windy-Oldenburg Trailhead provides access to the Oregon Cascades Recreation Area. The camp is at an elevation of 4,850 feet.
Campsites, facilities: There are five sites for tents only, 64 sites for tents or RVs up to 40 feet long, four multiple sites, and 12 sites that can be reserved together as a group site. Picnic tables and fire grills are provided. Drinking water, vault toilets, garbage service, boat-launching facilities, and firewood (may be gathered from the surrounding area) are available. Leashed pets are permitted.
Reservations, fees: Reservations are not accepted for single sites. Reservations are accepted for group sites at 877/444-6777 or www.recreation.gov ($10 reservation fee). Sites are $16 per night, $8 per night per additional vehicle; multiple sites are $30 per night, and the group site is $125 per night. Open May–September, weather permitting.
Directions: From Eugene, drive south on I-5 for five miles to Exit 188 and Highway 58. Turn east and drive 70 miles to Crescent Lake Highway (Forest Road 60). Turn right and drive eight miles west to the campground entrance road on the left. Turn left and drive one mile to the campground.
Contact: Deschutes National Forest, Crescent Ranger District, 541/433-3200, fax 541/433-3224, www.fs.fed.us.

183 CONTORTA POINT GROUP CAMP

Scenic rating: 8

on Crescent Lake in Deschutes National Forest

This campground (4,850 feet elevation) sits on the southern shore of Crescent Lake, where boating, swimming, and waterskiing are among the summer pastimes. A number of trails from the nearby Windy-Oldenburg Trailhead provide access to lakes in the Oregon Cascades Recreation Area. Motorized vehicles are restricted to open roads only.
Campsites, facilities: There are two group sites for tents or RVs up to 30 feet long that can accommodate up to 40 people each. There is no drinking water. Picnic tables and fire rings are provided. Vault toilets and garbage bins are available. Firewood can be gathered in surrounding forest. Boat docks and launching facilities are three miles away at Spring Campground. Leashed pets are permitted.
Reservations, fees: Reservations are accepted at 877/444-6777 or www.recreation.gov ($10 reservation fee). Sites are $65 per night. Open May–September, weather permitting.

Directions: From Eugene, drive south on I-5 for five miles to Exit 188 and Highway 58. Turn east and drive 70 miles to Crescent Lake Highway (Forest Road 60). Turn right and drive 9.9 miles to Forest Road 280. Turn left and drive one mile to the campground.

Contact: Deschutes National Forest, Crescent Ranger District, 541/433-3200, fax 541/433-3224, www.fs.fed.us.

184 WHITEFISH HORSE CAMP

Scenic rating: 5

on Whitefish Creek in Deschutes National Forest

This just might be the best horse camp in the state. Only horse camping is allowed here, and manure removal is required. High lines are not allowed; horses must be kept in stalls. On Whitefish Creek at the west end of Crescent Lake, this campground is set in lodgepole pine and has shaded sites. Although located in a flat area across the road from the lake, the campground has no lake view. Moderately to heavily used, it has access to about 100 miles of trail, leading to Diamond Peak Wilderness, the Metolius-Windigo National Recreation Trail, the Oregon Cascades Recreation Area, and many high mountain lakes. The camp sits at 4,850 feet elevation.

Campsites, facilities: There are 19 sites for tents or RVs up to 40 feet long. Picnic tables and fire rings are provided. Drinking water, garbage bins, vault toilets, horse corrals, and manure disposal site are available are available. Firewood may be gathered from the surrounding area. Leashed pets are permitted.

Reservations, fees: Reservations are accepted at 877/444-6777 or www.recreation.gov ($10 reservation fee). Sites are $14 per night for two stalls, $18 per night for four stalls, and $7 per night per additional vehicle. Open May–September, weather permitting.

Directions: From Eugene, drive south on I-5 for five miles to Exit 188 and Highway 58. Turn east and drive 70 miles to Crescent Lake Highway (Forest Road 60). Turn right (west) and drive 2.2 miles southwest. Stay to the right to remain on Forest Road 60, and drive six miles to the campground on the right.

Contact: Deschutes National Forest, Crescent Ranger District, 541/433-3200, fax 541/433-3224, www.fs.fed.us.

185 CRESCENT CREEK

Scenic rating: 7

on Crescent Creek in Deschutes National Forest

One of the Cascade's classic hidden campgrounds, Crescent Creek camp sits along the banks of its namesake at 4,500 feet elevation. The buzzwords here are pretty, developed, and private. A registered bird-watching area is nearby. Hunters are the primary users of this campground, mainly in the fall. Otherwise, it gets light use. There's some highway noise here, and even if you can't hear it, traffic is visible from some sites.

Campsites, facilities: There are nine sites for tents or RVs up to 40 feet long. Picnic tables and fire grills are provided. Vault toilets, drinking water, and garbage service are available. Firewood may be gathered from the surrounding area. Leashed pets are permitted.

Reservations, fees: Reservations are not accepted. Sites are $14 per night, $7 per night per additional vehicle. Open May–late September, weather permitting.

Directions: From Eugene, drive south on I-5 for five miles to Exit 188 and Highway 58. Turn east and drive 73 miles to County Road 61. Turn left (east) and drive three miles to the campground on the right.

Contact: Deschutes National Forest, Crescent Ranger District, 541/433-3200, fax 541/433-3224, www.fs.fed.us.

186 CORRAL SPRING

Scenic rating: 4

in Winema National Forest

This flat campground with no water source is located next to Corral Spring at 4,900 feet elevation. The main attraction is solitude; it's primitive, remote, and quiet. The landscape features stands of lodgepole pine, interspersed by several small meadows.

Campsites, facilities: There are six sites for tents or RVs up to 50 feet long. Picnic tables and fire grills are provided. Vault toilets are available. There is no drinking water, and garbage must be packed out. A store, café, coin laundry, and ice are within five miles. Leashed pets are permitted.

Reservations, fees: Reservations are not accepted. There is no fee for camping. Open mid-May–late October, weather permitting.

Directions: From Eugene, drive southeast on Highway 58 for 86 miles to U.S. 97. Turn south and drive five miles to Forest Road 9774 (2.5 miles north of Chemult). Turn right and drive two miles west to the campground.

Contact: Winema National Forest, Chemult Ranger District, 541/365-7001, fax 541/365-2206, www.fs.fed.us.

187 DIGIT POINT

Scenic rating: 7

on Miller Lake in Winema National Forest

This campground is nestled in a lodgepole pine and mountain hemlock forest at 5,600 feet elevation on the shore of Miller Lake, a popular spot for boating, fishing, and swimming. Nearby trails provide access to the Mount Thielsen Wilderness and the Pacific Crest Trail.

Campsites, facilities: There are 64 sites for tents or RVs up to 30 feet long. Picnic tables and fire grills are provided. Drinking water, flush toilets, garbage service and a dump station are available. Boat docks and launching facilities are nearby. Some facilities are wheelchair accessible. Leashed pets are permitted.

Reservations, fees: Reservations are not accepted. Sites are $12 per night, $5 per night per additional vehicle. Open Memorial Day–mid-October, weather permitting.

Directions: From Eugene, drive southeast on Highway 58 for 86 miles to U.S. 97. Turn south and drive seven miles to Forest Road 9772 (one mile north of Chemult). Turn right and drive 12 miles west to the campground.

Contact: Winema National Forest, Chemult Ranger District, 541/365-7001, fax 541/365-2206, www.fs.fed.us.

188 WALT HARING SNO-PARK

Scenic rating: 6

in Winema National Forest near Chemult

For eons, this has been a tiny, unknown, and free campground used as a staging area for snowmobiling and cross-country skiing in winter. In summer, it has primarily been a picnic site and layover spot. Note: In 2009, the Forest Service began improving the site and may start charging fees in 2010. The elevation is 4,700 feet.

Campsites, facilities: There are five sites for tents or RVs. Picnic tables and fire rings are provided. Drinking water, vault toilets, and an RV dump station are available. Some facilities are wheelchair accessible. Leashed pets are permitted.

Reservations, fees: No reservations are accepted. There is no fee, however, the Forest Service may start charging fees starting in 2010. If this is critical to your trip, call first. A sno-park permit is required. Open year-round.

Directions: From Eugene, drive southeast on

Highway 58 for 86 miles to U.S. 97. Turn south and drive seven miles to Forest Road 9772 (one mile north of Chemult). Turn right on Forest Road 9772 (Miller Lake Road) and drive 0.5 mile to the campground.

Contact: Winema National Forest, 541/365-7001, fax 541/365-2206.

189 CHARLES V. STANTON PARK

Scenic rating: 7

on the South Umpqua River

Charles V. Stanton Park, along the banks of the South Umpqua River, is an all-season spot with a nice beach for swimming in the summer and good steelhead fishing in the winter.

Campsites, facilities: There are 20 sites for tents or self-contained RVs (no hookups), 20 sites with full hookups for RVs up to 60 feet long, and one group area for up to 13 camping units. Picnic tables and fire pits or barbecues are provided. Drinking water, restrooms with flush toilets and showers, a dump station, pavilion, picnic area, and playground are available. Propane gas, a store, café, coin laundry, and ice are within one mile. Some facilities are wheelchair accessible. Leashed pets are permitted.

Reservations, fees: No reservations are accepted for single sites; reservations are required for the group site ($10 reservation fee) at 541/957-7001. Sites are $15–20 per night for single sites, $200 per night for the group site. Some credit cards are accepted. Open year-round.

Directions: Depending on which direction you're heading on I-5, there are two routes to reach this campground. In Canyonville northbound on I-5, take Exit 99 and drive one mile north on the frontage road to the campground on the right. Otherwise: In Canyonville southbound on I-5, take Exit 101. Turn right at the first stop sign, and almost immediately turn right again onto the frontage road. Drive one mile south on the frontage road to the campground on the left.

Contact: Charles V. Stanton Park, Douglas County Parks, 541/839-4483, fax 541/440-4500, www.co.douglas.or.us/parks.

190 CHIEF MIWALETA CAMPGROUND

Scenic rating: 7

on Galesville Reservoir, east of Azalea

If location is everything, then this camp has got it. Wooded sites are set along the shore of beautiful Gales Reservoir, providing a base camp for a trip filled with fishing, boating, hiking, camping, and picnicking. A pavilion can be reserved in the day-use area.

Campsites, facilities: There are 20 sites with full hookups for RVs up to 60 feet long (some pull-through), dispersed sites for tents, and one cabin. Picnic tables and fire rings are provided. Drinking water, vault toilets, and a boat ramp are available. Some facilities are wheelchair accessible. Leashed pets are permitted.

Reservations, fees: Reservations are accepted only for the cabin ($10 reservation fee) at 541/957-7001. RV sites are $20 per night, $3 per night per additional vehicle, tent sites are $15 per night, and the cabin is $32 per night. Some credit cards are accepted for reservations only. Open year-round.

Directions: From Azalea, take I-5 north about 0.5 mile to Exit 88 east to Upper Cow Creek Road. Merge onto Upper Cow Creek and drive eight miles to the campground on the left.

Contact: Chief Miwaleta County Campground, 541/837-3302, www.co.douglas.or.us/parks/campgrounds.asp.

191 MEADOW WOOD RV PARK

Scenic rating: 6

in Glendale

Meadow Wood is a good option for RVers looking for a camping spot along I-5. It features 80 wooded acres and all the amenities. Nearby attractions include a ghost town, gold panning, and Wolf Creek Tavern.

Campsites, facilities: There are 25 tent sites and 75 pull-through sites with full or partial hookups for RVs up to 40 feet long. Drinking water and picnic tables are provided. Restrooms with flush toilets and showers, propane gas, a dump station, modem access, firewood, a coin laundry, ice, a playground, and a seasonal heated swimming pool are available. Leashed pets are permitted.

Reservations, fees: Reservations are accepted at 800/606-1274. Sites are $12.50–25 per night. Monthly rentals are available. Open year-round.

Directions: From Grants Pass, drive north on I-5 to Exit 83 (near Glendale) and drive east for 0.25 mile to Autumn Lane. Turn right (south) on Autumn Lane and drive one mile to the park. Alternatively, if you are instead driving south from Roseburg, drive south on I-5 to Exit 86 (near Glendale). Take that exit and drive over the freeway and turn right onto the frontage road. Continue for three miles to Barton Road. Turn left (east) and drive one mile to Autumn Lane. Turn right (south) on Autumn Lane and drive 0.75 mile to the park.

Contact: Meadow Wood RV Park, 541/832-3114 or 800/606-1274, fax 541/832-2454.

192 WOLF CREEK PARK

Scenic rating: 6

near the town of Wolf Creek

This rustic campground is located on Wolf Creek near the historic Wolf Creek Inn. A hiking trail leads to the top of London Peak through old-growth forest. Although close to I-5 and the town of Wolf Creek, this spot gets low to average use.

Campsites, facilities: There are 19 sites for tents or RVs (no hookups) and 15 sites for tents or RVs up to 40 feet long (partial hookups). Picnic tables and fire pits are provided. Drinking water, vault toilets, a dump station, softball field, playground, horseshoe pits, disc golf, and a picnic shelter are available. A camp host is on-site. Supplies are available nearby. Some facilities are wheelchair accessible. Leashed pets are permitted.

Reservations, fees: Reservations are accepted ($8 reservation fee) at 800/452-5687 or www.reserveamerica.com. Sites are $19–20 per night, $5 per night per additional vehicle. Open year-round, but with no water November–early April.

Directions: From Grants Pass, drive north on I-5 for approximately 18 miles to exit 76/Wolf Creek. Take that exit to Wolf Creek Road. Turn left and drive 0.5 mile to the town of Wolf Creek and Main Street. Turn left and drive 0.25 mile to the park.

Contact: Josephine County Parks, 541/474-5285, fax 541/474-5288, www.co.josephine.or.us/parks/index.htm.

193 INDIAN MARY PARK

Scenic rating: 9

on the Rogue River

BEST

This park is the crown jewel of the Josephine County parks. Set right on the Rogue River at an elevation of 900–1,000 feet, the park offers disc golf (Frisbee golf), fishing, hiking trails, a historic mining town nearby, a picnic shelter, a swimming beach (unsupervised), and volleyball. Rogue River is famous for its rafting, which can be done with a commercial outfit or on your own.

Campsites, facilities: There are 34 sites for tents or self-contained RVs (no hookups), 58 sites for tents or RVs of up to 40 feet long (full or partial hookups), and two yurts. Picnic tables and fire pits are provided. Drinking water, restrooms with flush toilets and coin showers, garbage bins, a dump station, boat ramp, day-use area, a picnic shelter that can be reserved, playground, ice, and firewood are available. A camp host is on-site. A store and café are seven miles away, and a coin laundry is 16 miles away. Some facilities are wheelchair accessible. Leashed pets are permitted.

Reservations, fees: Reservations are accepted ($8 reservation fee) at 800/452-5687 or www.reserveamerica.com. Sites are $19–22 per night, $5 per night per additional vehicle; yurts are $30 per night. Open year-round.

Directions: From Grants Pass, drive north on I-5 for 3.5 miles to Exit 61 (Merlin-Galice Road). Take that exit and drive west on Merlin-Galice Road for 19 miles to Indian Mary Park on the right.

Contact: Josephine County Parks, 541/474-5285, fax 541/474-5288, www.co.josephine.or.us/parks/index.htm.

194 ELDERBERRY FLAT

Scenic rating: 7

on West Fork Evans Creek

This camp is virtually unknown except to the OHV crowd. On weekends, this is usually not the place to find quiet and serenity. OHV and motorcycle activity is common here. It is located on the banks of Evans Creek, about a 30-minute drive from I-5. Small and primitive, it has access to swimming holes along the creek. No fishing is allowed in the creek.

Campsites, facilities: There are nine primitive tent sites. Picnic tables and fire grills are provided. Vault toilets and garbage service are available, but there is no drinking water. Some facilities are wheelchair accessible. Leashed pets are permitted.

Reservations, fees: Reservations are not accepted. There is no fee for camping, but there is a 14-day stay limit. Open mid-April–mid-November.

Directions: From Grants Pass, drive south on I-5 for 10 miles to the Rogue River exit. Take that exit, turn right on Depot Street, and drive to Pine Street. Turn left and drive 18 miles (it becomes East Evans Creek Road) to West Fork Evans Creek Road. Turn left and drive nine miles to the campground.

Contact: Bureau of Land Management, Medford District, 541/618-2200, fax 541/618-2400, www.or.blm.gov/medford.

195 GRIFFIN PARK

Scenic rating: 7

on the Rogue River

This high-use campground and 16-acre park has grassy sites situated 100–150 yards from the Rogue River. The river current is slow in this area, so it is good for swimming and water play. Fishing and rafting are also popular. Hiking and bicycling are available nearby on Bureau of Land Management property.

Campsites, facilities: There are four sites for tents or RVs (no hookups), 15 sites for tents or RVs up to 40 feet long (full hookups), and one yurt. Picnic tables and fire pits are provided. Drinking water, restrooms with flush toilets and showers, a dump station, recreation field, playground, and horseshoe pits are available. A camp host is on-site. A boat ramp, convenience store, swimming area, and playground are within one mile. Some facilities are wheelchair accessible. Leashed pets are permitted.

Reservations, fees: Reservations are accepted ($8 reservation fee) at 800/452-5687 or www.reserveamerica.com. Sites are $19–22 per night, $5 per night per additional vehicle; yurts are $30 per night. Open year-round, but with no water November–early April.

Directions: From Grants Pass on I-5, take the U.S. 199 exit. Turn south on U.S. 199 and drive 6.7 miles to Riverbanks Road. Turn right and drive 6.2 miles to Griffin Park Road. Turn right and drive 0.5 mile to the park.

Contact: Josephine County Parks, 541/474-5285, fax 541/474-5288, www.co.josephine.or.us/parks/index.htm.

196 GRANTS PASS/ REDWOOD HIGHWAY

Scenic rating: 8

near Grants Pass

This KOA campground along a stream in the hills outside of Grants Pass attracts bird-watchers. It also makes a perfect layover spot for travelers who want to get away from the highway for a while. For an interesting side trip, drive south down scenic U.S. 199 to Cave Junction or Illinois River State Park.

Campsites, facilities: There are 40 sites for tents or RVs of any length (full hookups); some sites are pull-through. There is also one cabin. Picnic tables are provided, and tent sites have fire pits. Restrooms with showers, drinking water, a dump station, coin laundry, convenience store, ice, RV supplies, propane gas, and modem access are available. There are also a recreation hall, playground, and recreation field. Leashed pets are permitted with certain restrictions.

Reservations, fees: Reservations are accepted at 888/476-6508 and receive a 10 percent discount. Sites are $35–39 per night, plus $4 per person per night for more than two people. Some credit cards are accepted. Open year-round.

Directions: In Grants Pass on I-5, take the U.S. 199 exit. Turn southwest on U.S. 199 and drive 14.5 miles to the campground on the right (at Milepost 14.5).

Contact: Grants Pass/Redwood Highway KOA, 541/476-6508 or 888/476-6508.

197 SCHROEDER

Scenic rating: 9

on the Rogue River

Steelhead and salmon fishing, swimming, and boating are among the possibilities at this popular camp along the Rogue River. Just a short jog off the highway, it makes an excellent layover for I-5 travelers. A bonus for RVers is 50-amp service. The park is set close to Hellgate Excursions, which provides jet boat trips on the Rogue River. Tennis courts are close by.

Campsites, facilities: There are 22 sites for tents and RVs (no hookups), 29 sites for tents or RVs of any length (full hookups), and two yurts. Picnic tables and fire pits are provided. Restrooms with flush toilets and coin showers and a picnic shelter that can be reserved are available. Recreational facilities include ball fields, tennis and basketball courts, horseshoe pits, volleyball court, a dog park, picnic area, playground, and boat ramp. A camp host is on-site. Some facilities, including a fishing pier, are wheelchair accessible. Leashed pets are permitted.

Reservations, fees: Reservations are accepted ($8 reservation fee) at 800/452-5687 or www.reserveamerica.com. Sites are $19–22 per night, $5 per night per additional vehicle; yurts are $30 per night. Open year-round.

Directions: In Grants Pass on I-5, take Exit 55 to U.S. 199. Drive west on U.S. 199 for 0.7 mile to Redwood Avenue. Turn right and drive 1.5 miles to Willow Lane. Turn right and drive 0.9 mile to Schroeder Lane and the park.

Contact: Josephine County Parks, 541/474-5285, fax 541/474-5288, www.co.josephine.or.us/parks/index.htm.

198 ROGUE VALLEY OVERNITERS

Scenic rating: 5

near the Rogue River

This park is just off the freeway in Grants Pass, the jumping-off point for trips down the Rogue River. The summer heat in this part of Oregon can surprise visitors in late June and early July. This is a nice, comfortable park with shade trees. About half of the sites are taken by monthly renters.

Campsites, facilities: There are 30 sites for tents or RVs of any length (full hookups); some are pull-through sites. Cable TV and picnic tables are provided. Restrooms with flush toilets and showers, modem access, a dump station, and coin laundry are available. Propane gas, a store, café, and ice are available within one mile. Leashed pets are permitted.

Reservations, fees: Reservations are accepted. Sites are $33.30 per night, plus $2 per person per night for more than two people. Weekly and monthly rates are available. Open year-round.

Directions: In Grants Pass on I-5, take Exit 58 to 6th Street. Drive south on 6th Street for 0.25 mile to the park on the right.

Contact: Rogue Valley Overniters, 541/479-2208.

199 WHITEHORSE

Scenic rating: 9

near the Rogue River

This pleasant county park is set about a quarter mile from the banks of the Rogue River. It is one of several parks in the Grants Pass area that provide opportunities for salmon and steelhead fishing, hiking, and boating. This is a popular bird-watching area. Wildlife Images, a wildlife rehabilitation center, is nearby. Possible side trips include Crater Lake National Park (two hours away), Kerby Museum, and Oregon Caves.

Campsites, facilities: There are 34 sites for tents or RVs of any length (no hookups), eight sites for RVs of any any length (full hookups), and one yurt. Picnic tables and fire pits are provided. Restrooms with flush toilets and coin showers, a boat ramp, horseshoe pits, volleyball, a picnic shelter, and a playground are available. A camp host is on-site. Some facilities are wheelchair accessible. Leashed pets are permitted.

Reservations, fees: Reservations are accepted ($8 reservation fee) at 800/452-5687 or www.reserveamerica.com. Sites are $19–22 per night, $5 per night per additional vehicle, and $30 per night for the yurt. The group site is $30 per night for up to 12 people and $3 per person per night for additional people. Open year-round, but only to self-contained RVs in the winter.

Reservation note: When making a reservation for this campground, note that ReserveAmerica.com mistakenly lists it as White Horse, not Whitehorse, and its computer system will not recognize it as one word.

Directions: In Grants Pass on I-5, take Exit 58 to 6th Street. Drive south on 6th Street to G Street. Turn right (west) and drive approximately seven miles (the road becomes Upper River Road, then Lower River Road). The park is on the left at 7600 Lower River Road.

Contact: Josephine County Parks, 541/474-5285, fax 541/474-5288, www.co.josephine.or.us/parks/index.htm.

200 RIVER PARK RV RESORT

Scenic rating: 6

on the Rogue River

This park has a quiet, serene riverfront setting, yet it is close to all the conveniences of a small city. Highlights here include 700 feet of Rogue River frontage for trout fishing and swimming. It's one of several parks in the immediate area.

Campsites, facilities: There are three tent sites and 47 sites with full or partial hookups for RVs up to 40 feet long. Picnic tables are provided. Cable TV, restrooms with showers, a dump station, public phone, coin laundry, and ice are available. Leashed pets are permitted.

Reservations, fees: Reservations are accepted at 800/677-8857. Sites are $31–38 per night, $3.50 per person per night for more than two people, and $2 per night for an additional vehicle if not towed. Some credit cards are accepted. Open year-round.

Directions: In Grants Pass on I-5, take Exit 55 west to Highway 199. Drive west on Highway 199 for two miles to Parkdale. Turn left on Parkdale and drive one block to Highway 99. Turn left on Highway 99 and drive two miles to the park on the left.

Contact: River Park RV Resort, 541/479-0046 or 800/677-8857.

201 CHINOOK WINDS RV PARK

Scenic rating: 6

on the Rogue River

This campground along the Rogue River is close to chartered boat trips down the Rogue and a golf course. Fishing and swimming access are available from the campground. (Note: This park was previously known as Circle W RV Park.)

Campsites, facilities: There are 25 sites with full or partial hookups for RVs of any length; some are pull-through sites. Picnic tables and cable TV are provided. Restrooms with flush toilets and showers, a dump station, coin laundry, and ice are available. A boat dock is nearby. Leashed pets are permitted.

Reservations, fees: Reservations are accepted. Sites are $27–40 per night, plus $1.50 per person per night for more than two people. Some credit cards are accepted. Open year-round.

Directions: From Grants Pass, drive south on I-5 for 10 miles to Exit 48 at Rogue River. Take that exit west (over the bridge) to Highway 99. Turn right and drive west one mile to the park on the right.

Contact: Chinook Winds RV Park, 541/582-1686.

202 VALLEY OF THE ROGUE STATE PARK

Scenic rating: 7

on the Rogue River

With easy highway access, this popular campground along the banks of the Rogue River often fills to near capacity during the summer. Recreation options include fishing and boating. This spot makes a good base camp for taking in the Rogue Valley and surrounding attractions: Ashland's Shakespeare Festival, the Britt Music Festival, Crater Lake National Park, historic Jacksonville, and Oregon Caves National Monument.

Campsites, facilities: There are 147 sites with full or partial hookups for tents or RVs up to 75 feet long, some with pull-through sites, and 21 sites for tents. Three group tent areas for up to 25 people each and six yurts are available. Picnic tables and fire grills are provided. Restrooms with flush toilets and showers, drinking water, garbage bins, a dump station, firewood, Wi-Fi, coin laundry, a meeting hall, amphitheater, and playgrounds are available. A restaurant is nearby. Boat-launching facilities are nearby. Some facilities are wheelchair accessible. Leashed pets are permitted.

Reservations, fees: Reservations are accepted at 800/452-5687 or www.oregonstateparks.org ($8 reservation fee). Tent sites are $12–19 per night, RV sites are $16–24 per night, $5 per night per extra vehicle. Group areas are

$40–71 per night; yurts are $27–36 per night. Some credit cards are accepted. Open year-round.
Directions: From Grants Pass, drive south on I-5 for 12 miles to Exit 45B/Valley of the Rogue State Park. Take that exit, turn right, and drive a short distance to the park on the right.
Contact: Valley of the Rogue State Park, 541/582-1118 or 800/551-6949, www.oregonstateparks.org.

203 KOA GOLD N' ROGUE

Scenic rating: 6

on the Rogue River

This campground is set 0.5 mile from the Rogue River, with bike paths, a golf course, and the Oregon Vortex (the house of mystery) in the vicinity. It's one of the many campgrounds between Gold Hill and Grants Pass.
Campsites, facilities: There are 64 sites with full hookups for RVs of any length, 12 tent sites, and four cabins. Some sites are pull-through. Picnic tables are provided, and tent sites have fire rings. Restrooms with flush toilets and showers, modem access, propane gas, a dump station, firewood, a convenience store, coin laundry, ice, a playground, and a seasonal swimming pool are available. A café is within one mile, and boat-launching facilities are within five miles. Leashed pets are permitted.
Reservations, fees: Reservations are accepted at 800/562-7608. Sites are $25–38 per night, plus $2 per person per night for more than two people. Some credit cards are accepted. Open year-round.
Directions: From Medford, drive north on I-5 for 10 miles to South Gold Hill and Exit 40. Take that exit, turn right, and drive 0.25 mile to Blackwell Road. Turn right (on a paved road) and drive 0.25 mile to the park.
Contact: KOA Gold n' Rogue, 541/855-7710, www.koa.com.

204 LAKE SELMAC

Scenic rating: 9

on Lake Selmac

Nestled in a wooded, mountainous area, this 300-acre park offers boating, hiking, sailing, swimming, and good trophy bass fishing on beautiful, 160-acre Lake Selmac. Horse trails are also available. There are seasonal hosts and an assistant park ranger on-site.
Campsites, facilities: There are 94 sites for tents or RVs up to 40 feet long, some with full or partial hookups, and a group area for up to 50 people. There are also six horse camps with corrals and two yurts. Picnic tables and fire pits are provided. Drinking water, restrooms with coin showers, a dump station, convenience store, picnic area, horseshoe pits, playground, ball fields, two boat ramps, and a dock are available. Some facilities are wheelchair accessible. Leashed pets are permitted.
Reservations, fees: Reservations are accepted ($8 reservation fee) at 800/452-5687 or www.reserveamerica.com. Sites are $19–22 per night, $5 per night per additional vehicle, $19 per night for a horse site, $32 per night for a yurt, $32 per night for the first 12 people at the group site, and $3 per person per night for more than 12 people. Open year-round, with some facility limitations in winter.
Directions: In Grants Pass on I-5, take the U.S. 199 exit. Turn south on U.S. 199 and drive for 23 miles to Selma. Continue 0.5 mile to the Lake Selmac exit (Lakeshore Drive). Turn left (east) and drive 2.3 miles to the lake and the campground entrance.
Contact: Josephine County Parks, 541/474-5285, fax 541/474-5288, www.co.josephine.or.us/parks/index.htm.

205 LAKE SELMAC RESORT

Scenic rating: 7

on Lake Selmac

This resort borders the shore of Lake Selmac, a 160-acre lake. Fishing is great for largemouth bass (the state record has been set here three times). Bluegill, catfish, crappie, and trout are also catchable here. Fishing derbies are held during the summer. There is a 5-mph speed limit on the lake. Watch for waterfowl, including eagles, geese, osprey, and swans. A trail circles the lake, and bikers, hikers, and horses are welcome. A disc golf course is 1.5 miles away at the county park, and a golf course is about six miles away. Oregon Caves National Monument, about 30 miles away, makes a good side trip.

Campsites, facilities: There are 29 sites with partial hookups for tents or RVs of any length; most sites are pull-through. Drinking water, fire rings, and picnic tables are provided. Restrooms with flush toilets and showers, firewood, a general store, café, coin laundry, ice, propane, bait and tackle, miniature golf, and a playground are available. Boat docks and launching facilities are nearby, and rentals are on-site. Leashed pets are permitted.

Reservations, fees: Reservations are accepted. Sites are $30–35 per night, $3 per night per additional vehicle. Some credit cards are accepted. Open year-round, with limited winter facilities.

Directions: In Grants Pass on I-5, take the U.S. 199 exit. Turn southwest on U.S. 199 and drive 23 miles to Selma and the Lake Selmac exit (Lakeshore Drive). Turn left (east) and drive 2.5 miles to the lake and the resort on the left.

Contact: Lake Selmac Resort, 541/597-2277, www.lakeselmacresort.com.

206 MOUNTAIN MAN RV PARK

Scenic rating: 7

on the Illinois River

This park on the Illinois River provides good opportunities for swimming and boating (no motors are permitted). And yes, there is a mountain man here who often shows up in costume in the evening when camp groups build a fire. Great Cats World Park, a wildlife park, is 1.5 miles away. Other nearby side trips include Oregon Caves National Monument (21 miles) and Grants Pass (31 miles). Crescent City is 50 miles away. Note that a majority of the campground is taken by monthly rentals, with the remainder available for overnighters. This park was previously known as Town and Country RV Park.

Campsites, facilities: There are 51 sites for tents or RVs of any length (full hookups); some sites are pull-through. Picnic tables are provided, and some sites have fire rings. Cable TV, restrooms with showers, coin laundry, a community fire ring, and ice are available. Horseshoe pits and a clubhouse are also available. Leashed pets are permitted.

Reservations, fees: Reservations are accepted. Sites are $17–25 per night, plus $3 per person per night for more than two people. Monthly rates are available. Open year-round.

Directions: In Grants Pass on I-5, take the U.S. 199 exit. Go 30 miles west on U.S. 199 (past Cave Junction) to the park on the right.

Contact: Mountain Man RV Park, 541/592-2656 (phone or fax).

207 COUNTRY HILLS RESORT

Scenic rating: 7

near Oregon Caves National Monument

Lots of sites at this wooded camp border Sucker Creek, a popular spot for swimming. Several wineries are located within two miles. Lake Selmac and Oregon Caves National Monument provide nearby side-trip options.

Campsites, facilities: There are 12 tent sites and 20 sites with partial or full hookups for RVs of any length; some are pull-through sites. There are also six cabins and a five-unit motel. Picnic tables and fire rings are provided. Restrooms with flush toilets and coin showers, a dump station, modem access, drinking water, firewood, a convenience store, coin laundry, motel, seasonal ice cream parlor, seasonal café, and ice are available. Leashed pets are permitted.

Reservations, fees: Reservations are accepted. Sites are $16–21 per night, $3 per night per additional vehicle. Some credit cards are accepted. Open year-round.

Directions: In Grants Pass on I-5, take the U.S. 199 exit. Go 28 miles on U.S. 199 to the junction of Cave Junction and Highway 46/ Oregon Caves. Turn left on Highway 46 and drive eight miles to the resort on the right.

Contact: Country Hills Resort, 541/592-3406 (phone or fax).

208 GRAYBACK

Scenic rating: 7

near Oregon Caves National Monument in Siskiyou National Forest

This wooded campground (2,000 feet elevation) along the banks of Sucker Creek has sites with ample shade. It's a good choice if you're planning to visit Oregon Caves National Monument, about 10 miles away. The camp, set in a grove of old-growth firs, is also a prime place for bird-watching. A 0.5-mile trail cuts through the camp.

Campsites, facilities: There are 39 sites for tents and one RV site with partial hookups. Picnic tables, garbage bins, and fire grills are provided. Flush toilets and drinking water are available. Some facilities are wheelchair accessible, including a 0.5-mile trail. Leashed pets are permitted.

Reservations, fees: Reservations are not accepted. Sites are $16 per night, $5 per night per additional vehicle. Open May–September, weather permitting.

Directions: In Grants Pass on I-5, take Exit 55 for U.S. 199. Bear southwest on U.S. 199 for 30 miles to Cave Junction and Highway 46. Turn east on Highway 46 and drive 12 miles to the campground on the right.

Contact: Siskiyou National Forest, Wild Rivers Ranger District, 541/592-4000, fax 541/592-4010, www.fs.fed.us.

209 CAVE CREEK

Scenic rating: 7

near Oregon Caves National Monument in Siskiyou National Forest

No campground is closer to Oregon Caves National Monument than this U.S. Forest Service camp, a mere four miles away. There is even a two-mile trail out of camp that leads directly to the caves. The camp, at an elevation of 2,500 feet, lies in a grove of old-growth timber along the banks of Cave Creek, a small stream with some trout fishing opportunities (catch-and-release only). The sites are shaded, and an abundance of wildlife can be spotted in the area. Hiking opportunities abound.

Campsites, facilities: There are 18 sites for tents or RVs up to 16 feet long. Picnic tables and fire rings are provided. Drinking water, garbage bins, and vault toilets are available.

Showers are within eight miles. Leashed pets are permitted.

Reservations, fees: Reservations are not accepted. Sites are $10 per night, $4 per night per additional vehicle. Open mid-May–mid-September, weather permitting.

Directions: In Grants Pass on I-5, take Exit 55 for U.S. 199. Bear southwest on U.S. 199 for 30 miles to Cave Junction and Highway 46. Turn east on Highway 46 and drive 16 miles to the campground on the right.

Contact: Siskiyou National Forest, Wild Rivers Ranger District, 541/592-4000, fax 541/592-4010, www.fs.fed.us.

210 BOLAN LAKE

ATLAS 19 D5

Scenic rating: 9

on Bolan Lake in Siskiyou National Forest

BEST

Very few out-of-towners know about this camp, with pretty, shaded sites along the shore of 15-acre Bolan Lake. The lake is stocked with trout, and the fishing can be good. Only non-motorized boats are allowed. A trail from the lake leads up to a fire lookout and ties into miles of other trails, including the Bolan Lake Trail. This spot is truly a bird-watcher's paradise, with a variety of species to view. The camp is set at 5,500 feet elevation.

Campsites, facilities: There are 12 sites for tents or RVs up to 16 feet long. Picnic tables and fire grills are provided. Vault toilets and firewood are available. There is no drinking water. Leashed pets are permitted.

Reservations, fees: Reservations are not accepted. Sites are $5 per night per vehicle. Open June–early October, weather permitting.

Directions: From Grants Pass, drive south on U.S. 199 for 30 miles to Cave Junction and Rockydale Road (County Road 5560). Turn left (southeast) on Rockydale Road and drive eight miles to County Road 5828 (also called Waldo Road and Happy Camp Road). Turn southeast and drive 14 miles to Forest Road 4812. Turn left (east) and drive four miles to Forest Road 4812-040. Turn left (south) and drive two miles to the campground. This access road is very narrow and rough. Large RVs are strongly discouraged.

Contact: Siskiyou National Forest, Wild Rivers Ranger District, 541/592-4000, fax 541/592-4010, www.fs.fed.us.

South of Grants Pass near CA border
3¼ hrs (140 mi) from McKinleyville
leaves 240 mi to Bend

211 FAREWELL BEND

Scenic rating: 7

on the Upper Rogue River in Rogue River National Forest

Extremely popular Farewell Bend campground is set at an elevation of 3,400 feet along the banks of the Upper Rogue River near the Rogue River Gorge. A 0.25-mile barrier-free trail leads from camp to the Rogue Gorge Viewpoint and is definitely worth the trip. The Upper Rogue River Trail passes near camp. This spot attracts a lot of the campers visiting Crater Lake.

Campsites, facilities: There are 61 sites for tents or RVs up to 40 feet long. Picnic tables, fire grills, and fire rings are provided. Drinking water, firewood, and flush toilets are available. Some facilities are wheelchair accessible. Leashed pets are permitted.

Reservations, fees: Reservations are not accepted. Sites are $16 per night, $8 per night per additional vehicle. Open mid-May–late October, weather permitting.

Directions: From Medford, drive northeast on Highway 62 for 57 miles (near Union Creek) to the campground on the left.

Contact: Rogue River National Forest, Prospect Ranger District, 541/560-3400, fax 541/560-3444; Rogue Recreation, 541/560-3900, www.fs.fed.us.

212 UNION CREEK

Scenic rating: 8

near the Upper Rogue River in Rogue River National Forest

One of the most popular camps in the district, this spot is more developed than the nearby camps of Mill Creek, Natural Bridge, and River Bridge. It sits at 3,200 feet elevation along the banks of Union Creek, where the creek joins the Upper Rogue River. The Upper Rogue River Trail passes near camp. Interpretive programs are offered in the summer, and a convenience store and restaurant are within walking distance.

Campsites, facilities: There are 78 sites for tents or RVs up to 30 feet long, and three RV sites with full hookups. Picnic tables and fire grills are provided. A restroom with flush toilets, vault toilets, drinking water, and garbage service are available. Firewood is available for purchase. An amphitheater is available for programs. A store and restaurant are within walking distance. Some facilities are wheelchair accessible. Leashed pets are permitted.

Reservations, fees: Reservations are not accepted. Sites are $12 per night, $6 per night per additional vehicle. Open mid-May–mid-October, weather permitting.

Directions: From Medford, drive northeast on Highway 62 for 56 miles (near Union Creek) to the campground on the left.

Contact: Rogue River National Forest, Prospect Ranger District, 541/560-3400, fax 541/560-3444; Rogue Recreation, 541/560-3900, www.fs.fed.us.

213 NATURAL BRIDGE

Scenic rating: 8

on the Upper Rogue River Trail in Rogue River National Forest

BEST

Expect lots of company in midsummer at this popular camp, which sits at an elevation of 3,200 feet, where the Upper Rogue River runs underground. The Upper Rogue River Trail passes by the camp and follows the river for many miles to the Pacific Crest Trail in Crater Lake National Park. There is an interpretive area and a spectacular geological viewpoint adjacent to the camp. A 0.25-mile, barrier-free trail is also available.

Campsites, facilities: There are 17 sites for tents or RVs up to 30 feet long. Picnic tables, garbage service, and fire grills are provided. Vault toilets are available, but there is no drinking water. Some facilities are wheelchair accessible. Leashed pets are permitted.

Reservations, fees: Reservations are not accepted. Sites are $10 per night, $5 per night per additional vehicle. Open May–early November, weather permitting.

Directions: From Medford, drive northeast on Highway 62 for 55 miles (near Union Creek) to Forest Road 300. Turn left and drive one mile west to the campground on the right.

Contact: Rogue River National Forest, Prospect Ranger District, 541/560-3400, fax 541/560-3444; Rogue Recreation, 541/560-3900, www.fs.fed.us.

214 ABBOTT CREEK

Scenic rating: 8

on Abbott and Woodruff Creeks in Rogue River National Forest

BEST

Situated at the confluence of Abbott and Woodruff Creeks about two miles from the Upper Rogue River, this camp is a better choice for visitors with children than some of the others along the Rogue River. Abbott Creek is small and tame compared to the roaring Rogue. The elevation here is 3,100 feet.

Campsites, facilities: There are 25 sites for tents or RVs up to 22 feet long. Picnic tables, garbage service, and fire grills are provided. Drinking water, vault toilets, and firewood are available. Leashed pets are permitted.

Reservations, fees: Reservations are not accepted. Sites are $10 per night, $6 per night per additional vehicle. Open mid-May–late October, weather permitting.

Directions: From Medford, drive northeast on Highway 62 for 50 miles (near Union Creek) to Forest Road 68. Turn left and drive 3.5 miles west to the campground on the left.

Contact: Rogue River National Forest, Prospect Ranger District, 541/560-3400, fax 541/560-3444; Rogue Recreation, 541/560-3900, www.fs.fed.us.

215 MILL CREEK

Scenic rating: 7

near the Upper Rogue River in Rogue River National Forest

This campground (elevation of 2,800 feet) along the banks of Mill Creek, about two miles from the Upper Rogue River, features beautiful, private sites and heavy vegetation. One in a series of remote, primitive camps near Highway 62 missed by out-of-towners, this camp is an excellent choice for tenters.

Campsites, facilities: There are 10 sites for tents. Picnic tables, garbage service, and fire grills are provided. Vault toilets are available. There is no drinking water. Leashed pets are permitted.

Reservations, fees: Reservations are not accepted. Sites are $8 per night, $4 per night per additional vehicle. Open early May–November, weather permitting.

Directions: From Medford, drive north on Highway 62 for 46 miles (near Union Creek) to Forest Road 6200-030. Turn right (southeast) and drive one mile to the campground on the left.

Contact: Rogue River National Forest, Prospect Ranger District, 541/560-3400, fax 541/560-3444; Rogue Recreation, 541/560-3900, www.fs.fed.us.

216 RIVER BRIDGE

Scenic rating: 7

on the Upper Rogue River in Rogue River National Forest

River Bridge campground, situated at 2,900 feet elevation along the banks of the Upper Rogue River, is particularly scenic, with secluded sites and river views. This is a calmer part of the Wild and Scenic Upper Rogue River, but swimming and rafting are not recommended. The Upper Rogue River Trail passes by the camp and follows the river for many miles to the Pacific Crest Trail in Crater Lake National Park.

Campsites, facilities: There are eight sites for tents or RVs up to 22 feet long. Picnic tables, garbage service, and fireplaces are provided. Vault toilets are available, but there is no drinking water. Leashed pets are permitted.

Reservations, fees: Reservations are not accepted. Sites are $8 per night, $4 per night per additional vehicle. Open early May–November, weather permitting.

Directions: From Medford, drive northeast on Highway 62 (Crater Lake Highway) for 42 miles (before reaching Union Creek) to Forest Road 6210. Turn left and drive one mile to the campground on the right.

Contact: Rogue River National Forest, Prospect Ranger District, 541/560-3400, fax 541/560-3444; Rogue Recreation, 541/560-3900, www.fs.fed.us.

217 HUCKLEBERRY MOUNTAIN

Scenic rating: 6

near Crater Lake National Park in Rogue River National Forest

Here's a hideaway for Crater Lake visitors. The camp is located at the site of an old 1930s Civilian Conservation Corps camp, and an OHV trail runs through and next to the campground. Set at an elevation of 5,400 feet, this spot, about 15 miles from the entrance to Crater Lake National Park, really does get overlooked by highway travelers, so you have a good shot at privacy. About 10 miles of rough roads keep traffic down most of the time.

Campsites, facilities: There are 25 sites for tents or RVs up to 26 feet long. Picnic tables and fireplaces are provided. Drinking water and vault toilets are available. Garbage must be packed out. Leashed pets are permitted.

Reservations, fees: Reservations are not accepted. There is no fee for camping. Open June–late October, weather permitting.

Directions: From Medford, drive north on Highway 62 for 50 miles (near Union Creek) to Forest Road 60. Turn right and drive 12 miles to the campground.

Contact: Rogue River National Forest, Prospect Ranger District, 541/560-3400, fax 541/560-3444; Rogue Recreation, 541/560-3900, www.fs.fed.us.

218 MAZAMA

Scenic rating: 6

near the Pacific Crest Trail in Crater Lake National Park

One of two campgrounds at Crater Lake—the other being Lost Creek—this camp sits at 6,000 feet elevation and is known for cold nights, even in late June and early September. I once got caught in a snowstorm here at the opening in mid-June. A nearby store is a great convenience. Seasonal boat tours and junior ranger programs are available. The Pacific Crest Trail passes through the park, but the only trail access down to Crater Lake is at Cleetwood Cove. Note that winter access to the park is from the west only on Highway 62 to Rim Village.

Campsites, facilities: There are 200 sites for tents or self-contained RVs up to 32 feet long; there are no hookups. Picnic tables, fire grills, bear-proof food lockers, and garbage bins are provided. Drinking water, restrooms with flush toilets and coin showers, a dump station, coin laundry, gasoline, mini-mart, firewood, and ice are available. Some facilities are wheelchair accessible. Leashed pets are permitted in the campground and on paved roads only.

Reservations, fees: Reservations are not accepted. Sites are $14.75 per night, RV space is $15.75 per night, plus a $10 park-entrance fee per vehicle and $3 per person per night for more than two people. Some credit cards are accepted. Open early June–mid October, weather permitting.

Directions: From I-5 at Medford, turn east on Highway 62 and drive 72 miles into Crater Lake National Park and to Annie Springs junction. Turn left and drive a short distance to the national park entrance kiosk. Just beyond the kiosk, turn right to the campground and Mazama store entrance.

Contact: Crater Lake National Park, 541/594-3000, www.nps.gov/crla.

219 LOST CREEK

Scenic rating: 6

near the Crater Lake Pinnacles in Crater Lake National Park

In good weather, this is a prime spot in Crater Lake National Park; you avoid most of the crowd on Rim Drive. This campground is located near little Lost Creek and the Pinnacles, a series of spires. The only trail access down to Crater Lake is at Cleetwood Cove. Set in a lodgepole pine forest, the camp is more private than Mazama Campground. The roads in the campground are paved, and there is a possibility (hint, hint) that a black bear could visit your campsite. Be sure to follow bear precautions.

Campsites, facilities: There are 16 sites for tents. Picnic tables and fire grills are provided. Drinking water, flush toilets, and garbage bins are available. Leashed pets are permitted in the campground and on paved roads only.

Reservations, fees: Reservations are not accepted. Sites are $10 per night, plus a $10 park entrance fee per vehicle and $3 per person per night for more than two people. Open mid-July–mid-September, weather permitting.

Directions: From I-5 at Medford, turn east on Highway 62 and drive 72 miles into Crater Lake National Park and to Annie Springs junction. Turn left and drive less than one mile to the junction with Rim Drive. Turn right and drive east on Rim Drive for 8.5 miles to Pinnacles Road Junction. Turn right on Pinnacles Road and drive five miles to the campground.

Contact: Crater Lake National Park, 541/594-3000, fax 541/594-3010, www.nps.gov/crla.

220 FLY CASTERS RV PARK

Scenic rating: 6

on the Rogue River

This spot along the banks of the Rogue River is a good base camp for RVers who want to fish or hike. The county park, located across the river in Shady Cove, offers picnic facilities and a boat ramp. Lost Creek Lake is about a 15-minute drive northeast. Note that about half of the sites are taken by long-term rentals.

Campsites, facilities: There are 47 sites with full hookups for RVs of any length; two are pull-through sites. Picnic tables are provided. Restrooms with flush toilets and showers, propane gas, cable TV, wireless Internet service, a clubhouse, barbecue area, and coin laundry are available. A store, café, and ice are within one mile. Boat-launching facilities are nearby. Leashed pets are permitted.

Reservations, fees: Reservations are accepted. Sites are $25–38 per night. Some credit cards are accepted. Monthly rates are available. Open year-round.

Directions: From Medford, drive northeast on Highway 62 for 21 miles to the park on the left.

Contact: Fly Casters RV Park, 541/878-2749, fax 541/878-2742.

221 BEAR MOUNTAIN RV PARK

Scenic rating: 7

on the Rogue River

This campground is set in an open, grassy area on the Rogue River about six miles from Lost Creek Lake, where boat ramps and picnic areas are available for day use. The campsites are spacious and shaded.

Campsites, facilities: There is a grassy area for tent sites and 37 sites with full or partial hookups for RVs of any length. Drinking water and picnic tables are provided. Restrooms with flush toilets and showers, propane gas, coin laundry, ice, and a playground are available. A store and café are within one mile. Boat docks and launching facilities are nearby. Leashed pets are permitted.

Reservations, fees: Reservations are accepted at 541/878-2400 (from Oregon) or 800/586-2327 (from outside Oregon). Sites are $20–24 per night, plus $2 per person per night for more than two adults. Some credit cards are accepted. Open year-round.

Directions: From Medford, drive northeast on Highway 62 to the junction with Highway 227. Continue east on Highway 62 for 2.5 more miles to the park on the left.

Contact: Bear Mountain RV Park, 541/878-2400.

222 ROGUE ELK CAMPGROUND

Scenic rating: 8

on the Rogue River east of the city of Trail

Right on the Rogue River at an elevation of 1,476 feet, the park has creek swimming (unsupervised), a Douglas fir forest, fishing, hiking trails, rafting, and wildlife. With 33 acres of space and 0.75 mile of river frontage, this is Jackson County's most popular park. The forest is very beautiful here. Lost Creek Lake on Highway 62 makes a good side trip.

Campsites, facilities: There are 15 sites for tents or RVs of up to 25 feet long; some have partial hookups. Picnic tables and fire pits are provided. Drinking water, restrooms with flush toilets and coin showers, garbage bins, a dump station, boat ramp, and playground are available. A café, mini-mart, ice, coin laundry, and firewood are available within three miles. Some facilities are wheelchair accessible. Leashed pets are permitted.

Reservations, fees: Reservations are not accepted. Family sites are $18–32 per night and $1 per pet per night. Open mid-April–mid-October.

Directions: From Medford, take Exit 30 for the Crater Lake Highway (Highway 62) and drive northeast on Highway 62 for 29 miles to the park entrance on the right.

Contact: Jackson County Parks, 541/774-8183, fax 541/774-6320, www.jacksoncountyparks.com.

223 JOSEPH H. STEWART STATE PARK

Scenic rating: 7

on Lost Creek Reservoir

This state park is on the shore of Lost Creek Reservoir, about 40 miles from Crater Lake National Park, and is home to 11 miles of hiking and biking trails, a lake with a beach, boat rentals, and a marina. Grassy sites are spacious and sprinkled with conifers. The Cole River Hatchery is available for tours.

Note: At time of publication, a blue-green algae health advisory was in effect.

Campsites, facilities: There are 151 sites with partial hookups for tents or self-contained RVs, including some sites for RVs of any length, and 50 sites with water for tents or self-contained RVs. There are also two group areas for tents for up to 50 people each. Picnic tables and fire grills are provided. Restrooms with flush toilets and showers, garbage bins, drinking water, a dump station, firewood, and a playground with volleyball and horseshoes are available. Boat rentals, launching facilities, a swimming area, and a picnic area that can be reserved are nearby. Some facilities are wheelchair accessible. Leashed pets are permitted.

Reservations, fees: Reservations are accepted for the group sites at 800/452-5687 or www.oregonstateparks.org ($8 reservation fee) but are not accepted for single sites. Tent sites are $10–17 per night, sites for tents or RVs are $12–20 per night, $5 per night per additional vehicle. The group site is $40–71, plus $2.40–3 per person per night for more than 25 people. Some credit cards are accepted. Open year-round, weather permitting.

Directions: From Medford, drive northeast on Highway 62 for 34 miles to the Lost Creek Reservoir and the campground on the left.

Contact: Joseph H. Stewart State Park, 541/560-3334 or 800/551-6949, www.oregonstateparks.org.

224 WHISKEY SPRINGS

Scenic rating: 9

near Butte Falls in Rogue River National Forest

This campground at Whiskey Springs, near Fourbit Ford Campground, is one of the larger, more developed backwoods U.S. Forest Service camps in the area. A one-mile, wheelchair-accessible nature trail passes nearby. You can see beaver dams and woodpeckers here. The camp is set at 3,200 feet elevation.

Campsites, facilities: There are 36 sites for tents or RVs up to 30 feet long. Picnic tables, garbage service, and fire grills are provided. Drinking water and vault toilets are available. Some facilities are wheelchair accessible. Leashed pets are permitted.

Reservations, fees: Reservations are not accepted. Sites are $10 per night, $5 per night per additional vehicle. Open mid-May–September, weather permitting.

Directions: From Medford, drive northeast on Highway 62 for 14 miles to the Butte Falls Highway. Turn right and drive east for 16 miles to the town of Butte Falls. Continue southeast on Butte Falls Highway for nine miles to Forest Road 3065. Turn left on Forest Road 3065 and drive 300 yards to the campground on the left.

Contact: Rogue River National Forest, Butte Falls Ranger District, 541/865-2700, fax 541/865-2795, www.fs.fed.us.

225 IMNAHA

Scenic rating: 7

near the Sky Lakes Wilderness in Rogue River National Forest

Located along Imnaha Creek at an elevation of 3,800 feet, this campground makes a good base camp for a wilderness trip. Trailheads at the ends of the nearby forest roads lead east into the Sky Lakes Wilderness; there are also two shorter interpretive trails.

Campsites, facilities: There are four sites for tents or RVs up to 30 feet long. A cabin is also available. Picnic tables and fire grills are provided. Vault toilets, drinking water, and garbage service are available. Leashed pets are permitted.

Reservations, fees: Reservations are accepted only for the cabin at 877/444-6777 or www.recreation.gov ($10 reservation fee). Sites are $10 per night, $5 per night per additional vehicle, and $40 per night for the cabin. Open mid-May–October, weather permitting.

Directions: From Medford, drive northeast on Highway 62 for about 35 miles to Prospect and Mill Creek Drive. Turn right and drive one mile to County Road 992/Butte Falls Prospect Highway. Turn right and drive 2.5 miles to Forest Road 37. Turn left and drive 10 miles east to the campground.

Contact: Rogue River National Forest, Butte Falls Ranger District, 541/865-2700, fax 541/865-2795, www.fs.fed.us.

226 SOUTH FORK

Scenic rating: 7

on the South Rogue River in Rogue River National Forest

South Fork campground is set at an elevation of 4,000 feet along the South Rogue River. To the east, trails at the ends of the nearby forest roads provide access to the Sky Lakes Wilderness. The Southfork Trail, across the road from the campground, has a good biking trail in one direction and a hiking trail in the other. A map of Rogue River National Forest details all back roads, trails, and waters.

Campsites, facilities: There are two sites for tents and four sites for tents or RVs up to 16 feet long. Picnic tables, drinking water, garbage service, and fire grills are provided. Vault toilets are available. Leashed pets are permitted.

Reservations, fees: Reservations are not accepted. Sites are $10 per night, $5 per night per additional vehicle. Open early June–mid-November, weather permitting.
Directions: From Medford, drive northeast on Highway 62 for 14 miles to Butte Falls Highway. Turn right and drive 16 miles east to the town of Butte Falls. Continue one mile past Butte Falls to County Road 992 (Butte Falls Prospect Highway) and drive nine miles to Forest Road 34. Turn right and drive 8.5 miles to the campground on the right.
Contact: Rogue River National Forest, Butte Falls Ranger District, 541/865-2700, fax 541/865-2795, www.fs.fed.us.

227 MEDFORD OAKS RV PARK

Scenic rating: 6

near Eagle Point

This park is in a quiet, rural setting among the trees. Just a short hop off I-5, it's an excellent choice for travelers heading to or from California. The campground is located along the shore of a pond that provides good fishing. Most sites are filled with monthly renters.
Campsites, facilities: There are six sites for tents and 55 sites with full or partial hookups for RVs of any length; most sites are pull-through. There are also three cabins. Restrooms with coin showers, a dump station, modem access, coin laundry, limited groceries, ice, RV supplies, and propane gas are available. Recreational facilities include a seasonal, heated swimming pool, movies, horseshoe pits, table tennis, a recreation field for baseball and volleyball, and a playground. Leashed pets are allowed with certain restrictions.
Reservations, fees: Reservations are recommended. Sites are $28–33 per night. Group rates are available. Some credit cards are accepted. Open year-round.
Directions: From Medford, drive northeast on Highway 62 for five miles to Exit 30 and Highway 140. Turn east on Highway 140 and drive 6.8 miles to the park on the left.
Contact: Medford Oaks RV Park, 541/826-5103, fax 541/826-5984, www.medfordoaks.com.

228 FOURBIT FORD

Scenic rating: 6

on Fourbit Creek in Rogue River National Forest

Fourbit Ford campground, situated at an elevation of 3,200 feet along Fourbit Creek, is one in a series of hidden spots tucked away near County Road 821.
Campsites, facilities: There are seven sites for tents. Picnic tables and fire grills are provided. Vault toilets, drinking water, and garbage service are available. Leashed pets are permitted.
Reservations, fees: Reservations are not accepted. Sites are $10 per night, $5 per extra vehicle per night. Open mid-May–late September, weather permitting.
Directions: From Medford, drive northeast on Highway 62 for 14 miles to Butte Falls Highway. Turn right and drive 16 miles east to the town of Butte Falls and County Road 821. Turn left and drive nine miles southeast to Forest Road 3065. Turn left and drive one mile to the campground on the left.
Contact: Rogue River National Forest, Butte Falls Ranger District, 541/865-2700, fax 541/865-2795, www.fs.fed.us.

229 WILLOW LAKE RESORT

Scenic rating: 9

on Willow Lake

This campground sits on the shore of Willow Lake. Located at the base of Mount

McLoughlin at an elevation of 3,200 feet, it encompasses 927 wooded acres. The lake has fishing opportunities for bass, crappie, and trout. A hiking trail starts near camp. Waterskiing is allowed at the lake.

Campsites, facilities: There are 26 sites for tents or RVs (no hookups), 54 sites for tents or RVs (full or partial hookups), and a group area with 11 sites. There are also four cabins. Picnic tables and fire rings are provided. Restrooms with flush toilets and coin showers, a dump station, and firewood are available. A store, boat ramp, and boat rentals are on-site. Leashed pets are permitted.

Reservations, fees: Reservations are accepted for groups and cabins only at 541/560-3900. Sites are $15–25 per night, and it's $1 per pet per night. The group area is $175 per night. Open April–October.

Directions: From Medford, drive northeast on Highway 62 for 15 miles to Butte Falls Highway. Turn east and drive 25 miles to Willow Lake Road. Turn right (south) and drive two miles to the campground.

Contact: Rogue Recreation, 541/560-3900.

230 PARKER MEADOWS

Scenic rating: 7

on Parker Meadow in Rogue River National Forest

Fantastic views of nearby Mount McLoughlin are among the highlights of this rustic camp set at 5,000 feet elevation in a beautiful meadow. Trailheads at the ends of the forest roads lead into the Sky Lakes Wilderness. Parker Meadows is a nice spot, complete with water and lots of privacy between sites. Except during hunting season in the fall, this camp does not get much use.

Campsites, facilities: There are eight sites for tents or RVs up to 16 feet long. Picnic tables and fire grills are provided. Vault toilets, drinking water, and garbage service are available. Leashed pets are permitted.

Reservations, fees: Reservations are not accepted. Sites are $10 per night, $5 per night per additional vehicle. Open mid-June–late October, weather permitting.

Directions: From Medford, drive northeast on Highway 62 for 14 miles to Butte Falls Highway. Turn right and drive 16 miles east to the town of Butte Falls and County Road 821. Turn left and drive 10 miles southeast to Forest Road 37. Turn left and drive 11 miles to the campground on the left.

Contact: Rogue River National Forest, Butte Falls Ranger District, 541/865-2700, fax 541/865-2795, www.fs.fed.us.

231 ODESSA

Scenic rating: 4

near Klamath Lake in Winema National Forest

This campground (4,100 feet elevation) borders Odessa Creek, near the shore of Upper Klamath Lake. The lake is the main attraction, with fishing the main activity. The lake can provide excellent fishing for rainbow trout on both flies and Rapalas. Boating is also popular. Campsites sit among scattered mixed conifers and native brush.

Campsites, facilities: There are five tent sites. Picnic tables, garbage bins, and fire grills are provided. Vault toilets are available, but there is no drinking water. Leashed pets are permitted.

Reservations, fees: Reservations are not accepted. There is no fee for camping. Open year-round, weather permitting.

Directions: From Klamath Falls, drive west on Highway 140 about 18 miles to Forest Road 3639. Turn right (northeast) and drive one mile to the campground.

Contact: Fremont-Winema National Forests, Klamath Ranger District, 541/885-3400, fax 541/885-3452, www.fs.fed.us.

232 FOURMILE LAKE

Scenic rating: 8

at Fourmile Lake in Winema National Forest

This beautiful spot is the only camp on the shore of Fourmile Lake. Several nearby trails provide access to the Sky Lakes Wilderness. The Pacific Crest Trail passes about two miles from camp. Primitive and with lots of solitude, it attracts a calm and quiet crowd. Afternoon winds can be a problem, and in the evening, if the wind isn't blowing, the mosquitoes often arrive. Although this campground is near the foot of Mount McLoughlin (9,495 feet), there is no view of the mountain from here. Go to the east side of the lake for a good view.

Campsites, facilities: There are 25 sites for tents or RVs up to 22 feet long. Picnic tables, garbage bins, and fire grills are provided. Drinking water and vault toilets are available. Leashed pets are permitted.

Reservations, fees: Reservations are not accepted. Sites are $11 per night, $5.50 per night per additional vehicle. Open June–late September, weather permitting.

Directions: From Medford, drive northeast on Highway 62 for five miles to Exit 30 and Highway 140. Turn east on Highway 140 and drive approximately 40 miles to Forest Road 3661. Turn left (north) and drive six miles to the campground.

Contact: Fremont-Winema National Forests, Klamath Ranger District, 541/885-3400, fax 541/885-3452, www.fs.fed.us.

233 ROCKY POINT RESORT

Scenic rating: 7

on Upper Klamath Lake

Rocky Point Resort, at the Upper Klamath Wildlife Refuge, boasts 10 miles of canoe trails, along with opportunities for motorized boating and fishing. Ponderosa pines and Douglas firs create a quite picturesque setting for stellar sunsets and a peaceful retreat.

Campsites, facilities: There are 29 sites with partial or full hookups for RVs of any length, four tent sites, four cabins, and five motel rooms. Some sites are pull-through. Picnic tables and fire rings are provided. Restrooms with flush toilets and showers, drinking water, firewood, a convenience store, modem access, coin laundry, ice, a marina with boat gas, and boat and canoe rentals are available. There is a free boat launch and game area. A restaurant and lounge overlook the lake. Leashed pets are permitted.

Reservations, fees: Reservations are accepted. Sites are $28–30 per night, $4 per person per night for more than two people, $2 per pet per night, and $5 per night per additional vehicle. Some credit cards are accepted. Open April–November.

Directions: From Klamath Falls, drive northeast on Highway 140 for 25 miles to Rocky Point Road. Turn right and drive three miles to the resort on the right.

Contact: Rocky Point Resort, 541/356-2287, fax 541/356-2222, www.rockypointoregon.com.

234 WILLOW PRAIRIE

Scenic rating: 7

near Fish Lake in Rogue River National Forest

There are two campgrounds here, including one for equestrian campers. This spot is located near the origin of the west branch of Willow Creek and next to a beaver swamp and several large ponds that attract deer, ducks, elk, geese, and sandhill cranes. A number of riding trails pass nearby. A map of Rogue River National Forest details the back roads and can help you get here. Fish Lake is four miles south.

Campsites, facilities: There are 10 sites for tents or RVs up to 16 feet long, one primitive cabin with cots, and 10 equestrian sites. Picnic tables and fire grills are provided. Drinking water, vault toilets, and garbage service are available. The equestrian camp has 10 sites for tents or small RVs, two stock water troughs, and horse corrals. A store, café, ice, boat docks, launching facilities, and rentals are nearby. A camp host is on-site. Leashed pets are permitted.

Reservations, fees: Reservations are accepted only for the horse camp and cabin at 877/444-6777 or www.recreation.gov ($10 reservation fee). Sites are $10 per night, $5 per night per additional vehicle. Open late May–late October, weather permitting.

Directions: From Medford, drive northeast on Highway 62 for five miles to Exit 30 and Highway 140. Turn east on Highway 140 and drive 31.5 miles to Forest Road 37. Turn left and drive north 1.5 miles to Forest Road 3738. Turn left and drive one mile west to Forest Road 3735. Turn left and drive 100 yards to the campground. For the equestrian camp, continue for 0.25 mile to the campground entrance.

Contact: Rogue River National Forest, Butte Falls Ranger District, 541/865-2700, fax 541/865-2795, www.fs.fed.us.

235 NORTH FORK

Scenic rating: 7

near Fish Lake in Rogue River National Forest

Here is a small, pretty campground with easy access from the highway and proximity to Fish Lake. Situated on the north fork of Little Butte Creek at an elevation of 4,500 feet, it's fairly popular, so grab your spot early. Excellent fly-fishing can be found along the Fish Lake Trail, which leads directly out of camp.

Campsites, facilities: There are nine sites for tents or RVs up to 24 feet long. Picnic tables and fire grills are provided. Vault toilets and drinking water are available. Garbage must be packed out. A camp host is on-site. Boat docks, launching facilities, and rentals are nearby. Some facilities are wheelchair accessible. Leashed pets are permitted.

Reservations, fees: Reservations are not accepted. Sites are $8 per night, $4 per night per additional vehicle. Open May–mid-November, weather permitting.

Directions: From Medford, drive northeast on Highway 62 for five miles to Exit 30 and Highway 140. Turn east on Highway 140 and drive 31.5 miles to Forest Road 37. Turn right (south) and drive 0.5 mile to the campground.

Contact: Rogue River National Forest, Butte Falls District, 541/865-2700, fax 541/865-2795; Rogue Recreation, 541/560-3900, www.fs.fed.us.

236 FISH LAKE

Scenic rating: 8

on Fish Lake in Rogue River National Forest

Bicycling, boating, fishing, and hiking are among the recreation options at this campground on the north shore of Fish Lake. Easy, one-mile access to the Pacific Crest Trail is also available. If this campground is full, Doe Point and Fish Lake Resort are nearby.

Campsites, facilities: There are 19 sites for tents or RVs up to 40 feet long and two walk-in tent sites. Picnic tables, fire grills, and garbage bins are provided. Drinking water, flush toilets, a picnic shelter that can be reserved, a store, café, firewood, and ice are available. A camp host is on-site. Boat docks, launching facilities, boat rentals, coin laundry, dump station, and coin showers are nearby. Some facilities are wheelchair accessible. Leashed pets are permitted.

Reservations, fees: Reservations are accepted only for the picnic shelter at 541/560-3900. Sites are $16 per night, $8 per night per additional vehicle. Open mid-May–mid-October, weather permitting.

Directions: From Medford, drive northeast on Highway 62 for five miles to Exit 30 and Highway 140. Turn east on Highway 140 and drive 30 miles to the campground on the right.

Contact: Rogue River National Forest, Butte Falls District, 541/865-2700, fax 541/865-2795; Rogue Recreation, 541/560-3900, www.fs.fed.us.

237 DOE POINT

Scenic rating: 8

on Fish Lake in Rogue River National Forest

This campground (at 4,600 feet elevation) sits along the north shore of Fish Lake, nearly adjacent to Fish Lake Campground. Doe Point is slightly preferable because of its dense vegetation, offering shaded, quiet, well-screened sites. Privacy, rare at many campgrounds, can be found here. Recreation options include biking, boating, fishing, and hiking, plus an easy, one-mile access trail to the Pacific Crest Trail.

Campsites, facilities: There are five walk-in tent sites and 25 sites for tents or RVs up to 30 feet long. Picnic tables and fire grills are provided. Drinking water, garbage service, flush toilets, a store, café, firewood, and ice are available. Boat docks, launching facilities, boat rentals, showers, and a dump station are nearby. Some facilities are wheelchair accessible. Leashed pets are permitted.

Reservations, fees: Reservations are not accepted. Sites are $16 per night, $8 per night per additional vehicle. Open mid-May–late September, weather permitting.

Directions: From Medford, drive northeast on Highway 62 for five miles to Exit 30 and Highway 140. Turn east on Highway 140 and drive 30 miles to the campground on the right.

Contact: Rogue River National Forest, Butte Falls District, 541/865-2700, fax 541/865-2795, www.fs.fed.us; Rogue Recreation, 541/560-3900, www.fs.fed.us.

238 FISH LAKE RESORT

Scenic rating: 7

on Fish Lake

This resort along Fish Lake is privately operated under permit by the U.S. Forest Service and offers a resort-type feel, catering primarily to families. This is the largest and most developed of the three camps at Fish Lake. Bicycling, boating, fishing, and hiking are some of the activities here. Cozy cabins are available for rent. Boat speed on the lake is limited to 10 mph.

Campsites, facilities: There are 12 sites for tents, 46 sites with full hookups for RVs up to 38 feet long, and 11 cabins. Some sites are pull-through. Picnic tables, fire rings, drinking water, and garbage bins are provided. Restrooms with flush toilets and coin showers, propane gas, dump station, recreation hall, convenience store, café, coin laundry, ice, boat docks, boat rentals, and launching facilities are available. Leashed pets are permitted.

Reservations, fees: Reservations are accepted at 541/949-8500. Tent sites are $18–40 per night, and RV sites are $32–34 per night. Some credit cards are accepted. Open year-round, weather permitting, with limited winter facilities.

Directions: From Medford, take I-5 to Exit 30 and go to Highway 140. Turn east on Highway 140 and drive 30 miles to Fish Lake Road. Turn right (south) and drive 0.5 mile to the resort on the left.

Contact: Fish Lake Resort, 541/949-8500, www.fishlakeresort.net.

239 LAKE OF THE WOODS RESORT

Scenic rating: 9

on Lake of the Woods

BEST

On beautiful Lake of the Woods, this resort offers fishing (four kinds of trout, catfish, and bass) and boating in a secluded forest setting. It's on one of the most beautiful lakes in the Cascade Mountains, surrounded by tall pine trees. A family-oriented campground, it has all the amenities. In the winter, snowmobiling and cross-country skiing are popular. Attractions in the area include the Mountain Lakes Wilderness and the Pacific Crest Trail.

Campsites, facilities: There are 27 sites with full or partial hookups for tents or RVs up to 35 feet long and 26 cabins. Picnic tables and fire rings are provided. Restrooms with showers, a dump station, coin laundry, ice, snacks, a restaurant, lounge, and propane gas are available. There are also a boat ramp, dock, marina, boat and mountain bike rentals, and a barbecue area. Leashed pets are permitted.

Reservations, fees: Reservations are accepted at 866/201-4194. Sites are $28–35 per night, $7 per night per additional vehicle, and $1 per pet per night. Some credit cards are accepted. Open during summer season; call for winter schedule.

Directions: In Medford on I-5, take Exit 14 to Highway 62. Go six miles on Highway 62 to Highway 140/Lake of the Woods. Drive 59.6 miles on Lake of the Woods Road to the resort on the left.

Contact: Lake of the Woods Resort, 541/949-8300, fax 541/949-8229, www.lakeofthewoodsresort.com.

240 ASPEN POINT

Scenic rating: 8

on Lake of the Woods in Winema National Forest

BEST

This campground (at 5,000 feet elevation) is near the north shore of Lake of the Woods, adjacent to Lake of the Woods Resort. It's heavily timbered with old-growth fir and has a great view of Mount McLoughlin (9,495 feet). A hiking trail just north of camp leads north for several miles, meandering around Fourmile Lake and extending into the Sky Lakes Wilderness. Other trails nearby head into the Mountain Lakes Wilderness. Boating, fishing, swimming, and waterskiing are among the activities here. Note that of the 60 campsites, 20 are available by reservation; the rest are first-come, first-served.

Campsites, facilities: There are 18 single sites and two double sites for tents or RVs up to 55 feet long. Picnic tables, garbage bins, and fire grills are provided. Drinking water, a dump station, and flush toilets are available. Boat docks, launching facilities, and rentals are nearby. Some facilities are wheelchair accessible. Leashed pets are permitted.

Reservations, fees: Reservations are accepted at 877/444-6777 or www.recreation.gov ($10 reservation fee). Single sites are $16–17 per night, $34 for double sites, and $8 per night per additional vehicle. The group sites is $90–95 per night. Open late May–early September, weather permitting.

Directions: In Ashland on I-5, take Exit 14 to Highway 66. Drive east for less than a mile to Dead Indian Memorial Road. Turn left (east) and drive 40 miles to Lake of the Woods. Continue along the east shore to the campground turnoff on the left.

Contact: Fremont-Winema National Forests, Klamath Ranger District, 541/885-3400, fax 541/885-3452, www.fs.fed.us.

241 SUNSET

Scenic rating: 8

near Lake of the Woods in Winema National Forest

Sunset campground (at 5,000 feet elevation) near the eastern shore of Lake of the Woods is fully developed and offers a myriad of recreation options. It's popular for both fishing and boating. Of the 67 sites, 20 are available by reservation.

Campsites, facilities: There are 67 sites for tents or RVs up to 50 feet long. Picnic tables, garbage bins, and fire grills are provided. Drinking water and flush toilets are available. Boat docks, launching facilities, and rentals are nearby. Some facilities are wheelchair accessible. Leashed pets are permitted.

Reservations, fees: Reservations are accepted at 877/444-6777 or www.recreation.gov ($10 reservation fee). Sites are $17 per night, $8 per night per additional vehicle. Open late May–early September.

Directions: In Ashland on I-5, take Exit 14 to Highway 66. Drive east for less than a mile to Dead Indian Memorial Road. Turn left (east) and drive 40 miles to Lake of the Woods. Continue along the east shore to Forest Road 3738. Turn left (west) and drive 0.5 mile to the camp.

Contact: Fremont-Winema National Forests, Klamath Ranger District, 541/885-3400, fax 541/885-3452, www.fs.fed.us.

242 CANTRALL-BUCKLEY PARK & GROUP CAMP

Scenic rating: 8

on the Applegate River

This county park outside of Medford offers pleasant, shady sites in a wooded setting. Encompassing 88 acres of land, the camp has 1.75 miles of frontage along the Applegate River, which has good trout fishing.

Campsites, facilities: There are 42 sites for tents or self-contained RVs up to 25 feet long and one group area for 60–100 people. Picnic tables and fire pits are provided. Drinking water, restrooms with flush toilets and coin showers, and a picnic area that can be reserved are available. Recreational facilities include horseshoes, a playground, and a recreation field. Leashed pets are permitted.

Reservations, fees: Reservations are accepted only for the group site at 541/774-8183. Sites are $12 per night, $1 per pet per night, and $65 per night for the group site. Some credit cards are accepted with reservations only. Open mid-April–mid-October.

Directions: In Medford on I-5, take the Jacksonville exit to the Jacksonville Highway. Drive west on the Jacksonville Highway (Highway 238) for seven miles to Jacksonsville. Bear left on Highway 238 and drive to Hamilton Road. Turn left (south) on Hamilton Road and drive approximately 0.4 mile to Cantrall Road. Turn right on Cantrall and drive approximately 0.5 mile to the campground.

Contact: Jackson County Parks, 541/774-8183, fax 541/774-6320, www.jacksoncountyparks.com.

243 THE WELLSPRINGS

Scenic rating: 5

near Ashland

This wooded campground has mineral hot springs that empty into a swimming pool. Hot mineral baths are available in private rooms. Massages, sauna use, and swimming are also available for a fee. This is an old Native American birthing ground. Nearby recreation options include a bike path, a golf course, hiking trails, and tennis courts. Boating, fishing, and waterskiing are within 10 miles.

Campsites, facilities: There is a large grassy area for tents, 28 sites with full hookups for RVs of any length, and five tepees. Some sites are pull-through. Picnic tables and fire rings are provided. Restrooms with flush toilets and showers, coin laundry, ice, volleyball, massage therapists, a soaking pool, a swimming pool, and a sauna are available. Propane gas is within one mile. Leashed pets are permitted with deposit.

Reservations, fees: Reservations are not accepted. Tent sites are $15 per night, RV sites are $20 per night, $3–6 per person per night for more than two people, and tepees are $25 per night. Some credit cards are accepted. Open year-round.

Directions: From Ashland, drive north on I-5 to Exit 19. Take that exit and drive west for 0.25 mile to the stoplight at Highway 99. Turn right and drive 500 feet to the campground on the left.

Contact: The WellSprings, 541/482-3776.

244 GLENYAN CAMPGROUND OF ASHLAND

Scenic rating: 7

near Emigrant Lake

This campground, located within seven miles of Ashland and less than one mile from Emigrant Lake, offers shady sites. Recreation options in the area include a golf course and tennis courts. It's an easy jump from I-5 at Ashland.

Campsites, facilities: There are 22 tent sites and 46 sites with full or partial hookups for tents or RVs of any length. Drinking water, fire rings, and picnic tables are provided. Restrooms with flush toilets and showers, propane gas, a dump station, wireless Internet service, firewood, a recreation hall, convenience store, coin laundry, ice, a playground, and a seasonal heated swimming pool are available. Leashed pets are permitted.

Reservations, fees: Reservations are accepted at 877/453-6926. Sites are $29–32 per night, plus $2 per person per night for more than five people. Some credit cards are accepted. Open year-round.

Directions: From Ashland, drive east on Highway 66 for 3.5 miles to the campground on the right.

Contact: Glenyan Campground of Ashland, 541/488-1785, www.glenyancampground.com.

245 DALEY CREEK

Scenic rating: 6

on Daley Creek in Rogue River National Forest

Daley Creek campground is a primitive alternative to some of the more developed spots in the area. Situated at 4,500 feet elevation, the camp borders the banks of Daley Creek near the confluence of Beaver Dam and Daley Creek. Sites are scattered among old-growth Douglas and white fir, and the Beaver Dam Trail heads right out of camp, running along the creek. Fishing can be decent downstream from here.

Campsites, facilities: There are six sites for tents or RVs up to 18 feet long. Picnic tables and fire grills are provided. There is no drinking water, and garbage must be packed out. Some facilities are wheelchair accessible. Leashed pets are permitted.

Reservations, fees: Reservations are not accepted. Sites are $8 per night, $4 per night per additional vehicle. Open early May–mid-November, weather permitting.

Directions: In Ashland on I-5, take Exit 14 to Highway 66. Drive east for less than a mile to Dead Indian Memorial Road. Turn left (east) and drive 22 miles to Forest Road 37. Turn left (north) and drive 1.5 miles to the campground.

Contact: Rogue River National Forest, Ashland Ranger District, 541/552-2900, fax 541/552-2922, www.fs.fed.us.

246 BEAVER DAM

Scenic rating: 5

on Beaver Dam Creek in Rogue River National Forest

This campground sits at an elevation of 4,500 feet along Beaver Dam Creek. Look for beaver dams. There's not much screening between sites, but it's a pretty, rustic, and quiet spot, with unusual vegetation along the creek for botany fans. The trailhead for the Beaver Dam Trail is also here. The camp is adjacent to Daley Creek Campground.

Campsites, facilities: There are four sites for tents or RVs up to 16 feet long. Picnic tables and fire grills are provided. There is no drinking water, and garbage must be packed out. Leashed pets are permitted.

Reservations, fees: Reservations are not accepted. Sites are $8 per night, $4 per night per additional vehicle. Open early May–early November, weather permitting.

Directions: In Medford on I-5, take Exit 14 to Highway 66. Drive east for less than a mile to Dead Indian Memorial Road. Turn left (east) and drive 22 miles to Forest Road 37. Turn left (north) and drive 1.5 miles to the campground.

Contact: Rogue River National Forest, Ashland Ranger District, 541/552-2900, fax 541/552-2922, www.fs.fed.us.

247 HOWARD PRAIRIE LAKE RESORT

Scenic rating: 7

on Howard Prairie Lake

This wooded campground is located along the shore of Howard Prairie Lake, where boating, fishing, hiking, and swimming are among the recreation options. This is one of the largest campgrounds in over 100 miles.

Campsites, facilities: There are 150 sites with full or partial hookups for tents or RVs of any length and 20 furnished RV rentals. Some sites are pull-through. Picnic tables and fire rings are provided. Restrooms with flush toilets and showers, propane gas, a dump station, firewood, 24-hour security, a convenience store, café, coin laundry, boat docks, boat rentals, moorage, and launching facilities are available. Leashed pets are permitted.

Reservations, fees: Reservations are not accepted. Sites are $20–29 per night, plus $5 per person per night for more than two people. Some credit cards are accepted. Open mid-April–October.

Directions: In Ashland on I-5, take Exit 14 to Highway 66 and drive for less than a mile to Dead Indian Memorial Road. Turn left and drive 17 miles to Hyatt Prairie Road. Turn right and drive 3.5 miles to the resort.

Contact: Howard Prairie Lake Resort, 541/482-1979, fax 541/488-7485, www.howardprairieresort.com.

248 HOWARD PRAIRIE LAKE: LILY GLEN

Scenic rating: 6

near Howard Prairie Lake

Set along the shore of Howard Prairie Lake, this horse camp is a secluded, primitive getaway. Trout fishing is available. Tubb Springs Wayside State Park and the nearby Rogue River National Forest are possible side trips. There is also nearby access to the Pacific Crest Trail. The elevation is 4,500 feet.

Campsites, facilities: There are 26 sites for tents or self-contained RVs and two group sites for up to 75 people. Picnic tables and fire grills are provided. Drinking water, vault toilets, and corrals are available. Some facilities are wheelchair accessible. Leashed pets are permitted.

Reservations, fees: Reservations are accepted for group sites at 541/774-8183 but are not accepted for family sites. Sites are $16 per night, $6 per night per additional vehicle, $1 per pet per night, and $2 per horse per night for more than two horses; group sites are $75–150 per night. Some credit cards are accepted for reservations. Open mid-April–October, weather permitting.

Directions: In Ashland on I-5, take Exit 14 to Highway 66. Drive east for less than a mile to Dead Indian Memorial Road. Turn left (east) and drive 21 miles to the campground on the right.

Contact: Howard Prairie Lake Recreational Area, Jackson County Parks, 541/774-8183, fax 541/774-6320, www.jacksoncountyparks.com.

249 HOWARD PRAIRIE LAKE: GRIZZLY

Scenic rating: 7

near Howard Prairie Lake

One of a series of four county campgrounds at Howard Prairie Lake, Grizzly features well-spaced campsites amid a forest and lake setting. The lake level is known to fluctuate; in low-water years, this camp is sometimes shut down. It gets moderate use. The elevation is 4,550 feet.

Campsites, facilities: There are 29 sites for tents or RVs (no hookups). Picnic tables and fire rings are provided. Drinking water, vault toilets, and garbage bins are available. A boat ramp is nearby. A store, café, laundry facilities, and boat rentals are available within two miles. Some facilities are wheelchair accessible. Leashed pets are permitted.

Reservations, fees: Reservations are not accepted. Sites are $14 per night, $6 per night per additional vehicle, and $1 per pet per night. Open mid-April–October, weather permitting.

Directions: In Ashland on I-5, take Exit 14 to Highway 66. Drive east for less than a mile to Dead Indian Memorial Road. Turn left (east) and drive 17 miles to Howard Prairie Road. Turn right (south) and drive eight miles to Howard Prairie Dam Road. Turn left (east) and drive 0.25 mile to the campground.

Contact: Howard Prairie Lake Recreational Area, Jackson County Parks, 541/774-8183, fax 541/774-6320, www.jacksoncountyparks.com.

250 HOWARD PRAIRIE LAKE: WILLOW POINT

Scenic rating: 7

near Howard Prairie Lake

Willow Point is the most popular of the four county campgrounds on Howard Prairie Lake. Similar to Grizzly, it offers flat tent sites in an area well covered by trees. The lake is stocked with about 100,000 trout annually.

Campsites, facilities: There are 40 sites for tents or self-contained RVs. Picnic tables and fire rings are provided. Drinking water, vault toilets, and garbage bins are available. A boat ramp is nearby. A store, café, laundry facilities, and boat rentals are available within four miles. Some facilities are wheelchair accessible. Leashed pets are permitted.

Reservations, fees: No reservations are accepted. Sites are $16 per night, $6 per night per additional vehicle, and $1 per pet per night. Open mid-April–October.

Directions: In Ashland on I-5, take Exit 14 to Highway 66. Drive east for less than a mile to Dead Indian Memorial Road. Turn left (east) and drive 17 miles to Howard Prairie Road. Turn right (south) and drive three miles to the reservoir.

Contact: Howard Prairie Lake Recreational Area, Jackson County Parks, 541/774-8183, fax 541/774-6320, www.jacksoncountyparks.com.

251 HOWARD PRAIRIE LAKE: KLUM LANDING

Scenic rating: 7

near Howard Prairie Lake

Klum Landing is one of four county campgrounds on Howard Prairie Lake. A bonus at this one is that coin-operated showers are available. Sugar Pine Group Camp is more primitive and is situated away from the lake.

Campsites, facilities: At Klum Landing, there are 32 sites for tents or self-contained RVs. Picnic tables and fire rings are provided. Drinking water, garbage bins, and restrooms with flush toilets and coin showers are available; some facilities are wheelchair accessible. Sugar Pine can accommodate up to 100 people in tents or self-contained RVs. Vault toilets are available, and the facilities are not wheelchair accessible. A boat ramp is nearby. A store, café, laundry facilities, and boat rentals are available at Howard Prairie Lake Resort. Leashed pets are permitted.

Reservations, fees: Reservations are not accepted for Klum Landing. Sites are $18 per night, $6 per night per additional vehicle, and $1 per pet per night. Reservations are accepted for Sugar Pine Group at 541/774-8183. The group camp is $150–200 per night. Open mid-April–October.

Directions: In Ashland on I-5, take Exit 14 to Highway 66. Drive east for less than a mile to Dead Indian Memorial Road. Turn left (east) and drive 17 miles to Howard Prairie Road. Turn right (south) and drive eight miles to Howard Prairie Dam Road. Turn left (east) and drive 0.25 mile to Sugar Pine Group Camp on the right. Continue 0.75 mile to reach Klum Landing.

Contact: Jackson County Parks, 541/774-8183, fax 541/774-6320, www.jacksoncountyparks.com.

252 EMIGRANT CAMPGROUND

Scenic rating: 8

on Emigrant Lake

This camp is nestled among the trees above Emigrant Lake, a well-known recreational area. Activities at this park include boating, fishing, hiking, swimming, and waterskiing. There are also two 280-foot water slides. The park has its own swimming cove (unsupervised). Side-trip possibilities include exploring nearby Mount Ashland, where a ski area operates in the winter, as well as visiting Ashland's world-renowned Shakespeare Festival, the Britt Music Festival, and historic Jacksonville.

Campsites, facilities: There are 42 sites for tents or self-contained RVs, 32 sites for RVs of any length (50-amp full hookups), an overflow area, and one group camp area for up to 100 people. Restrooms with flush toilets, coin showers, a dump station, snacks in summer, and a barbecue are available. A group picnic and day-use area that can be reserved are also available. Recreational facilities include horseshoe pits, volleyball, and a playground. Two boat ramps are provided. Laundry and food are within six miles. Some facilities are wheelchair accessible. Leashed pets are permitted in designated areas only.

Reservations, fees: Reservations are accepted for RV sites and the group site at 541/774-8183. Tent sites are $18 per night, RV sites with full hookups are $26 per night, $6 per night per additional vehicle, and $1 per pet per night. The group site is $125–175 per night. Some credit cards are accepted for reservations. Open mid-March–mid-October, weather permitting.

Directions: From Ashland, drive east on Highway 66 for five miles to the campground on the left.

Contact: Jackson County Parks, 541/774-8183, fax 541/774-6320, www.jacksoncountyparks.com.

253 HYATT LAKE

Scenic rating: 8

on Hyatt Lake

Hyatt Lake campground is situated on the south end of Hyatt Reservoir, which has six miles of shoreline. Fishing is good for brook and rainbow trout and smallmouth bass. The boat speed limit here is 10 mph. The Pacific Crest Trail runs next to the campground. Another campground option is Wildcat, about two miles north, with 12 semi-primitive sites.

Campsites, facilities: There are 54 sites for tents or RVs up to 40 feet long, five horse campsites, one group site for up to 50 people, and 12 walk-in tent sites. Picnic tables and fire grills are provided. Drinking water, restrooms with flush toilets and showers, garbage service, dump station, fish-cleaning station, group kitchen, day-use area, softball fields, volleyball, a playground, horseshoe pits, and two boat ramps are available. Some facilities are wheelchair accessible. Leashed pets are permitted.

Reservations, fees: Reservations are accepted only for the group camp or horse camp at 541/482-2031 or 541/618-2306. Sites are $12–15 per night, $3 per night per additional vehicle, with a 14-day stay limit. Campsites with horse facilities are $10 per night; the group site is $95 per night. Sites at nearby primitive Wildcat Campground are $7 per night. Pacific Crest Trail hikers pay $2 per person per night for camping. Open late April–October, weather permitting.

Directions: From Ashland, drive east on Highway 66 for 17 miles to East Hyatt Lake Road. Turn north and drive three miles to the campground entrance on the left.

Contact: Bureau of Land Management, Ashland Resource Area, 541/618-2200, fax 541/618-2400, www.blm.gov.

254 TOPSY

Scenic rating: 7

on the Upper Klamath River

This campground is on Boyle Reservoir near the Upper Klamath River, a good spot for trout fishing. Swimming is not recommended because of the murky water. This is a top river for rafters (experts only, or non-experts with professional, licensed guides). There are Class IV and V rapids about four miles southwest at Caldera, Hells Corner, and Satan's Gate. I flipped at Caldera and ended up swimming for it, finally getting out at an eddy. Luckily, I was wearing a dry suit and the best lifejacket available, perfect fitting, which saved my butt.

Campsites, facilities: There are 13 sites for RVs up to 40 feet long. Picnic tables and fire grills are provided. Drinking water, vault toilets, garbage service, and a dump station are available. Boat-launching facilities are nearby. A camp host is on-site in season. Some facilities are wheelchair accessible. Leashed pets are permitted.

Reservations, fees: Reservations are not accepted. Sites are $7 per night, $4 per night per additional vehicle, with a 14-day stay limit. Open mid-May–mid-September, weather permitting.

Directions: From Klamath Falls, drive west on Highway 66 for 20 miles to Topsy Road. Turn south on Topsy Road and drive 1.5 miles to the campground on the right.

Contact: Bureau of Land Management, Klamath Falls Resource Area, 541/883-6916, fax 541/884-2097, www.blm.gov.

255 JACKSON

Scenic rating: 7

on the Applegate River in Rogue River National Forest

Jackson campground is nestled in an old mining area at 1,700 feet elevation. Situated between the Applegate River and the road, under a canopy of ponderosa pine, it features a swimming hole and good trout fishing. An interpretive trail is across the road from the campground. Mine tailings can be seen from the camp. Trailers and large RVs are not allowed.

Campsites, facilities: There are eight sites for tents. Picnic tables and fire rings are provided. Drinking water (summer only), garbage service (summer only), and flush toilets are available. Some facilities are wheelchair accessible. Leashed pets are permitted.

Reservations, fees: Reservations are not accepted. Sites are $10 per night, $5 per night per

additional vehicle. Open year-round, weather permitting, with limited winter services.
Directions: In Medford on I-5, take the Jacksonville exit to the Jacksonville Highway. Drive west on the Jacksonville Highway (Highway 238) for seven miles to Jacksonville. Bear left on Highway 238 and drive eight miles to the town of Ruch and Upper Applegate Road (County Road 10). Turn left and drive 10 miles to the campground on the right.
Contact: Rogue River National Forest, Siskiyou Mountains District, 541/899-1812, fax 541/899-3888, www.fs.fed.us; concessionaire, 541/899-9220.

256 BEAVER SULPHUR GROUP

Scenic rating: 7

on Beaver Creek in Rogue River National Forest

This group camp is well hidden along the banks of Beaver Creek. It is set at an elevation of 2,100 feet and situated in an area with mixed tree cover, including tall Douglas fir, live oak, and maple. The camp is about nine miles from Applegate Reservoir, features attractive shaded sites, and offers easy access to the creek. Some recreational mining is done here; access is provided with a campground reservation.
Campsites, facilities: There is one group site for up to 50 people. Picnic tables and fire grills are provided. Vault toilets and garbage bins (summer only) are available. There is no drinking water. Some facilities are wheelchair accessible. Leashed pets are permitted.
Reservations, fees: Reservations are accepted at 877/444-6777 or www.recreation.gov ($10 reservation fee). The site is $50 per night. Open May–mid-September, weather permitting.
Directions: In Medford on I-5, take the Jacksonville exit to the Jacksonville Highway. Drive west on the Jacksonville Highway (Highway 238) for seven miles to Jacksonville. Bear left on Highway 238 and drive eight miles to the town of Ruch and Upper Applegate Road (County Road 10). Turn left (south) and drive 9.5 miles to Forest Road 20. Continue three miles to the campground on the right.
Contact: Rogue River National Forest, Siskiyou Mountains District, 541/899-1812, fax 541/899-3888, www.fs.fed.us.

257 HART-TISH RECREATION AREA WALK-IN

Scenic rating: 7

on Applegate Lake, Rogue River National Forest

This concessionaire-managed campground on Applegate Lake has shaded sites and a great view of the lake. Bald eagles and osprey nest in the area, and it's a treat to watch them fish. A nearby boat launch and boat rentals are available. The walk-in sites are only 200 yards from the parking area.
Campsites, facilities: There are eight walk-in tent sites and eight parking-lot sites for RVs up to 45 feet long. Picnic tables and fire pits are provided. Drinking water, flush toilets, garbage bins, and firewood are available. A day-use area is nearby. A small general store and kayak and bicycle rentals are nearby. Some facilities are wheelchair accessible. Leashed pets are permitted.
Reservations, fees: Reservations are accepted at 877/444-6777 or www.recreation.gov ($10 reservation fee). Sites are $10 per night, $5 per night per additional vehicle. Open mid-April–September, weather permitting.
Directions: In Medford on I-5, take the Jacksonville exit to the Jacksonville Highway. Drive west on the Jacksonville Highway (Highway 238) for seven miles to Jacksonville. Bear left on Highway 238 and drive eight miles to the town of Ruch and Upper Applegate Road (County Road 10). Turn left (south) and drive 15.5 miles to the campground on the left.

Contact: Rogue River National Forest, Siskiyou Mountains District, 541/899-1812, fax 541/899-3888, www.fs.fed.us; concessionaire, 541/899-9220.

258 WATKINS

Scenic rating: 6

on Applegate Reservoir in Rogue River National Forest

On the southwest shore of Applegate Reservoir at an elevation of 2,000 feet, this campground, like Carberry Walk-In and French Gulch, is small and quite primitive—yet pretty—and offers all the same recreation options. Few campers know about this spot, so it usually doesn't fill up quickly. There are good views of the lake and the surrounding Siskiyou Mountains. The Seattle Bar day-use area at the lake is approximately two miles away.

Campsites, facilities: There are 14 walk-in sites for tents. Picnic tables, garbage bins, and fire grills are provided. There is no drinking water. Vault toilets are available. A general store, boat docks, and launching facilities are within two miles. Leashed pets are permitted.

Reservations, fees: Reservations are not accepted. Sites are $10 per night, $5 per night per additional vehicle. Open late May–early September.

Directions: In Medford on I-5, take the Jacksonville exit to the Jacksonville Highway. Drive west on the Jacksonville Highway (Highway 238) for seven miles to Jacksonville. Bear left on Highway 238 and drive eight miles to the town of Ruch and Upper Applegate Road (County Road 10). Turn left (south) and drive 17 miles to the campground.

Contact: Rogue River National Forest, Siskiyou Mountains District, 541/899-1812, fax 541/899-3888, www.fs.fed.us; concessionaire, 541/899-9220.

259 CARBERRY WALK-IN

Scenic rating: 5

near Applegate Reservoir in Rogue River National Forest

You'll find recreational opportunities aplenty, including boating, fishing, hiking, mountain biking, and swimming, at this campground on Cougar Creek near the southwest shore of Applegate Reservoir. Dense forest covers the campsites, providing much-needed shade. This camp is similar to Watkins Walk-in.

Campsites, facilities: There are 11 walk-in sites for tents and three spaces in the parking lot for RVs up to 25 feet long. Picnic tables and fire grills are provided. Vault toilets and drinking water are available. A general store, firewood, boat docks, and launching facilities are within two miles. Some facilities are wheelchair accessible. Leashed pets are permitted.

Reservations, fees: Reservations are not accepted. Sites are $10 per night, $5 per night per additional vehicle. Open late May–early September, weather permitting.

Directions: In Medford on I-5, take the Jacksonville exit to the Jacksonville Highway. Drive west on the Jacksonville Highway (Highway 238) for seven miles to Jacksonville. Bear left on Highway 238 and drive eight miles to the town of Ruch and Upper Applegate Road (County Road 10). Turn left (south) and drive 18 miles to the campground parking area. A short walk is required.

Contact: Rogue River National Forest, Siskiyou Mountains District, 541/899-1812, fax 541/899-3888, www.fs.fed.us; concessionaire, 541/899-9220.

260 SQUAW LAKE HIKE-IN

Scenic rating: 10

on Squaw Lake in Rogue River National Forest

BEST

"Paradise Found" should be the name of this campground. Numerous trails crisscross the area around this camp (3,000 feet elevation). The setting—the shore of spectacular Squaw Lake—is more intimate than that of larger Applegate Reservoir to the west. This spot has a mix of developed and primitive sites and is also more popular. In fact, it's the only campground in the district that requires reservations. This area attracts the canoe/kayak crowd. Be sure to call ahead for a space. Campers with disabilities are welcome, but arrangements should be made in advance with the local U.S. Forest Service office.

Campsites, facilities: There are 17 walk-in sites for tents and two family group sites that can accommodate up to 10 people each. Picnic tables and fire grills are provided. Vault toilets are available. Drinking water is available at one end of the camp during the summer only. Garbage must be packed out. Leashed pets are permitted.

Reservations, fees: Reservations are accepted at 877/444-6777 or www.recreation.gov ($10 reservation fee). Sites are $10 per night and group sites are $20–30 per night. Open mid-May–mid-September, weather permitting.

Directions: In Medford on I-5, take the Jacksonville exit to the Jacksonville Highway. Drive west on the Jacksonville Highway (Highway 238) for seven miles to Jacksonville. Bear left on Highway 238 and drive eight miles to the town of Ruch and Upper Applegate Road (County Road 10). Turn left (south) and drive 15 miles to Forest Road 1075. Continue eight miles to Squaw Lake and the trailhead. Hike one mile to the campsites.

Contact: Rogue River National Forest, Siskiyou Mountains District, 541/899-1812, fax 541/899-3888, www.fs.fed.us.

261 WRANGLE

Scenic rating: 10

near the Pacific Crest Trail in Rogue River National Forest

This campground is located at the headwaters of Glade Creek in the Siskiyou Mountains at an elevation of 6,400 feet. The Pacific Crest Trail passes near camp. Dutchman Peak Lookout, built in the late 1920s and featured in the National Historic Register, is within five miles. This lovely campground, in a beautiful, high country setting, boasts huge Shasta red firs and views of the Siskiyou Mountains. Wrangle is along the Scenic Siskiyou Loop driving tour.

Campsites, facilities: There are five sites for tents. Picnic tables and fire grills are provided. Vault toilets, a pole shelter, and a community kitchen are available. There is no drinking water, and garbage must be packed out. Leashed pets are permitted.

Reservations, fees: Reservations are not accepted. There is no fee for camping. Open early July–late October, weather permitting.

Directions: In Ashland on I-5, take the Jacksonville exit. Drive east on the Jacksonville Highway to Jacksonville and Highway 238. Bear left on Highway 238 and drive eight miles to the town of Ruch and County Road 10 (Upper Applegate Road). Turn left and drive 9.5 miles to Forest Road 20. Turn left and drive 21 miles to Forest Road 2030. Continue one mile on Forest Road 2030 to the campground.

Contact: Rogue River National Forest, Siskiyou Mountains District, 541/899-1812, fax 541/899-3888, www.fs.fed.us.

262 MOUNT ASHLAND

Scenic rating: 8

on the Pacific Crest Trail in Klamath National Forest

BEST

Set at 6,600 feet elevation along the Pacific Crest Trail, this beautiful camp is heavily wooded and has abundant wildlife. On a clear day, enjoy great lookouts from nearby Siskiyou Peak, particularly to the south, where California's 14,162-foot Mount Shasta is an awesome sight. Mount Ashland Ski Resort is one mile east of the campground.

Campsites, facilities: There are nine sites for tents or RVs up to 15 feet long, with extremely limited space for RVs. Picnic tables and fire grills are provided. Vault toilets are available. There is no drinking water. Garbage must be packed out. Leashed pets are permitted.

Reservations, fees: Reservations are not accepted. There is no fee for camping but donations are accepted. Open May–late October, weather permitting.

Directions: From Ashland, drive south on I-5 for 12 miles to Mount Ashland Ski Park Road (County Road 993). Turn west and drive 10 miles (the road becomes Forest Road 20) to the campground.

Contact: Klamath National Forest, Happy Camp/Oak Knoll Ranger District, 530/493-2243, fax 530/493-1796, www.fs.fed.us.

263 JACKSON F. KIMBALL STATE PARK

Scenic rating: 7

on the Wood River

This primitive state campground at the headwaters of the Wood River is another nice spot just far enough off the main drag to remain a secret. A trail from camp leads to a nearby spring. Fishing from canoe is good on the Wood River.

Campsites, facilities: There are 10 primitive sites for tents or self-contained RVs up to 45 feet long. Picnic tables, fire grills, and garbage bins are provided. Vault toilets are available. There is no drinking water. Leashed pets are permitted.

Reservations, fees: Reservations are not accepted. Sites are $6–10 per night, $5 per night per additional vehicle. Open year-round, weather permitting.

Directions: From Klamath Falls, drive north on U.S. 97 for 21 miles to Highway 62. Turn left (northwest) on Highway 62 and drive 10 miles to Highway 232/Sun Pass Road (near Fort Klamath). Turn right (north) and drive three miles to the campground.

Contact: Collier Memorial State Park, 541/783-2471 or 800/551-6949, www.oregonstateparks.org. (Jackson F. Kimball is managed by Collier Memorial State Park.)

264 CRATER LAKE RESORT

Scenic rating: 6

on the Wood River

The campground at Crater Lake Resort is dotted with huge pine trees on the banks of the beautiful, crystal-clear Fort Creek. It's located just outside Fort Klamath, the site of numerous military campaigns against the Modoc people in the late 1800s.

Campsites, facilities: There are 14 sites with full or partial hookups for RVs of any length, six tent sites, nine cabins, and one log cabin. Drinking water, picnic tables, and fire rings are provided. Restrooms with flush toilets and showers, modem access, a recreation hall, and coin laundry are available. Propane gas, a store, café, and ice are within one mile. Leashed pets are permitted.

Reservations, fees: Reservations are accepted. RV sites are $25 per night, $2 per person per night for more than two people, and $2 per pet per night. Tent sites are $5 per person per night. Some credit cards are accepted. Open mid-April–mid-October.

Directions: From Klamath Falls, drive north on U.S. 97 for 21 miles to Highway 62. Bear left on Highway 62 and drive 12.5 miles north to the resort (just before reaching Fort Klamath).

Contact: Crater Lake Resort, 541/381-2349, www.craterlakeresort.com.

265 COLLIER MEMORIAL STATE PARK

Scenic rating: 7

on the Williamson River

This campground sits at the confluence of Spring Creek and the Williamson River, both of which are superior trout streams. An area for equestrian campers is situated at a trailhead for horses. A nature trail is also available. The park features a pioneer village and a logging museum. Movies about old-time logging and other activities are shown on weekend nights during the summer.

Campsites, facilities: There are 18 sites for tents or self-contained RVs up to 50 feet long (no hookups), 50 sites for tents or RVs of any length (full hookups), and an area for up to four groups of equestrian campers. Some sites are pull-through. Picnic tables, fire grills, garbage bins, and drinking water are provided. Restrooms with flush toilets and showers, a dump station, firewood, coin laundry, playground, and day-use hitching area are available. Some facilities are wheelchair accessible. Leashed pets are permitted.

Reservations, fees: Reservations are not accepted. Tent sites are $11–18 per night, RV sites are $13–21 per night, $5 per night per additional vehicle. The equestrian area is $12–18 per night and $1.50 per night per horse. Some credit cards are accepted. Open year-round, weather permitting.

Directions: From Klamath Falls, drive north on U.S. 97 for 28 miles to the park (well signed).

Contact: Collier Memorial State Park, 541/783-2471 or 800/551-6949, www.oregonstateparks.org.

266 WILLIAMSON RIVER

Scenic rating: 6

near Collier Memorial State Park in Winema National Forest

Another great little spot is discovered, this one at 4,200 feet elevation, with excellent trout fishing along the banks of the Williamson River, a world-famous fly-fishing river. Mosquitoes are numerous in spring and early summer, which can drive people away. A map of Winema National Forest details the back roads and trails. Collier Memorial State Park provides a nearby side-trip option.

Campsites, facilities: There are 10 sites for tents or RVs up to 30 feet long. Picnic tables, garbage bins, and fire grills are provided. Drinking water and vault toilets are available. A restaurant is within five miles. Some facilities are wheelchair accessible. Leashed pets are permitted.

Reservations, fees: Reservations are not accepted. Sites are $8 per night, $2 per night per additional vehicle. Open late April–late November, weather permitting.

Directions: From Klamath Falls, drive north on U.S. 97 for 30 miles to Chiloquin. Continue north on U.S. 97 for 5.5 miles to Forest Road 9730. Turn right (northeast) and drive one mile to the campground.

Contact: Fremont-Winema National Forests, Klamath Ranger District, 541/885-3400, fax 541/885-3452, www.fs.fed.us.

267 POTTER'S PARK

Scenic rating: 6

on the Sprague River

This park on a bluff overlooking the Sprague River is in a wooded setting and bordered by the Winema National Forest. Canoeing and rafting are options here. For the most part, the area east of Klamath Lake doesn't get much attention.

Campsites, facilities: There are 17 tent sites and 22 sites with full hookups for RVs of any length. Drinking water, picnic tables, and fire pits are provided. Restrooms with flush toilets and showers, firewood, a convenience store, coin laundry, pay telephone, and ice are available. Leashed pets are permitted.

Reservations, fees: Reservations are accepted. Sites are $15 per night, plus $2.50 per person per night for more than one adult. Monthly rates are available for RV sites. Open year-round, with limited winter facilities.

Directions: From Klamath Falls, drive north on U.S. 97 for 27 miles to Chiloquin and Sprague River Highway. Turn right (east) on Sprague River Highway and drive 12 miles to the park on the right.

Contact: Potter's Park, 541/783-2253.

268 WALT'S RV PARK

Scenic rating: 7

on the Williamson River

This heavily treed campground, across the highway from the Williamson River near Collier Memorial State Park, is one of three camps in the immediate area. The Williamson River has excellent trout fishing. For those looking for a more remote setting, head east to Potter's Park.

Campsites, facilities: There are 20 tent sites and 16 sites with full or partial hookups for RVs up to 40 feet long; some are pull-through sites. Drinking water, picnic tables, and fire pits are provided. Restrooms with flush toilets and showers, firewood, coin laundry, and ice are available. A café is within 0.25 mile, and there is a store in Chiloquin. Leashed pets are permitted.

Reservations, fees: Reservations are accepted. Sites are $13.75–17.75 per night, $1 per person per night for more than two people, and $1 per night for air-conditioning. Open year-round, weather permitting.

Directions: From Klamath Falls, drive north on U.S. 97 for 24 miles to Chiloquin Junction. Continue north for 0.25 mile to the campground (adjacent to the Chiloquin Ranger Station) on the left.

Contact: Walt's RV Park, 541/783-2537, www.waltsrvpark.com.

269 AGENCY LAKE RESORT

Scenic rating: 5

on Agency Lake

This campground sits along Agency Lake in an open, grassy area with some shaded sites. The resort has more than 700 feet of lakefront property, offering world-class trout fishing. Look across the lake and watch the sun set on the Cascades. Note that some sites are filled with monthly renters.

Campsites, facilities: There are 15 tent sites and 25 sites with full or partial hookups for tents or RVs of any length, three cabins, and one rental trailer. Drinking water and picnic tables are provided. Restrooms with flush toilets and showers, a general store, ice, boat docks, launching facilities, and marine gas are available. Leashed pets are permitted.

Reservations, fees: Reservations are accepted. RV sites are $16–20 per night; tent sites are $12–13 per night. Some credit cards are accepted. Open year-round, weather permitting.

Directions: From Klamath Falls, drive north on U.S. 97 for 17 miles to Modoc Point Road. Turn left and drive about 10 miles to the resort on the left.

Contact: Agency Lake Resort, 541/783-2489, www.agencylakeresort.net.

OREGON'S SOUTHERN CASCADES HIKING

© SEAN PATRICK HILL

BEST HIKES

Desert Hiking
Smith Rock State Park, **page 172.**
Newberry Lava Tubes, **page 217.**

Hikes for Kids
Shevlin Park, **page 185.**

Hikes for Views
The Obsidian Trail, **page 177.**
Green Lakes via Fall Creek, **page 181.**
Mount Thielsen, **page 210.**
Mount Scott, **page 233.**
Pilot Rock, **page 248.**

Hikes Through Old-Growth Forests
Lookout Creek Old-Growth Trail, **page 161.**

Self-Guided Nature Walks
Lava Cast Forest, **page 219.**

Short Backpacking Trips
Patjens Lakes, **page 170.**
Pacific Crest Trail to Matthieu Lakes, **page 174.**
Divide Lake, **page 198.**

Non-Technical Summit Hikes
Black Crater, **page 174.**
South Sister Summit, **page 182.**
Mount Bailey, **page 211.**
Mount McLoughlin, **page 241.**

Waterfall Hikes
Sahalie and Koosah Falls, **page 160.**
Proxy Falls/Linton Lake, **page 178.**
Tumalo Falls, **page 184.**
Salt Creek Falls and Vivian Lake, **page 195.**
Deschutes River Trail/Dillon and Benham Falls, **page 216.**

Wheelchair-Accessible Trails
Natural Bridge and the Rogue Gorge, **page 231.**
OC&E Woods Line Linear State Park, **page 249.**

The Cascade Mountains, extending from British Columbia to California, make their breathtaking sweep straight through the center of the state and are home to a series of fantastic volcanic peaks and dense, old-growth forests. Here you can hike along mountain rivers, visit fire watchtowers, or climb into alpine meadows lush with summer flowers. Reach some of the highest elevations in Oregon, including a non-technical – but difficult – climb of South Sister, Oregon's third-highest peak. Don't forget Crater Lake National Park, one of the prides of the state.

To the southwest, the Siskiyou Mountains feel more like California: Open forests of ponderosa pine, a rugged granite landscape, and whitewater stretches of the Rogue River lie in an entirely different and drier climate. In this billions-of-years-old landscape, you'll find rattlesnakes, mountain lions, and the California pitcher plant, a bug-devouring oddity found in these mountains.

In these two zones, you'll find the majority of Oregon's claim to the Pacific Crest Trail. This well-maintained path traverses the edge of the Siskiyou Mountains before cutting over to the Cascades, where it passes through a bevy of wilderness areas and the national park, and along innumerable streams and lakes. Many of the trails in this section use the PCT as an entry point or a destination in and of itself. And if you like mountains, the PCT brushes by all the biggies: Mount Jefferson, Three Fingered Jack, Mount Washington, the Three Sisters, Diamond Peak, Mount Thielsen, and Mount McLoughlin. You'll skirt Crater Lake, the Sky Lakes, Odell Lake, and Waldo Lake.

Just remember that weather is finicky in these mountains. Snow typically buries many of the trails from late November until as late as July, at least for high elevations. But there is plenty of surrounding area to explore, and year-round trails abound in the foothills both east and west of the divide.

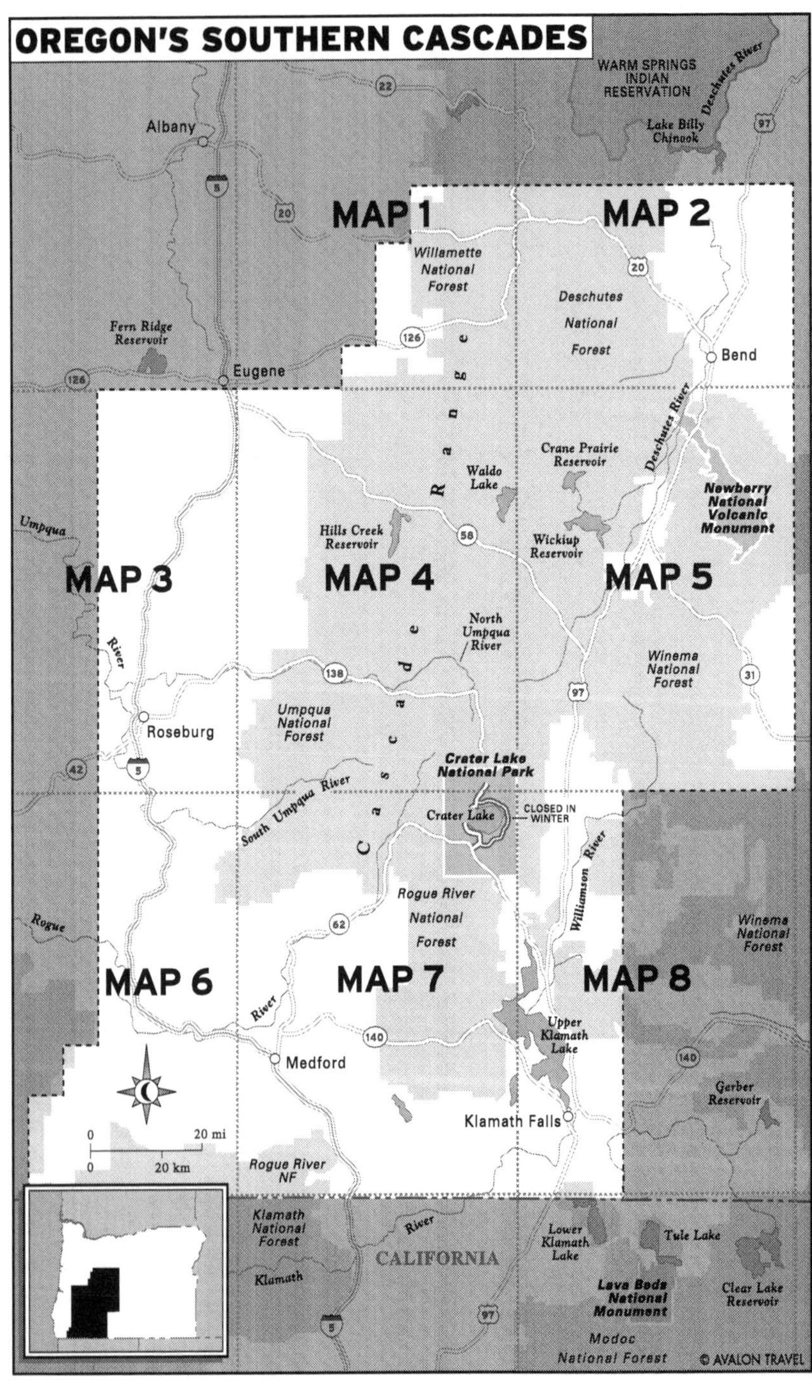

OREGON'S SOUTHERN CASCADES
WARM SPRINGS INDIAN RESERVATION
Deschutes River
Lake Billy Chinook
Albany
MAP 1
MAP 2
Willamette National Forest
Deschutes National Forest
Fern Ridge Reservoir
Eugene
Bend
Cascade Range
Deschutes River
Crane Prairie Reservoir
Waldo Lake
Newberry National Volcanic Monument
Umpqua
Hills Creek Reservoir
Wickiup Reservoir
MAP 3
MAP 4
MAP 5
North Umpqua River
River
Winema National Forest
Roseburg
Umpqua National Forest
Crater Lake National Park
South Umpqua River
Crater Lake
CLOSED IN WINTER
Williamson River
Rogue River National Forest
Rogue
Winema National Forest
MAP 6
MAP 7
MAP 8
River
Upper Klamath Lake
Medford
Gerber Reservoir
Klamath Falls
0
20 mi
0
20 km
Rogue River NF
Klamath National Forest
River
CALIFORNIA
Lower Klamath Lake
Tule Lake
Klamath
Lava Beds National Monument
Clear Lake Reservoir
Modoc National Forest
© AVALON TRAVEL

Map 1

Hikes 1-19

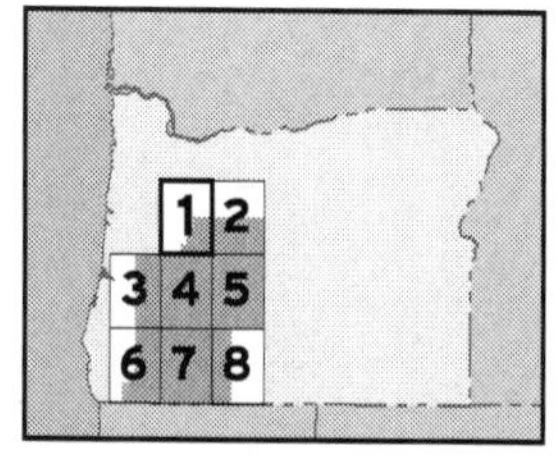

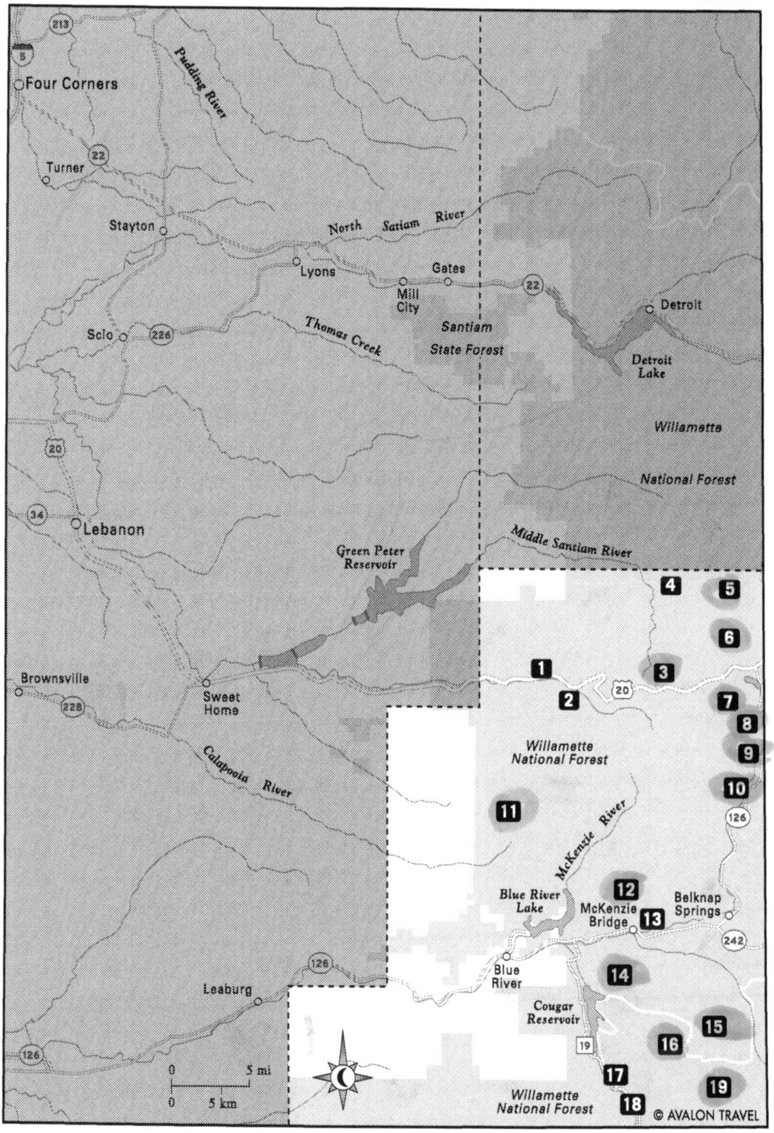

213
5
Four Corners
Pudding River
22
Turner
Stayton
North Santiam River
Lyons
Gates
Mill City
22
Detroit
Scio
226
Thomas Creek
Santiam State Forest
Detroit Lake
Willamette National Forest
20
34
Lebanon
Middle Santiam River
Green Peter Reservoir
4
5
6
1
3
Brownsville
Sweet Home
20
2
7
228
8
Willamette National Forest
9
Calapooia River
10
11
126
McKenzie River
12
Blue River Lake
McKenzie Bridge
13
Belknap Springs
242
126
Blue River
14
Leaburg
Cougar Reservoir
15
16
126
19
0 5 mi
0 5 km
17
19
Willamette National Forest
18
© AVALON TRAVEL

Map 2

Hikes 20-47

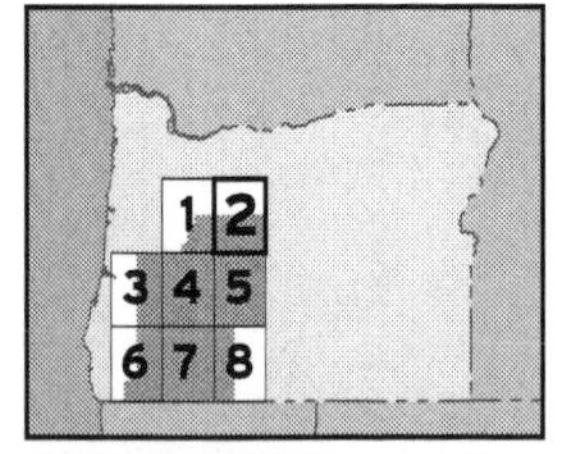

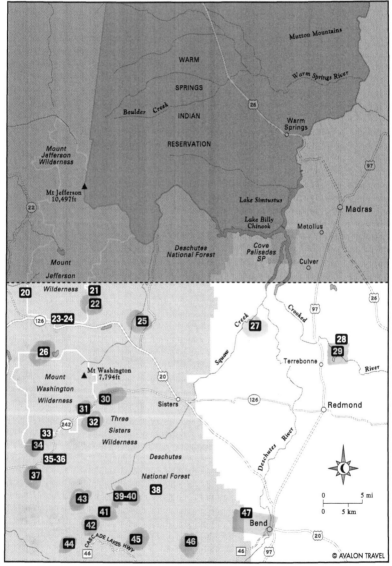

WARM SPRINGS INDIAN RESERVATION
Mutton Mountains
Warm Springs River
Boulder Creek
Warm Springs
Mount Jefferson Wilderness
Mt Jefferson 10,497ft
Lake Simtustus
Lake Billy Chinook
Madras
Metolius
Culver
Deschutes National Forest
Cove Palisades SP
20 21 22 23-24 25 26 27 28 29 30 31 32 33 34 35-36 37 38 39-40 41 42 43 44 45 46 47
Crooked River
Squaw Creek
Terrebonne
Mt Washington 7,794ft
Mount Washington Wilderness
Sisters
Redmond
Three Sisters Wilderness
Deschutes River
Deschutes National Forest
Cascade Lakes Hwy
Bend
0 5 mi
0 5 km
22 26 97 126 20 242 46

Map 3

Hike 48

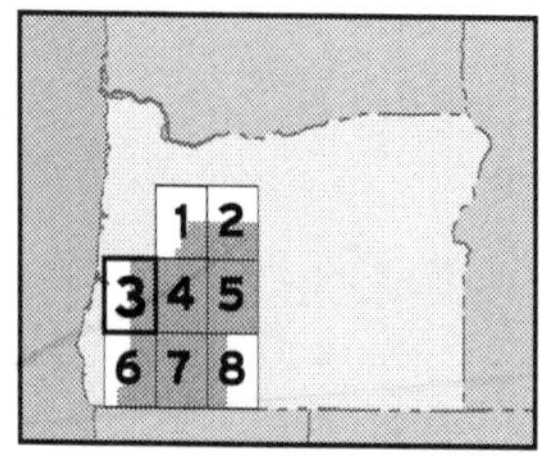
1 2
3 4 5
6 7 8

Siuslaw
National
Forest
Smith
River
Siuslaw
River
Creswell
5
Cottage
Grove
Cottage
Grove Lake
38
38
99
Elkton
Yoncalla
Umpqua
5
138
Oakland
Sutherlin
River
48
Umpqua
River
North
Winchester
138
S Fork
Coos
River
Roseburg
Green
East Fork Coquille River
42
42
5
0 5 mi
0 5 km
Myrtle
Creek
South Myrtle Creek
© AVALON TRAVEL

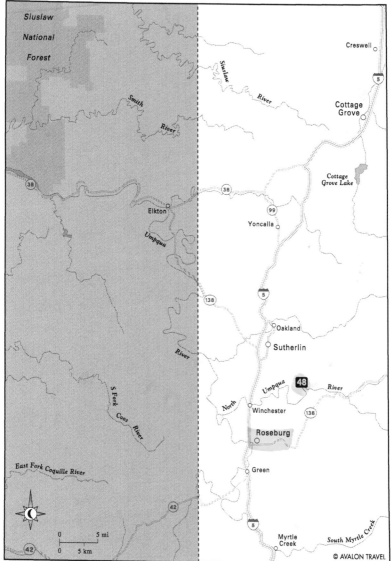

Map 4

Hikes 49-93

1
2
3
4
5
6
7
8

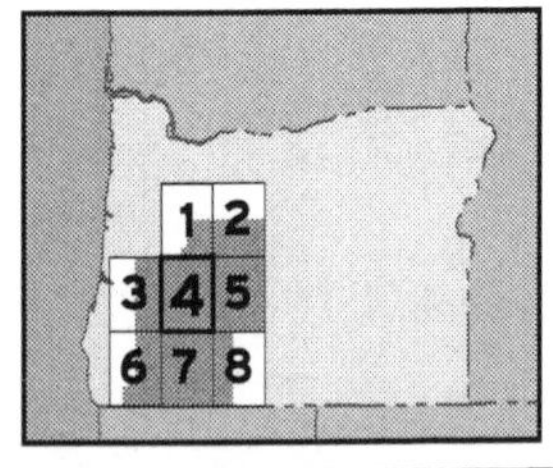

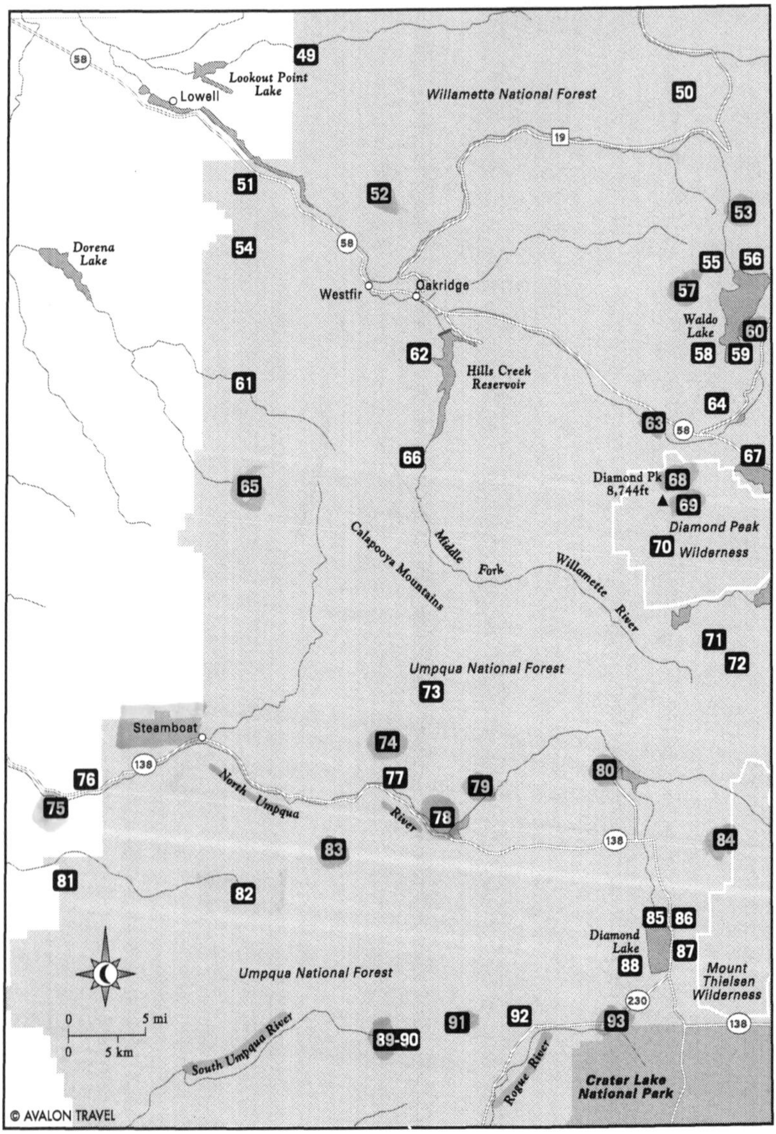

Lookout Point Lake
Lowell
Willamette National Forest
Dorena Lake
Westfir
Oakridge
Hills Creek Reservoir
Waldo Lake
Diamond Pk 8,744ft
Diamond Peak Wilderness
Calapooya Mountains
Middle Fork Willamette River
Umpqua National Forest
Steamboat
North Umpqua River
Diamond Lake
Mount Thielsen Wilderness
Umpqua National Forest
South Umpqua River
Rogue River
Crater Lake National Park
0 5 mi
0 5 km
58
19
138
230
49
50
51
52
53
54
55
56
57
58
59
60
61
62
63
64
65
66
67
68
69
70
71
72
73
74
75
76
77
78
79
80
81
82
83
84
85
86
87
88
89-90
91
92
93
© AVALON TRAVEL

Map 5

Hikes 94-108

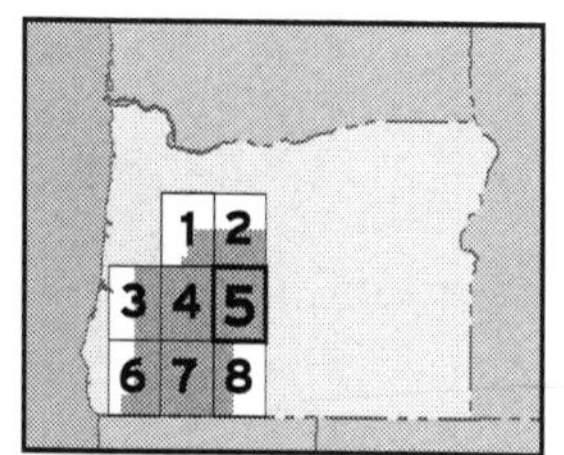

94
95
46
CASCADE LAKES HWY
96
20
97
Deschutes
National Forest
97
Sunriver
99
98
46
40
River
Deschutes
National
Forest
100
42
Crane
Prairie
Reservoir
Newberry Nat'l
Volcanic Monument
101
Deschutes
East
Lake
102
Paulina
Lake
103
105
104
PAULINA-EAST LAKE RD
106
Davis
Lake
Wickiup
Reservoir
River
Odell
Lake
46
Deschutes
Little
31
Deschutes
National Forest
107
Crescent
Lake
58
97
Winema
National
108
FR 9772
Chemult
31
Forest
Silver
Lake
138
97
0
5 mi
0
5 km

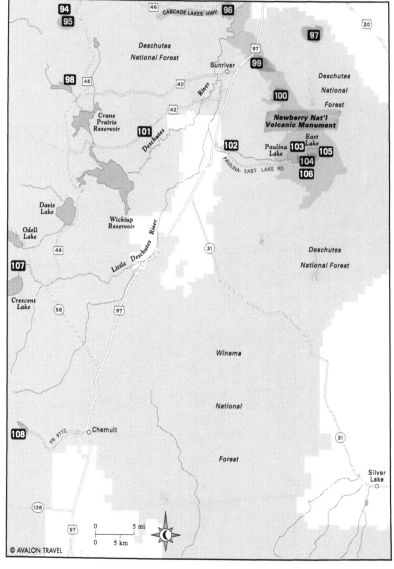

Map 6

Hikes 109-119

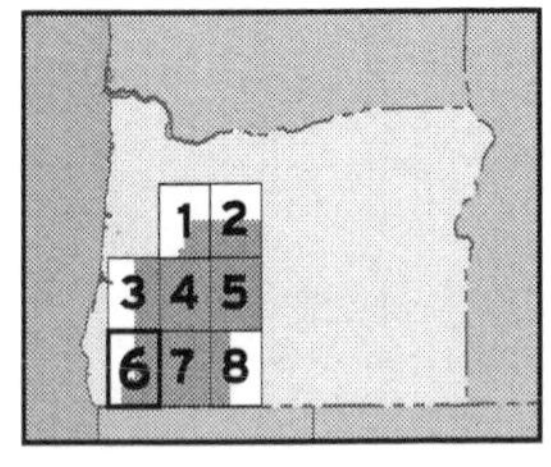

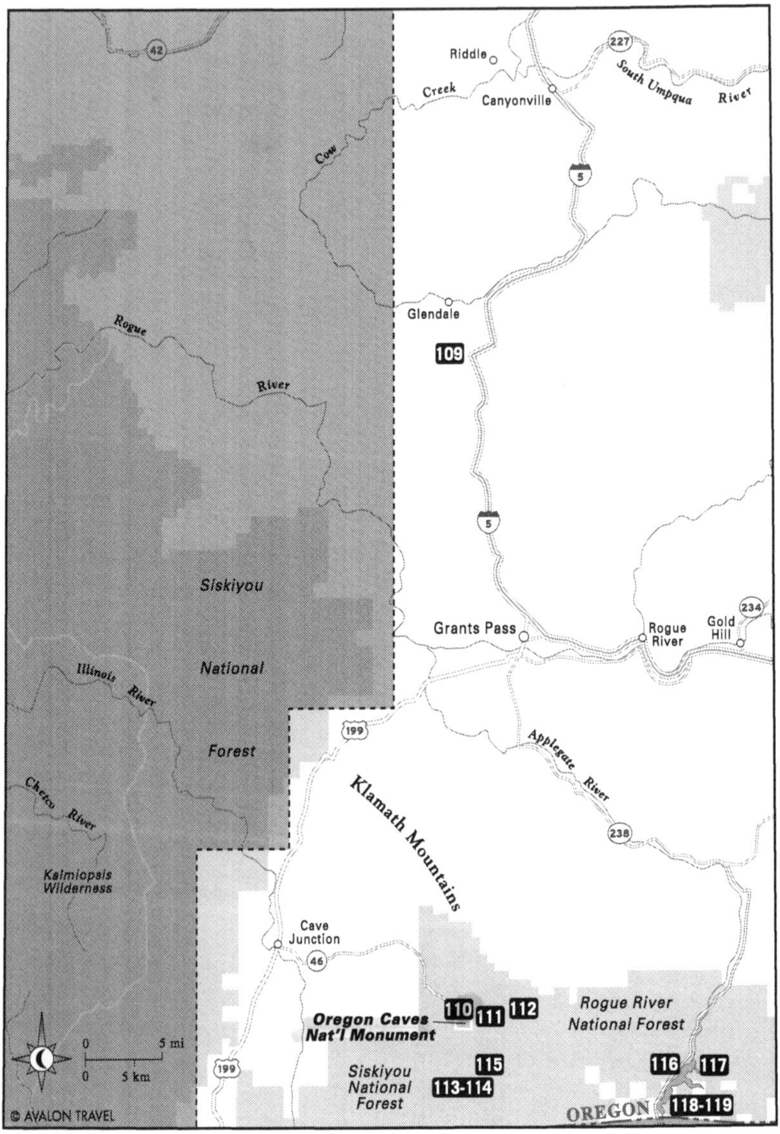

HIKING

Riddle
Canyonville
Creek
South Umpqua River
227
42
5
Cow
Glendale
109
Rogue
River
Siskiyou
National
Forest
Grants Pass
Rogue River
Gold Hill
234
Illinois River
199
Applegate River
Klamath Mountains
Chetco River
238
Kalmiopsis Wilderness
Cave Junction
46
110
111
112
Oregon Caves Nat'l Monument
Rogue River National Forest
0 5 mi
0 5 km
199
Siskiyou National Forest
115
113-114
116
117
118-119
OREGON

Map 7

Hikes 120-156

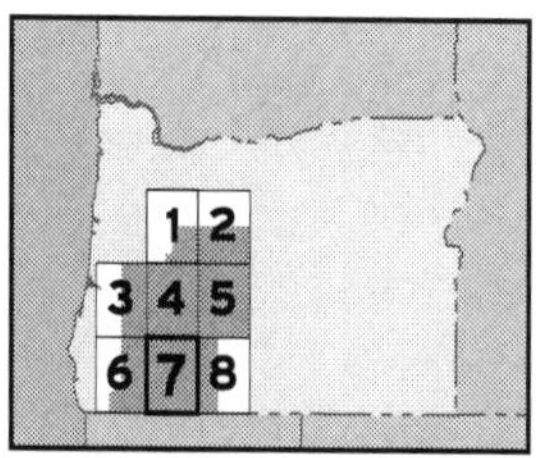

120
121
230
126
Crater Lake National Park
125
Crater Lake
127
Rogue River National Forest
122
123
124
62
128
129
130
132
131
227
134
133
62
Rogue
62
Lost Creek Reservoir
135
Trail
136-137
138
River
139
Shady Cove
Sky Lakes Wilderness
National
140
62
Butte Falls
Upper Klamath NWR
141
142
Forest
234
Eagle Point
White City
Upper Klamath Lake
143
144
140
5
145
140
140
146
Fish Lake
147
148
Central Point
Lake of the Woods
Mountain Lakes Wilderness
149
Medford
Jacksonville
Phoenix
Aspen Lake
Howard Prairie Lake
Talent
Ashland
150
151
152
Hyatt Res
Emigrant Lake
66
Pinehurst
66
5
Mt. Ashland 7,533ft
153
154
155
Rogue River National Forest
0 5 mi
0 5 km
156
OREGON

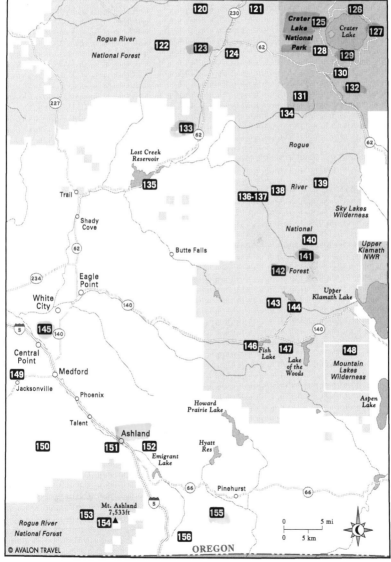

Map 8

Hikes 157-158

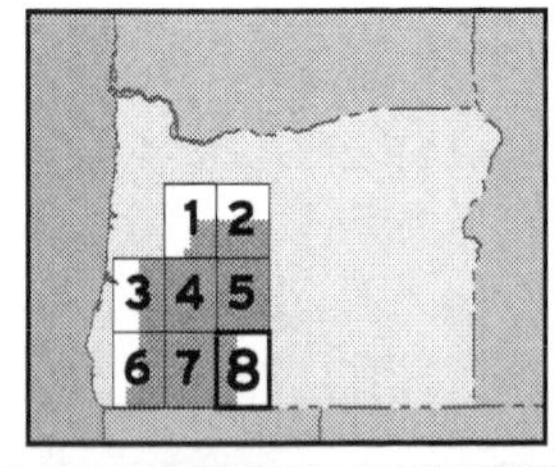

Crater Lake National Park
97
SUN MTN RD
Winema National Forest
River
Winema
Williamson
62
62
National
Chiloquin
Agency Lake
Forest
Modoc Point
Upper Klamath Lake
97
140
Klamath Falls
157
Altamont
158
Round Lake
66
39
97

OREGON
Thompson Reservoir
Fremont
National
Forest
Winema
National
Forest
Williamson
River
Sprague River
140
140
140
Fremont National Forest
Bonanza
Gerber Reservoir
0 5 mi
0 5 km
Merrill
Malin

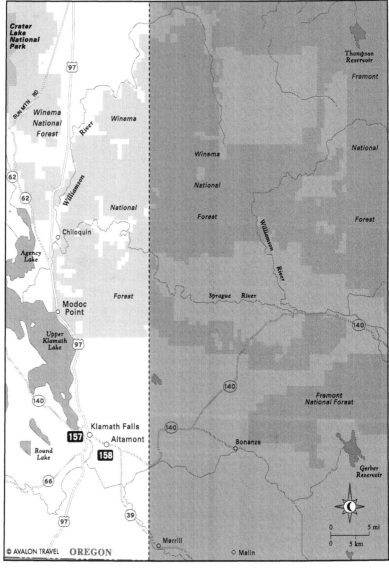

1 ROOSTER ROCK

4.2-6.6 mi/1.5-4.0 hr

west of Santiam Pass in Menagerie Wilderness

This towering pillar of basalt and andesite is a popular destination for rock climbers, as are many of the spires in the Menagerie Wilderness: Rabbit Ears, Turkey Monster, Chicken Rock, The Eggs, The Siamese Twins, and the Royal Arch, to name a few. Each is a challenge in its own right. If you're not the mountain-climbing type but want to see what all the fuss is about, there are two ways in.

The shorter but harsher route is up the Rooster Rock Trailhead, climbing 1.6 miles up 1,500 feet to the junction with the Trout Creek Trail. From here, go right up 0.5 mile to a viewpoint near Rooster Rock.

The longer, but somewhat more gradual way, is from the Trout Creek Trailhead, climbing 1,600 feet over a distance of 2.8 miles to the Rooster Rock Trail, heading to the left and uphill the remaining 0.5 mile.

User Groups: Hikers and dogs. No horses or mountain bikes allowed. No wheelchair facilities.

Permits: A free self-issue Wilderness Permit is required and is available at both trailheads. Parking and access are free at the Rooster Rock Trailhead. A federal Northwest Forest Pass is required to park at the Trout Creek Trailhead; the cost is $5 a day or $30 for an annual pass. You can buy a day pass at the trailhead, at ranger stations, or through private vendors.

Maps: For a map of the Willamette National Forest and the Mount Jefferson Wilderness, contact Willamette National Forest Headquarters, 3106 Pierce Parkway, Suite D, Springfield, OR, 97477, 541/225-6300. For a topographic map, ask the USGS for Upper Soda.

Directions: From Sweet Home, go east on U.S. 20 for 21 miles just past Trout Creek Campground near milepost 49. Park at a pullout on the north side of the highway. The Rooster Rock Trailhead is 2.6 miles farther east on U.S. 20 at a pullout.

Contact: Willamette National Forest, Sweet Home Ranger District, 4431 Highway 20, Sweet Home, OR, 97386, 541/367-5168.

2 SANTIAM WAGON ROAD

4.8 mi round-trip or 19.5 mi one-way/2.5 hr-2 days 3 6

west of Santiam Pass in Willamette National Forest

This stretch of the historic Santiam Wagon Road is famous not only for its history of travelers between the cattle farms of the Willamette Valley and the mining towns of Eastern Oregon, but also for a 1905 Transcontinental automobile race in which the new-fangled horseless carriages descended the steep mountains with trees tied to the autos to slow their descent of Sevenmile Hill. Some sections of the wagon trail are remarkably well preserved, while others become a jumble of logging roads. The trail can be taken in a series of segments, each with its own flavor. The entire stretch extends from the westernmost trailhead on U.S. 20 across from the Mountain House Restaurant to the easternmost trailhead at Fish Lake near the Santiam Pass, 19.5 miles in all.

The easiest and most historic route is from the trailhead across from the Mountain House Restaurant to House Rock, a 4.8-mile round-trip hike to a boulder that dwarfs everything around it and that served as shelter for entire pioneer families. Hike in 2.0 miles from Highway 20 along the most intact section of the old wagon road to the beginning of the loop, then head in either direction 0.8 mile around House Rock, located in the House Rock Campground.

To extend this segment to an 11.8-mile round-trip, continue from the loop on the Santiam Wagon Road to a viewpoint knoll atop Sevenmile Hill overlooking a canyon. Continue from the House Rock Campground 0.8 mile east to a gate, following the old wagon route. Go 0.3 mile to the left on Road 2044, cross the river, then turn right at the next gate to continue 2.3 mile to the knoll. If you continue one more mile, you will arrive at the Sevenmile Trailhead, where there are dispersed campsites. Otherwise, return as you came, bypassing the loop by staying to the left as you near the campground.

You could also start the hike by parking at the House Rock Campground, walking the 0.8-mile loop around House Rock and continuing on to the Sevenmile Knoll 3.4 miles past the loop, returning as you came.

Of course, you could continue further. The 4.2-mile stretch between Sevenmile Trailhead and Tombstone Pass has views to Iron Mountain, but the next 6.5-mile segment between Tombstone Pass and Hackleman Creek Road is not as interesting, as it follows newer roads that supplanted the original wagon road. The final 3.6-mile segment, however, follows an intact portion of the road to the trail's end at Fish Lake, where you'll find a historic guard station; note that parking is not allowed at Fish Lake, so park at the Hackleman Creek Road trailhead instead.

User Groups: Hikers, dogs, and horses. Mountain bikes allowed on some segments. No wheelchair facilities.

Permits: Permits are not required. Parking and access are free at the trailhead across from Mountain House Restaurant, House Rock Campground, and Hackleman Creek Road. A federal Northwest Forest Pass is required to park at the Sevenmile Trailhead; the cost is $5 a day or $30 for an annual pass. You can buy a day pass at the trailhead, at ranger stations, or through private vendors.

Maps: For a map of the Willamette National Forest and the Mount Jefferson Wilderness, contact Willamette National Forest Headquarters, 3106 Pierce Parkway, Suite D, Springfield, OR, 97477, 541/225-6300. For a topographic map, ask the USGS for Harter Mountain and Echo Mountain.

Directions: To begin the hike at Mountain House Restaurant, drive east from Sweet Home about 23 miles to the old restaurant between mileposts 52 and 53, going just beyond it to a parking area by a green gate on the south shoulder. To begin at House Rock Campground, drive east of Sweet Home 25 miles on U.S. 20 and turn right at a sign for House Rock Campground for 0.2 mile, then right again at the campground entrance for 0.2 mile to the trailhead. To reach the Sevenmile Trailhead, drive east of Sweet Home about 30.3 miles on U.S. 20 and turn right on spur Road 024, driving to the trailhead at road's end. The easternmost trailhead is on Hackleman Creek Road 2672, about 40 miles east of Sweet Home on U.S. 20; turn right onto Road 2672 and follow signs to the trailhead on the left.

Contact: Willamette National Forest, Sweet Home Ranger District, 4431 Highway 20, Sweet Home, OR, 97386, 541/367-5168.

3 IRON MOUNTAIN

3.4 mi/1.5 hr

west of Santiam Pass in Willamette National Forest

Despite its sturdy name, Iron Mountain is most famous for its wildflowers. With more than 300 species of flowering plants—including steer's head, scarlet gilia, glacier lilies, and blue flax—this peak is a designated Special Interest Area. Much of the trail follows Cone Peak, which will amaze and delight you with its array of summer colors. Bring a camera. You can visit the staffed lookout tower atop Iron Mountain's dangerous peaks. Be careful! One staffer fell to his death, and the entire tower blew off once in a winter storm. Stay away from the edge and keep a close eye on kids and dogs.

For the full loop, start at the Tombstone Pass Trailhead and go toward the nature trail and follow this 0.6 mile, crossing the highway. From here, the trail climbs 800 feet through stands of rare Alaska cedar into the meadows for 1.8 miles. From the meadows, you'll see Iron Mountain. Continue 1.5 miles along the trail to a junction. Go left and uphill, a steep 650-foot climb in 0.7 mile to the watchtower. To return, go back down Iron Mountain and take two lefts, then continue down one mile, crossing the highway again, to the Santiam Wagon Road Trail, going left 0.3 mile back to the Tombstone lot.

User Groups: Hikers and dogs. No horses or mountain bikes allowed. No wheelchair facilities.

Permits: Permits are not required. A federal Northwest Forest Pass is required to park here; the cost is $5 a day or $30 for an annual pass. You can buy a day pass at the trailhead, at ranger stations, or through private vendors.

Maps: You can purchase a Middle Santiam Wilderness Map from Geo-Graphics. For a map of the Willamette National Forest and the Mount Jefferson Wilderness, contact Willamette National Forest Headquarters, 3106 Pierce Parkway, Suite D, Springfield, OR, 97477, 541/225-6300. For a topographic map, ask the USGS for Harter Mountain.

Directions: Drive east of Sweet Home 36 miles on U.S. 20, parking at Tombstone Pass between mileposts 63 and 64.

Contact: Willamette National Forest, Sweet Home Ranger District, 4431 Highway 20, Sweet Home, OR, 97386, 541/367-5168.

4 MIDDLE SANTIAM RIVER

13.0 mi/7.0 hr  3 7

northwest of Santiam Pass in Willamette National Forest

Virtually hidden in the Cascade foothills beyond a maze of logging roads, the Middle Santiam Wilderness encompasses everything great about the Oregon Cascades. Of course, negotiating this area of rain-gorged creeks means several crossings without bridges. In low water, you may be able to cross on logs. If no logs are there to help, wading shoes will help. Some of the road that skirts this wilderness area was utterly demolished in a series of landslides, extending your journey somewhat. Nevertheless, you could take this trail as far as you'd like: the Shedd Camp Shelter, Pyramid Creek, or distant Donaca Lake all make excellent destinations, depending on your endurance.

From the Chimney Peak Trailhead, it's an easy 0.7 mile to the shake-roofed shelter and the Middle Santiam River, with 20-foot Shelter Falls. From here you'll have to cross the river and continue 0.3 mile to a junction with the South Pyramid Creek Trail. Stay left another two miles to another crossing on Pyramid Creek. If you're going on, continue 0.8 mile and cross Road 2041, then head into the wilderness area for 2.7 miles to Donaca Lake, which was dammed long ago by a massive landslide—look for boulders and snags of dead trees in the lake. Return as you came.

User Groups: Hikers, dogs, and horses. No mountain bikes allowed. No wheelchair facilities.

Permits: A free self-issue Wilderness Permit is required and is available at the trailhead. Parking and access are free.

Maps: You can purchase a Middle Santiam Wilderness Map from Geo-Graphics. For a map of the Willamette National Forest and the Mount Jefferson Wilderness, contact Willamette National Forest Headquarters, 3106 Pierce Parkway, Suite D, Springfield, OR, 97477, 541/225-6300. For a topographic map, ask the USGS for Harter Mountain.

Directions: From Sweet Home, drive 24 miles east on U.S. 20. Just beyond milepost 52, turn left on Soda Fork Road 2041 and stay on this road for eight miles to a six-way junction. Go straight, staying on Road 2041 for another 4.5 miles to a three-way fork. Take the middle Road 646 for 0.6 mile to its end at a lot for the Chimney Peak Trail.

Contact: Willamette National Forest, Sweet Home Ranger District, 4431 Highway 20, Sweet Home, OR, 97386, 541/367-5168.

5 THE PYRAMIDS

4.0 mi/2.0 hr 

northwest of Santiam Pass in Willamette National Forest

Why go to Egypt when you can just come visit Oregon's version of the pyramids? These glaciated peaks in the Old Cascades, a mountain range far younger than the bigger, snow-clad peaks, provide a view stretching from Mount Hood in the north to Diamond Peak in the south. The climb to Middle Pyramid crosses terrain ranging from woodland slopes to wildflower meadows. Vanilla leaf, bleeding hearts, columbine, and the tall white lily stalks of hellebore keep you company along the way.

From the trailhead, cross a creek to the Old Cascades Crest Trail and go right uphill for 1.8 miles, steeply climbing switchbacks near the end. At a saddle, head uphill on a fainter path 0.2 mile to the 5,618-foot peak and the site of an old watchtower. Straddled between North and South Pyramid, you'll have views of the whole countryside.

User Groups: Hikers and dogs. No horses or mountain bikes allowed. No wheelchair facilities.

Permits: Permits are not required. Parking and access are free.

Maps: For a map of the Willamette National Forest and the Mount Jefferson Wilderness, contact Willamette National Forest Headquarters, 3106 Pierce Parkway, Suite D, Springfield, OR, 97477, 541/225-6300. For a topographic map, ask the USGS for Coffin Mountain.

Directions: From Salem, drive 77 miles east on OR 22. Between mileposts 76 and 77, go right on Lava Lake Meadow Road 2067 and follow this route 1.9 miles. Cross Park Creek and turn right, following a sign for the Pyramids Trail. Follow Road 560 for 3.5 miles to its end at a parking lot.

Contact: Willamette National Forest, Sweet Home Ranger District, 4431 Highway 20, Sweet Home, OR, 97386, 541/367-5168.

6 CRESCENT MOUNTAIN

8.6 mi/4.5 hr 

west of Santiam Pass in Willamette National Forest

This aptly named mountain is just what it says it is: an enormous crescent-shaped bowl rimmed by a mighty peak, cradling little Crescent Lake and its outlet creek. The views from up here encompass Three-Fingered Jack, Mount Washington, and the Three Sisters. To get to the peak, and the last remnants of a watchtower, you'll cross a broad meadow on the Old Cascades Crest Trail to the 5,750-foot summit.

Follow the Old Cascades Crest Trail 1.1 miles to a crossing of Maude Creek then begin to climb for the next 3.2 miles to Crescent Mountain's high point along a ridge of subalpine fir and mountain hemlock.

User Groups: Hikers, dogs, and horses. No mountain bikes allowed. No wheelchair facilities.

Permits: Permits are not required. Parking and access are free.

Maps: For a map of the Willamette National Forest and the Mount Jefferson Wilderness, contact Willamette National Forest Headquarters, 3106 Pierce Parkway, Suite D, Springfield, OR, 97477, 541/225-6300. For a topographic map, ask the USGS for Echo Mountain.

Directions: Drive east of Sweet Home 43 miles on U.S. 20. Near milepost 71, turn left on Lava Lake Road for one mile, then left on Road 508 for 0.7 mile to a trailhead lot.

Contact: Willamette National Forest, Sweet Home Ranger District, 4431 Highway 20, Sweet Home, OR, 97386, 541/367-5168.

HIKING

7 BROWDER RIDGE

8.4 mi/5.0 hr

west of Santiam Pass in Willamette National Forest

Amazing views, mountain wildflower meadows, old-growth forests... why don't people come here more often? Why ask? This summit-topping trail commands views of the Southern Cascade peaks from Jefferson to the Three Sisters, and if you're lucky you might not see another soul.

From the Gate Creek Trailhead, climb 3.1 miles up nearly 1,600 feet to a junction. Go right here, up another 0.9 mile and 250 feet along Browder Ridge. A cross-country summit is possible by climbing the last 0.2 mile the remaining 300 feet to a summit.

User Groups: Hikers, dogs, and horses. No mountain bikes allowed. No wheelchair facilities.

Permits: Permits are not required. Parking and access are free.

Maps: For a map of the Willamette National Forest and the Mount Jefferson Wilderness, contact Willamette National Forest Headquarters, 3106 Pierce Parkway, Suite D, Springfield, OR, 97477, 541/225-6300. For a topographic map, ask the USGS for Tamolitch Falls.

Directions: Drive east of Sweet Home 41 miles on U.S. 20. Near milepost 68, go south on Hackelman Creek Road for 1.7 miles, then turn right on Road 1598 for 2.8 miles to the trailhead.

Contact: Willamette National Forest, Sweet Home Ranger District, 4431 Highway 20, Sweet Home, OR, 97386, 541/367-5168.

8 CLEAR LAKE

5.4 mi/2.5 hr

southwest of Santiam Pass in Willamette National Forest

The source of the wild McKenzie River is the cold Clear Lake, fed by a giant spring emerging from an ancient lava flow. The lake itself was once a forest: the lava flow dammed an ancient river and flooded this tree-filled hollow, creating a kind of ghost forest of preserved white snags beneath the calm water. This is also the topmost stretch of the McKenzie River Trail, but you can do it in a loop around the lake. You'll pass picturesque views of the lake and the mountains, and be able to spot a variety of wildflowers in the forest.

Start at the Clear Lake Resort, heading north on the trail. The first 1.5 miles curves around Ikenick Creek and meets with the sometimes dry Fish Lake Creek. In another 0.5 mile you'll come to the massive springs that feed the lake. The next 2.2 miles crosses the lava flows and passes the campground before reaching a junction. To the left, the McKenzie River Trail heads to the waterfalls, but to continue the loop go right the last 1.2 miles to the lot, watching for views to the Three Sisters and Mount Washington.

User Groups: Hikers, dogs, and bicycles. No horses allowed. No wheelchair facilities.

Permits: Permits are not required. Parking and access are free.

Maps: For a map of the Willamette National Forest, contact Willamette National Forest Headquarters, 3106 Pierce Parkway, Suite D, Springfield, OR, 97477, 541/225-6300. For a topographic map, ask the USGS for Tamolitch Falls.

Directions: Drive east on OR 126 from McKenzie Bridge 20 miles. Between mileposts 3 and 4, turn east at the Clear Lake Resort sign, driving the paved loop road 0.4 mile to the parking lot.

Contact: Willamette National Forest, McKenzie River Ranger District, 57600 McKenzie Highway, McKenzie Bridge, OR, 97413, 541/822-3381.

9 SAHALIE AND KOOSAH FALLS

2.6 mi/1.0 hr 1 9

south of Clear Lake on the McKenzie River

BEST

In the Chinook language, a Native American trade jargon that gives many local places their colorful names, both "Sahalie" and "Koosah" mean sky or heaven—which makes these two dramatic waterfalls aptly named, as they are without a doubt two of the most beautiful waterfalls in all of Oregon. What formed them is a series of lava flows from the nearby Cascades, over which the river plunges twice before it slows behind the dam at the Carmen Reservoir. The convenient pullout and viewpoint at Sahalie Falls offers access to an excellent loop around both falls, so you can see them from opposite sides of the river. You'll also see the forest, lava outcrops, and spring trilliums and calypso orchids along the way.

From the lot, walk down to the viewpoint of double-plumed Sahalie Falls, then head downstream to the left, descending easily to sheer Koosah Falls in 0.5 mile. Keep going another 0.4 mile to the road, cross the bridge to the right, and head to the right again on the spur trail, arriving at the junction with the McKenzie River Trail. The next 1.3 miles passes the waterfalls again before arriving at an upper footbridge. Go right over the bridge, then right again for the 0.4-mile return to the pullout.

User Groups: Hikers, dogs, and bicycles. No horses allowed. There is wheelchair access to the overlook at Sahalie Falls.

Permits: Permits are not required. Parking and access are free.

Maps: For a map of the Willamette National Forest, contact Willamette National Forest

© SEAN PATRICK HILL

Koosah Falls on the McKenzie River

Headquarters, 3106 Pierce Parkway, Suite D, Springfield, OR, 97477, 541/225-6300. For a topographic map, ask the USGS for Tamolitch Falls.

Directions: Drive 19 miles east of McKenzie Bridge on OR 126. Near milepost 5, go left into the Sahalie Falls Overlook parking area.

Contact: Willamette National Forest, McKenzie River Ranger District, 57600 McKenzie Highway, McKenzie Bridge, OR, 97413, 541/822-3381.

10 TAMOLITCH POOL

4.2 mi/2.0 hr 

north of McKenzie Bridge on the McKenzie River

The upper reaches of the McKenzie River were shaped by a series of 6,000-year-old lava flows that poured down from the area around Mount

Washington, shifting, damming, and even covering the river. In the stretch above Tamolitch Pool—a Chinook word for "bucket"—the McKenzie River actually runs underground for three miles, ending at this strangely empty waterfall. At the base of the seeming invisible falls, a pool composed of colors simply unimaginable lies still as the sky, a haunting blue and emerald green. At the edge of this silent pool, the river roars to life, cascading on its long journey from the mountains. A beautiful walk in a rugged canyon, this is an excellent hike for kids you want to impress.

From the Trail Bridge Reservoir road 655, head north on the McKenzie River Trail for 2.1 miles to reach the viewpoint of Tamolitch Pool, then return as you came.

User Groups: Hikers, dogs, and bicycles. No horses allowed. No wheelchair facilities.

Permits: Permits are not required. Parking and access are free.

Maps: For a map of the Willamette National Forest, contact Willamette National Forest Headquarters, 3106 Pierce Parkway, Suite D, Springfield, OR, 97477, 541/225-6300. For a topographic map, ask the USGS for Tamolitch Falls.

Directions: Drive 14 miles east of McKenzie Bridge on OR 126 to Trailbridge Reservoir, and turn left at a sign for the Trailbridge Campground. Cross the bridge and turn right on Road 655. After 0.3 mile, park at a trailhead sign.

Contact: Willamette National Forest, McKenzie River Ranger District, 57600 McKenzie Highway, McKenzie Bridge, OR, 97413, 541/822-3381.

11 TIDBITS MOUNTAIN

4.0 mi/2.0 hr 2 8

north of Blue River in Willamette National Forest

You couldn't ask much more of a hike: views to the snow-capped peaks of the Three Sisters and all the way down to the Willamette Valley, even a close-up view of one of Tidbits' two peaks. Old-growth forests line the trail, as do flowering rhododendrons and beargrass, a type of lily, and big Cascade lilies. On top, the trail passes the ruins of an old Forest Service shelter and the remains of a stairway that you won't need to get to the top.

From the trailhead, the Tidbits Mountain Trail climbs steadily 1.3 miles to a saddle with both the shelter ruins and a trail junction. Continue to the left 0.5 mile, nearly circling Tidbits Mountain, to a four-way junction. Go left and climb 0.2 mile to the summit. You can explore around the peak a bit, too.

User Groups: Hikers, dogs, horses, and mountain bikes. No wheelchair facilities.

Permits: Permits are not required. Parking and access are free.

Maps: For a map of the Willamette National Forest, contact Willamette National Forest Headquarters, 3106 Pierce Parkway, Suite D, Springfield, OR, 97477, 541/225-6300. For a topographic map, ask the USGS for Tidbits Mountain.

Directions: From Springfield, drive 44 miles east on OR 126, passing Blue River. Near milepost 44, turn left onto Road 15, following signs for Blue River Reservoir and going 4.8 miles. At pavement's end, continue on Road 1509 for 8 miles, passing a water tank, then go left on steep Road 877 for 0.2 mile to a left-hand spur parking area.

Contact: Willamette National Forest, McKenzie River Ranger District, 57600 McKenzie Highway, McKenzie Bridge, OR, 97413, 541/822-3381.

12 LOOKOUT CREEK OLD-GROWTH TRAIL

7.0 mi/3.5 hr 2 6

north of McKenzie Bridge in Willamette National Forest

BEST

The H. J. Andrews Experimental Forest in the Blue River drainage is part of an ecological research program of Oregon State University and the National Science Foundation. This rugged trail enters a forest of old-growth Douglas fir, red cedar, and Pacific yew. Feel blessed that Oregon has preserved places like this for future generations; indeed, this is the whole purpose of the Experimental Forest.

Cross Lookout Creek and head into the woods. If you're looking for a turnaround point, a 3,000-foot rock pinnacle marks the 1.6-mile mark. Otherwise, it's another 1.9 miles to the end of the trail at an upper trailhead on the 1506 road.

User Groups: Hikers and dogs. No horses or mountain bikes allowed. No wheelchair access.

Permits: Permits are not required. Parking and access are free.

Maps: For a map of the Willamette National Forest, contact Willamette National Forest Headquarters, 3106 Pierce Parkway, Suite D, Springfield, OR, 97477, 541/225-6300. For a topographic map, ask the USGS for Tamolitch Falls.

Directions: From Eugene, drive 40 miles east on OR 126 to Blue River, then go beyond town three miles to FS Road 15. Turn left and go four miles to Lookout Creek Road 1506, turning right and driving seven miles to the parking area.

Contact: Willamette National Forest, McKenzie River Ranger District, 57600 McKenzie Highway, McKenzie Bridge, OR, 97413, 541/822-3381.

13 MCKENZIE RIVER NATIONAL RECREATION TRAIL

26.5 mi one-way/2 days 3 9

between Clear Lake and McKenzie Bridge in Willamette National Forest

Backpackers rejoice! This amazing stretch of the Wild and Scenic McKenzie River is brimming with not only day trips, but excellent opportunities for extended hikes. With maintained campgrounds along the way—and more primitive spots, if you can find them—it's tempting to do the whole trail. Along the way you'll find white-water rapids, hot springs, waterfalls, and lava fields culminating in the river's source at lovely Clear Lake. Access points abound along the way (see *Clear Lake, Sahalie and Koosah Falls,* and *Tamolitch Pool* listings in this chapter) and you're never too far from the road, though once you set out you'll find yourself worlds away.

Some basic mileage numbers: From the start of the trail to the McKenzie Ranger Station, a route paralleling the highway, is one mile. From the Ranger Station to Belknap Hot Springs, a private resort where you can pay to swim, is 3.9 miles, with Paradise Campground in-between. From Belknap to the natural hot springs at Deer Creek is five miles; you'll cross the river on a road and arrive at Deer Creek Road. From Deer Creek to the campground at Trail Bridge Reservoir is 3.3 miles. From Trail Bridge to Tamolitch Pool is 3.9 miles. From Tamolitch to Carmen Reservoir is 3.4 miles (along this stretch the river runs underground). From Carmen to the crossing of Highway 126, passing both Sahalie and Koosah Falls is two miles. From the highway to the upper trailhead, passing Clear Lake and Coldwater Cover Campground is four miles.

User Groups: Hikers, dogs, and bicycles. No horses allowed. No wheelchair facilities.

Permits: Permits are not required. Parking and access are free.

Maps: For a map of the Willamette National Forest, contact Willamette National Forest Headquarters, 3106 Pierce Parkway, Suite D, Springfield, OR, 97477, 541/225-6300. For a topographic map, ask the USGS for Tamolitch Falls.

Directions: To get to the lower trailhead at McKenzie Ranger Station, go 2.2 miles east of McKenzie Bridge on OR 126 and park at the station. To get to the upper trailhead, drive east on OR 126 from McKenzie Bridge about 21 miles, passing the entrance for Clear Lake Resort to the well-marked trailhead on the right.

Contact: Willamette National Forest, McKenzie River Ranger District, 57600 McKenzie Highway, McKenzie Bridge, OR, 97413, 541/822-3381.

14 CASTLE ROCK

2.0-11.4 mi/1.0-6.0 hr 2 8

south of Blue River in Willamette National Forest

There are two main ways to climb Castle Rock: the easy way and the hard way. It's a matter of both distance and elevation gain, but the end point is the same: an excellent view down to the McKenzie River canyon and east to the Three Sisters. The peak itself, the remnant of a long-extinct volcano, has sheer cliffs at the summit, and you can look down into the peaks of the Douglas fir trees. To try the easy hike, follow the driving directions and head up the trail a mere mile to the summit.

For the difficult hike, you'll start at a lower trailhead. Once on Kings Road, instead of turning onto Road 480, continue 1.3 miles past it to the trailhead on the right. From here, the King Castle Trail sets off four miles, crosses Road 480, continues up 0.7 mile through a clear-cut, then arrives at the upper trailhead, with its remaining mile to the top.

User Groups: Hikers, dogs, horses, and mountain bikes. No wheelchair facilities.

Permits: Permits are not required. Parking and access are free.

Maps: For a map of the Willamette National Forest, contact Willamette National Forest Headquarters, 3106 Pierce Parkway, Suite D, Springfield, OR, 97477, 541/225-6300. For a topographic map, ask the USGS for McKenzie Bridge.

Directions: From Springfield, drive 45 miles east on OR 126 and turn right onto the Aufderheide Road 19. At the next fork in 0.5 mile, stay straight onto Road 410, and in another 0.4 mile go left onto Kings Road 2639 for 0.5 mile. Turn right on Road 480 and continue uphill 5.8 miles to road's end at the upper trailhead.

Contact: Willamette National Forest, McKenzie River Ranger District, 57600 McKenzie Highway, McKenzie Bridge, OR, 97413, 541/822-3381.

15 OLALLIE MOUNTAIN/ OLALLIE RIDGE

7.2-12.2 mi/4.0-6.0 hr

south of McKenzie Bridge in Three Sisters Wilderness

When all is said and done, the Olallie Trail stretches 9.7 miles end to end, making this a great option for backpackers (another trailhead is located 6.0 miles away at Horsepasture Saddle; see *Horsepasture Mountain and Olallie Ridge* listing in this chapter). From this trail, you can bushwhack to a hidden lake, find the remains of an old guard station in Olallie Meadows, and climb to one of only two lookouts left in this wilderness, a 14-square-foot cabin with stunning views. Not only that, but the door is usually unlocked, opening it up for backpackers. You'll find the big metal fire locator still there, and the panoramic view is unequalled.

From Pat Saddle Trailhead, enter the Three Sisters Wilderness on the Olallie Trail. In 0.5 mile, cross Mosquito Creek (heading off-trail and upstream 0.2 mile leads to Wolverine Lake, but use your route-finding skills). Continue on the Olallie Trail 1.6 miles to a pass and junction. Head right 1.5 miles and up 700 feet to the lookout for a 7.2 mile round-trip hike, returning as you came.

Other options for extended trips abound. From the lookout tower, return to the Olallie Trail junction. Going right 0.9 mile farther leads to the guard station ruins in Olallie Meadows. In another 0.6 mile past the meadows, a left-hand junction goes 10.2 miles to Horse Lake, and the Bear Flat Trail heads to the right, making for a potential loop around Olallie Mountain by following it 6.9 miles to a junction with the French Pete Creek Trail, then heading right 2.9 mile back to the Pat Saddle Trailhead.

User Groups: Hikers, dogs, and horses. No mountain bikes allowed. No wheelchair facilities.

Permits: A free self-issue Wilderness Permit is required and is available at the trailhead. Parking and access are free.

Maps: A map of the Three Sisters Wilderness is available for purchase from Geo-Graphics. For a map of the Willamette National Forest, contact Willamette National Forest Headquarters, 3106 Pierce Parkway, Suite D, Springfield, OR, 97477, 541/225-6300. For a topographic map, ask the USGS for French Mountain.

Directions: From Springfield, drive 45 miles east on OR 126 and turn right onto the Aufderheide Road 19. At the next fork in 0.5 mile, go right on Road 19 for 10 miles to the French Pete Trailhead on the left. To begin at the top, start at the Pat Saddle Trailhead: From Springfield, drive 45 miles east on OR 126 and turn right onto the Aufderheide Road 19. At the next fork in 0.5 mile, go right on Road 19 for 2.8 miles to the reservoir. Turn left across the Cougar Dam on Road 1993 for 2.6 miles, then fork left and stay on Road 1993 another 11.3 miles to the Pat Saddle Trailhead on the left.

Contact: Willamette National Forest, McKenzie River Ranger District, 57600 McKenzie Highway, McKenzie Bridge, OR, 97413, 541/822-3381.

16 HORSEPASTURE MOUNTAIN AND OLALLIE RIDGE

2.8 mi/1.0 hr

south of McKenzie Bridge in Willamette National Forest

One entry to the Three Sisters Wilderness is Olallie Ridge, which leads up to the boundary just before Olallie Mountain. Only the mountain retains the name Horsepasture—named because horseback wilderness rangers once camped here. The camp is long gone, though huckleberries—once harvested by Native Americans in the area—remain. Olallie, in fact, is a Chinook word for "berry."

For views as far as Mount Jefferson and Mount Hood, go left from the trailhead up 1.4 miles to the 5,660-foot summit. This easy hike also offers access to the Olallie Trail, which extends six miles from the Horsepasture Saddle to the Pat Saddle Trailhead.

User Groups: Hikers, dogs, horses, and mountain bikes. No wheelchair facilities.

Permits: Permits are not required. Parking and access are free.

Maps: A map of the Three Sisters Wilderness is available for purchase from Geo-Graphics. For a map of the Willamette National Forest, contact Willamette National Forest Headquarters, 3106 Pierce Parkway, Suite D, Springfield, OR, 97477, 541/225-6300. For a topographic map, ask the USGS for French Mountain.

Directions: From Springfield, drive 50 miles east on OR 126 to McKenzie Bridge. Cross the river and turn right on Horse Creek Road 2638 for 1.7 miles. Turn right on Road 1993 for 8.6 miles and park at the Horsepasture Trailhead on the right.

Contact: Willamette National Forest, McKenzie River Ranger District, 57600 McKenzie Highway, McKenzie Bridge, OR, 97413, 541/822-3381.

17 FRENCH PETE CREEK

9.8 mi one-way/4.0 hr

south of Cougar Reservoir in Three Sisters Wilderness

This lovely mountain creek makes a good day hike and provides entrance to the high country. In 1.7 miles, the French Pete Trail reaches the first ford. The next 1.3 miles runs along the opposite shore to a second ford. Beyond this the trail is not maintained, but runs another 1.8 miles to the five-mile marker. From here, continue another 4.8 miles to the Pat Saddle Trailhead, following Pat Creek rather than French Pete.

User Groups: Hikers, dogs, and horses. No mountain bikes allowed. No wheelchair facilities.

Permits: A free self-issue Wilderness Permit is required and is available at the trailhead. Parking and access are free.

Maps: A map of the Three Sisters Wilderness is available for purchase from Geo-Graphics. For a map of the Willamette National Forest, contact Willamette National Forest Headquarters, 3106 Pierce Parkway, Suite D, Springfield, OR, 97477, 541/225-6300. For a topographic map, ask the USGS for Cougar Reservoir.

Directions: From Springfield, drive 45 miles east on OR 126 and turn right onto the Aufderheide Road 19. At the next fork in 0.5 mile, go right on Road 19 for 10 miles to the French Pete Trailhead on the left.

Contact: Willamette National Forest, McKenzie River Ranger District, 57600 McKenzie Highway, McKenzie Bridge, OR, 97413, 541/822-3381.

18 REBEL ROCK

12.3 mi/7.0 hr

south of Cougar Reservoir in Three Sisters Wilderness

One of two lookouts left in the Three Sisters Wilderness (the other is on Olallie Mountain), Rebel Rock Lookout is perched on a 5,000-foot promontory overlooking Mount Bachelor. You won't spot this from the wooded trail, however, so you'll have to be alert for its spur trail. This loop as a whole is a great entrance to the Three Sisters country, with a trail veering off at Rebel Rock (which is not where the tower is, actually) into the deeper wilderness. This loop, though, is nothing to sneeze at: it will require some fortitude, as it travels more than 12 miles and climbs 3,300 feet along the way.

Start on the Rebel Creek Trail to the left at the trailhead, crossing two bridges and a true old-growth forest in the first 1.1 miles. The next 4.6 miles climbs away from the creek and up the canyon slope and into hemlock woods to a junction. Go right on the Rebel Rock Trail for 1.8 miles, watching to the left for the pillar of Rebel Rock. Watch for four rock cairns on the left and a faint path; follow this a short distance to the lookout. Continue on the main trail 0.5 mile to a viewpoint of the Three Sisters and Mount Jefferson. The trail descends to a meadow and continues the remaining 4.3 miles following Trail Creek back to the trailhead.

User Groups: Hikers, dogs, and horses. No mountain bikes allowed. No wheelchair facilities.

Permits: A free self-issue Wilderness Permit is required and is available at the trailhead. Parking and access are free.

Maps: A map of the Three Sisters Wilderness is available for purchase from Geo-Graphics. For a map of the Willamette National Forest, contact Willamette National Forest Headquarters, 3106 Pierce Parkway, Suite D, Springfield, OR, 97477, 541/225-6300. For a topographic map, ask the USGS for Chucksney Mountain and Grasshopper Mountain.

Directions: From Springfield, drive 45 miles east on OR 126 and turn right onto the Aufderheide Road 19. At the next fork in 0.5 mile, go right on Road 19 for 13 miles to the Rebel Creek Trailhead on the left.

Contact: Willamette National Forest, McKenzie River Ranger District, 57600 McKenzie Highway, McKenzie Bridge, OR, 97413, 541/822-3381.

19 LOWDER MOUNTAIN

5.6 mi/3.0 hr

south of McKenzie Bridge in Three Sisters Wilderness

From the summit of Lowder Mountain, you will see mountains from the Three Sisters to Mount Hood. You can camp on the plains atop the peak, with its sheer drop over the cliffs down to inaccessible Karl and Ruth Lakes, nearly 2,000 feet below. If you choose to camp here, be sure to bring enough water.

From the trailhead, head to the left on the Lowder Mountain Trail (the right-hand trail goes to a quaking aspen swamp) and go uphill, passing through three view-laden meadows in the first two miles. At a junction, go left and climb steeply up a series of switchbacks for 0.5 mile. When you reach the plain, go another 0.3 mile, almost to the forest, then turn uphill 0.2 mile to the cliffs.

User Groups: Hikers, dogs, and horses. No mountain bikes allowed. No wheelchair facilities.

Permits: A free self-issue Wilderness Permit is required and is available at the trailhead. Parking and access are free.

Maps: A map of the Three Sisters Wilderness is available for purchase from Geo-Graphics. For a map of the Willamette National Forest, contact Willamette National Forest Headquarters, 3106 Pierce Parkway, Suite D, Springfield, OR, 97477, 541/225-6300. For a topographic map, ask the USGS for French Mountain.

Directions: From Springfield, drive 45 miles east on OR 126 and turn right onto the Aufderheide Road 19. At the next fork in 0.5 mile, go right on Road 19 for 2.8 miles to the reservoir. Turn left across the Cougar Dam on Road 1993 for 2.6 miles, then fork left and stay on Road 1993 another 9.2 miles to the Lowder Mountain Trailhead on the right.

Contact: Willamette National Forest, McKenzie River Ranger District, 57600 McKenzie Highway, McKenzie Bridge, OR, 97413, 541/822-3381.

20 DUFFY AND MOWICH LAKES

8.8–11.8 mi/4.5–6.0 hr

west of Three Fingered Jack in Mount Jefferson Wilderness

Like all the Cascade Mountain wilderness areas, Mount Jefferson's flanks are studded with beautiful mountain lakes of all shapes and sizes. In 2003, the unfortunate B&B Complex Fire roared through this area, reducing much of the forest to snags and ash. Don't let that stop you: This area is still untouched in places, and the lakes are as cool and clear as ever. Two lakes lie along this entrance to backpacking adventures: Duffy Lake, below the pointed peak of Duffy Butte, and Mowich Lake, with one side untouched by fire. From little Alice Lake you can climb Red Butte and continue on to the Eight Lakes Basin. Or, you can head to nearby Santiam Lake for a stunning view of Three Fingered Jack.

From the trailhead, follow the Duffy Trail along the North Santiam River bed up 3.3 miles, staying left at a junction, to Duffy Lake. From here, continue along Duffy Lake, keeping to the left 1.1 miles to Mowich Lake, then another mile to Alice Lake. An obvious cross-country path climbs 0.5 mile up Red Butte here. From there, the Blue Lake Trail continues on to Eight Lakes Basin.

For a look at the alpine meadows around Santiam Lake, source of the North Santiam River, start from the outlet of Duffy Lake and go 0.2 mile to a spur trail on the right, following it one mile to Santiam Lake at the bottom of Three Fingered Jack's long slope from its craggy heights.

User Groups: Hikers, dogs, and horses. No mountain bikes allowed. No wheelchair facilities.

Permits: A free self-issue Wilderness Permit is required and is available at the trailhead. Parking and access are free.

Maps: You can purchase a Mount Jefferson Wilderness Map from Geo-Graphics. For a

map of the Willamette National Forest and the Mount Jefferson Wilderness, contact Willamette National Forest Headquarters, 3106 Pierce Parkway, Suite D, Springfield, OR, 97477, 541/225-6300. For a topographic map, ask the USGS for Santiam Junction.
Directions: From Salem, drive 76 miles east on OR 22. Near milepost 76, turn east on Big Meadows Road 2267 for three miles to road's end.
Contact: Willamette National Forest, Detroit Ranger District, HC73, Box 320, Mill City, OR, 97360, 503/854-4239.

21 ROCKPILE LAKE

10.8–13.2 mi/4.0–6.0 hr

north of Three Fingered Jack in Mount Jefferson Wilderness

The 2003 B&B Complex Fire truly devastated this area, so you'll need to confirm trail conditions before hiking in these parts. Rockpile Lake Trail follows the massive Bear Valley steadily up to the Pacific Crest Trail and little Rockpile Lake, with access in either direction to great views along the Cascade Crest. If trails are in working order, it is possible to do a great loop around Bear Valley, stopping by little Minto Lake along the way.

From the trailhead follow the Rockpile Lake Trail to the right. In 0.3 mile, stay left at a junction, then stay left again in another 2.3 mile. From the second junction, climb steadily for 2.8 miles up 1,000 feet to the Pacific Crest Trail and Rockpile Lake to the right. Return as you came.

If the loop trail is open, and if you'd like to follow some stunning vistas along this high ridge, head south on the PCT for 3.4 miles to Minto Lake on the right. To the left, the Bear Valley Trail descends 4.4 miles into huckleberry groves and past Bear Valley Lake to the trailhead.
User Groups: Hikers, dogs, and horses. No mountain bikes allowed. No wheelchair facilities.
Permits: A free self-issue Wilderness Permit is required and is available at the trailhead. Parking and access are free.
Maps: You can purchase a Mount Jefferson Wilderness Map from Geo-Graphics. For a map of the Deschutes National Forest and the Mount Jefferson Wilderness, contact Deschutes National Forest Headquarters, 1001 SW Emkay Drive, Bend, OR, 97702, 541/383-5300. For a topographic map, ask the USGS for Marion Lake.
Directions: From Sisters, drive 12 miles west on U.S. 20 to about milepost 88. Turn right on Road 12 at a sign for Mount Jefferson Wilderness Trailheads. Drive north 3.7 miles on Road 12 and continue straight on Road 1230 for 1.5 miles, then turn left on Road 1234 for 0.8 mile. Turn right on Road 1235 for 3.9 miles to road's end.
Contact: Deschutes National Forest, Sisters Ranger District, P.O. Box 249, Sisters, OR, 97759, 541/549-7700.

22 CANYON CREEK MEADOWS

7.5 mi/4.0 hr 3 9

east of Three Fingered Jack in Mount Jefferson Wilderness

For a worthy alpine meadow experience, and to get a look at a glacial-silt lake among an array of wildflowers, the Canyon Creek Meadows is it. By the grace of nature, the meadows were spared by the 2003 fire that decimated other parts of the wilderness, including the area around Jack Lake and the trailhead here. Did I mention you will also be standing beneath the towering crags of Three Fingered Jack? The creek begins in a cirque in the bowl of the mountain, surrounded by gravel walls. This trail, going from burn to forest to meadow to alpine rockfall, even a pitch to a saddle with a view over the mountain range to the south, allows you to visit just about every kind of ecosystem in this range. The meadows, too, are suitable for backpacking.

From Jack Lake, head up the Wasco Lake Trail 0.4 mile to a junction. Here the trail splits into the Canyon Creek Meadows Loop, and the USFS asks that you go to the left first, and return on the opposite loop. So go left 1.7 miles, leaving the burn and reaching the lower meadow. Go left another 1.5 miles, reaching the upper meadow and an alpine wonderland. If you follow the trail to the end, you'll climb a ridge above the meadows, climbing steeply to the saddle on the shoulder of the mountain. When you return, go left at the loop junction. Head 0.9 mile along the creek to a junction. If you'd like to visit Wasco Lake, go left 0.7 mile, watching for the waterfalls off the trail. Then return to this junction and go right 1.5 miles back to Jack Lake.

User Groups: Hikers, dogs, and horses. No mountain bikes allowed. No wheelchair facilities.

Permits: A free self-issue Wilderness Permit is required and is available at the trailhead. A federal Northwest Forest Pass is required to park here; the cost is $5 a day or $30 for an annual pass. You can buy a day pass at the trailhead, at ranger stations, or through private vendors.

Maps: You can purchase a Mount Jefferson Wilderness Map from Geo-Graphics. For a map of the Deschutes National Forest and the Mount Jefferson Wilderness, contact Deschutes National Forest Headquarters, 1001 SW Emkay Drive, Bend, OR, 97702, 541/383-5300. For a topographic map, ask the USGS for Three Fingered Jack.

Directions: From Sisters, drive 12 miles west on U.S. 20 to about milepost 88. Turn right on Road 12 at a sign for Mount Jefferson Wilderness Trailheads. Drive north 3.7 miles on Road 12 and continue straight on Road 1230 for 1.5 miles, then turn left on Road 1234 and going five miles to the trailhead at Jack Lake Campground.

Contact: Deschutes National Forest, Sisters Ranger District, P.O. Box 249, Sisters, OR, 97759, 541/549-7700.

23 PACIFIC CREST TRAIL TO THREE FINGERED JACK

10.5 mi/5.5 hr

south of Three Fingered Jack in Mount Jefferson Wilderness

Three Fingered Jack is a dark-hued volcanic core that resembles a frightening fortress. It rises abruptly from the surrounding mountains and practically begs rock climbers to try their luck. Most likely, one look will make you lose all nerve. Instead, this Pacific Crest Trail stretch offers a commanding look at this massive peak, and an entrance to the Mount Jefferson Wilderness. The forest was burned here in a 2003 fire, but that opened up the views as this trail follows the ridgeline. From the PCT trailhead, follow the PCT north 5.2 miles to a close-up viewpoint of the mountain. From there, you can return the way you came—or continue on as far as you like.

User Groups: Hikers, dogs, and horses. No mountain bikes allowed. No wheelchair facilities.

Permits: A free self-issue Wilderness Permit is required and is available at the trailhead. A federal Northwest Forest Pass is required to park here; the cost is $5 a day or $30 for an annual pass. You can buy a day pass at the trailhead, at ranger stations, or through private vendors.

Maps: You can purchase a Mount Jefferson Wilderness Map from Geo-Graphics. For a map of the Willamette National Forest and the Mount Jefferson Wilderness, contact Willamette National Forest Headquarters, 3106 Pierce Parkway, Suite D, Springfield, OR, 97477, 541/225-6300. For a topographic map, ask the USGS for Three Fingered Jack.

Directions: The trailhead is located 20 miles west of Sisters on U.S. 20 at the Santiam Pass, accessible from either Sisters to the east or Eugene/Springfield/OR 126 or OR 22/Salem to the east.

Contact: Willamette National Forest, Detroit Ranger District, HC73, Box 320, Mill City, OR, 97360, 503/854-4239.

24 BERLEY AND SANTIAM LAKES

10.2 mi/4.5 hr 2 8

south of Three Fingered Jack in Mount Jefferson Wilderness

The original trail to these lakes, which began at the ruins of the abandoned Santiam Lodge, was permanently closed after the 2003 wildfire that decimated this section of the Mount Jefferson Wilderness. There is another way to get to the two rock-rimmed tarns known as the Berley Lakes and to picturesque Santiam Lake at the base of Three Fingered Jack. This trail runs along a section of the Skyline Trail.

From the PCT trailhead on U.S. 20, go north 1.2 miles to a left-hand junction and go left 0.5 mile on this connector trail. Then go right 1.5 miles on the Santiam Lake Trail and watch for an unmarked turnoff to the left heading 0.3 mile to and along the lower and larger Berley Lake; follow this trail to another side trail and find the upper lake. Return to the Santiam Trail and go left another 1.9 miles to a right-hand turnoff for Santiam Lake.

User Groups: Hikers, dogs, and horses. No mountain bikes allowed. No wheelchair facilities.

Permits: A free self-issue Wilderness Permit is required and is available at the trailhead. A federal Northwest Forest Pass is required to park here; the cost is $5 a day or $30 for an annual pass. You can buy a day pass at the trailhead, at ranger stations, or through private vendors.

Maps: You can purchase a Mount Jefferson Wilderness Map from Geo-Graphics. For a map of the Willamette National Forest and the Mount Jefferson Wilderness, contact Willamette National Forest Headquarters, 3106 Pierce Parkway, Suite D, Springfield, OR, 97477, 541/225-6300. For a topographic map, ask the USGS for Santiam Lake.

Directions: The trailhead is located 20 miles west of Sisters on U.S. 20 at the Santiam Pass, accessible from either Sisters to the east or Eugene/Springfield/OR 126 or OR 22/Salem to the east.

Contact: Willamette National Forest, Detroit Ranger District, HC73, Box 320, Mill City, OR, 97360, 503/854-4239.

25 BLACK BUTTE

3.8 mi/2.5 hr 3 8

north of Sisters in Deschutes National Forest

Set aside to the east of the bulk of the Cascades, Black Butte seems an oddball mountain. For one thing, this dominant 6,436-foot butte retains its perfectly symmetrical shape, a huge rounded mound set near peaks far more eroded than its stern face. This has less to do with age than with weather: the peaks to the west create a rainshadow that has largely kept this mountain from being weathered. This makes for a fairly easy climb, which explains why Black Butte hosts one of the few surviving fire watchtowers in the Cascade Mountains, with a view worth a summer spent spotting fires. Atop Black Butte, you can check out the old cupola-style lookout and get a glimpse of the new one. A second lookout built by the Civilian Conservation Corps in 1934 was destroyed in a storm. Beyond the edges of the peak, you'll have an expansive view of the Cascades, Green Ridge, and the Metolius River far below.

The trail is a straightforward lunge for the peak up 1.9 miles of trail that climbs steadily, even steeply at times. Follow it through the ponderosa pine forests onto the open prairies of wildflowers.

User Groups: Hikers, dogs, and horses. No mountain bikes allowed. No wheelchair facilities.

Permits: A federal Northwest Forest Pass is

HIKING

© SEAN PATRICK HILL

historic Black Butte lookout

required to park here; the cost is $5 a day or $30 for an annual pass. You can buy a day pass at the trailhead, at ranger stations, or through private vendors.

Maps: For a map of the Deschutes National Forest contact Deschutes National Forest Headquarters, 1001 SW Emkay Drive, Bend, OR, 97702, 541/383-5300. For a topographic map, ask the USGS for Black Butte.

Directions: From Sisters, drive 5.5 miles west on U.S. 20 to Green Ridge Road 11. Turn right and follow this road north 3.8 miles, then turn left on Road 1110, following it 5.1 miles uphill to the parking area at road's end.

Contact: Deschutes National Forest, Sisters Ranger District, P.O. Box 249, Sisters, OR, 97759, 541/549-7700.

26 PATJENS LAKES

6.0 mi/3.0 hr 2 8

at Big Lake in Mount Washington Wilderness

BEST

Big Lake earns its name and makes for a destination for car campers and, in the winter, cross-country skiers. For hikers, adventure lies beyond the big lake in the Mount Washington Wilderness, with meadows, ponds, slopes of bracken ferns, and the Patjens Lakes hidden nicely back in Hidden Valley, with its view of Mount Washington's spire. The Patjens Lake Loop Trail follows the shore of Big Lake too, past a beach and towards views of broad and flat-topped Hayrick Butte. For backpackers, this makes a good entry into this little-explored wilderness.

From the trailhead, follow signs for Patjens Lakes, staying right at the first junction and left at the second for 1.8 miles to a saddle. Continue 1.7 miles into the midst of the lakes, the third of four being a perfect place to stop and eat. Continue 1.5 miles through Hidden Valley to a beach on Big Lake, going left along the shore one mile back to the trailhead.

User Groups: Hikers, dogs, and horses. No mountain bikes allowed. No wheelchair facilities.

Permits: A free self-issue Wilderness Permit is required and is available at the trailhead. Parking and access are free.

Maps: For a map of the Willamette National

Forest and the Mount Washington Wilderness, contact Willamette National Forest Headquarters, 3106 Pierce Parkway, Suite D, Springfield, OR, 97477, 541/225-6300. For a topographic map, ask the USGS for Clear Lake.

Directions: Drive U.S. 20 to the Santiam Pass and turn south on Big Lake Road four miles to a trailhead on the right.

Contact: Willamette National Forest, McKenzie River Ranger District, 57600 McKenzie Highway, McKenzie Bridge, OR, 97413, 541/822-3381.

27 ALDER SPRINGS

6.0 mi/2.5 hr

northeast of Sisters in Crooked River National Grassland

The creek formerly known as "Squaw Creek" is now called "Whychus Creek," derived from a Sahaptin word meaning "the place we cross the water." It's a fitting name for this hike, since you'll have to ford the creek to travel this trail in a remote canyon down to its confluence with the Deschutes River. Along the way the trail passes a dry waterfall and a massive spring that flows out of a cliff and down through a grove of alder into the main creek. At the confluence, note the incredible rock formations high on the canyon walls, and watch for more springs.

From the trailhead, go downhill on the Alder Springs Trail to a junction in 0.2 mile, continuing to the right for 1.2 miles along the canyon rim and finally down to the creek itself. Ford the creek and continue 1.6 miles downstream on the opposite shore to the confluence of the Deschutes and its massive, water-smoothed boulders.

User Groups: Hikers and dogs on leash only. No horses or mountain bikes. No wheelchair facilities.

Permits: Permits are not required. Parking and access are free.

Maps: For a topographic map, ask the USGS for Steelhead Falls.

Directions: From Sisters, drive east on U.S. 20 and veer left on OR 126 toward Redmond. Go 4.6 miles and turn left on Goodrich Road for 8.1 miles. At milepost 7, go left on Road 6360 through a green gate (remember to close the gate behind you). Go 4.1 miles and turn right at an Alder Springs sign, going 0.8 mile to road's end.

Contact: Crooked River National Grassland, 813 SW Highway 97, Madras, OR, 97741, 541/475-9272.

28 GRAY BUTTE

4.8-7.1 mi/2.5-3.0 hr

north of Redmond in Crooked River National Grassland

The lopsided pyramid that looms behind the crags of Smith Rock State Park is Gray Butte, and this not-well-known trailhead offers a free entrance to Smith Rock State Park (see next listing). From the saddle between the butte and the ridge that gently slopes down to the Crooked River canyon, this vista-rich trail looks out over the desert and Cascade Mountains and crosses a pass where you can find rare bitterroot flowers in spring. The root of these tiny flowers provided Native Americans with a valuable food.

From the Gray Butte Saddle Trailhead, follow the trail away from Gray Butte 1.4 miles to a pass. Pass by the dirt roads and continue one mile to the dirt Burma Road. You can continue on an unofficial trail to a viewpoint and along the ridge into Smith Rock, a 1.5-mile walk to the Crooked River.

A longer tour, perhaps better for mountain bikes, especially in summer, loops for a 7.1-mile ride around Gray Butte itself. From the Gray Butte Saddle Trailhead, go back to the four-way junction and go straight on a dirt road. The trail crosses this road, circling the butte. The longest stretch of walking trail goes 3.4 mile to the left, ending at the McCoin Orchard Trailhead. From here follow Road 57 down 0.7 mile, veering right on Road 5710 for 1.4 miles, then going right again on Road 5720 over the cattle guard and veering off on the trail to the right for the remaining 1.6 miles.

User Groups: Hikers, dogs, horses, and mountain bikes. No wheelchair facilities.

Permits: Permits are not required. Parking and access are free.

Maps: For a topographic map, ask the USGS for Gray Butte.

Directions: From Redmond, drive six miles north on U.S. 97 to Terrebonne and a sign for Smith Rock State Park. Turn east on Smith Rock Way for 5.9 miles to a junction, and go left on Lone Pine Road for 3.4 miles. At a sign for Gray Butte Trailhead go left on Road 5720 for 1.6 miles to a four-way junction. Turn left and park on the right by the trailhead.

Contact: Crooked River National Grassland, 813 SW Highway 97, Madras, OR, 97741, 541/475-9272.

29 SMITH ROCK STATE PARK

3.7-6.3 mi/1.5-3.5 hr

north of Redmond

BEST

In a state rich with state parks, Smith Rock ranks in the upper echelon. Simply put, this is one of Oregon's most magnificent parks, an intense land of river canyon, rock formations, wildlife, and ponderosa pines. What makes it famous is its allure to rock climbers, and on any given spring, summer, or fall day—sometimes even winter, one of the best times to hike here—you're sure to see climbers on the many dizzying walls. The kingpin of these climbs is the welded tuff ash formation known as Monkey Face, which, from the right angle, resembles exactly that. Within view of all the climbing, aeries of golden eagles nestle in the cliff faces. Deer wander here, as do coyote and other animals. And arcing gracefully through it all is the Crooked River, oxbowing around this one-of-a-kind rock formation. You can easily spend a full day here, or two, and a walk-in campground for backpackers and climbers makes that a temptation. Two hikes crown the

Smith Rock State Park

park and visit everything you could want to see. Just be aware of the dangers here; people have died in this park by falling from the cliffs. Play it safe and stay on the trail.

To climb over Misery Ridge and visit Monkey Face close up, start from the parking area and descend 0.4 mile into the canyon and cross the footbridge. Continue to the left and up the Misery Ridge Trail 0.5 mile up staircases and a steep trail to the crest. Follow the trail to a junction, where a left-hand user trail goes down a ridge to a view of Monkey Face. You should not attempt this if you are afraid of heights. Continue on the Misery Ridge Trail down the opposite side of the ridge on a long series of steep switchbacks, then along the cliffs above the river to a junction with the river trail, 0.7 mile in all. From here you can explore at whim; going left along the river 1.7 miles will bring you back to the footbridge and the remaining 0.4 mile to the lot.

For a longer walk, hike 0.4 mile to the footbridge and follow the river downstream 2.2 miles, passing the climbing walls and huge boulders. Past Monkey Face and at a huge boulder, turn right up a path climbing a steep gully, following it 1.5 miles up and along the ridge to the Burma Road. From the road, going straight leads to Gray Butte (see listing in this chapter). For the loop, go right on Burma Road and descend back into the canyon 0.7 mile to the trail junction on the right, and follow this trail 1.1 mile back to the footbridge and the remaining 0.4 mile back to the parking lot.

User Groups: Hikers and dogs on leash only. No horses or mountain bikes. No wheelchair facilities.

Permits: Permits are not required. A $3 day-use fee is collected at a self-serve kiosk, or you can get an annual Oregon Parks and Recreation pass for $25; contact Oregon Parks and Recreation, 800/551-6949.

Maps: For a free park brochure, call Oregon Parks and Recreation, 800/551-6949, or download a free map at www.oregonstateparks.org. For a topographic map, ask the USGS for Gray Butte.

Directions: From Redmond, drive six miles north on U.S. 97 to Terrebonne and a sign for Smith Rock State Park. Turn east on Smith Rock Way and follow signs 3.3 miles to the parking area.

Contact: Oregon Parks and Recreation Department, 1115 Commercial Street Northeast, Salem, OR, 97301, 800/551-6949, www.oregonstateparks.org.

30 PACIFIC CREST TRAIL TO LITTLE BELKNAP CRATER

5.2 mi/2.5 hr 2 9

in the McKenzie Pass in Mount Washington Wilderness

If you want to get a sense of what walking on a barren planet like, say, Mars is like (especially after the photographs from that red planet), all you have to do is walk onto the McKenzie Pass. At first view of these lava fields, it's hard not to be shocked. You'll feel a certain awe here, as the size of these flows staggers the imagination. You'll have a whole new respect for those that built the Pacific Crest Trail, carving its route over the black, jumbled basalt. You'll also get a sense of what volcanics really look like up close. An easy tour heads out onto the flow toward the Little Belknap Crater. Atop its knob, a series of lava caves plunge into the peak, and the views extend to far bigger Belknap Crater and Mount Washington and the Sisters. With a sharp eye you can spot "lava bombs"—which solidified in the shapes of tears as they were hurled through the air. Bring plenty of sunblock and water on this trail, especially in summer.

From the PCT trailhead, head north. The trail begins at the foot of a forested island in the lava, then crosses a second island, the trail heading 2.4 miles to the Little Belknap Crater. A cairn marks the right-hand side trail that climbs 0.2 mile up the crater. The PCT continues on along the base of Mount Washington and rises to the Santiam Pass.

User Groups: Hikers, dogs, and horses. No mountain bikes allowed. No wheelchair facilities.

Permits: A free self-issue Wilderness Permit is required and is available at the trailhead. A federal Northwest Forest Pass is required to park here; the cost is $5 a day or $30 for an annual pass. You can buy a day pass at the trailhead, at ranger stations, or through private vendors.

Maps: For a map of the Deschutes National Forest and the Mount Washington Wilderness, contact Deschutes National Forest Headquarters, 1001 SW Emkay Drive, Bend, OR, 97702, 541/383-5300. For a topographic map, ask the USGS for Mount Washington.

Directions: From McKenzie Bridge, drive east on OR 126 to the McKenzie Pass Highway 242. Follow the highway to a trailhead sign near milepost 77. From Sisters, drive OR 242 west 0.5 mile beyond the McKenzie Pass.

Contact: Deschutes National Forest, Sisters Ranger District, P.O. Box 249, Sisters, OR, 97759, 541/549-7700.

31 BLACK CRATER

7.4 mi/4.0 hr 4 9

in the McKenzie Pass in Three Sisters Wilderness

BEST

From the town of Sisters, the massive silhouette of Black Crater is imposing and dominant on the skyline. This monumental volcanic peak, carved into 500-foot-cliffs atop its peak by Ice Age glaciers, is a killer climb. From the top, you'll secure a view extending from Mount Hood to the Three Sisters atop a windswept peak of stunted, whitebark pine—one of the best views of the High Cascades anywhere.

The Black Crater Trail climbs 2,500 feet in 3.7 miles, crossing a glacier-carved valley on the crater's flank then climbing steeply up switchbacks to the craggy peak.

User Groups: Hikers, dogs, and horses. No mountain bikes allowed. No wheelchair facilities.

Permits: A free self-issue Wilderness Permit is required and is available at the trailhead. A federal Northwest Forest Pass is required to park here; the cost is $5 a day or $30 for an annual pass. You can buy a day pass at the trailhead, at ranger stations, or through private vendors.

Maps: A map of the Three Sisters Wilderness is available for purchase from Geo-Graphics. For a map of the Deschutes National Forest and the Three Sisters Wilderness, contact Deschutes National Forest Headquarters, 1001 SW Emkay Drive, Bend, OR, 97702, 541/383-5300. For a topographic map, ask the USGS for Black Crater.

Directions: From Sisters, drive west on the McKenzie Pass Highway 242. Between mileposts 80 and 81, turn left into the Black Crater Trailhead parking area.

Contact: Deschutes National Forest, Sisters Ranger District, P.O. Box 249, Sisters, OR, 97759, 541/549-7700.

32 PACIFIC CREST TRAIL TO MATTHIEU LAKES

6.0 mi/3.0 hr 2 7

in the McKenzie Pass in Three Sisters Wilderness

BEST

Although you could enter the Three Sisters Wilderness at the McKenzie Pass trailhead for the Pacific Crest Trail, that would result in a longer walk over black, jagged lava. A closer trailhead reaches the PCT quickly and sets out north for a loop around the two Matthieu Lakes. The northern lake is set in a deep forest, but the southern lake, the smaller one, is set high in Scott Pass with views to North Sister. Both of these lakes make for good camps (though regulations require that camps be 250 feet from the shore), and the swimming here is exquisite. It also makes for a launching point to other explorations including the Scott Trail and the mountains themselves.

From the Lava Camp Trailhead, set out toward the PCT for 0.2 mile and go left. Follow the PCT 0.7 mile to a junction. Get the high ground out of the way and go to the left on the PCT for 2.1 miles, with views down to North Matthieu Lake. At the next junction, go left on the PCT toward Scott Pass and South Matthieu Lake. To continue farther, note that the next junction splits; to the left, access to distant Green Lakes, and to the right the PCT continues toward Yapoah Crater and the Scott Trail. To return, go back to the junction before South Matthieu and go left 0.7 mile on the North Matthieu Lake Trail to reach the lower lake. Continue 1.4 miles to return to the PCT and the 0.9 mile back to the trailhead.

User Groups: Hikers, dogs, and horses. No mountain bikes allowed. No wheelchair facilities.

Permits: A free self-issue Wilderness Permit is required and is available at the trailhead. A federal Northwest Forest Pass is required to park here; the cost is $5 a day or $30 for an annual pass. You can buy a day pass at the trailhead, at ranger stations, or through private vendors.

Maps: A map of the Three Sisters Wilderness is available for purchase from Geo-Graphics. For a map of the Deschutes National Forest and the Three Sisters Wilderness, contact Deschutes National Forest Headquarters, 1001 SW Emkay Drive, Bend, OR, 97702, 541/383-5300. For a topographic map, ask the USGS for North Sister.

Directions: From Sisters, drive west on the McKenzie Pass Highway 242. Near milepost 78, turn left at a sign for Lava Lake Camp and follow Road 900 for 0.3 mile, then turn right for the PCT parking.

Contact: Deschutes National Forest, Sisters Ranger District, P.O. Box 249, Sisters, OR, 97759, 541/549-7700.

33 HAND LAKE AND OLD MCKENZIE WAGON ROAD

2.6 mi/1.0 hr — 1, 7

in the McKenzie Pass in Mount Washington Wilderness

Though you can visit Hand Lake via the Benson Trail (see *Benson Lake and Scott Mountain*, next listing), it's easy to get there from the highway trailhead. This way you can spend a little time here exploring this strange lake that pools up against a rugged lava flow, and a piece of the old McKenzie Wagon Road chipped through that same flow by John Craig in 1871, meant to be a shortcut. You'll have to go off trail to find it, but with a landmark as substantial as this lava flow it presents no problem.

The stretch of hike goes an easy 0.5 mile along the Hand Lake Trail into the wilderness to the Hand Lake Shelter, with its view of Hand Lake and two of the Three Sisters. At a junction, go right (the left leads to Scott Lake and its campground) and walk 0.6 mile along the lake and lava flow. Watch for a series of rock cairns and the 15-foot-wide berth in the flow to the right. Cross on this old wagon road then follow the flow to the right, eventually finding Hand Lake again in one mile. Return the 0.5 mile to the trailhead.

User Groups: Hikers, dogs, and horses. No mountain bikes allowed. No wheelchair facilities.

Permits: A free self-issue Wilderness Permit is required and is available at the trailhead. Parking and access are free.

Maps: For a map of the Willamette National Forest and the Mount Washington Wilderness, contact Willamette National Forest Headquarters, 3106 Pierce Parkway, Suite D, Springfield, OR, 97477, 541/225-6300. For a topographic map, ask the USGS for North Sister.

Directions: From McKenzie Bridge, drive east on OR 126 to the McKenzie Pass Highway 242. Follow the highway to a trailhead sign between mileposts 72 and 73. From Sisters, drive OR 242 west 4.5 miles beyond the McKenzie Pass.

Contact: Willamette National Forest, McKenzie River Ranger District, 57600 McKenzie Highway, McKenzie Bridge, OR, 97413, 541/822-3381.

34 BENSON LAKE AND SCOTT MOUNTAIN

8.2–9.7 mi/4.0–4.5 hr 3 9

in the McKenzie Pass in Mount Washington Wilderness

When summer in the Central Oregon desert heats up, it's good to know that easy respite lies in any one of the mountain lakes strewn over the Cascade Crest. Benson Lake, for one, is a swimmer's dream: cold, clear, and deep. Beyond Benson Lake are even more lakes, the congregation of little pools known as the Tenas Lakes, set atop a plateau with a view out over the western range. If that's not enough of a day, try climbing Scott Mountain for an amazing view over the lava-rubble fields of the McKenzie Pass, with a perfect view of six Cascade peaks. To lengthen the trail even further, you can link to a loop past Hand Lake (see *Hand Lake and Old McKenzie Wagon Road,* previous listing) for a 9.7-mile jaunt that's great for backpacking.

Start out from the lot at Scott Lake and follow the Benson Trail straight for 1.4 miles to broad Benson Lake. In another 1.1 miles, the trail reaches a left-hand spur to the Tenas Lakes, a series of lovely rock bowls. To climb Scott Mountain, continue on 0.9 mile, staying right at a junction leading to The Knobs, to another junction on Scott Mountain itself. From here, go left and up 300 feet and 0.7 mile to the peak. This makes a fine turnaround point for the 8.2-mile hike, but you could continue on the Benson Trail another 1.8 miles to a junction, then go right 1.6 miles to Hand Lake, and continue to the right past the shelter for the remaining 1.5 miles to Scott Lake, making for a 9.7-mile loop.

User Groups: Hikers, dogs, and horses. No mountain bikes allowed. No wheelchair facilities.

Permits: A free self-issue Wilderness Permit is required and is available at the trailhead. A federal Northwest Forest Pass is required to park here; the cost is $5 a day or $30 for an annual pass. You can buy a day pass at the trailhead, at ranger stations, or through private vendors.

Maps: For a map of the Willamette National Forest and the Mount Washington Wilderness, contact Willamette National Forest Headquarters, 3106 Pierce Parkway, Suite D, Springfield, OR, 97477, 541/225-6300. For a topographic map, ask the USGS for Linton Lake.

Directions: From McKenzie Bridge, drive east on OR 126 to the McKenzie Pass Highway 242. Follow the highway to a sign for Scott Lake between mileposts 71 and 72 and turn left, following Road 260 for 1.5 miles to its end. From Sisters, drive OR 242 west 5.6 miles beyond the McKenzie Pass.

Contact: Willamette National Forest, McKenzie River Ranger District, 57600 McKenzie Highway, McKenzie Bridge, OR, 97413, 541/822-3381.

35 SCOTT TRAIL TO FOUR-IN-ONE CONE

9.0 mi/5.0 mi 3  8

in the McKenzie Pass in Three Sisters Wilderness

The Scott Trail was blazed by Captain Felix Scott, who arduously led a wagon train across this volcanic landscape in 1862. This modern hiking trail follows his route and leads backpackers into the Three Sisters Wilderness, opening up their own world of exploration. Hike across a lava flow erupted from the Four-in-One Cone, four cinder cones with a view of North and Middle Sister and the surrounding

© SEAN PATRICK HILL

Sunshine Meadows in the Three Sisters Wilderness

volcanic landscape. You can also go farther and connect to the Pacific Crest Trail. Keep in mind that this trail is largely exposed to the sun—bring adequate water, headgear, and sunblock.

From the trailhead, cross the McKenzie Pass Highway and start on the Scott Trail, staying left at the first junction (the right leads to the Obsidian Trailhead and Frog Camp) and continue 2.7 miles. The next 1.4 miles crosses a rugged lava flow and the forested island in its midst, then arrives at a cairn beside the cinder cones. Climb to the left for a view of the mountains, 0.4 mile along the Four-in-One Cone's rim. From the cairn, it is another 0.8 mile up the Scott Trail to its junction with the PCT.

User Groups: Hikers, dogs, and horses. No mountain bikes allowed. No wheelchair facilities.

Permits: A free self-issue Wilderness Permit is required and is available at the trailhead. Parking and access are free.

Maps: A map of the Three Sisters Wilderness is available for purchase from Geo-Graphics. For a map of the Willamette National Forest and the Three Sisters Wilderness, contact Willamette National Forest Headquarters, 3106 Pierce Parkway, Suite D, Springfield, OR, 97477, 541/225-6300. For a topographic map, ask the USGS for North Sister.

Directions: From McKenzie Bridge, drive east on OR 126 to the McKenzie Pass Highway 242. Follow the highway to a sign for Scott Lake between mileposts 71 and 72 and turn left, then right into a parking area. From Sisters, drive OR 242 west 5.6 miles beyond the McKenzie Pass.

Contact: Willamette National Forest, McKenzie River Ranger District, 57600 McKenzie Highway, McKenzie Bridge, OR, 97413, 541/822-3381.

HIKING

36 THE OBSIDIAN TRAIL

12.0 mi/6.0 hr 3 10

west of McKenzie Pass in Three Sisters Wilderness

BEST

The Obsidian Trail in the Three Sisters Wilderness sees a multitude of visitors—including those who come to climb 10,047-foot Middle Sister, Oregon's fourth-highest mountain. Because of the trail's popularity, the Forest Service requires a special permit that can be attained in advance from the McKenzie Ranger Station. What makes it such a desirable destination are the meadows known as Sunshine, which offer some of the rarest landscape to be found anywhere. The trail passes 4.1 miles through deep forests and over jagged rivers of lava fields that poured down from nearby Collier Cone. Volcanic black glass abounds here, making it obvious how this trail acquired its name. Atop the Obsidian Cliffs, the alpine plateau sparkles with acres of glittering chips. You'll pass 20-foot Obsidian Falls tumbling into a forest that by late summer is full of the mop-head blooms of western pasque flower, known as "old man of the mountain." From the Sunshine Meadows around Glacier Creek, climbers ascend to summit Middle Sister. Backpacking and camping affords many opportunities for day trips. To the south lie the Linton Meadows, the Wickiup Plain, and South Sister. To the north, the PCT crosses the ridge of Little Brother and deep lava flows to the volcanic moonscape beneath North Sister and a steep climb up the Collier Cone.

Starting from the McKenzie Pass Highway, go 4.1 miles on the Obsidian Trail through forests and over lava fields. Immediately after crossing the White Branch Creek, take a right at a junction, staying on the Obsidian Trail for 1.7 miles. Once on the PCT, turn left for 1.4 miles to continue to Sunshine. A 0.7-mile spur trail heading downhill along Glacier Creek completes the loop, returning to the last 4.1-mile stretch of the Obsidian Trail back to the trailhead.

User Groups: Hikers, dogs, and horses. No mountain bikes allowed. No wheelchair facilities.

Permits: A Limited Entry Permit is required for overnight and day visits to the Pamelia Lake area; contact the USFS for information. A federal Northwest Forest Pass is required to park here; the cost is $5 a day or $30 for an annual pass. You can buy a day pass at the trailhead, at ranger stations, or through private vendors.

Maps: A map of the Three Sisters Wilderness is available for purchase from Geo-Graphics. For a map of the Willamette National Forest and the Three Sisters Wilderness, contact Willamette National Forest Headquarters, 3106 Pierce Parkway, Suite D, Springfield, OR, 97477, 541/225-6300. For a topographic map, ask the USGS for North Sister.

Directions: From McKenzie Bridge, drive east on OR 126 to the McKenzie Pass Highway 242. Follow the highway to a sign for the Obsidian Trail between mileposts 70 and 71 and turn right 0.4 mile into a parking area. From Sisters, drive OR 242 west 6.2 miles beyond the McKenzie Pass.

Contact: Willamette National Forest, McKenzie River Ranger District, 57600 McKenzie Highway, McKenzie Bridge, OR, 97413, 541/822-3381.

37 PROXY FALLS/ LINTON LAKE

4.8 mi/2.5 hr 1 8

west of McKenzie Pass in Three Sisters Wilderness

BEST

There's a reason you may have trouble finding parking here. These two easy hikes into the Three Sisters Wilderness are located just off the beautiful and heavily traveled McKenzie Pass Highway (a gateway to many fantastic hikes). That's no reason to pass up these two hikes, though, and their relative brevity makes it a good idea to do both.

The one-mile Proxy Falls loop should be hiked counterclockwise, as per Forest Service request; the loop visits Lower Proxy Falls, a tall cascade over a lava wall, and Upper Proxy Falls, which ends abruptly in a pool without a visible outlet (the water travels underground from here).

The Linton Lake Trail enters the woods and heads 1.4 miles to the edge of the lake at an ancient lava flow. You can continue 0.5 mile farther along the lakeshore to a beach. In the distance you can hear Linton Falls tumbling out of the hills.

User Groups: Hikers and dogs. No horses or mountain bikes. No wheelchair facilities.

Permits: A free self-issue Wilderness Permit is required and is available at the trailhead. A federal Northwest Forest Pass is required to park here; the cost is $5 a day or $30 for an annual pass. You can buy a day pass at the trailhead, at ranger stations, or through private vendors.

Maps: A map of the Three Sisters Wilderness is available for purchase from Geo-Graphics. For a map of the Willamette National Forest and the Three Sisters Wilderness, contact

Willamette National Forest Headquarters, 3106 Pierce Parkway, Suite D, Springfield, OR, 97477, 541/225-6300. For a topographic map, ask the USGS for Linton Lake.

Directions: From McKenzie Bridge, drive east on OR 126 to the McKenzie Pass Highway 242. For the Proxy Falls Trailhead follow this highway nine miles, and park on the roadside between mileposts 64 and 65. For the Linton Lake Trailhead, drive another 1.6 miles past Proxy Falls and park on the left. From Sisters, drive OR 242 west 13.5 miles beyond the McKenzie Pass.

Contact: Willamette National Forest, McKenzie River Ranger District, 57600 McKenzie Highway, McKenzie Bridge, OR, 97413, 541/822-3381.

38 CAMP LAKE AND CHAMBERS LAKES

14.2 mi/7.0 hr 4 10

southwest of Sisters in Three Sisters Wilderness

Although this trail starts out hot and dry in a viewless, lodgepole pine forest, all that quickly changes. Soon enough the trail traverses one of the most stunning landscapes in the state, ambling along beneath North and Middle Sister, with views to South Sister and Broken Top. The heights are breathtaking, and the destination of Camp Lake, set in the alpine saddle between Middle and South Sister, is almost too beautiful to bear. It's hard to exaggerate this place's wonder—and to know that you could go even farther into the wilderness (with a map and compass, of course), and head for the trail-less Chambers Lakes higher in the saddle, makes this a true wilderness destination.

Start on the Pole Creek Trail, going 1.4 miles to a junction that heads to Scott Pass. Stay left and continue 0.6 mile to Soap Creek. At the junction here, go right (the left heads for Green Lakes) another 2.6 miles. At this point, a side trail to the left leads 0.8 mile down to Demaris Lake, a possible side trip. Otherwise, continue 2.5 miles to trail's end at Camp Lake. To find the Chambers Lakes, watch for user trails and consult your map.

User Groups: Hikers, dogs, and horses. No mountain bikes allowed. No wheelchair facilities.

Permits: A free self-issue Wilderness Permit is required and is available at the trailhead. Parking and access are free.

Maps: A map of the Three Sisters Wilderness is available for purchase from Geo-Graphics. For a map of the Deschutes National Forest and the Three Sisters Wilderness, contact Deschutes National Forest Headquarters, 1001 SW Emkay Drive, Bend, OR, 97702, 541/383-5300. For a topographic map, ask the USGS for North Sister.

Directions: From Sisters, drive 1.4 miles west of Sisters on Highway 242 then turn left on Road 15 for 10.5 miles, following signs for the Pole Creek Trailhead.

Contact: Deschutes National Forest, Sisters Ranger District, P.O. Box 249, Sisters, OR, 97759, 541/549-7700.

39 PARK MEADOW

7.6 mi/4.0 hr 2 8

southwest of Sisters in Three Sisters Wilderness

This unassuming trail beneath the Tam McArthur Rim is a back door to the very popular Green Lakes area (see *Green Lakes via Broken Top Trail* and *Green Lakes via Fall Creek* listings in this chapter). Park Meadow lies in the midst of thick woods with views to the nearby mountains. But the trail continues on, and with some path-finding skills you may be able to find nearly invisible Golden Lake nearly a mile off the trail, and could follow a series of tarns on the flanks of Broken Top.

The beginning of the Park Meadow Trail follows an old road 1.1 miles along the Snow Creek Ditch. Once the trail proper begins, it descends 2.7 miles to Whychus Creek (stay straight at a four-way intersection along the way). From here it's 1.1 miles to Park Meadow, fed by Park Creek, which is fed, in turn, by the Bend Glacier on Broken Top. From here the trail continues to Green Lakes, and following it you could wander off trail to the south to find Golden Lake with its impressive views, a waterfall, and sky-reflecting tarns high on the mountain.

User Groups: Hikers, dogs, and horses. No mountain bikes allowed. No wheelchair facilities.

Permits: A free self-issue Wilderness Permit is required and is available at the trailhead. Parking and access are free.

Maps: A map of the Three Sisters Wilderness is available for purchase from Geo-Graphics. For a map of the Deschutes National Forest and the Three Sisters Wilderness, contact Deschutes National Forest Headquarters, 1001 SW Emkay Drive, Bend, OR, 97702, 541/383-5300. For a topographic map, ask the USGS for Broken Top.

Directions: From Sisters, go south on Elm Street, which becomes Road 16, for 14.3 mostly paved miles to the Park Meadow Trailhead.

Contact: Deschutes National Forest, Sisters Ranger District, P.O. Box 249, Sisters, OR, 97759, 541/549-7700.

40 TAM MCARTHUR RIM

9.4 mi/4.0 hr

southwest of Sisters in Three Sisters Wilderness

Tam McArthur Rim is the rim of a massive, long-dead volcano. It's far higher than most mountains in the state, making this is one of the best viewpoints in Oregon, with vistas as far as Mount Adams in Washington State—and everything in between. The rim itself drops impressively over 500-foot cliffs to the lakes below, and at the far end of the ridge lies Broken Top. With care, you can extend this hike along that ridge, which gets narrower as you go, to a hidden lake beneath the steep slope of craggy Broken Top.

North Sister from the Tam McArthur Rim

From the trailhead, climb the Tam McArthur Rim Trail steadily through the woods nearly 600 feet and 0.7 mile to the rim. Continue 1.8 miles to a right-hand junction, which leads to an overlook on a long tongue of lava. From here, continue 2.2 miles, the trail becoming increasingly faint, to the lava plug of Broken Hand. The trail traverses the left side and continues on to the mountain itself, but only the sure-footed should attempt it.

User Groups: Hikers, dogs, and horses. No mountain bikes allowed. No wheelchair facilities.

Permits: A free self-issue Wilderness Permit is required and is available at the trailhead. A federal Northwest Forest Pass is required to park here; the cost is $5 a day or $30 for an annual pass. You can buy a day pass at the trailhead, at ranger stations, or through private vendors.

Maps: A map of the Three Sisters Wilderness is available for purchase from Geo-Graphics. For a map of the Deschutes National Forest and the Three Sisters Wilderness, contact Deschutes National Forest Headquarters, 1001 SW Emkay Drive, Bend, OR, 97702, 541/383-5300. For a topographic map, ask the USGS for Broken Top.
Directions: From Sisters, go south on Elm Street, which becomes Road 16, for 15.7 mostly paved miles to the trailhead on the left.
Contact: Deschutes National Forest, Sisters Ranger District, P.O. Box 249, Sisters, OR, 97759, 541/549-7700.

41 GREEN LAKES VIA BROKEN TOP TRAIL

9.6 mi/5.5 hr

west of Bend in the Three Sisters Wilderness

Getting to this trailhead requires one of the worst drives possible. Since you'll have to contend with badly rutted and steep dirt roads, washouts, shock-busting potholes, you'll want to drive something with clearance and you'll want to take it slow. The Broken Top Trail passes before the colossal crater of its namesake mountain, a desolate and rocky castle surrounded by meadows of wildflowers so intense you'd never think the two belonged together. Larkspur, columbine, and other varieties dot these high alpine meadows. Views extend out to Mount Bachelor and more distant peaks.

From the trailhead, follow the Broken Top Trail, not taking any side trails, until you reach Green Lakes in 4.8 miles. Watch for the Cayuse Crater along the way, a cinder vent along the trail at the end of a long ridge. Return as you came.
User Groups: Hikers, dogs on leash only, and horses. No mountain bikes allowed. No wheelchair facilities.
Permits: A free self-issue Wilderness Permit is required and is available at the trailhead. A federal Northwest Forest Pass is required to park here; the cost is $5 a day or $30 for an annual pass. You can buy a day pass at the trailhead, at ranger stations, or through private vendors.
Maps: A map of the Three Sisters Wilderness is available for purchase from Geo-Graphics. For a map of the Deschutes National Forest and the Three Sisters Wilderness, contact Deschutes National Forest Headquarters, 1001 SW Emkay Drive, Bend, OR, 97702, 541/383-5300. For a topographic map, ask the USGS for Broken Top.
Directions: From Bend, drive 23.7 miles west on the Cascade Lakes Highway and turn right at a sign for Todd Lake onto Road 370. After 0.5 mile, continue on Road 370 (the gate stays closed most of the year) for 3.5 terrible miles to Road 380, going left on this road 1.3 miles to its end at the Broken Top Trailhead.
Contact: Deschutes National Forest, Bend-Fort Rock Ranger District, 1230 NE 3rd Street, Suite A-262, Bend, OR, 97701, 541/383-4000.

42 GREEN LAKES VIA FALL CREEK

8.4-11.4 mi/4.5-6.0 hr 3 10

west of Mount Bachelor in Three Sisters Wilderness

BEST

Whereas other areas of the Three Sisters Wilderness are virtually empty, this trail—leading to what has to be one of the most beautiful places in the world—almost never is. The three Green Lakes lie in a valley between South Sister and Broken Top, with unparalleled views of both. To get there, you'll follow the loud and vivacious Fall Creek, which tumbles and tumbles on its way down, almost an endless waterfall; when it does level out, you'll pass a massive obsidian flow that glows in the sun. No wonder it's so popular.

This area has seen a lot of visitor damage over the years, so make sure you camp at a designated area marked by a post and stick to marked trails. You could do this trip in an out-and-back fashion, or make a loop of it using the Broken Top and Soda Creek Trails (recommended if you're backpacking).

From the trailhead, follow the Fall Creek Trail two miles, stay straight at a junction, and continue 2.2 miles to the next junction. Crest a rise and you'll see the Green Lakes, which you can visit by continuing another 1.2 miles. Return to the junction with the Broken Top Trail. You can return as you came or go left toward Broken Top for 2.7 miles, then right at a sign for Fall Creek Trailhead for 0.8 mile, then follow the Soda Creek Trail to the right down 3.7 miles to the lot.

User Groups: Hikers, dogs on leash only, and horses. No mountain bikes allowed. No wheelchair facilities.

Permits: A free self-issue Wilderness Permit is required and is available at the trailhead. A federal Northwest Forest Pass is required to park here; the cost is $5 a day or $30 for an annual pass. You can buy a day pass at the trailhead, at ranger stations, or through private vendors.

Maps: A map of the Three Sisters Wilderness is available for purchase from Geo-Graphics. For a map of the Deschutes National Forest and the Three Sisters Wilderness, contact Deschutes National Forest Headquarters, 1001 SW Emkay Drive, Bend, OR, 97702, 541/383-5300. For a topographic map, ask the USGS for Trout Creek Butte and Broken Top.

Directions: From Bend, drive 26.4 miles west on the Cascade Lakes Highway and turn right at a Green Lakes Trailhead sign to a parking area.

Contact: Deschutes National Forest, Bend-Fort Rock Ranger District, 1230 NE 3rd Street, Suite A-262, Bend, OR, 97701, 541/383-4000.

43 SOUTH SISTER SUMMIT

11.0–12.6 mi/1–2 days 5 10

west of Mount Bachelor in Three Sisters Wilderness

BEST

Of all the alpine climbs you could do in Oregon, and of all the peaks you could bag without needing equipment or real mountaineering expertise, South Sister is king. At the same time, you must make serious considerations and take precautions. Altitude sickness affects some more than others, and this trail will lift you 10,358 feet into the atmosphere on Oregon's third-highest mountain. You'll need all day to do it, too; starting early is never a bad idea. The most direct route—and most challenging—begins at the Devil's Lake Trailhead. It's easy to turn this into a backpacking multi-day pitch simply by securing a campsite near Moraine Lake, a little lake with a big view of South Sister and nearby Broken Top. Hike up, pitch a tent, and gather your strength: You'll need it. Be safe and check the weather before attempting an ascent. Any clouds are usually bad clouds. Also, a note on dogs: Because cinders are sharp and can badly cut a dog's paws, it's best to spare them this climb.

From the Devil's Lake Trailhead, climb 1.5 miles on the South Sister climbing trail, heading up a gully, gradually growing steeper, to a four-way junction at the first view of South Sister. To the right, the 0.8-mile side trail leads down to Moraine Lake, where camping is regulated (choose a spot marked with a post). To continue on the climb, go forward up the climber's trail 1.8 miles to the head of the canyon on the right. The next 1.1 miles climbs steeply up the mountain before arriving at a lake beneath the Lewis Glacier. The final grinding slog is up 0.7 mile of sliding cinder to the rim. Once at the top, follow the rim counter-clockwise 0.4 mile to the summit. From here, you'll see half the state of Oregon and, in the crater, Teardrop Pool—the highest lake in Oregon.

User Groups: Hikers, dogs on leash only, and horses. No mountain bikes allowed. No wheelchair facilities.

Permits: A free self-issue Wilderness Permit is required and is available at the trailhead. A federal Northwest Forest Pass is required to park here; the cost is $5 a day or $30 for an annual pass. You can buy a day pass at the trailhead, at ranger stations, or through private vendors.

Maps: A map of the Three Sisters Wilderness is available for purchase from Geo-Graphics. For a map of the Deschutes National Forest and the Three Sisters Wilderness, contact Deschutes National Forest Headquarters, 1001 SW Emkay Drive, Bend, OR, 97702, 541/383-5300. For a topographic map, ask the USGS for South Sister.

Directions: From Bend, drive 28.5 miles west on the Cascade Lakes Highway and turn left at a Devil's Lake Trailhead sign to a parking area.

Contact: Deschutes National Forest, Bend-Fort Rock Ranger District, 1230 NE 3rd Street, Suite A-262, Bend, OR, 97701, 541/383-4000.

44 SISTERS MIRROR LAKE AND WICKIUP PLAIN

8.3–11.3 mi/4.0–5.0 hr  3 9

west of Mount Bachelor in the Three Sisters Wilderness

The Pacific Crest Trail passes breathtakingly close to South Sister, the third-highest mountain in Oregon, via the broad Wickiup Plain. In this alpine wonderland, you'll see expansive lava flows, smaller peaks, craters, and rolling meadows. It is strange, really, to find this corner of the Three Sisters Wilderness so bereft of crowds. This loop trail leads to backpacking sites near a bundle of lakes, the most well known of which is Sisters Mirror Lake; it somewhat reflects nearby South Sister, whose rounded crown peeks over the tree line. A small peninsula juts out into the lake, but camping is banned in this one spot. Instead, poke around some of the side trails to find plenty of other spots nearby.

From the trailhead, go 0.4 mile on the Mirror Lakes Trail to a four-way junction, staying straight for 2.7 miles to the PCT. The trail crosses Sink Creek and passes several ponds and Kokostick Butte. At the PCT, go left 0.2 mile along Sisters Mirror Lake. To find the other lakes, Lancelot and Denude, go back to the north shore and follow a user trail 0.4 mile. To make a loop from the Wickiup Plain, return to the four-way junction just north of Mirror Lake and continue north on the PCT. In 0.2 mile, you have a choice. For the shorter loop along the edge of the plain, go right here for 1.4 miles to the Wickiup Plains Trail, right at the next junction for one mile, then right again for 1.6 miles along the Elk-Devils Trail to the first four-way junction; go left 0.4 mile back to the lot. For a longer hike, continue on the PCT another 1.6 miles into the Wickiup meadows toward Le Conte Crater, beside the shimmering lava rock mesa. At a junction, go right towards Devil's Lake for 1.1 miles, then straight on the Wickiup Plains Trail for 0.5 mile, continuing left on this path for one mile. Now follow signs for Elk Lake to the right for 1.6 miles, and finally take the final left to return to the Mirror Lakes Trailhead.

User Groups: Hikers, dogs, and horses. No mountain bikes allowed. No wheelchair facilities.

Permits: A free self-issue Wilderness Permit is required and is available at the trailhead. A federal Northwest Forest Pass is required to park here; the cost is $5 a day or $30 for an annual pass. You can buy a day pass at the trailhead, at ranger stations, or through private vendors.

Maps: A map of the Three Sisters Wilderness is available for purchase from Geo-Graphics. For a map of the Deschutes National Forest and the Three Sisters Wilderness, contact Deschutes National Forest Headquarters, 1001 SW Emkay Drive, Bend, OR, 97702, 541/383-5300. For a topographic map, ask the USGS for South Sister.

Directions: From Bend, drive 29.8 miles west

on the Cascade Lakes Highway and turn right at a Trailhead sign to a parking area.

Contact: Deschutes National Forest, Bend-Fort Rock Ranger District, 1230 NE 3rd Street, Suite A-262, Bend, OR, 97701, 541/383-4000.

45 TUMALO MOUNTAIN

3.6 mi/2.5 hr

west of Bend in Deschutes National Forest

This fairly straightforward climb offers views of surrounding peaks, but is far easier to climb than the others—though it is a 1,200-foot gain in elevation in less than two miles. The view down into Tumalo's eroded crater makes it worth it. From the Sno-Park, follow the Tumalo Mountain Trail up 1.8 miles to the peak.

User Groups: Hikers and dogs only. No horses or mountain bikes allowed. No wheelchair facilities.

Permits: No permits are required. Parking and access are free.

Maps: For a map of the Deschutes National Forest, contact Deschutes National Forest Headquarters, 1001 SW Emkay Drive, Bend, OR, 97702, 541/383-5300. For a topographic map, ask the USGS for Broken Top.

Directions: From Bend, drive 21.7 miles west on the Cascade Lakes Highway and turn right at the Dutchman Flat parking area.

Contact: Deschutes National Forest, Bend-Fort Rock Ranger District, 1230 NE 3rd Street, Suite A-262, Bend, OR, 97701, 541/383-4000.

46 TUMALO FALLS

6.8 mi/3.5 hr

west of Bend in Deschutes National Forest

BEST

The people who call Bend home are lucky to live such a short distance from such incredible beauty. Here, for instance, at the end of a long paved road into the forest is not one, but several waterfalls on Tumalo Creek, which flows all the way down to Bend, passing through Shevlin Park. In 1979, a wildfire started by a campfire burned off six-square-miles of stately trees. It's amazing how much the forest has recovered, and this hike doesn't stay long in the burn before getting into the good high-country forests.

Follow the South Fork Trail 0.2 mile to the right to find the top of 97-foot Tumalo Falls. Continue along the creek another 3.2 miles, passing four sets of waterfalls along the way. At a junction, go left on the Swampy Lakes Trail 2.1 miles on a high ridge (note that this trail enters the Bend Watershed, and that animals and mountain bikes are not allowed). Then follow the Bridge Creek Trail to the left 1.3 miles back to the lot.

User Groups: Hikers, dogs, horses, and mountain bikes. No mountain bikes or animals allowed in the Bend Watershed. There is a wheelchair-accessible trail to an overlook of Tumalo Falls.

Permits: A federal Northwest Forest Pass is required to park here; the cost is $5 a day or $30 for an annual pass. You can buy a day pass at the trailhead, at ranger stations, or through private vendors.

Maps: For a map of the Deschutes National Forest, contact Deschutes National Forest Headquarters, 1001 SW Emkay Drive, Bend, OR, 97702, 541/383-5300. For a topographic map, ask the USGS for Tumalo Falls.

Directions: From the west side of Bend, follow Skyliner Road 9.8 miles to its end at the OMSI camp, and turn right on dirt Road 4603 for 3.4 miles to the picnic area and trailhead.

Contact: Deschutes National Forest, Bend-Fort Rock Ranger District, 1230 NE 3rd Street, Suite A-262, Bend, OR, 97701, 541/383-4000.

47 SHEVLIN PARK

4.7–5.0 mi/2.0–2.5 hr 1 7

west of Bend

BEST

Suffice it to say that this has to be one of the country's best city parks—and it's not even in the city. Instead, it stretches out in a canyon along Tumalo Creek, a cold mountain river that passes under stately ponderosa pine, quaking aspen, Douglas fir, and Engelmann spruce. In spring and summer, wildflowers abound here, and you could spend all day trying out side trails, looking up gulches, and exploring farther up Tumalo Creek, where a biking trail leads all the way to Tumalo Falls. But for an easy start, try this loop trail that follows the canyon rim in a scenic loop around all the park's perks. The burn the trail passes over is the result of a 1990 forest fire that just missed destroying the forested canyon. Already, trees are growing back strong.

From the lot, head toward the creek on the Shevlin Loop Trail along the stand of aspen trees, crossing the creek on a footbridge and climbing the ridge to the burn. After the first 0.9 mile, the trail meets an old road. Follow this road a bit, then head back onto trail for one mile, dropping down into the canyon to a side creek flowing past enormous boulders. Cross the creek and continue 0.6 mile through denser woods of Douglas fir to a crossing of Tumalo Creek. Continue over the old road (though going left follows the creek back a ways into National Forest land) and follow this trail along the opposite side of the canyon 1.5 miles to the top of Red Tuff Gulch and a supply yard. Then walk the final 0.7 mile back to your vehicle.

For another walk, this one along the creek, follow the 2.5-mile Tumalo Creek Trail out-and-back; it passes footbridges connecting to the Loop Trail, a covered bridge, and historic Fremont Meadows before launching into the National Forest.

User Groups: Hikers, dogs on leash only, and mountain bikes. No horses allowed. Paved portions of the park are wheelchair accessible.

Permits: No permits are required. Parking and access are free.

Maps: For a downloadable map, go to www.bendparksandrec.org. For a topographic map, ask the USGS for Shevlin Park.

Directions: From downtown Bend, follow Newport Avenue (which becomes Shevlin Park Road) 3.9 miles. Just after crossing Tumalo Creek, turn left at a bend in the road and park in the first lot.

Contact: Bend Parks and Recreation, 200 NW Pacific Park Lane, Bend, OR, 97701, 541/389-7275.

48 NORTH BANK DEER PRESERVE

6.9 mi/3.5 hr 2 8

north of Roseburg on the North Umpqua River

The Columbia white-tailed deer once roamed widely in Western Oregon, but by the 1970s populations had dwindled to two pockets: one on the Columbia River, and the other along this bend of the Umpqua River. This 10,000-acre former ranch is now a wildlife preserve where you can certainly see wildlife, not to mention an assortment of landscapes from rolling forests and oak savannah to giant madrone trees and creek-carved chasms. The trail rises and falls, climbing two knobs high above the preserve. Watch for pennyroyal, blue-eyed grass, mariposa lilies, and cat's ear. Note that chiggers are a problem here, so wear long pants.

From the west access, hike straight onto an old road and up 1.8 miles to the 1,480-foot peak of South Knob. A right-hand trail leads to Whistler's Overlook over the Umpqua River, a good place to spot osprey, and will add three miles round-trip to your hike. From South Knob continue 1.5 miles over Middle Ridge to 1,816-foot Middle Knob. Keep going another 0.5 mile, sticking to the left, to a saddle. From here, go left for 2.3 miles through woods along Chasm Creek to a road. Turn left on the road for 0.8 mile back to the car, going to the left of the gate for the last stretch of trail.

User Groups: Hikers, horses, and bicycles. Dogs are discouraged. No wheelchair facilities.

Permits: Permits are not required. Parking and access are free.

Maps: For a topographic map, ask the USGS for Winchester and Oak Creek Valley.

Directions: From Roseburg, drive I-5 north four miles to Winchester (Exit 129). Turn left toward Wilbur for two miles, then turn right on North Bank Road for 5.5 miles. Beyond a gated road on the left, watch for a gravel lot on the left.

Contact: Bureau of Land Management, Roseburg District, 777 NW Garden Valley Boulevard, Roseburg, OR, 97471, 541/440-4930.

49 FALL CREEK NATIONAL RECREATION TRAIL

9.0-13.7 mi one-way/3.0 hr-2 days

2 7

southeast of Eugene in Willamette National Forest

Open all year, this forested hike follows Fall Creek through a lush riparian zone, passing side streams and a small cave once used by Native Americans. A good beginning is to hike a nine-mile section of the trail to what was formerly a 90-foot log bridge, now gone. There is a primitive campsite about halfway out, which could make for a good backpacking spot. There are many access points along the way, but a good stretch begins at the westernmost point in an old-growth forest, and soon traverses out over a 2003 burn on its way upstream. With the bridge out about 9.5 miles upstream, it is possible to access the higher trailhead from the upper stretches of Road 18, hiking downstream to an old-growth grove on Marine Creek.

From the trailhead at the Dolly Varden Campground, follow the creek 2.9 miles through an old-growth forest of ferns and firs along the forested bank to a footbridge at Timber Creek. Along the way, the trail sometimes drops to gravel beaches and to a swimming hole two miles in. After the footbridge, the trail enters the burn from the 2003 Clark Fire, continuing another 0.6 mile to Road 18. Go left across the bridge, and continue upstream on the trail on the far side. In 1.1 miles, the trail passes the cave on Slick Creek and a possible camping area. Continuing another 0.4 mile, the trail forks; to the right is the Bedrock Campground, but the bridge to it is gone. Stay left, going 0.7 mile up a series of switchbacks to a junction with the Jones Creek Trail on the left, closed due to fire damage. The Fall Creek Trail exits the burn, staying high above the creek for one mile, then descending to the creekside again for 3.3 miles to gravel road 1828. This makes the best turnaround point, though continuing 0.5 mile on the trail will bring you to the spot the bridge once spanned, but the bridge being out and the creek being unfordable here makes this a fine ending.

The final 4.2 miles of trail beyond the missing bridge can be reached from Road 1833.

User Groups: Hikers and dogs only. No horses or mountain bikes allowed. No wheelchair facilities.

Permits: Permits are not required. Parking and access are free.

Maps: For a map of the Willamette National Forest, contact Willamette National Forest Headquarters, 3106 Pierce Parkway, Suite D, Springfield, OR, 97477, 541/225-6300. For a topographic map, ask the USGS for Saddleblanket Mountain.

Directions: From Eugene, drive east on Highway 58 for 14 miles and turn left across Dexter Reservoir at the covered bridge. Take Jasper-Lowell Road 2.8 miles through Lowell, following signs for Fall Creek. Turn right on Big Fall Creek Road for 10.3 miles, parking at a trail sign on the right just before the Dolly Varden Campground. To shuttle this as a 9-mile one-way walk, continue past the Dolly Varden Campground 8 miles and turn left on Road 1828 to the trailhead.

To reach the uppermost trailhead, follow Road 18 past Dolly Varden Campground another 12 miles, turn right on Road 1833 and cross a bridge. The trailhead is on the left.

Contact: Willamette National Forest, Middle Fork Ranger District, 46375 Highway 58, Westfir, OR, 97492, 541/782-2283.

50 CHUCKSNEY MOUNTAIN

10.3 mi/5.5 hr 3 8

northeast of Oakridge in Willamette National Forest

From the peak of Chucksney Mountain, views extend to the Three Sisters, Broken Top, and Mount Bachelor in the east. The meadows atop the peak are home to wildflowers such as pearly everlasting, coneflower, and larkspur. You'll work for this peak, though, as you climb 2,000 feet in less than five miles, but on the way down the trail visits the headwaters of Box Canyon Creek and follows the stream down.

From the horse camp trailhead, follow the trail in 0.3 mile, keeping right at all junctions until you reach the Chucksney Mountain Loop Trail. Go right on this trail for 2.4 miles to a side trail on the right with views of the eastern peaks. Continue 0.6 mile to a crest, then switchback down into a large cirque and back out again for 1.7 miles to the 5,600-foot summit. Continue across the meadowed ridge 1.4 miles to the Grasshopper Trail. Go left for one mile to the meadows at the headwaters of Box Canyon Creek, then another 2.6 miles back down to the end of the loop, turning right 0.3 mile back to the horse camp.

User Groups: Hikers, dogs, horses, and mountain bikes. No wheelchair facilities.

Permits: Permits are not required. Parking and access are free.

Maps: For a map of the Willamette National Forest, contact Willamette National Forest Headquarters, 3106 Pierce Parkway, Suite D, Springfield, OR, 97477, 541/225-6300. For a topographic map, ask the USGS for Chucksney Mountain.

Directions: From Blue River, drive four miles east on OR 126 to Road 19 and turn south for 25.5 miles to Box Canyon Horse Camp. From Westfir, drive 32 miles north on Road 19 to Box Canyon Horse Camp.

Contact: Willamette National Forest, McKenzie River Ranger District, 57600 McKenzie Highway, McKenzie Bridge, OR, 97413, 541/822-3381.

51 GOODMAN CREEK AND EAGLE'S REST

13.4 mi/6.0 hr 3 7

south of Lookout Point Reservoir in Willamette National Forest

This popular trail is popular for several reasons: It's easily accessible from the Eugene/Springfield area, it's an easy hike for families, and it passes through an old-growth forest along Goodman Creek to a pretty waterfall and swimming hole. Continuing beyond the lower part of the trail on to Eagles Rest, passing a marshy swale of skunk cabbage and a shelter, you'll leave the crowds behind and make for a view over the Lost Creek Valley, standing high above the Lookout Point Reservoir.

From the trailhead, stick to the right-hand junction after 0.2 mile and follow the Goodman Creek arm of the Lookout Point Reservoir. In 1.8 miles, watch for an unmarked trail to the left leading to the waterfall and swimming hole. To continue on to Eagles Rest stay on the Goodman Trail, crossing the creek and continuing 1.2 miles along the creek, then crossing a side creek and climbing the next mile to a road crossing and the Eagles Rest Trailhead. Climb 700 feet over 1.5 miles of second-growth woods

HIKING

to the Ash Swale Shelter by its boggy marsh. Continue 0.3 mile up, cross another road, then ascend the final 0.7 mile to the rocky peak of Eagles Rest.

User Groups: Hikers, dogs, horses, and mountain bikes. No wheelchair facilities.

Permits: Permits are not required. Parking and access are free.

Maps: For a map of the Willamette National Forest, contact Willamette National Forest Headquarters, 3106 Pierce Parkway, Suite D, Springfield, OR, 97477, 541/225-6300. For a topographic map, ask the USGS for Mount June.

Directions: From Eugene, follow Highway 58 east to milepost 21, and park on the right at a trailhead sign.

Contact: Willamette National Forest, Middle Fork Ranger District, 46375 Highway 58, Westfir, OR, 97492, 541/782-2283.

52 TIRE MOUNTAIN

7.6 mi/3.0 hr

north of Oakridge in Willamette National Forest

On the large, flat top of Tire Mountain a fire watchtower once stood atop a platform on a topped tree. The mountain itself is named for a nearby creek, which in turn was named for a wagon wheel someone left there. Today the trail accessing this mountain is part of the Eugene to Pacific Crest Trail system, which quite handily connects that nearby city to the mountains. Along this trail, wildflower meadows spread out over the ridge and views open to the distant Cascade peaks.

From the left side of the road, start up the Alpine Trail, going 1.2 miles into an old-growth forest then a meadow at 4,000 feet with views to the Three Sisters, Mount Bachelor, and Diamond Peak. At the junction, go right on the easy and level Tire Mountain Trail for two miles, crossing another steep mountainside meadow and two smaller meadows on the way to the peak. A side trail to the left leads 0.6 mile to the 4,329-foot summit.

User Groups: Hikers, dogs, horses, and mountain bikes. No wheelchair facilities.

Permits: Permits are not required. Parking and access are free.

Maps: For a map of the Willamette National Forest, contact Willamette National Forest Headquarters, 3106 Pierce Parkway, Suite D, Springfield, OR, 97477, 541/225-6300. For a topographic map, ask the USGS for Westfir East and West.

Directions: From Eugene, follow Highway 58 east 30 miles then go left toward Westfir for 0.3 mile. At a three-way junction, go left 1.8 miles toward Westfir to a red covered bridge and go straight on Road 19 for 4.5 miles. Turn left on Road 1912 for 6.8 miles to Windy Pass, going straight onto Road 1910 for 0.3 mile, then right on Road 1911 for 0.4 mile to the Alpine Trail on the left.

Contact: Willamette National Forest, Middle Fork Ranger District, 46375 Highway 58, Westfir, OR, 97492, 541/782-2283.

53 ERMA BELL LAKES

8.4 mi/4.5 hr 2 8

northeast of Oakridge in Three Sisters Wilderness

This trail has every right to be heavily used: Located just inside the Three Sisters Wilderness, the trail crosses Skookum Creek (Chinook for "powerful"), and loops around five major lakes, including the three Erma Bell Lakes, the lower and middle of which are joined by a waterfall falling over a rock ledge. As for the lakes themselves, they are wonderfully wild and without the usual trampling of shoreline trails. This doesn't mean there's no camping to be had, though it is prohibited on Lower Erma Bell Lake. Respect the rules and stay at least 200 yards away from lakeshores when pitching a tent.

From the Skookum Creek Campground, cross the creek and head into the wilderness on the Erma Bell Lake Trail 0.6 mile to a junction. Follow the right-hand main trail 1.1 miles to Lower Erma Bell Lake, another 0.4 mile past the waterfall to Middle Erma Bell Lake, and another 0.7 mile to Upper Erma Bell Lake on the right. Continue 0.7 mile to a junction, staying left on the Erma Bell Trail (the right-hand trail goes less than a mile past Mud Lake and Edna Lake to the Taylor Burn Campground). In another 0.7 mile, begin the loop by staying left on the Williams Lake Trail, then go 0.4 mile to Williams Lake. From here the trail gradually descends 2.4 miles through forest to the Irish Mountain Trail junction. Stay to the left another 0.3 mile to Otter Lake, then finish the loop in 0.3 mile. Return to Skookum Creek by going right 0.6 mile.

User Groups: Hikers, dogs, and horses. No mountain bikes allowed. The trail to Lower Erma Bell Lake is wheelchair accessible.

Permits: A free self-issue Wilderness Permit is required and is available at the trailhead. A federal Northwest Forest Pass is required to park here; the cost is $5 a day or $30 for an annual pass. You can buy a day pass at the trailhead, at ranger stations, or through private vendors.

Maps: A map of the Three Sisters Wilderness is available for purchase from Geo-Graphics. For a map of the Willamette National Forest and Three Sisters Wilderness, contact Willamette National Forest Headquarters, 3106 Pierce Parkway, Suite D, Springfield, OR, 97477, 541/225-6300. For a topographic map, ask the USGS for Waldo Mountain.

Directions: From McKenzie Highway 126, turn south on Road 19 toward the Cougar Reservoir for 25.6 miles. Pass Box Canyon Guard Station and go left on Road 1957 to Skookum Campground. The trail begins from the campground parking lot.

Contact: Willamette National Forest, Middle Fork Ranger District, 46375 Highway 58, Westfir, OR, 97492, 541/782-2283.

54 MOUNT JUNE AND HARDESTY MOUNTAIN

9.6-10.0 mi/5.0 hr 3 8

south of Lookout Point Reservoir in Willamette National Forest

The name Hardesty Mountain has a certain ring to it, mostly because you have to be pretty hardy to attempt this steep climb. Eugene hikers slog up Hardesty Mountain Trail when they need a real bout of exercise. You'll find, though, that Hardesty has no views, the old lookout site being overgrown with trees. If you begin at Mount June, though, you'll traverse from one peak to the next and passing the 50-foot block of Sawtooth Rock with its shallow cave.

To climb Hardesty Mountain the tough way, start at the Highway 58 trailhead, keeping to the left at the junction in 0.2 mile. This Hardesty Mountain Trail climbs 3,300 feet in 4.8 miles to the summit, passing the Eula Ridge Trail on the left near the top. The final 0.2 mile goes to the left where the trail meets the Cutoff Trail on the right. Return as you came.

To start from Mount June, follow the Mount June Trail 0.7 mile. At a junction, climb 0.5 mile to the left to top 4,618-foot Mount June, which has views extending as far as Mount Hood. Return to the main trail and continue to the right another 0.7 mile on the Sawtooth Trail. Go right one mile through a wildflower meadow past the spire to another junction after some switchbacks, and stay left on the Sawtooth Trail another 2.2 miles to a three-way junction. From here, it is possible to do a short loop around the peak of Hardesty Mountain, going left 0.2 mile on the Hardesty Cutoff Trail, then right over the peak, then right another 0.2 mile back to the Sawtooth Trail. Return as you came.

User Groups: Hikers, dogs, and horses. No mountain bikes allowed. No wheelchair facilities.

Permits: Permits are not required. Parking and access are free.
Maps: For a map of the Umpqua National Forest, contact Umpqua National Forest, 2900 NW Stewart Parkway, Roseburg, OR, 97470, 541/672-6601; for a map of the Willamette National Forest, contact Willamette National Forest Headquarters, 3106 Pierce Parkway, Suite D, Springfield, OR, 97477, 541/225-6300. For a topographic map, ask the USGS for Mount June.
Directions: For the lower trailhead to Hardesty Mountain, start from Eugene and follow Highway 58 east to milepost 21, and park on the right at a trailhead sign. For the upper trailhead to Mount June, follow Highway 58 east from Eugene 11.4 miles to the Dexter Dam and turn right toward Lost Creek. After 3.7 miles, keep left onto Eagles Rest Road, following this road 7.8 miles to a fork. Keep left on Road 20-1-14 for 6.1 miles and turn left on Road 1721 for 0.1 mile, then left on Road 941 for 0.4 mile to the trailhead sign on the right.
Contact: Umpqua National Forest, Cottage Grove Ranger District, 78405 Cedar Park Road, Cottage Grove, OR, 97424, 541/767-5000; Willamette National Forest, Middle Fork Ranger District, 46375 Highway 58, Westfir, OR, 97492, 541/782-2283.

55 EDDEELEO LAKES

9.2–16 mi/4.0 hr–2 days

north of Waldo Lake in Waldo Lake Wilderness

The strange name of these lakes is not so strange when you separate the syllables into three names: Ed, Dee, and Leo. These were three Forest Service workers who carried in fish to these lakes to stock them. The two lakes that carry their names are still being fished today. Lined up along the base of long Winchester Ridge, along with three other lakes, these lakes are jewels along a stone wall. Extending this trip makes for a good backpacking jaunt to Waldo Lake, the very large namesake of this wilderness area.

To begin, follow the Winchester Trail 0.8 mile, then take a left turn at a junction for 0.3 mile, then go right at the Blair Lake Trail junction for 1.1 miles to reach Lower Quinn Lake and another junction leading to Taylor Burn Campground. Stay right on the Six Lakes Trail to visit the lakes. The first mile passes a loop on the right to Upper Quinn Lake and arrives at the head of aptly named Long Lake. Follow this lake for most of the next 1.4 miles to the edge of Lower Eddeeleo Lake, and another 1.5 miles to Upper Eddeeleo. This can serve as a turnaround point.

If you're backpacking, continue 2.7 miles to the Waldo Shore Trail, then go south to Elbow Lake for 2.4 miles. At Elbow Lake, turn right on Trail 3585 for 0.8 mile, then right at the next junction on a cutoff trail for 300 yards, then left toward Waldo Mountain for 0.5 mile, then right on the Winchester Ridge Trail for 5.7 miles back to the Winchester Trail junction, then left 0.8 mile back to the trailhead.
User Groups: Hikers, dogs, and horses. No mountain bikes allowed. No wheelchair facilities.
Permits: A free self-issue Wilderness Permit is required and is available at the trailhead. Parking and access are free.
Maps: For a map of the Willamette National Forest and Waldo Lake Wilderness, contact Willamette National Forest Headquarters, 3106 Pierce Parkway, Suite D, Springfield, OR, 97477, 541/225-6300. For a topographic map, ask the USGS for Waldo Mountain.
Directions: From Highway 58 at Oakridge, turn north on Crestview Street for 0.2 mile to East 1st Street, going right. Follow this road, which becomes Salmon Creek Road 24, for 11 miles, then veer left on Road 2417 for 10.9 miles. Turn left at Road 254 for 0.3 mile, following signs for Winchester Trail. Park on the right at a parking lot.
Contact: Willamette National Forest, Middle Fork Ranger District, 46375 Highway 58, Westfir, OR, 97492, 541/782-2283.

56 RIGDON LAKES

8.0 mi/4.0 hr — 2 — 7

north of Waldo Lake in Waldo Lake Wilderness

Though the 1996 fires that burned through the north shore of Waldo Lake made the area a ghostly version of a forest, it does not follow that the area is off-limits. Burns have their own beauty and after time manage to regenerate. To access the Rigdon Lakes, you'll follow the 10-square-mile Waldo Lake, nearly surrounded by wilderness, on your way to Rigdon Butte and the lakes in its shadow. As long as you're here, why not make a loop of it? Visit Lake Kiwa and return on the far side of the butte, to the lake's outlet, the headwaters of the North Fork Middle Fork Willamette River—a mouthful, I know.

From the North Waldo Trailhead head west, ignoring a horse trail on the right, but noting instead a one-mile shoreline trail on the left that rejoins the main trail 0.7 mile later on the North Waldo Trail. Continue on this easy shoreline walk one mile past numerous ponds to the Rigdon Lakes Trail on the left. Go left 0.7 mile to Upper Rigdon Lake, circled on the far side by a user trail connecting to a 0.6-mile climb of Rigdon Butte. The final 1.3 miles of the Rigdon Lakes Trail passes Lower Rigdon Lake, Lake Kiwa, and little Ernie Lake before joining the Wahanna Trail. Go left at this junction 1.3 miles through the burned woods to a junction; go straight to the head of this fork of the Willamette. Otherwise, turn left and go 1.3 miles back along Waldo Lake to the beginning of the loop, then 1.7 miles back to the campground.

User Groups: Hikers, dogs, and horses. No mountain bikes allowed. No wheelchair facilities.

Permits: A free self-issue Wilderness Permit is required and is available at the trailhead. A federal Northwest Forest Pass is required to park here; the cost is $5 a day or $30 for an annual pass. You can buy a day pass at the trailhead, at ranger stations, or through private vendors.

Maps: For a map of the Willamette National Forest and Waldo Lake Wilderness, contact Willamette National Forest Headquarters, 3106 Pierce Parkway, Suite D, Springfield, OR, 97477, 541/225-6300. For a topographic map, ask the USGS for Waldo Mountain.

Directions: From Highway 58 go three miles west of the Willamette Pass and turn north on Road 5897 toward Waldo Lake for 13 miles to the North Waldo Campground. Park at a sign for the Waldo Lake Trail.

Contact: Willamette National Forest, Middle Fork Ranger District, 46375 Highway 58, Westfir, OR, 97492, 541/782-2283.

57 WALDO MOUNTAIN LOOKOUT

7.9-8.8 mi/4.0-5.0 hr — 3 — 8

northwest of Waldo Lake in Waldo Lake Wilderness

Waldo Lake, at 10 square miles, is so large that it's hard to get a sense of scale when you're standing on the shoreline. From the lookout atop Waldo Mountain, though, you'll have clear view down to the sparkling water and nearby peaks, including The Twins, Maiden Peak, Fuji Mountain, Diamond Peak, and the distant Three Sisters. The 1957 cabin, staffed in summer, is listed on the National Historic Lookout Register. A figure eight of trails on this mountain's flanks passes through a wildflower meadow, with a side trip to the pair of Salmon Lakes and a 20-foot waterfall. A number of loops are possible, so a map is essential in this wilderness area.

From the trailhead, enter the forest of big grand fir and hemlock for 200 yards to a junction, staying left on the Waldo Mountain Trail. The trail climbs gradually 1.9 miles up through beargrass plumes and sub-alpine trees to a T-junction, where you'll continue up one mile and almost 600 feet to the 6,357-foot summit. From here there are two ways to get down and form one of two loops.

The first way down is to return down the peak the way you came for one mile, keeping left at the next two junctions for 1.2 miles to Waldo Meadows and a T-junction. To return to the car, go right 2.5 miles on the Waldo Meadows Trail back to the trailhead. To find Upper and Lower Salmon Lakes, go left 100 feet to a signed trail on the right, going down 0.5 mile to the Upper Lake.

The second way down from the mountain, a longer loop, requires you to continue up and over the far side of the peak, descending 1.4 miles to a junction (ignore the left-hand Winchester Ridge Trail along the way). At the intersection, with Lake Chetco nearby to the left, instead go right 1.7 miles to Waldo Meadows, staying right at junctions to Elbow Lake and the Salmon Lakes, then continuing as above 2.5 miles back to the trailhead.

User Groups: Hikers, dogs, and horses. No mountain bikes allowed. No wheelchair facilities.

Permits: A free self-issue Wilderness Permit is required and is available at the trailhead. Parking and access are free.

Maps: For a map of the Willamette National Forest and Waldo Lake Wilderness, contact Willamette National Forest Headquarters, 3106 Pierce Parkway, Suite D, Springfield, OR, 97477, 541/225-6300. For a topographic map, ask the USGS for Waldo Mountain.

Directions: From Highway 58 at Oakridge, turn north on Crestview Street for 0.2 mile to East 1st Street, going right. Follow this road, which becomes Salmon Creek Road 24, for 11 miles, then veer left on Road 2417 for six miles. Turn right on Road 2424 and go 3.7 miles to the trailhead.

Contact: Willamette National Forest, Middle Fork Ranger District, 46375 Highway 58, Westfir, OR, 97492, 541/782-2283.

HIKING

58 LILLIAN FALLS AND KLOVDAHL BAY

7.6 mi/4.5 hr — 2 — 7

west of Waldo Lake in Waldo Lake Wilderness

Access to the western shore of Waldo Lake can be a long journey if you start from the eastern shore, where the road and campgrounds are. A backdoor entrance along Black Creek is just as easy, and opens up the network of trails inside the wilderness area bordering the shoreline. A short, easy jaunt leads to Lillian Falls, and a longer more rugged hike climbs to Klovdahl Bay on the eastern shore. Oddly, neither Black Creek, Nettle Creek, nor Klovdahl Creek are outlets for Waldo Lake—it has only one outlet in its northwestern corner; the creeks in this area slip away, fed instead by winter snows. But one Simon Klovdahl tried in 1912 to dynamite a tunnel from Waldo to the Black Creek Canyon, an irrigation and hydroelectric power scheme that failed.

Start out on the trail along Black Creek, climbing easily for 1.2 miles to the base of Lillian Falls. From here the trail switchbacks up 0.7 mile and begins to climb more fiercely, leveling off in a valley along Nettle Creek then climbing again to Klovdahl Creek and above the Waldo shore for 1.9 miles before descending to the Waldo Lake Trail and Klovdahl Bay.

User Groups: Hikers, dogs, and horses. No mountain bikes all owed. No wheelchair facilities.

Permits: A free self-issue Wilderness Permit is required and is available at the trailhead. Parking and access are free.

Maps: For a map of the Willamette National Forest and Waldo Lake Wilderness, contact Willamette National Forest Headquarters, 3106 Pierce Parkway, Suite D, Springfield, OR, 97477, 541/225-6300. For a topographic map, ask the USGS for Waldo Lake.

Directions: From Highway 58 at Oakridge, turn north on Crestview Street for 0.2 mile to East 1st Street, going right. Follow this road, which becomes Salmon Creek Road 24, for 11 miles, keeping right at a Y-junction and staying on Road 24 for another 3.2 miles, then going straight on Road 2421 for 8.2 miles to road's end.

Contact: Willamette National Forest, Middle Fork Ranger District, 46375 Highway 58, Westfir, OR, 97492, 541/782-2283.

59 WALDO LAKE SHORE

21.5 mi/2-3 days 4 8

on Waldo Lake north of Willamette Pass

The best way to circumnavigate huge Waldo Lake, the second-largest freshwater lake in Oregon, is by mountain bike, and many do attempt its single-track challenge. The 21-plus-mile Jim Weaver Loop Trail mostly follows the lakeshore, though for a substantial portion it ducks a bit away from the lake into deep woods that are heavy with huckleberries in the late summer. This is also a backpacker's dream; there are camps aplenty dispersed along the shore, as well as secluded beaches reachable only by foot or boat. On top of that, the side trails radiate out from the northern, western, and southern shore into the Waldo Lake Wilderness, a maze of peaks and lakes good for extended trips. The Jim Weaver Trail is best accessed from either the Shadow Bay Campground or North Waldo Campground. Watch for bikes along the way!

User Groups: Hikers, dogs, horses, and mountain bikes. No wheelchair facilities.

Permits: Permits are not required. A federal Northwest Forest Pass is required to park here; the cost is $5 a day or $30 for an annual pass. You can buy a day pass at the trailhead, at ranger stations, or through private vendors.

Maps: For a map of the Willamette National Forest and Waldo Lake Wilderness, contact Willamette National Forest Headquarters, 3106 Pierce Parkway, Suite D, Springfield, OR, 97477, 541/225-6300. For a topographic map, ask the USGS for Waldo Lake.

Directions: To find the Shadow Bay Trailhead, drive Highway 58 three miles west of the Willamette Pass to milepost 59 and turn on Road 5897 for 6.7 miles, following signs for Waldo Lake. Turn left into the Shadow Bay Campground, continuing two miles to the boat ramp parking. To find the North Waldo Trailhead, continue 6.3 miles farther on Road 5897 to the North Waldo Campground and park at the Waldo Lake Trailhead.

Contact: Willamette National Forest, Middle Fork Ranger District, 46375 Highway 58, Westfir, OR, 97492, 541/782-2283.

60 THE TWINS

6.6 mi/3.0 hr 2 9

east of Waldo Lake in Willamette National Forest

The peak of The Twins, with its distinct dual volcanic flanks and crater, is easy enough to spot from the east or west. Accessible from the Pacific Crest Trail, this 7,360-foot peak offers an outstanding view of Waldo Lake to the west, the Three Sisters to the north, and Diamond Peak to the south. The trail is an easy one-shot climb from the trailhead: Ascend the first 450 feet through lodgepole pine and mountain hemlock forest in 1.6 miles to the PCT junction, and continue straight 1.7 miles and 1,160 feet to the north summit. With a bit of path-finding, you can explore the crater and top the south summit as well.

User Groups: Hikers, dogs, horses, and mountain bikes. No wheelchair facilities.

Permits: Permits are not required. A federal Northwest Forest Pass is required to park here; the cost is $5 a day or $30 for an annual pass. You can buy a day pass at the trailhead, at ranger stations, or through private vendors.

Maps: For a map of the Willamette National Forest, contact Willamette National Forest Headquarters, 3106 Pierce Parkway, Suite D, Springfield, OR, 97477, 541/225-6300. For a topographic map, ask the USGS for The Twins.

Directions: Drive Highway 58 three miles past the Willamette Pass to milepost 59 and turn on Road 5897 for 6.2 miles, following signs for Waldo Lake. Park at the Twin Peaks Trailhead on the right.
Contact: Willamette National Forest, Middle Fork Ranger District, 46375 Highway 58, Westfir, OR, 97492, 541/782-2283.

61 BRICE CREEK

5.5–7.5 mi one-way/2.5–3.5 hr

2 7

east of Cottage Grove in Umpqua National Forest

In the Cascade Mountains above Cottage Grove, this lovely rushing creek bounds out of the forest in a forested canyon. Rain or shine, this trail is accessible all year, and it even has some primitive campsites along Road 22, not to mention bigger campgrounds and a backpacking spot along the far side of the creek. The trail stays on the far side of the creek away from the road, making for a quiet hike. There is also the option at the upper reach of the trail to loop around the two Trestle Creek Falls, adding two miles to the trip.

From the lower trailhead, follow the creek upstream 1.5 miles along the canyon and into old-growth forest. Ignore a side trail over the creek that goes to the Cedar Creek Campground, and continue 2.6 miles, passing a series of waterfalls over a rock shelf and the primitive Boy Scout Camp to another bridge crossing to the Lund Park Campground. The trail continues upstream 0.6 mile to the beginning of the loop. Going straight along the creek another 0.5 mile leads to Trestle Creek (for an interesting side-trip, follow a left-hand trail up 0.3 mile to a view of the lower falls). Continue another 0.3 mile up the Brice Creek Trail to its end at the upper trailhead.

A loop option leading to two waterfalls is also available at Trestle Creek. From the upper trailhead, this 3.4-mile loop makes for an easier trip that can be coupled with a longer excursion downstream on the Brice Creek Trail. At the end of the Brice Creek Trail at the upper trailhead, note the side trail going uphill. Following this steep trail up nearly 1,000 feet you'll reach the Upper Trestle Creek Falls, pass behind them, and descend another mile to the Brice Creek Trail. Go left to return to the upper trailhead, passing the side trail to the lower waterfall, or go right for any length along the remaining 4.7 miles of the Brice Creek Trail.

User Groups: Hikers, dogs, and horses. No mountain bikes allowed. No wheelchair facilities.
Permits: Permits are not required. Parking and access are free.
Maps: For a map of the Umpqua National Forest, contact Umpqua National Forest, 2900 NW Stewart Parkway, Roseburg, OR, 97470, 541/672-6601. For a topographic map, ask the USGS for Rose Hill.
Directions: To find the lower trailhead, drive I-5 south of Eugene to Cottage Grove (exit 174), and follow signs east to Dorena Lake on Row River Road, which becomes Road 22, for 21.7 miles to a parking lot on the right. For the upper trailhead at the Trestle Creek Falls Loop, continue past the lower trailhead on Road 22 for another 5.5 miles to the next bridge and parking for the trailhead.
Contact: Umpqua National Forest, Cottage Grove Ranger District, 78405 Cedar Park Road, Cottage Grove, OR, 97424, 541/767-5000.

62 LARISON CREEK

12.6 mi/6.0 hr

on Hills Creek Reservoir in Willamette National Forest

This easy trail up Larison Creek weaves its way into some pretty stunning old-growth above the Hills Creek Reservoir. Douglas fir, red cedar, and the fabled yew trees—which Native Americans used for bows—all grow here.

You'll find a primitive campsite and a waterfall as you enter this deep, green canyon.

The trail begins along Larison Cove, an arm of the Hills Creek Reservoir; hillsides here are livid with poison oak. After 1.5 miles, the Larison Creek Trail reaches the end of the cove and a camping and picnic area. The trail then climbs gradually another 1.5 miles to a small waterfall and pool on the left. The next 2.2 miles leaves the creek and crosses a clear-cut before returning to the creek, crossing it near a creek fork. The last 1.1 miles climbs steeply up to trail's end at a dirt road. Return as you came.

User Groups: Hikers, dogs, horses, and mountain bikes. No wheelchair facilities.

Permits: Permits are not required. A federal Northwest Forest Pass is required to park here; the cost is $5 a day or $30 for an annual pass. You can buy a day pass at the trailhead, at ranger stations, or through private vendors.

Maps: For a map of the Willamette National Forest, contact Willamette National Forest Headquarters, 3106 Pierce Parkway, Suite D, Springfield, OR, 97477, 541/225-6300. For a topographic map, ask the USGS for Oakridge.

Directions: From Oakridge, drive 1.8 miles east on Highway 58. Between mileposts 37 and 38, turn south toward Hills Creek Dam on Road 23. In 0.5 mile, turn right on Road 21 for 3.3 miles to the trailhead on the right.

Contact: Willamette National Forest, Middle Fork Ranger District, 46375 Highway 58, Westfir, OR, 97492, 541/782-2283.

63 SALT CREEK FALLS AND VIVIAN LAKE

8.0 mi/4.0 hr 3 9

in the Willamette Pass in Diamond Peak Wilderness

BEST

Fall Creek, Diamond Creek, and Salt Creek—talk about waterfalls. Salt Creek Falls, showering over a basalt flow 286 feet into the canyon below, are the second highest in Oregon. Diamond Creek Falls and the double-tiered Fall Creek Falls also grace this trail into Diamond Peak Wilderness. At the top lies muddy-bottomed Vivian Lake, with its towering white pine trees and view of nearby Mount Yoran, a volcanic plug dominating the skyline. Besides flowering rhododendrons, huckleberries grow in such profusion along this trail that it's doubtful you'll get anywhere quickly, but watch out as you're stumbling through the bushes like a hungry bear—ground wasps call this area home, and I can attest that they pack quite a sting.

From the lot for Salt Creek Falls, take a quick tour of the observation trail on the north side of the creek. Then go upstream and cross a footbridge. At a junction, go right on the Diamond Creek Falls Trail for 1.8 miles along the canyon rim, passing strangely named Too Much Bear Lake and a viewpoint of a tall waterfall streaming into Salt Creek's canyon. To see Diamond Creek Falls, take a right-hand signed side trail down 0.2 mile to see the 100-

Vivian Lake in Diamond Peak Wilderness

foot fan-shaped falls. Return to the main trail and keep to the right, switchbacking up to a junction. Go right and begin steadily climbing along Fall Creek on the Vivian Lake Trail. In 1.3 miles, the trail reaches two viewpoints of Fall Creek Falls. The next mile is a more gradual grade, coming to a side trail on the right leading to Vivian Lake. From here, backpackers can continue on to Notch Lake and other trail connections into Diamond Peak Wilderness. For a return loop, return on the Vivian Lake Trail down 2.3 miles to the junction, this time going right 1.2 miles back to Salt Creek.

User Groups: Hikers, dogs, and horses. No mountain bikes allowed. No wheelchair facilities.

Permits: A free self-issue Wilderness Permit is required and is available at the trailhead. A federal Northwest Forest Pass is required to park here; the cost is $5 a day or $30 for an annual pass. You can buy a day pass at the trailhead, at ranger stations, or through private vendors.

Maps: For a map of the Willamette National Forest, contact Willamette National Forest Headquarters, 3106 Pierce Parkway, Suite D, Springfield, OR, 97477, 541/225-6300. For a topographic map, ask the USGS for Diamond Peak.

Directions: From Oakridge, drive Highway 58 east to milepost 57 and turn right at a sign for Salt Creek Falls. Follow this paved road to the parking lot at its end.

Contact: Willamette National Forest, Middle Fork Ranger District, 46375 Highway 58, Westfir, OR, 97492, 541/782-2283.

64 FUJI MOUNTAIN

3.0–11.2 mi/1.5–4.0 hr

south of Waldo Lake in Waldo Lake Wilderness

The dominant peak of Fuji Mountain has a lot going for it. At 7,144 feet, it towers above the surrounding countryside, and with its 360-degree view of the surrounding Cascade Mountains, it has quite the stupendous view, reaching as far as the peak of Mount Hood in the north to Mount Thielsen in the south. The view also extends clear across monumental Waldo Lake, the reason this made a great lookout point long ago.

For the easier trailhead off Road 5883, follow the trail into the forest 0.3 mile to a junction and turn left on the Fuji Mountain Trail. The trail gets gradually steeper, climbing 1.2 miles to the peak.

For the more difficult climb, start from the trailhead on Road 5897, climbing one mile on the Fuji Mountain Trail to the forested plateau. In another two miles, the trail reaches Birthday Lake (warm in summer and a great place for a cool-down swim on the way down the mountain). In another 0.4 mile, it passes little Verde Lake on the left and comes to a junction. Go left 100 feet to a second junction, going right one mile and climbing to the junction with the Road 5883 spur trail. Keep right, and continue 1.2 miles to the top.

User Groups: Hikers, dogs, and horses. No mountain bikes allowed. No wheelchair facilities.

Permits: A federal Northwest Forest Pass is required to park here; the cost is $5 a day or $30 for an annual pass. You can buy a day pass at the trailhead, at ranger stations, or through private vendors.

Maps: For a map of the Willamette National Forest, contact Willamette National Forest Headquarters, 3106 Pierce Parkway, Suite D, Springfield, OR, 97477, 541/225-6300. For a topographic map, ask the USGS for Waldo Lake.

Directions: To find the shorter trail, begin in Oakridge and drive 15 miles east on Highway 58 to Eagle Creek Road 5883, between mileposts 50 and 51. Turn left on Road 5897 for 10.3 miles to the trailhead on the left. For the more difficult trail, continue on Highway 58 to milepost 59, and turn left on Road 5897, following signs for Waldo Lake. In two miles, park on the left at the trailhead.

Contact: Willamette National Forest, Middle Fork Ranger District, 46375 Highway 58, Westfir, OR, 97492, 541/782-2283.

65 BOHEMIA MOUNTAIN

1.6 mi/1.0 hr 1 8

east of Cottage Grove in Umpqua National Forest

If you think the road to Bohemia Mountain is long and rough, imagine what it must have been like for the miners who once lived in Bohemia City. This old mining town, now one of Oregon's many ghost towns, sits at the base of its namesake mountain. Residents drilled the Musick Mine looking for gold, which was discovered here by a Czech immigrant in 1863. Only one building remains: the old post office, visible from the peak. You can make your way to it, being careful not to cross any private land, by bushwhacking down a hillside and heading for the last remnant of a town that operated from 1880 to 1930.

Follow the Bohemia Mountain Trail up 0.8 mile and 700 feet to the peak, where views stretch from Mount Shasta in the south to Mount Hood in the north. If this isn't enough for you, you can return to the Bohemia Saddle and follow the road one mile up to the watchtower on Fairview Peak.

User Groups: Hikers and dogs only. No horses or mountain bikes allowed. No wheelchair facilities.

Permits: Permits are not required. Parking and access are free.

Maps: For a map of the Umpqua National Forest, contact Umpqua National Forest, 2900 NW Stewart Parkway, Roseburg, OR, 97470, 541/672-6601. For a topographic map, ask the USGS for Fairview Peak.

Directions: Drive I-5 south of Eugene to Cottage Grove (Exit 174) and follow signs east to Dorena Lake on Row River Road, which becomes Road 22, for 30.5 miles. Turn right on Road 2212 at a sign for Fairview Peak and go 8.4 miles to Champion Saddle, then turn left on Road 2460. Follow this steep and rough road 1.1 miles to a junction in Bohemia Saddle. Park at the saddle and walk 100 yards to the left to the Bohemia Mountain Trail.

Contact: Umpqua National Forest, Cottage Grove Ranger District, 78405 Cedar Park Road, Cottage Grove, OR, 97424, 541/767-5000.

66 MIDDLE FORK WILLAMETTE RIVER

33.1 mi one-way/3 days 5 8

south of Hills Creek Reservoir in Willamette National Forest

The Hills Creek Reservoir catches all of the Middle Fork Willamette River, the main branch of this colossal and important Oregon river. With plenty of established campgrounds along the way, it's possible to spend days here exploring the trail in segments. Backpackers may be tempted to try it in longer stretches along any of the points between the reservoir and Timpanogas Lake, the river's headwaters. Along the way are a series of springs—Chuckle Springs and Indigo Springs—that add to the river's bulk. With all the mixed stands of conifers, wildflowers, and waterfalls, there's plenty to see and explore. The total elevation gain for the trail is 4,000 feet, so plan ahead with a map.

The trail segments are as follows: Sand Prairie to Road 2127, 5.1 miles; Road 2127 to Road 2133, 5.2 miles; Road 2133 to 2143, 4.7 miles; Road 2143 to Indigo Springs, three miles; Indigo Springs to 2153, including Chuckle Springs, 6.8 miles; Road 2153 to Road 2154, 7.1 miles; Road 2154 to Timpanogas Lake, 0.3 mile; from Timpanogas Lake to the Pacific Crest Trail, 4.5 miles.

User Groups: Hikers, dogs, and horses. No mountain bikes allowed in wilderness area. No wheelchair facilities.

Permits: A free self-issue Wilderness Permit is required to enter the uppermost section in Waldo Lake Wilderness and is available at the trailhead; otherwise, permits are not required. Parking and access are free.

Maps: For a map of the Willamette National Forest, contact Willamette National Forest Headquarters, 3106 Pierce Parkway, Suite D, Springfield, OR, 97477, 541/225-6300. For a topographic map, ask the USGS for Rigdon Point.

Directions: To find the lower trailhead from Oakridge, drive 1.8 miles east on Highway 58. Between mileposts 37 and 38, turn south toward Hills Creek Dam on Road 23. In 0.5 mile, turn right on Road 21 for 11 miles to the Sand Prairie Campground access. Along this route are many trailheads for the Middle Fork Willamette River Trail, including points at Roads 2120, 2127, 2133, 2143, 2153, and Timpanogas Lake. The uppermost trailhead is found at the Timpanogas Campground: From the lower trailhead, continue on Road 21 another 2.5 miles and turn left on Timpanogas Road 2154, following signs for Timpanogas Lake for 9.3 miles to the campground and a trailhead parking area on the right.

Contact: Willamette National Forest, Middle Fork Ranger District, 46375 Highway 58, Westfir, OR, 97492, 541/782-2283.

67 ROSARY LAKES AND MAIDEN PEAK

5.4–19.0 mi/2.0 hr–2 days 5 9

in the Willamette Pass in Willamette National Forest

Of all the peaks in the Waldo Lake area, none stands higher than 7,818-foot Maiden Peak, easily visible from afar for its long, sloping sides and prominent spire near the summit. Looming above Odell Lake, it seems a daunting climb, yet a number of trails crisscross its flanks, including the Pacific Crest Trail, the main access point. Along the way, the trail passes the picturesque Rosary Lakes, a shelter, and little Maiden Lake.

Start by going north on the PCT for 2.7 gradual miles to Rosary Lakes, switchbacking up just before the lakes. Pass the three lakes over 1.4 miles, then keep straight on the PCT, climbing to Maiden Saddle. Keep right on the PCT and continue 1.8 miles to the log cabin Maiden Peak Shelter, built by the Eugene Nordic Club and Forest Service crews during the 1990s. Continue another 0.7 mile on the PCT to a junction. To climb Maiden Peak, turn right here on the Maiden Peak Trail, which climbs 1,700 feet in 2.7 miles to a left-hand, 0.3-mile summit trail climbing the final 300 feet to the crater. Return to the Maiden Peak Trail and continue forward on it to make a loop, descending 1,200 feet in 1.7 miles to a junction, going right toward Maiden Lake. After 0.6 mile, pass the lake and continue 2.3 miles back to the PCT. Go left to return to the highway and parking lot.

User Groups: Hikers, dogs, and horses. No mountain bikes allowed. No wheelchair facilities.

Permits: Permits are not required. Parking and access are free.

Maps: For a map of the Willamette National Forest, contact Willamette National Forest Headquarters, 3106 Pierce Parkway, Suite D, Springfield, OR, 97477, 541/225-6300. For a topographic map, ask the USGS for Willamette Pass and Odell Lake.

Directions: From Oakridge, drive east on Highway 58 to the Pacific Crest Trail lot 0.3 mile east of the Willamette Pass Ski Area.

Contact: Deschutes National Forest, Crescent Ranger District, 136471 Highway 97 North, P.O. Box 208, Crescent, OR, 97733, 541/433-3200.

68 DIVIDE LAKE

8.0 mi/4.0 hr 3 8

southeast of Hills Creek Reservoir in Diamond Peak Wilderness

It's hard to say if Divide Lake is a secret, but not many people seem to go there. For

© SEAN PATRICK HILL

Mount Yoran and Divide Lake

through-hikers on the Pacific Crest Trail, it lies hidden behind the long wall of the Cascade Divide. The Divide Lake Trail itself is somewhat remote, lying west of Diamond Peak at the far end of a long, lonely drive. The trailhead, awash in huckleberries, seems a good sign that this is something special. And it is. The views of Diamond Peak, so close it's startling, provide ever-present company, and views extend to the north out to the Three Sisters. At the end of the trail, huddled beneath the massive volcanic plug of Mount Yoran, is Divide Lake, a perfect pond for camping and swimming. You can continue up the trail and climb out on the Cascade Divide, a wall that abruptly ends at a steep precipice where you can stand with a foot in two watersheds.

Start on the Vivian Lake Trail, going 0.8 mile to Notch Lake, a lovely series of ponds rimmed with mountain heather. Just 0.2 mile past these lakes, go right on the Mount Yoran Trail for three miles (steep at times) to Divide Lake, perfect for a backpacking camp. From here, the trail switchbacks 0.8 mile up and over the Cascade Divide to meet the PCT.

User Groups: Hikers, dogs, and horses. No mountain bikes allowed. No wheelchair facilities.

Permits: A free self-issue Wilderness Permit is required and is available at the trailhead. Parking and access are free.

Maps: For a map of the Willamette National Forest, contact Willamette National Forest Headquarters, 3106 Pierce Parkway, Suite D, Springfield, OR, 97477, 541/225-6300. For a topographic map, ask the USGS for Diamond Peak.

Directions: To find the lower trailhead from Oakridge, drive 1.8 miles east on Highway 58. Between mileposts 37 and 38, turn south toward Hills Creek Dam on Road 23. Stay on Road 23 for 19.5 miles to a pass at Hemlock Butte. Turn left on a spur road to the trailhead parking area.

Contact: Willamette National Forest, Middle Fork Ranger District, 46375 Highway 58, Westfir, OR, 97492, 541/782-2283.

69 YORAN LAKE

12.0 mi/6.0 hr — 3 — 8

south of Odell Lake in Diamond Peak Wilderness

For travelers on Highway 58, one of the most beautiful sights is the view of Diamond Peak rising above enormous Odell Lake. Here's a chance at a much closer view, with long, red Diamond Peak lifting above clear and glassy, tree-rimmed Yoran Lake, a clear and glassy lake. There are plenty of opportunities here for backpackers to take a load off for the night—and there's more than one lake to choose from. Scattered along the Pacific Crest Trail are a bevy of beautiful lakes, each with its own personality: Midnight, Arrowhead, Hidden, and Lils, and a number of small ponds to boot. If you come in via the Pacific Crest Trail, you'll have to bushwhack your way a few hundred yards to big Yoran Lake, where you can continue on a loop past very lovely Karen Lake, then descend along Trapper Creek through thick woods of white pine, Douglas fir, and rhododendron.

The trail begins at Pengra Pass on the Pacific Crest Trail. Go toward Midnight Lake, 1.4 miles into the woods. Continue on the PCT a steady 3.2 miles past Arrowhead Lake on the right and Hidden Lake on the left, with views of Diamond Peak ahead. When you reach Lils Lake, go just beyond it and point your compass true south, passing the lake and a small pond, crest a rise, cross a meadow, and then find the lakeshore of Yoran Lake. Follow the left side of the lake past some campsites to its far end and the Yoran Lake Trail. Head left on the trail to stop by Karen Lake, continuing 4.3 miles to a junction. Go left one mile, eventually joining the dirt road back to Pengra Pass.

User Groups: Hikers, dogs, and horses. No mountain bikes allowed. No wheelchair facilities.

Permits: A free self-issue Wilderness Permit is required and is available at the trailhead. Parking and access are free.

Maps: For a map of the Deschutes National Forest, contact Deschutes National Forest Headquarters, 1001 SW Emkay Drive, Bend, OR, 97702, 541/383-5300. For a topographic map, ask the USGS for Willamette Pass.

Directions: From Oakridge, drive east on Highway 58. West of Willamette Pass 0.5 mile, turn right at a sign for Gold Lake Sno-Park onto Abernethy Road for one mile. Fork left on Road 300, and in another 0.2 mile fork left on a dirt road and park 200 yards down this road at a sign for Midnight Lake.

Contact: Deschutes National Forest, Crescent Ranger District, 136471 Highway 97 North, P.O. Box 208, Crescent, OR, 97733, 541/433-3200.

70 DIAMOND PEAK

12.0 mi/1 day

south of Hills Creek Reservoir in Diamond Peak Wilderness

Of all the peaks in the Central Oregon Cascades, Diamond Peak seems the most unassuming. Due to its relative anonymity and distance from major urban areas, this wilderness area does not see the crowds that other areas of the forest do. This is to the benefit of not only the area, but also the hiker and backpacker who comes here. There is much to love about Diamond Peak Wilderness: quiet lakes, stately forests, and, of course, the long and graceful peak that sits in the center of it all. What's more, you can summit 8,744-foot Diamond Peak via a little known climber's trail on its south ridge. Along the way, there are opportunities for resting at two lovely and untrammeled lakes. If you do choose to climb the mountain, come prepared with a map, compass, and path-finding skills. What you'll find on top are views over Waldo Lake, the Three Sisters, Mount Jefferson, and far off, the tip of Mount Hood.

Start off on the Rockpile Trail 1.3 miles to a four-way junction, continuing straight another 1.2 miles, passing the Diamond Rockpile ridge on the left. At the next intersection, either way leads to a lake; to the left 0.2 mile is the larger Marie Lake, and to the right, the main trail continues to a right-hand side trail to little Rockpile Lake. Continue on the main trail 0.5 mile to reach the Pacific Crest Trail. Go left for 1.2 miles to a sharp right-hand turn on a corner atop an open ridge—if you have a GPS device, mark this spot. A series of rock cairns guides climbers up to tree line, then follow the ridge up and over the false summit one mile from the PCT. The next section follows a hogback and is sketchy—be careful. This route arrives at the true summit in 0.4 mile. Return as you came. For those not at ease with the climb, you can continue hiking along the PCT along the slope of Diamond Peak.

HIKING

User Groups: Hikers, dogs, and horses. No mountain bikes allowed. No wheelchair facilities.

Permits: A free self-issue Wilderness Permit is required and is available at the trailhead. Parking and access are free.

Maps: For a map of the Willamette National Forest, contact Willamette National Forest Headquarters, 3106 Pierce Parkway, Suite D, Springfield, OR, 97477, 541/225-6300. For a topographic map, ask the USGS for Diamond Peak.

Directions: To find the lower trailhead from Oakridge, drive 1.8 miles east on Highway 58. Between mileposts 37 and 38, turn south toward Hills Creek Dam on Road 23. In 0.5 mile go right on Road 21, staying on this route for 29.2 miles. In 0.4 mile past Indigo Springs Campground, go left on Pioneer Gulch Road 2149 for 3.5 miles, then right on Rockpile Road 2160 for 2.3 miles to a sign for the Rockpile Trail, parking beyond the trailhead on the right shoulder.

Contact: Willamette National Forest, Middle Fork Ranger District, 46375 Highway 58, Westfir, OR, 97492, 541/782-2283.

71 WINDY LAKES

11.2 mi/5.0 hr 

south of Crescent Lake in Oregon Cascades Recreation Area

Just south of Diamond Peak Wilderness is the largely unknown Oregon Cascades Recreation Area. You'd be hard pressed to find any other area in these mountains with so many lakes and ponds. The real jewels are at the end of the trail, where the Windy Lakes fan out below the massive wall of Cowhorn Mountain. Many of these lakes are deep, great for swimming, and certainly make great camping spots. Just be aware that early summer brings mosquitoes.

Begin on the Meek Lake Trail, crossing Summit Creek in 0.2 mile and arriving at Meek Lake in another 0.3 mile. From there the trail ambles into a pond-strewn forest for most of the next 2.4 miles. At a junction, go left to continue toward Windy Lakes (the right-hand junction heads to Summit Lake). After 1.6 miles the trail reaches North Windy Lake, and a right-hand side trail leads down to East Windy Lake. At the intersection with the Crescent Lake Trail, go right toward South Windy Lake. In 0.9 mile the trail skirts East Windy, passes another lake, then reaches its end at South Windy Lake. Return as you came.

User Groups: Hikers, dogs, horses, and mountain bikes.

Permits: Permits are not required. Parking and access are free.

Maps: For a map of the Deschutes National Forest, contact Deschutes National Forest Headquarters, 1001 SW Emkay Drive, Bend, OR, 97702, 541/383-5300. For a topographic map, ask the USGS for Cowhorn Mountain.

Directions: Drive Highway 58, going seven miles east of the Willamette Pass to Crescent Junction, turning right on Road 60 for 2.2 miles. At an intersection, turn right to stay on this road for another five miles. Turn right on dirt Road 6010 to Summit Lake. Follow this road 3.9 miles to the Meek Lake Trail on the left.

Contact: Deschutes National Forest, Crescent Ranger District, 136471 Highway 97 North, P.O. Box 208, Crescent, OR, 97733, 541/433-3200.

72 COWHORN MOUNTAIN LOOP

11.9 mi/6.0 hr 

south of Hills Creek Reservoir in Willamette National Forest

Two mountain peaks, worn down by time, stand sentry over the source of the Middle Fork Willamette River. In their shadow, Timpanogas and Indigo Lakes glisten in the light. Sawtooth Mountain stands more than 1,000 feet above Indigo Lake, but the goal here is

HIKING

Cowhorn Mountain, which once really did have a horn (it fell off in a 1911 storm). A magnificent loop climbs to the Pacific Crest Trail and scrambles to the 7,664 peak of Cowhorn with its amazing view north to the Three Sisters and south to Crater Lake.

Begin by following the Indigo Lake Trail 0.7 mile to a junction, staying to the left another 1.2 miles to Indigo, where a one-mile trail circles the lake. Continue on the main trail up a series of steady-climbing switchbacks 1.7 miles to a pass. To the right, a climber's trail heads up two miles and 600 feet to Sawtooth Mountain. Go left on the Windy Pass Trail 2.1 miles to a junction; to climb to the peak of Cowhorn go right 0.3 mile to the Pacific Crest Trail, then right on the PCT 0.3 mile to a scramble trail by a rock cairn following a ridge up the steep climb 0.4 mile. To descend on the loop, return to the Windy Pass Trail and go right and down 2.7 miles to a junction, and turn left toward Timpanogas Lake for 1.1 miles. At the lake, go right 0.4 mile back to the campground.

User Groups: Hikers, dogs, and mountain bikes. No horses allowed. No wheelchair facilities.

Permits: Permits are not required. Parking and access are free.

Maps: For a map of the Willamette National Forest, contact Willamette National Forest Headquarters, 3106 Pierce Parkway, Suite D, Springfield, OR, 97477, 541/225-6300. For a topographic map, ask the USGS for Cowhorn Mountain.

Directions: To find the lower trailhead from Oakridge, drive 1.8 miles east on Highway 58. Between mileposts 37 and 38, turn south toward Hills Creek Dam on Road 23. In 0.5 mile, turn right on Road 21 for 31.2 miles. Turn right on Timpanogas Road 2154, going 9.3 miles to the Timpanogas Campground on the left. Drive into the campground and watch for the trailhead sign on the right.

Contact: Willamette National Forest, Middle Fork Ranger District, 46375 Highway 58, Westfir, OR, 97492, 541/782-2283.

HIKING

73 BULLPUP LAKE AND BULLDOG ROCK

1.4-7.0 mi/1.0-3.5 hr

north of North Umpqua River in Umpqua National Forest

The Calapooya Mountains form a high divide between the watershed of the North Umpqua and the Willamette Rivers. One entry point to this heavily eroded lava mountain range is via Bullpup Lake, an easy destination in itself, with a shake-roofed shelter on the shore and towering andesite cliffs above it. Top that slope and the views quickly extend out to the Cascade Range, and you can go on farther to the Bear Camp Shelter, passing Bulldog Rock along the way.

The initial hike extends only 0.4 mile to Bullpup Lake and the shelter, and you can circle the lake on a 0.6-mile loop. At the far end of that loop (going left is the shortest, at 0.2-mile) you can continue up the slope and on the Bulldog Rock Trail 2.8 miles to a view of Bulldog Rock, and another 2.2 miles beyond that to the Bear Camp Shelter.

User Groups: Hikers, dogs, horses, and mountain bikes. No wheelchair facilities.

Permits: Permits are not required. Parking and access are free.

Maps: For a map of the Umpqua National Forest, contact Umpqua National Forest, 2900 NW Stewart Parkway, Roseburg, OR, 97470, 541/672-6601. For a topographic map, ask the USGS for Chiltcoot Mountain and Reynolds Ridge.

Directions: From Roseburg, drive east on OR 138 for 38.4 miles and turn left on Steamboat Creek Road for 10.4 miles to a fork. Go right on Bend Creek-Washboard Road 3817 for 2.2 miles, then right on Road 3850 for 5.6 miles, then left on Road 200 for 0.1 mile, and finally left on Road 300 for four miles to the trail parking area on the right.

Contact: Umpqua National Forest, North Umpqua Ranger District, 18782 North Umpqua Highway, Glide, OR, 97443, 541/496-3532.

74 ILLAHEE ROCK LOOKOUT

1.4 mi/1.0 hr 1 8

north of Boulder Creek Wilderness in Umpqua National Forest

Not one, but two fire lookout towers are set atop 5,382-foot Illahee Rock. The newer one was built in 1958, and its 40-foot-high lookout is staffed each summer. The older one is a cupola-style lookout building, built in 1925 and housed in a lightning cage. This easy 1.4-mile round-trip climbs 500 feet to the towers, with high-point views extending out over a number of Cascade peaks.

User Groups: Hikers, dogs, horses, and mountain bikes. No wheelchair facilities.

Permits: Permits are not required. Parking and access are free.

Maps: For a map of the Umpqua National Forest, contact Umpqua National Forest, 2900 NW Stewart Parkway, Roseburg, OR, 97470, 541/672-6601. For a topographic map, ask the USGS for Illahee Rock.

Directions: From Roseburg, drive 47 miles on OR 138 and turn left on Illahee Road 4760 for eight miles. Go straight on Road 100 for 1.3 miles, then left on the steep and rocky Road 104 to its end.

Contact: Umpqua National Forest, North Umpqua Ranger District, 18782 North Umpqua Highway, Glide, OR, 97443, 541/496-3532.

75 NORTH UMPQUA NATIONAL RECREATION TRAIL

3.5-79.0 mi/1-10 days  5 8

east of Roseburg on the North Umpqua River

Just past Idleyld Park in the canyon of the North Umpqua River begins a trail and backpacking adventure. The North Umpqua National Recreation Trail follows the river 79 miles, passing waterfalls, rapids, and

Toketee Falls on the North Umpqua River

gorges, crossing creeks, and meeting up with several side trails leading to old homesteads and shelters. You can even access hot springs along the way. The trail follows the river up to its headwaters at Maidu Lake high in the Cascades, with many access points along the good steady trip. You'll pass through unique forests of sugar pine, Shasta red fir, and incense cedar. Be sure to contact the USFS and BLM about trail conditions; at the time of this writing, the Calf Segment is closed due to unsafe conditions.

The Umpqua Trail is segmented into sections suitable for day hikes or backpacking trips. The Swiftwater Trailhead accesses the 15.5-mile Tioga section along the south bank of the river, ending at the Wright Creek Trailhead. From here, it's 5.5 miles to the Mott Trailhead, then 5.0 miles to the Panther Trailhead. The next 3.7-mile section to Calf Creek Trailhead is closed as of now. The 3.6-mile section to Marsters Trailhead is open, however. From here, the trail follows the north bank of the river 4.1 miles through the Jessie Wright section to the Soda Springs Trailhead, then the longer 9.6-mile Deer Leap section to the Toketee Lake Trailhead. From here the trail leaves Highway 138, going 3.5 miles to the Hot Springs Trailhead, and on 13.0 miles into the strangely named Dread and Terror Section to the White Mule Trailhead, another 6.3 miles through the Lemolo section to the Kelsay Valley Trailhead, and finally 9.0 miles through the Maidu segment to the Digit Point Trailhead and the end of the trail.

User Groups: Hikers, dogs, horses, and mountain bikes. No wheelchair facilities.

Permits: Permits are not required. Parking and access are free for most trailheads, excepting Umpqua Hot Springs.

Maps: For a map of the Umpqua National Forest, contact Umpqua National Forest, 2900 NW Stewart Parkway, Roseburg, OR, 97470, 541/672-6601. For a topographic map, ask the USGS for Old Fairview, Mace Mountain, Steamboat, Illahee Rock, Toketee Falls, Lemolo Lake, Tolo Mountain, and Burn Butte.

Directions: To access the Tioga Trailhead, the westernmost entry for the North Umpqua Trail, follow OR 138 east from Roseburg 22 miles. One mile past Idleyld Park, turn right at a "Swiftwater Park" sign, cross the river, and park at the Tioga Trailhead. Trailheads are numerous along Highway 138 and Forest Service Road 3401.

Contact: Bureau of Land Management, Roseburg District, 777 NW Garden Valley Boulevard, Roseburg, OR, 97471, 541/440-4930, or Umpqua National Forest, 2900 NW Stewart Parkway, Roseburg, OR, 97470, 541/672-6601.

76 SUSAN CREEK FALLS AND FALL CREEK FALLS

3.8 mi/1.5 hr 1 7

east of Roseburg on the North Umpqua River

If you're in the area of the North Umpqua River and looking for a place to stretch your legs or just take in the fresh air, try these two waterfalls just off Highway 138. The 70-foot Susan Creek Falls tumble over the canyon wall, on top of which is a fenced area of Indian mounds, where tribes reputedly held vision quests for their youth. A bit further east is Fall Creek Falls, with a side trail leading to a columnar basalt outcrop called Jobs Garden. Both trails are easily hiked together, though from two different trailheads.

The Susan Creek Falls Trail sets out 0.7 mile up to a viewpoint of the trail, and continues 0.3 mile to the top of the canyon and the Indian mounds. The Fall Creek Falls Trail climbs 0.9 mile to the top of the falls, with a side trail to Jobs Garden at the 0.3-mile mark.

User Groups: Hikers and dogs only. No horses or mountain bikes. Susan Creek Falls is wheelchair accessible.

Permits: Permits are not required. Parking and access are free.

Maps: For a topographic map, ask the USGS for Old Fairview and Mace Mountain.

Directions: To access Susan Creek Falls, drive east of Roseburg 28.3 miles on OR 138 to the Susan Creek Recreation Area lot on the right. To access Fall Creek Falls, drive another 3.9 miles east of Susan Creek on OR 138 and park at a trailhead sign on the left.

Contact: Bureau of Land Management, Roseburg District, 777 NW Garden Valley Boulevard, Roseburg, OR, 97471, 541/440-4930, or Umpqua National Forest, North Umpqua Ranger District, 18782 North Umpqua Highway, Glide, OR, 97443, 541/496-3532.

77 BOULDER CREEK

8.0–21.6 mi/3.0 hr–2 days 3  7

north of the North Umpqua River in Boulder Creek Wilderness

Above the North Umpqua River, this low-elevation wilderness area is open year-round and makes for excellent backpacking. There is camping available on a plateau of ponderosa pines at the top of the Boulder Creek canyon. From this plateau, trails radiate in all directions; hike into this area to get a taste of what these mountains offer.

Go under the giant pipe and head up the Pine Bench Trail 0.4 mile, then go left 1.5 miles to top Pine Bench. Once you reach another trail junction, go right 0.4 mile to a viewpoint with a spring and camping area. Continue on 1.7 miles to a crossing of Boulder Creek, a good turnaround point. Backpackers can follow the Boulder Creek Trail another 6.8 miles, fording the creek three times then grinding uphill on a series of switchbacks to its end. Return as you came.

User Groups: Hikers, dogs, and horses. No mountain bikes allowed. No wheelchair facilities.

Permits: A free self-issue Wilderness Permit is required and is available at the trailhead. Parking and access are free.

Maps: For a map of the Umpqua National Forest and Boulder Creek Wilderness, contact Umpqua National Forest, 2900 NW Stewart Parkway, Roseburg, OR, 97470, 541/672-6601. For a topographic map, ask the USGS for Illahee Rock.

Directions: From Roseburg, drive 54.7 miles east on OR 138. Between mileposts 54 and 55, turn left at a sign for Spring Creek then immediately left on Soda Springs Road, following this gravel road 1.4 miles to a trailhead parking area on the left.

Contact: Umpqua National Forest, Diamond Lake Ranger District, 2020 Toketee Ranger Station Road, Idleyld Park, OR, 97477, 541/498-2531.

78 TOKETEE AND WATSON FALLS

1.4 mi/0.5 hr 

west of Toketee Ranger Station in Umpqua National Forest

These two easy trails head to two of the Umpqua Canyon's most famous falls. Toketee Falls is a heavily photographed (and heavily visited) plunge along the North Umpqua River, the water spills in two tiers, one falling 40 feet into a bowl and the other 80 feet over a notch in some of the most beautiful examples of hexagonal columnar basalt anywhere. From the trailhead, you'll head 0.8 mile out and back to a viewpoint overlooking this deep gorge.

You'll see Watson Falls, the highest in southwest Oregon, not from the top but from the bottom of the 272-foot plunge. Watson makes a fun 0.6-mile loop and passes a viewpoint at the base of the falls.

User Groups: Hikers and dogs only. No wheelchair facilities.

Permits: Permits are not required. Parking and access are free.

Maps: For a map of the Umpqua National Forest and Boulder Creek Wilderness, contact Umpqua National Forest, 2900 NW Stewart Parkway, Roseburg, OR, 97470, 541/672-6601. For a topographic map, ask the USGS for Illahee Rock.

Directions: To access Toketee Falls, drive 58.6 miles east of Roseburg on OR 138 and turn north on Toketee-Rigdon Road 34. Turn left at each junction for 0.4 mile to a parking area. To access Watson Falls, drive 60.9 miles east of Roseburg on OR 138 and turn south on Fish Creek Road 37 to a lot on the right.

Contact: Umpqua National Forest, Diamond Lake Ranger District, 2020 Toketee Ranger Station Road, Idleyld Park, OR, 97477, 541/498-2531.

79 UMPQUA HOT SPRINGS

0.6 mi/0.25 hr 

north of Toketee Ranger Station in Umpqua National Forest

Along this stretch of the North Umpqua River Trail, a spur heads off to one of the most famous hot springs in Oregon: the sheltered pool of Umpqua Hot Springs. A number of pools have been dug into the orange travertine deposits that form this cascading cliff down to the North Umpqua River and its old-growth forests. Recently, the bridge has been removed over the river, but by the time of this publication it may have already been replaced. If not, you can hike in from a trailhead on Road 3401 just before the road crosses the river, which adds 1.6 miles to the hike but also adds a profusion of spring-flowering rhododendron bushes.

From the lot, follow the trail toward the river to a crossing and up the hill for 0.1 mile. At the junction, go right 0.2 mile to the shelter atop the cliff and the hot springs. The hot springs are clothing-optional.

User Groups: Hikers only. No wheelchair facilities.

Permits: Permits are not required. A federal Northwest Forest Pass is required to park here; the cost is $5 a day or $30 for an annual pass. You can buy a day pass at the trailhead, at ranger stations, or through private vendors.

Maps: For a map of the Umpqua National Forest and Boulder Creek Wilderness, contact Umpqua National Forest, 2900 NW Stewart Parkway, Roseburg, OR, 97470, 541/672-6601. For a topographic map, ask the USGS for Illahee Rock.

Directions: Drive 58.6 miles east of Roseburg on OR 138 and turn north on Toketee-Rigdon Road 34. Keep left along the lake and continue two miles, forking right on Thorn Prairie Road to a large lot on the left.

Contact: Umpqua National Forest, Diamond Lake Ranger District, 2020 Toketee Ranger Station Road, Idleyld Park, OR, 97477, 541/498-2531.

80 LEMOLO FALLS

3.4 mi/1.5 hr 

north of Toketee Ranger Station in Umpqua National Forest

On this upper reach of the North Umpqua Trail, near the oddly named Dread and Terror Ridge, the river plunges over 100-foot Lemolo Falls and into a canyon. This woodsy hike begins at the spot the trail crosses Road 2610. Start the section of trail south of the road, crossing a canal. In 1.7 miles you'll reach a viewpoint of the falls, then continue another 0.7 mile to a footbridge crossing of the river. From here, the trail continues on another 10 miles towards the Umpqua Hot Springs.

User Groups: Hikers, dogs, horses, and mountain bikes. No wheelchair facilities.

Permits: Permits are not required. Parking and access are free.

Maps: For a map of the Umpqua National Forest, contact Umpqua National Forest, 2900 NW Stewart Parkway, Roseburg, OR, 97470, 541/672-6601. For a topographic map, ask the USGS for Lemolo Lake.

Directions: Drive east of Roseburg 70 miles on OR 138 and turn north on Road 2610 towards Lemolo Lake Recreation Area. After five miles cross the dam and go left on Road 2610 for 0.6 mile to a parking area.

Contact: Umpqua National Forest, Diamond Lake Ranger District, 2020 Toketee Ranger Station Road, Idleyld Park, OR, 97477, 541/498-2531.

81 WOLF CREEK FALLS

2.6 mi/1.0 hr 1 7

southeast of Glide on the Little River

The so-called "Land of Umpqua" (as the tourism advertisements like to call it) is, above all, a land of waterfalls. There are so many waterfalls feeding the North Umpqua River Canyon that it would be quite impossible to do them all even in a week's time. But here and there, you can catch some of the finest. The 70-foot Wolf Creek Falls feeds the Little River and makes for a good 2.6-mile in-and-out hike from the trailhead. In the rainy season, the falls really pound, but in the dryer months you'll get a chance to see some of the carved-out bedrock beneath the plunge.

User Groups: Hikers and dogs only. No wheelchair facilities.

Permits: Permits are not required. Parking and access are free.

Maps: For a topographic map, ask the USGS for Red Butte.

Directions: From Roseburg, drive east on OR 138 toward Glide. At milepost 16, go right on Little River Road for 10.4 miles and park at the Wolf Creek Trail parking on the right.

Contact: Bureau of Land Management, Roseburg District, 777 NW Garden Valley Boulevard, Roseburg, OR, 97471, 541/440-4930.

82 HEMLOCK LAKE

7.2 mi/3.5 hr 

southeast of Glide in Umpqua National Forest

Beyond the reservoir of Hemlock Lake lie some of the most beautiful alpine meadows in this part of the world. Hellebore, also known as corn lily, bloom their tall sprouts in a series of meadows dotted by Douglas fir and Shasta red fir. In the Yellow Jacket Glade you'll find shooting stars (the flower, not the falling stardust) and trilliums, and in other sections you'll see marsh marigolds, yellow fawn lilies, bunchberry, and violets.

Starting on the Hemlock Creek Trail you'll quickly come to a junction; go right then left on the Yellow Jacket Loop Trail for a 1.1-mile tour of Hemlock Meadows. At a junction, it's worth it to go right up 0.8 mile to 5,310-foot Flat Rock with its views of the rim of Crater Lake, Diamond Peak, Mount Thielsen, and Mount Bailey. Head back to Yellow Jacket and go right at the junction through Yellowjacket Glade, continuing 2.9 miles along a viewpoint ridge and paralleling Road 625 to the next junction, heading left on the faint path and passing Dead Cow Lake. Stay left at the next two junctions for 1.6 miles, reaching the shore of Hemlock Lake and returning to the parking area.

User Groups: Hikers, dogs, horses, and mountain bikes. No wheelchair facilities.

Permits: Permits are not required. Parking and access are free.

Maps: For a map of the Umpqua National Forest, contact Umpqua National Forest, 2900 NW Stewart Parkway, Roseburg, OR, 97470, 541/672-6601. For a topographic map, ask the USGS for Quartz Mountain.

Directions: Drive east of Roseburg on OR 138 to milepost 16 and turn right on Little River Road, which becomes Road 27. Follow this road 18.8 miles on pavement and 11.5 miles on gravel to Hemlock Lake, crossing the dam to an intersection and the trailhead.

Contact: Umpqua National Forest, North Umpqua Ranger District, 18782 North Umpqua Highway, Glide, OR, 97443, 541/496-3532.

83 TWIN LAKES AND TWIN LAKES MOUNTAIN

3.2-5.4 mi/1.5-3.0 hr 

south of the North Umpqua River in Umpqua National Forest

If you are a novice backpacker, or just want a quick trip, or are camping with kids, make Twin Lakes your destination. Once you're settled in and the tent is pitched, you can ramble off on a couple side trails: Twin Lakes Mountain, for example, is a fairly easy climb to a viewpoint above the lakes that also looks out over the Cascade Mountains. You can also just circle the lakes to find a couple old shelters. Beyond lies the largely roadless Boulder Creek Wilderness.

From the trailhead, hike in 0.6 mile on

the Twin Lakes Trail to a junction, with a viewpoint of three Cascade peaks along the way. Turn right then a quick left for 0.3 mile to an old shelter. To the right at this junction are six campsites with picnic tables, and this Twin Lakes Loop Trail joins a loop around the larger of the two lakes, 0.7 mile in all. At the far end of the lake, a spur trail joins a 0.7-mile loop trail around the smaller lake, with another log shelter along the way.

To climb Twin Lakes Mountain head back from the old shelter on the larger lake toward the parking area. At the junction, go right and then stay right for 1.1 miles to a viewpoint. Another 0.6 mile and this trail ends at Road 530.

User Groups: Hikers, dogs, horses, and mountain bikes. No wheelchair facilities.

Permits: Permits are not required. Parking and access are free.

Maps: For a map of the Umpqua National Forest, contact Umpqua National Forest, 2900 NW Stewart Parkway, Roseburg, OR, 97470, 541/672-6601. For a topographic map, ask the USGS for Twin Lakes Mountain.

Directions: From Roseburg, drive 49 miles east on OR 138. Cross the North Umpqua River on Marsters Bridge and go right on Wilson Creek Road 4770, following this gravel road nine miles to the trailhead parking at road's end.

Contact: Umpqua National Forest, North Umpqua Ranger District, 18782 North Umpqua Highway, Glide, OR, 97443, 541/496-3532.

84 TIPSOO PEAK

6.2 mi/2.5 hr

northeast of Diamond Lake in Mount Thielsen Wilderness

Nearby Crater Lake National Park and Diamond Lake attract a lot of tourists, but this alpine area begs for exploration. Just inside Mount Thielsen Wilderness is 8,034-foot Tipsoo Peak, a pretty substantial peak with the accompanying view it deserves. What's more, this trail leads right to its summit with a breathtaking view of the alpine territory around it, including the pumice plains dotted with clumps of trees, not to mention a view of peaks extending from Mount Shasta in California to the Three Sisters in Central Oregon, with Mount Thielsen's domineering spire clearly marking the centerpiece of this wilderness.

The Tipsoo Peak Trail itself is a single track heading up 3.1 miles to the summit. It is possible, with a compass, to hike cross-country across Tipsoo Meadow 0.5 mile to the Pacific Crest Trail. From there, Maidu and Miller Lakes are five miles to the north, Howlock Meadows only 1.6 miles south, and the access to the Mount Thielsen climbing trail five miles beyond that.

User Groups: Hikers, dogs, and horses. No mountain bikes allowed. No wheelchair facilities.

Permits: A free self-issue Wilderness Permit is required and is available at the trailhead. A federal Northwest Forest Pass is required to park here; the cost is $5 a day or $30 for an annual pass. You can buy a day pass at the trailhead, at ranger stations, or through private vendors.

Maps: For a map of the Umpqua National Forest and Mount Thielsen Wilderness, contact Umpqua National Forest, 2900 NW Stewart Parkway, Roseburg, OR, 97470, 541/672-6601. For a topographic map, ask the USGS for Mount Thielsen.

Directions: Drive east of Roseburg 75 miles on OR 138. Near milepost 75, turn east on Cinnamon Butte Road 4793 and go 1.7 miles. Go straight on Wits End Road 100 for 3.2 miles to a Tipsoo Trail sign on the right.

Contact: Umpqua National Forest, Diamond Lake Ranger District, 2020 Toketee Ranger Station Road, Idleyld Park, OR, 97477, 541/498-2531.

85 DIAMOND LAKE

11.5 mi/5.0 hr 2 7

on Diamond Lake in Umpqua National Forest

It's easy to see why 3,015-acre Diamond Lake is one of the most popular destinations in the area, even more so than nearby Crater Lake National Park. Two mountains hover at opposite sides above the placid waters: Mount Thielsen and Mount Bailey. There are hundreds of campsites along the lake—well-established car campsites, needless to say—and picnic areas and boat ramps. There are, too, a few side trails to little Teal Lake and Horse Lake. All in all, the Diamond Lake Trail is a good trail if you're staying here. Plus, the entire route is paved, making it accessible to all and a good route for bikes. And if you're in the mood for a swim, Diamond Lake's 20-foot average depth means it warms up quickly, unlike so many of the other Cascade high-mountain lakes.

You can go either way along the loop trail. The east side follows routes through the large Diamond Lake Campground for most of its 3.8 miles to the South Shore Picnic Area. The south side continues 1.9 miles to a crossing of Road 4795, with side trails to two small lakes and along Silent Creek. The west side of the lakeshore is mostly private land, and the trail goes 2.9 miles above the road, but with views to Mount Thielsen. After crossing the road again near Thielsen View Campground and going another 1.2 miles to the road crossing at Lake Creek. The final uninterrupted stretch travels 1.7 miles along the north shore back to the lodge.

User Groups: Hikers, dogs, and mountain bikes. No horses allowed. The paved lakeshore loop is wheelchair accessible.

Permits: Permits are not required. Parking and access are free.

Maps: For a map of the Umpqua National Forest, contact Umpqua National Forest, 2900 NW Stewart Parkway, Roseburg, OR, 97470, 541/672-6601. For a topographic map, ask the USGS for Diamond Lake.

Directions: To find the Diamond Lake Lodge, drive east of Roseburg 78.6 miles east on OR 138 to a sign for Diamond Lake, and turn right on Road 6592, following signs for the Lodge, turning right and going past a boat ramp to the parking area.

Contact: Umpqua National Forest, Diamond Lake Ranger District, 2020 Toketee Ranger Station Road, Idleyld Park, OR, 97477, 541/498-2531.

86 THIELSEN CREEK AND HOWLOCK MOUNTAIN

11.4–15.7 mi/6.0–8.0 hr 

northeast of Diamond Lake in Mount Thielsen Wilderness

A series of meadows in the Mount Thielsen Wilderness lie strewn along Thielsen Creek and the Pacific Crest Trail, and the hardy hiker can visit one, two, or all three of them in a single hike. Along the way, there's plenty to see in this alpine country, including Mount Thielsen itself looming above this country like a church spire. The Howlock Mountain Trail provides the opportunity for a long loop, with extended opportunities for backpacking available, too.

The Howlock Mountain Trail starts at the trailhead, ducking through a tunnel under the highway, and continuing 1.1 miles to a junction with the Spruce Ridge Trail. Stay left on the Thielsen Creek Trail another 2.4 miles through a hot, dusty country of lodgepole pines and manzanita bushes to Timothy Meadows and Thielsen Creek. To continue on to Thielsen Meadow, go right 2.2 miles along Thielsen Creek to the junction of the Pacific Crest Trail.

From here, you can return as you came, or for an outstanding loop, go north and left on the PCT for three miles along the base of Howlock Mountain to Howlock Meadows, then left 3.5 miles back to Timothy Meadows.

User Groups: Hikers, dogs, and horses. No mountain bikes allowed. No wheelchair facilities.

Permits: A free self-issue Wilderness Permit is required and is available at the trailhead. A federal Northwest Forest Pass is required to park here; the cost is $5 a day or $30 for an annual pass. You can buy a day pass at the trailhead, at ranger stations, or through private vendors.

Maps: For a map of the Umpqua National Forest and Mount Thielsen Wilderness, contact Umpqua National Forest, 2900 NW Stewart Parkway, Roseburg, OR, 97470, 541/672-6601. For a topographic map, ask the USGS for Mount Thielsen.

Directions: From Roseburg, drive 78.6 miles east on OR 138 to a sign for Diamond Lake, and turn right on Road 6592 for 0.3 mile to a parking area on the left.

Contact: Umpqua National Forest, Diamond Lake Ranger District, 2020 Toketee Ranger Station Road, Idleyld Park, OR, 97477, 541/498-2531.

87 MOUNT THIELSEN

10.0 mi/6.0 hr 5 10

northeast of Diamond Lake in Mount Thielsen Wilderness

BEST

Mount Thielsen's peak, a towering 9,182 feet in the sky, has earned the nickname "Lightning Rod of the Cascades" for no uncertain reason. What was once an 11,000-foot-high volcano has been whittled down by glaciers to its single lava plug, an andesite core left after 100,000 years. What you'll find on the peak are the lightning-melted spots of fulgurite, a re-crystalized glassy rock that pocks the summit boulders. Named for a pioneer railroad engineer, Thielsen is no climb for the weak-hearted. It demands endurance, stamina, sureness of hands, and outright skill; the final ascent is a dangerous technical climb that requires ropes and climbing partners to aid you. Any ascent past the topmost ledge, a Class 4 rock climb, is done at your own risk. *Only experienced climbers should attempt this final pitch.* Should you make it, you'll find a canister summit register at the top.

From the Mount Thielsen Trailhead, climb 1.4 miles into the forest, staying right at a junction with the Spruce Ridge Trail, and continuing another 2.4 miles into the Wilderness Area to a junction with the PCT. To attempt the summit, continue straight up the ridge 1.2 miles on a climber's trail, spiraling to the right around the eastern ledge at the base of the 80-foot peak. The drop from this ledge to the east is thousands of feet, a dizzying view down to the deserts of Eastern Oregon. *Do not climb to the peak without rock climbing experience; rockfall and exposure make this pitch dangerous.* To ascend to the peak requires climbing up the series of cracks and fissures in the rock, wedging your way up to the peak. To be sure, the peak is an unnerving experience and only for the stout-hearted. The shoulder beneath the peak has expansive views across the Cascade Range, down into Crater Lake, and out and over Diamond Lake to the west.

User Groups: Hikers only. Dogs are not recommended. Horses can access the PCT from the nearby Howlock Mountain Trailhead. No mountain bikes allowed. No wheelchair facilities.

Permits: A free self-issue Wilderness Permit is required and is available at the trailhead. A federal Northwest Forest Pass is required to park here; the cost is $5 a day or $30 for an annual pass. You can buy a day pass at the trailhead, at ranger stations, or through private vendors.

Maps: For a map of the Umpqua National Forest and Mount Thielsen Wilderness, contact Umpqua National Forest, 2900 NW Stewart Parkway, Roseburg, OR, 97470, 541/672-6601. For a topographic map, ask the USGS for Mount Thielsen.

Directions: From Roseburg, drive 81.6 miles east on OR 138 to a large trailhead parking area on the left.

Contact: Umpqua National Forest, Diamond Lake Ranger District, 2020 Toketee Ranger Station Road, Idleyld Park, OR, 97477, 541/498-2531.

88 MOUNT BAILEY

9.8 mi/5.0 hr 4 9

west of Diamond Lake in Umpqua National Forest

BEST

The Mount Bailey National Recreation Trail follows what in winter becomes a Nordic trail. Blue diamonds lead the way to some alpine ski runs on this dome-shaped mountain above Diamond Lake. But in summer, this mountain makes a fairly easy summit—no gear or technical expertise required. All you'll need is a little stamina to make it up the crater rim to an 8,368-foot view of the Cascade Mountains in all directions. From Road 300, the trail climbs steadily up 2.2 miles to cross another dirt road, then begins to really climb up the mountain's ridge for 2.7 miles and up 2,300 feet to the south summit with its small crater and finally the true summit.

User Groups: Hikers and dogs only. No wheelchair facilities.

Permits: Permits are not required. Parking and access are free.

Maps: For a map of the Umpqua National Forest, contact Umpqua National Forest, 2900 NW Stewart Parkway, Roseburg, OR, 97470, 541/672-6601. For a topographic map, ask the USGS for Diamond Lake.

Directions: Drive east of Roseburg 78.6 miles on OR 138 to a sign for Diamond Lake, and turn right on Road 6592, following this road to the South Shore Picnic Area. Turn right on Road 4795 for 1.7 miles and turn left on Road 300 for 0.4 mile to a parking area.

Contact: Umpqua National Forest, Diamond Lake Ranger District, 2020 Toketee Ranger Station Road, Idleyld Park, OR, 97477, 541/498-2531.

89 BUCKEYE AND CLIFF LAKES

3.4-8.9 mi/1.5-4.5 hr 2 8

in the Rogue-Umpqua Divide Wilderness

In this 16- to 25-million-year-old mountain range, the forest has had time to get a foothold in this lovely bottom of high lakes. Even a massive landslide that befell this valley when Grasshopper Mountain collapsed 1,000 years ago has been repaired by the trees. Beneath what is left of that mountain, Buckeye and Cliff Lakes warm in the afternoon sun and invite backpackers. Being so close to Fish Lake (see next listing), you can easily turn this into a multi-day trip. For a different entry into the Rogue-Umpqua Divide Wilderness, try starting this trail from the Skimmerhorn Trailhead. You'll climb to a high meadow above the lakes.

To access the Lakes Trail from the Skimmerhorn Trailhead, hike in 0.2 mile and keep left at the first junction, going another 0.7 mile and keeping right at the next junction with the Indian Trail. After 0.1 mile go left at the next junction with the Acker Divide Trail for 0.4 mile, arriving at Buckeye Lake. In 0.3 mile arrive at Cliff Lake. From here, you can return as you came.

To continue on a longer loop to Grasshopper Mountain, continue another 0.3 mile past Cliff Lake to a junction. Now go right on the Grasshopper Trail and climb onto a high plateau of mixed conifer for one mile to Grasshopper Meadow. A right-hand junction leads 0.6 mile and 300 feet up to Grasshopper Mountain and good views. Going straight here leads to a junction with the Acker Divide Trail; go right on this trail and down 0.9 mile to a trailhead near Road 550 and go right, continuing on the Acker Divide Trail. In 0.4 mile find Mosquito Camp; continue on 1.7 miles, passing Little Fish Lake, and rejoining the Lakes Trail. Go left one mile to the trailhead.

User Groups: Hikers, dogs, and horses. No mountain bikes allowed. No wheelchair facilities.

Permits: A free self-issue Wilderness Permit is required and is available at the trailhead. Parking and access are free.
Maps: For a map of the Umpqua National Forest and Rogue-Umpqua Divide Wilderness, contact Umpqua National Forest, 2900 NW Stewart Parkway, Roseburg, OR, 97470, 541/672-6601. For a topographic map, ask the USGS for Buckeye Lake.
Directions: From Roseburg, drive 25 miles north on I-5 to the Canyonville exit 98, following signs towards Crater Lake. In Canyonville, turn east on 3rd Street and follow this road, which becomes the Tiller-Trail Highway, 23.3 miles to Tiller. Go through town and turn left on Road 46 for 24.2 miles, then go right on Road 2823. Follow Skimmerhorn Trailhead signs for 2.4 miles to a right turn on Road 2830 and go 3.9 miles. Turn left on Road 600 for 1.8 miles to road's end at the trailhead.
Contact: Umpqua National Forest, Tiller Ranger District, 27812 Tiller Trail Highway, Tiller, OR, 97484, 541/825-3201.

90 FISH LAKE

12.6 mi/7.0 hr 3 9

in the Rogue-Umpqua Divide Wilderness

This loop serves as an introduction to the Rogue-Umpqua Divide Wilderness, following a rugged landscape where the key word is "Highrock"—as in Highrock Creek, Highrock Meadow, and Highrock Mountain. Fish Lake, true to its name in regards to the fish, is a good destination for backpackers, as there are several camping sites along the lake, and access to a multitude of lakes and trails beyond. Take this trail up the dramatic andesite cliff-strewn backbone of Rocky Ridge for a peak experience.

From the Beaver Swamp Trailhead take the right-hand Beaver Swamp Trail in 1.5 miles to Fish Lake, staying left at a junction. When you reach the lake, go left around the lake and continue on the Fish Lake Trail past camping spots 1.3 miles to a junction, staying left again for another three miles to the lovely Highrock Meadows beneath Highrock Mountain. At the next junction, go left on the Rogue Umpqua Divide Trail toward Rocky Ridge, staying left at a junction in 0.4 mile and continuing up the steep climb for 3.2 miles, over Standoff Point and several viewpoints. Keep left at the next junction and descend past more viewpoints 3.2 miles to the trailhead
User Groups: Hikers, dogs, and horses. No mountain bikes allowed. No wheelchair facilities.
Permits: A free self-issue Wilderness Permit is required and is available at the trailhead. Parking and access are free.
Maps: For a map of the Umpqua National Forest and Rogue-Umpqua Divide Wilderness, contact Umpqua National Forest, 2900 NW Stewart Parkway, Roseburg, OR, 97470, 541/672-6601. For a topographic map, ask the USGS for Buckeye Lake.
Directions: From Roseburg, drive 25 miles north on I-5 to the Canyonville exit (Exit 98), following signs towards Crater Lake. In Canyonville, turn east on 3rd Street and follow this road, which becomes the Tiller-Trail Highway, 23.3 miles to Tiller. Go through town and turn left on Road 46 for 24.2 miles, then go right on Road 2823. Follow Fish Lake Trailhead signs for 2.4 miles to a right turn on Road 2830 and go 3.9 miles, then go left on Road 2840 for 0.5 mile. Continue past the Fish Lake Trailhead another 4.6 miles to the Beaver Swamp Trailhead.
Contact: Umpqua National Forest, Tiller Ranger District, 27812 Tiller Trail Highway, Tiller, OR, 97484, 541/825-3201.

91 RATTLESNAKE MOUNTAIN

5.2–5.6 mi/3.0 hr 

in the Rogue-Umpqua Divide Wilderness

In the heart of the Rogue-Umpqua Divide Wilderness, the wildflowers of Fish Creek

Valley see few visitors, which is fortunate for the intrepid explorer looking for a little quiet time. The meadows along Fish Creek are only the beginning; above them, a loop trail reaches Windy Gap and its awesome views, and a side trail climbs Rattlesnake Mountain, second highest in the Rogue Umpqua Divide Wilderness, with views out to nearby Mount Thielsen, Mount Scott, Mount Bailey, and Mount McLoughlin.

From the Happy Camp Trailhead, follow Fish Creek 0.7 mile along the Rogue Umpqua Divide Trail to a junction and go left on the Whitehorse Meadow Trail, climbing along a creek one mile to Windy Gap and a four-way junction. The right-hand Rattlesnake Way Trail (also known as the Rattlesnake Mountain Trail) climbs one mile and 1,000 feet to a viewpoint on Rattlesnake Mountain. Return as you came, for 5.6 miles in all.

For a loop option, which turns out to be 0.4 mile shorter, go back to Windy Gap and take the Castle Creek Trail, which heads along the ridge 0.4 mile to a junction. Go left, staying on Trail 1576, to descend 1.1 miles back to Happy Camp.

User Groups: Hikers, dogs, and horses. No mountain bikes allowed. No wheelchair facilities.

Permits: A free self-issue Wilderness Permit is required and is available at the trailhead. Parking and access are free.

Maps: For a map of the Umpqua National Forest and Rogue-Umpqua Divide Wilderness, contact Umpqua National Forest, 2900 NW Stewart Parkway, Roseburg, OR, 97470, 541/672-6601. For a topographic map, ask the USGS for Fish Mountain.

Directions: From Roseburg, drive east on OR 138, and between mileposts 60 and 61 turn right on Fish Creek Road 37 for 13 miles. Turn right on Incense Cedar Loop Road 800 for 3.5 miles, then right on Fish Creek Valley Road 870 for 4.2 miles to a "Rogue-Umpqua Trail" sign on the right. Park 100 yards farther down the road.

Contact: Umpqua National Forest, Diamond Lake Ranger District, 2020 Toketee Ranger Station Road, Idleyld Park, OR, 97477, 541/498-2531.

92 MUIR CREEK TO BUCK CANYON

15.0-22.8 mi/7.0 hr-2 days

in the Rogue-Umpqua Divide Wilderness

The relatively uncrowded Rogue-Umpqua Divide Wilderness is a must-do for the backpacking crowd. About the only visitors this area sees in the summer are the cows that are allowed to graze here. But don't let that dissuade you: This trail up Muir Creek and into Buck Canyon opens a door to numerous backpacking sites, beautiful meadows, and Buck Canyon. From here you can traverse out to other areas like Rattlesnake Mountain and Hershberger Mountain. This trail system begins within a stone's throw of a paved highway, yet you'd never know it was there. With some path-finding skills, you can make your way in a loop around theis wilderness and bushwhack a bit back to your car.

Starting from the highway, follow the Muir Creek Trail 2.7 miles to an overlook of Muir Falls, then continue one mile, keeping left at a junction, then 1.4 miles, keeping left at another trailhead junction. From here hike 1.6 miles into Buck Canyon and Hummingbird Meadows. The next junction has a right-hand turn to cross the creek and pass Wiley Camp; from here the main trail continues to follow Muir Creek another 0.8 mile past some falls, the crumbling Devil's Slide, and an upper meadow. For a day's exploration, this is adequate. Backpackers can continue on another 3.9 miles for three more camps and the Alkali Meadows and connections to trails fanning out from there.

User Groups: Hikers, dogs, and horses. No mountain bikes allowed. No wheelchair facilities.

Permits: A free self-issue Wilderness Permit is required and is available at the trailhead. Parking and access are free.
Maps: For a map of the Rogue River National Forest and the Rogue-Umpqua Divide Wilderness, contact the Rogue River-Siskiyou National Forest, 3040 Biddle Road, Medford, OR, 97504, 541/618-2200. For a topographic map, ask the USGS for Fish Mountain.
Directions: From Medford, drive 57 miles east on OR 62, going left onto Highway 230 for 10.3 miles. Just before the Muir Creek Bridge, park in a lot on the left.
Contact: Rogue River National Forest, Prospect Ranger District, 47201 Highway 62, Prospect, OR, 97536, 541/560-3400.

93 BOUNDARY SPRINGS AND UPPER ROGUE RIVER TRAIL

5.0-18.6 mi/2.0 hr-1 day 

on the Upper Rogue River and in Crater Lake National Park

From a massive series of springs just inside the boundary of Crater Lake National Park, the Rogue River begins its journey through the southern Cascade Mountains. Almost immediately, the river sets out into a forested canyon, plunging over Rough Rider Falls and No Name Falls. From there, the trail goes on and on, allowing for a long backpacking adventure along several access points. For a sampling of the Rogue's wonders, start from the easy pullout at the head of the canyon. Then you can plan out a longer trip along the Upper Rogue River Trail, following this Wild and Scenic River from the Crater Rim to the town of Prospect.

To see the Boundary Springs, follow the Upper Rogue River Trail in from the Crater Rim Viewpoint lot 0.5 mile to a junction. Go left on the Boundary Springs Trail 1.9 miles to the springs. Return as you came, or continue on to the viewpoint.

To descend instead into the Rogue Canyon and hike the uppermost segment of this famous trail, begin from the same trailhead, following the Upper Rogue Trail, and go to the right from this first junction. In 4.2 miles you'll march along the canyon rim and reach Rough Rider Falls, and in another 2.2 you'll go into the canyon itself to see No Name Falls. A final stretch of the trail continues through the forest another 1.7 miles to a lower trailhead at the Hamaker Campground.

The entire length of the Upper Rogue River Trail is 47.9 miles, with numerous access points along the way. Contact the Rogue River-Siskiyou National Forest (www.fs.fed.us/r6/rogue-siskiyou) for maps and information.
User Groups: Hikers and dogs only. No horses or mountain bikes allowed. No wheelchair facilities.
Permits: Permits are not required. Parking and access are free.
Maps: For a map of the Rogue River National Forest, contact the Rogue River-Siskiyou National Forest, 3040 Biddle Road, Medford, OR, 97504, 541/618-2200. For a topographic map, ask the USGS for Pumice Desert West and Hamaker Butte.
Directions: To reach the upper trailhead, start from Medford, drive 57 miles on OR 62 and continue on Highway 230 for 18.6 miles to the Crater Rim Viewpoint on the right. For the lower trailhead, go north on 230 approximately 14 miles from the junction with Highway 62. Turn right on Road 6530, and follow it one mile to Road 900. Continue 0.5 mile on Road 900. The trail begins east of the Hamaker Campground.
Contact: Rogue River National Forest, Prospect Ranger District, 47201 Highway 62, Prospect, OR, 97536, 541/560-3400.

94 HORSE LAKE

7.2–8.8 mi/4.0–4.5 hr 

west of Mount Bachelor in the Three Sisters Wilderness

In the stretches of the Three Sisters Wilderness south of the peaks themselves, the landscape is a dense forest punctuated by lakes. No wonder they call the main access road the Cascade Lakes Highway; this entire area east of the Cascade Divide is rife with ponds and lakes, many suitable for swimming. Starting from big Elk Lake, a superb loop trail passes through the forests to visit Horse Lake with its rocky peninsula, then returning past two smaller lakes, Colt and Sunset. Be prepared to walk through a burn, resulting from fire that torched this area in 1999.

From the trailhead, start on the right-hand Horse Lake Trail, immediately entering the wilderness area. In 1.3 miles, the trail crosses the Pacific Crest Trail. Continue straight on the Horse Lake Trail two miles to a T-junction with a sign for Horse Lake. After viewing the lake, you have a choice; to continue on the loop, go south from this junction toward Dumbbell Lake 0.1 mile, stay left at the next junction, and continue 0.3 mile to another junction, going to the left toward Sunset Lake.

To circle Horse Lake on a loop, however, go forward to the lake and to the right instead and watch for a side trail which circles the lake over 1.7 miles, keeping left at a junction 0.3 mile after the peninsula until you reach another junction. Go right toward Dumbbell Lake 0.3 mile, then go left away from Dumbbell Lake, going toward Sunset Lake instead.

Both options bring you to the same place. Now, to continue from either of these two options, start down the trail toward Sunset Lake, watching on the left for a faint trail to Colt Lake, and just beyond a trail to the right for Sunset Lake. Stay on this main trail 1.3 miles to a junction with the PCT. Go left on the PCT for 1.2 miles, then right on the Island Meadow Trail one mile back to the trailhead.

User Groups: Hikers, dogs, and horses. No mountain bikes allowed. No wheelchair facilities.

Permits: A free self-issue Wilderness Permit is required and is available at the trailhead. A federal Northwest Forest Pass is required to park here; the cost is $5 a day or $30 for an annual pass. You can buy a day pass at the trailhead, at ranger stations, or through private vendors.

Maps: A map of the Three Sisters Wilderness is available for purchase from Geo-Graphics. For a map of the Deschutes National Forest and the Three Sisters Wilderness, contact Deschutes National Forest Headquarters, 1001 SW Emkay Drive, Bend, OR, 97702, 541/383-5300. For a topographic map, ask the USGS for South Sister.

Directions: From Bend, drive the Cascades Lake Highway 32.7 miles west to the Elk Lake Trailhead on the right, following the 0.3-mile spur road to the parking area.

Contact: Deschutes National Forest, Bend-Fort Rock Ranger District, 1230 NE 3rd Street, Suite A-262, Bend, OR, 97701, 541/383-4000.

95 SIX LAKES TRAIL

2.0–19.0 mi/1.0 hr–1 day 

southwest of Mount Bachelor in the Three Sisters Wilderness

There are so many lakes along the Six Lakes Trail that it's hard to say which six give the trail its name. You'll pass two big ones, Blow and Doris, right off, then continue into a virtual maze of lakes both big and small. Bring a map and a backpack, and have your pick. Two other obvious goals are Cliff Lake and Mink Lake, both with rustic shelters. The Pacific Crest Trail curves right through this basin, allowing access to other hikes in the area, including Horse Lake and Sisters Mirror Lake to the north. Consider this hike either as a straight in-and-out, or with the possibility for a number of loops.

HIKING

From the Six Lakes Trailhead, follow the trail one mile to Blow Lake, and another 1.4 miles to Doris Lake. In another 0.9 mile, stay right at a junction, climb a pass and descend to the PCT in 2.1 miles. Go left on the PCT 1.6 miles to an unmarked side trail on the left to Cliff Lake's shelter, just before a junction to Porky Lake. To continue to Mink Lake, leave the PCT and go right toward Porky Lake 1.6 miles, then left to Mink Lake's old shelter. A loop trail around Mink Lake is 2.6 miles.

From here, possibilities for loops can be done a number of ways. From Mink Lake, go right away from Porky Lake, then stay left on the main trail 1.2 miles to the PCT. Go left on the PCT 2.2 miles, passing five lakes to return to Cliff Lake. Another way is to leave Mink Lake towards Porky Lake, then go left 1.2 miles to Goose Lake, then right for 2.2 miles past smaller lakes to the PCT. Go straight to return to the trailhead.

User Groups: Hikers, dogs, and horses. No mountain bikes allowed. No wheelchair facilities.

Permits: A free self-issue Wilderness Permit is required and is available at the trailhead. A federal Northwest Forest Pass is required to park here; the cost is $5 a day or $30 for an annual pass. You can buy a day pass at the trailhead, at ranger stations, or through private vendors.

Maps: A map of the Three Sisters Wilderness is available for purchase from Geo-Graphics. For a map of the Deschutes National Forest and the Three Sisters Wilderness, contact Deschutes National Forest Headquarters, 1001 SW Emkay Drive, Bend, OR, 97702, 541/383-5300. For a topographic map, ask the USGS for Elk Lake and Packsaddle Mountain.

Directions: From Bend, drive the Cascades Lake Highway 34.7 miles west to the Six Lakes Trailhead on the right, following the spur road to the parking area.

Contact: Deschutes National Forest, Bend-Fort Rock Ranger District, 1230 NE 3rd Street, Suite A-262, Bend, OR, 97701, 541/383-4000.

96 DESCHUTES RIVER TRAIL/DILLON AND BENHAM FALLS

4.4-17.4 mi/2.0 hr-1 day 3 9

southwest of Bend in the Deschutes National Forest

BEST

The city of Bend is blessed to have this Upper Deschutes River Trail. From here, the river makes its way to the center of town, languidly flowing behind a dam, creating Mirror Pond, but in the ponderosa pine forests of the lower Cascades, the river is a pounding cataract of falls and eddies, and at other times gentle as a pond. The landscape is one of lava flows, which constantly force the river into its shapes and drops—the remnants of a massive flow from nearby Lava Butte. It is possible to do the trail up and down in a day, and shuttling is easy enough; along the way, too, are a number of access points, making for combinations of hikes leading to the best points: Lava Island Falls and the Lava Island Cave, Dillon Falls and Ryan Ranch Meadow, and the absolutely beautiful Benham Falls.

From the Meadow picnic area, climb 0.5 mile on the Deschutes River Trail to a slough, keeping left along the river 0.6 mile to the cave and Lava Island Falls. Continue 1.1 woodsy miles to a view of Big Eddy Rapids, and another 1.1 miles to the Aspen Picnic Area. The next 0.9 mile enters pine woods and climbs to a viewpoint of Dillon Falls' long cascade. Follow the road to Ryan Ranch Meadows, with views to the lava on the opposite shore, and continue 2.3 miles to the Slough Day-Use Area. The next 1.5 miles climbs into cooler, denser woods and arrives at Benham Falls overlook. From here, the trail follows an old logging railroad grade 0.7 mile to a crossing of the Deschutes, arriving at the Benham West Day-Use Area, with a few more loop trails angling into the woods to an old mill site.

User Groups: Hikers, dogs on leash only, horses, and mountain bikes uphill only. The

Big Eddy Rapids, Dillon Falls, and Benham Falls West Area are wheelchair accessible.

Permits: Permits are not required. A federal Northwest Forest Pass is required to park here; the cost is $5 a day or $30 for an annual pass. You can buy a day pass at the trailhead, at ranger stations, or through private vendors.

Maps: For a map of the Deschutes National Forest, contact Deschutes National Forest Headquarters, 1001 SW Emkay Drive, Bend, OR, 97702, 541/383-5300. For a topographic map, ask the USGS for Benham Falls.

Directions: From Bend, take the Cascades Lake Highway 6.2 miles west to a sign for Meadow Day Use Area and turn left on gravel FS Road 100 for 1.3 miles to the road's end for the lower trailhead. To access other sites, continue another 1.6 mile on Cascade Lakes Highway then turn left on Conklin Road/Road 41. Go 2.6 miles and turn left on Road 4120 for 0.5 mile, then right on Road 4120 for 3.1 miles to the trailhead at road's end.

Contact: Deschutes National Forest, Bend-Fort Rock Ranger District, 1230 NE 3rd Street, Suite A-262, Bend, OR, 97701, 541/383-4000.

97 NEWBERRY LAVA TUBES

0.4-1.2 mi/1.0-2.0 hr 2 8

east of Bend in the Deschutes National Forest

BEST

These trails require hiking underground. "Spelunking" gives an impression of clambering around in chambers, but that's not what Central Oregon caves are about—although you can do that too. These volcanic-formed caves are "lava tubes," formed when rivers of lava from nearby Newberry Caldera cooled on top, but left the lava flowing underneath. In time, the lava drained and left these rounded wormholes descending under the basalt roofs. Three caves along China Hat Road in the dry, burned forests east of Bend are open for walking—come prepared with warm clothes and a flashlight with plenty of batteries. Boyd Cave is shortest, Skeleton Cave a little longer. The Wind Cave is most difficult, but has a skylight, which is how the bats enter—thus, Wind Cave is closed from November to late April to protect their habitat.

The Boyd Cave is the easiest at 0.2 mile. Simply descend the stairs and follow the broad cave back to its low ceiling. The Skeleton Cave is more ambitious; go down the stairs and hike in 0.4 mile to a junction. The left tunnel peters out in a short distance, though you can get on your belly and go farther. The right path continues another 0.2 mile to its end. Wind Cave is most difficult of all, requiring climbing and descending massive jumbles of boulders 0.1 mile to the skylight room, and continuing 0.5 mile to its end.

User Groups: Hikers only. No dogs, horses, or mountain bikes allowed. No wheelchair facilities.

Permits: Permits are not required. Parking and access are free.

Maps: For a map of the Deschutes National Forest, contact Deschutes National Forest Headquarters, 1001 SW Emkay Drive, Bend, OR, 97702, 541/383-5300. For a topographic map, ask the USGS for Kelsey Butte.

Directions: Drive four miles south of Bend on U.S. 97 and turn left on China Hat Road 18. In nine miles, turn left at a sign for Boyd Cave. Another 0.5 mile beyond this turn, go left on Road 1819 for 1.6 miles to the Skeleton Cave. Another two miles east on China Hat, turn left at a sign for Wind Cave and park at the lot.

Contact: Deschutes National Forest, Bend-Fort Rock Ranger District, 1230 NE 3rd Street, Suite A-262, Bend, OR, 97701, 541/383-4000.

98 MUSKRAT LAKE CABIN

10.0-11.2 mi/3.5-4.0 hr 2 7

north of Cultus Lake in Three Sisters Wilderness

At this southeastern corner of the Three Sisters Wilderness, you'll be lucky to see anyone. Sure, it's far from the peaks, but close as it is to popular Cultus Lake, a wind-whipped lake high on the divide, visitors just don't seem to wander down here. The Winopee Trail follows the shore of this massive lake for a stretch, with possibilities for backpacking, then dives into the wilderness to access a number of lakes. The two large Teddy Lakes are an easy side trip, but the goal is a decrepit cabin on Muskrat Lake; it once was suitable for camping—with a stove, a loft, windows, and cupboards—but vandals have rendered unusable. It's worth a visit though, as this corner of the wilderness is quiet and deep.

Follow the Winopee Trail 2.9 miles along the shore of Cultus Lake, keeping left at the first junction to Corral Lakes, then heading right toward Winopee Lake 0.7 mile to a junction. To the right, two Teddy Lakes lie along a 0.6-mile trail. Continue left 1.4 miles to reach the cabin at Muskrat Lake.

User Groups: Hikers, dogs, and horses. No mountain bikes allowed. No wheelchair facilities.

Permits: A free self-issue Wilderness Permit is required and is available at the trailhead. A federal Northwest Forest Pass is required to park here; the cost is $5 a day or $30 for an annual pass. You can buy a day pass at the trailhead, at ranger stations, or through private vendors.

Maps: A map of the Three Sisters Wilderness is available for purchase from Geo-Graphics. For a map of the Deschutes National Forest and the Three Sisters Wilderness, contact Deschutes National Forest Headquarters, 1001 SW Emkay Drive, Bend, OR, 97702, 541/383-5300. For a topographic map, ask the USGS for Irish Mountain.

Directions: From Bend, drive the Cascades Lake Highway 44 miles west to the Cultus Lake Resort on the right. Turn right on Road 4635 for 1.8 miles, then go right on Road 100 toward the campground, keeping right on a Dead End road and parking at the trailhead in 0.5 mile.

Contact: Deschutes National Forest, Bend-Fort Rock Ranger District, 1230 NE 3rd Street, Suite A-262, Bend, OR, 97701, 541/383-4000.

99 LAVA RIVER CAVE

2.2 mi/1.5 hr

southeast of Bend in the Newberry National Volcanic Monument

Like Boyd, Skeleton, and Wind Caves (see *Newberry Lava Tubes* listing in this chapter), the Lava River Cave is a lava tube, only this one is the queen bee. A full 1.1 miles long, it actually goes beneath Highway 97, and features a double-tiered cave and strange formations of the Sand Garden that form castles on the floor as Mount Mazama ash leaks in from above. You may find crowds here visiting such notable places as Echo Hall and Low Bridge Lane, but it's worth joining the fray to see one of Oregon's treasures. The cave makes for an easy excursions, and guided tours are available.

User Groups: Hikers only. No dogs, horses, or mountain bikes. No wheelchair facilities.

Permits: Permits are not required. A federal Northwest Forest Pass is required to park here; the cost is $5 a day or $30 for an annual pass. You can buy a day pass at the trailhead, at ranger stations, or through private vendors. Lanterns can be rented for $2.

Maps: For a map of the Deschutes National Forest, contact Deschutes National Forest Headquarters, 1001 SW Emkay Drive, Bend, OR, 97702, 541/383-5300. For a topographic map, ask the USGS for Lava Butte.

Directions: From Bend, drive 11 miles south on U.S. 97 and turn left at a sign for Lava

River Cave. Between May and October, you can drive 0.3 mile to the fee booth; the rest of the year the road is gated, but you can walk it.

Contact: Deschutes National Forest, Bend-Fort Rock Ranger District, 1230 NE 3rd Street, Suite A-262, Bend, OR, 97701, 541/383-4000.

100 LAVA CAST FOREST

1.0 mi/1.0 hr 

southeast of Bend in the Newberry National Volcanic Monument

BEST

Make this a destination if you're touring the entire Lava Lands complex. Lava Cast Forest makes an interesting educational outing with the kids, or if you're looking to entertain visitor—if they can stand the awful washboard gravel road to get there. This easy, paved one-mile loop crosses the lava landscape of the Newberry Caldera's eruption, with views to that great shield volcano itself. The "lava casts" are actually stone cast of ancient trees—when the lava pooled around them and cooled, the tree it embraced burned and left perfect casts, some wells in the ground deep enough to stand in up to your chest, or in some cases knocked them over, leaving tubes and tunnels you can look through horizontally.

User Groups: Hikers and dogs. No horses or mountain bikes allowed. The entire trail is wheelchair accessible.

Permits: Permits are not required. A federal Northwest Forest Pass is required to park here; the cost is $5 a day or $30 for an annual pass. You can buy a day pass at the trailhead, at ranger stations, or through private vendors.

Maps: For a map of the Deschutes National Forest, contact Deschutes National Forest Headquarters, 1001 SW Emkay Drive, Bend, OR, 97702, 541/383-5300. For a topographic map, ask the USGS for Lava Cast Forest.

Directions: From Bend, drive 13.2 miles south on U.S. 97 and turn left on Road 9720, following this miserable road nine miles to its end at the trailhead.

Contact: Deschutes National Forest, Bend-Fort Rock Ranger District, 1230 NE 3rd Street, Suite A-262, Bend, OR, 97701, 541/383-4000.

101 FALL RIVER

7.0 mi/3.0 hr 

southwest of Sunriver in the Deschutes National Forest

Fall River is amazingly quiet and absolutely lovely. It seems only anglers appreciate its charm, but bird-lovers and hikers should, too. This easy hike follows the river up and down along its bends and riffles, right up to the point where the river emerges from the ground in its entirety. Just above this massive spring sits the quiet Fall River Guard Station (another possible place to begin the hike, though you'll be following old user trails to get to the main trail). Near the campground, a footbridge crosses a deep pool and leads to a reflective spot at a bench, a good place to admire the pines and listen to the water birds.

The main trail begins behind campsite #8, ambling 2.4 miles downstream for a stretch following an old road, before petering out near private land. From the picnic area of the campground, hike down to the footbridge. On the opposite side, go left 0.4 mile to the viewpoint. Cross the bridge once more, and set out upstream to the left to make your way 0.7 mile to the springs behind the guard station.

User Groups: Hikers, dogs, horses, and mountain bikes. No wheelchair facilities.

Permits: Permits are not required. Parking and access are free.

Maps: For a map of the Deschutes National Forest, contact Deschutes National Forest Headquarters, 1001 SW Emkay Drive, Bend, OR, 97702, 541/383-5300. For a topographic map, ask the USGS for Pistol Butte.

Directions: From Bend, drive 16 miles south

on U.S. 97 and turn right on Vandevert Road, following signs for Fall River. In one mile, turn left on South Century Drive for 0.9 mile, then right on Road 42 for 9.7 miles. Just before milepost 13, turn left and park in the Fall River Campground.

Contact: Deschutes National Forest, Bend-Fort Rock Ranger District, 1230 NE 3rd Street, Suite A-262, Bend, OR, 97701, 541/383-4000.

102 PAULINA CREEK TRAIL

9.2-17.0 mi/5.0 hr-2 days 3 8

east of LaPine in the Deschutes National Forest

Paulina Creek, fed by Paulina Lake in the collapsed volcano of the Newberry Caldera, falls in a double plume over the lip of the crater and begins a long descent down to the Deschutes River. A trail follows it through burned woods and out to a viewpoint of not only the uppermost falls, but two others as well. At the right time of year, expect to see salmon meandering beneath those massive top falls, thick enough you'd think you could walk over them. Two trailheads give access to the whole stretch—one going up, and one coming down. A shuttle is easy enough, as both trailheads start of the main road. If you do shuttle, you could easily start from the top and make your way to the bottom.

From the Paulina Falls Picnic Area, take the left trail and follow it 0.2 mile to a viewpoint. After this great view of the double falls, return to the junction and head upstream 0.3 mile to a road at the mouth of Paulina Lake. Go left, crossing the bridge, then go left to access the creek trail. In 3.3 miles you'll reach a lower falls, and in another 2.4 miles reach the falls at McKay Crossing with a campground to the right down the road. The last 2.8 miles continues to a crossing, joins an old road, and ends at the Ogden Trailhead.

From the Ogden Trailhead, a loop option is available. From the Ogden Camp, head back up a trail and take a short spur trail to the right, then follow gravel road 2120 for 2.8 miles upstream. Cross a road and continue 5.0 miles on what is now trail. Watch for mountain bikes! This trail returns to the lot at the Paulina Creek Falls Overlook.

User Groups: Hikers, dogs, horses, and mountain bikes. No wheelchair facilities.

Permits: Permits are not required. Parking and access are free from the Ogden Camp Trailhead, but a federal Northwest Forest Pass is required to park at the Paulina Falls Trailhead; the cost is $5 a day or $30 for an annual pass. You can buy a day pass at the trailhead, at ranger stations, or through private vendors.

Maps: For a map of the Deschutes National Forest, contact Deschutes National Forest Headquarters, 1001 SW Emkay Drive, Bend, OR, 97702, 541/383-5300. For a topographic map, ask the USGS for Paulina Peak and Anns Butte.

Directions: From Bend, drive 22 miles south on U.S. 97 and turn left on Road 21 toward the Newberry Caldera. For the Ogden Trailhead, follow Road 21 for 2.8 miles and turn left at the Ogden Group Camp and park at the lot for the Peter Skene Ogden Trail. For the Paulina Falls Viewpoint, continue on Road 21 for 9.4 miles and turn left into the Paulina Falls Picnic Area.

Contact: Deschutes National Forest, Bend-Fort Rock Ranger District, 1230 NE 3rd Street, Suite A-262, Bend, OR, 97701, 541/383-4000.

103 PAULINA LAKE

8.6 mi/3.0 hr 

in the Newberry National Volcanic Monument

The Newberry Caldera is rather like a small Crater Lake, though Newberry's crater is filled with not one but two lakes: Paulina and East. Paulina Lake has a trail around it, and it's quite a walk. The trail passes a smaller crater, a pumice cone, an obsidian flow, and a lakeside hot spring. For pretty much the whole hike, Paulina Peak is a massive presence at the south side of the water. This leisurely hike is the longest in the Newberry Caldera National Volcanic Monument, and is a must-do for dayhikers, campers, and even backpackers.

From the trailhead, set out along the lakeshore to the left. In 1.2 miles the trail crosses an obsidian lava flow and comes to a camping area on the right. In another 1.4 miles the trail passes more camping sites and a beach where hot springs bubble. The next 1.7 miles follows the lakeshore through the woods before arriving at the Paulina Lake Lodge. Continue on the trail, crossing the bridge over Paulina Creek, then continuing along the lakeshore 2.4 miles, passing two campgrounds. The trail crosses the entrance road to Little Crater Campground and climbs to the peak of Little Crater, then descends 1.9 miles back to the trailhead.

User Groups: Hikers and dogs. No horses or mountain bikes allowed. No wheelchair access.

Permits: Permits are not required. A federal Northwest Forest Pass is required to park here; the cost is $5 a day or $30 for an annual pass. You can buy a day pass at the trailhead, at ranger stations, or through private vendors.

Maps: For a map of the Deschutes National Forest, contact Deschutes National Forest Headquarters, 1001 SW Emkay Drive, Bend, OR, 97702, 541/383-5300. For a topographic map, ask the USGS for Paulina Peak.

Directions: From Bend, drive 22 miles south on U.S. 97 and turn left on Road 21 toward the Newberry Caldera. Follow Road 21 for 14.5 miles and turn left at the Little Crater Campground and follow this road 0.9 mile to the trailhead at road's end.

Contact: Deschutes National Forest, Bend-Fort Rock Ranger District, 1230 NE 3rd Street, Suite A-262, Bend, OR, 97701, 541/383-4000.

104 BIG OBSIDIAN FLOW

0.8 mi/0.5 hr 1 8

in the Newberry National Volcanic Monument

Breathtakingly short but nonetheless breathtaking, this terribly easy 0.8-mile trails loops into Oregon's most recent volcanic eruption, a sweeping and swirling flow of obsidian, a black volcanic glass that shines in the sun. When doing any of the other hikes in the Newberry Volcanic National Monument, make sure to include this one.

User Groups: Hikers only. No dogs, horses, or mountain bikes. No wheelchair facilities.

Permits: Permits are not required. A federal Northwest Forest Pass is required to park here; the cost is $5 a day or $30 for an annual pass. You can buy a day pass at the trailhead, at ranger stations, or through private vendors.

Maps: For a map of the Deschutes National Forest, contact Deschutes National Forest Headquarters, 1001 SW Emkay Drive, Bend, OR, 97702, 541/383-5300. For a topographic map, ask the USGS for East Lake.

Directions: From Bend, drive 22 miles south on U.S. 97 and turn left on Road 21 toward the Newberry Caldera. Follow Road 21 for 14.8 miles and turn right into the Obsidian Trail parking lot.

Contact: Deschutes National Forest, Bend-Fort Rock Ranger District, 1230 NE 3rd Street, Suite A-262, Bend, OR, 97701, 541/383-4000.

105 CINDER HILL AND THE DOME

1.4-7.2 mi/0.5-3.5 hr 2 8

in the Newberry National Volcanic Monument

The Newberry Caldera—a National Volcanic Monument—is well worth exploring. It's also a great place to camp. Whether you're here overnight or just for the day, make it a big day and hike as much of it as you can. There are plenty of short trails, and the trail to The Dome ranks high up there: the easy 0.7 mile climbs up to its crater rim with views to the Cascade peaks and Fort Rock Valley.

For a longer hike, climb to Cinder Hill, following its trail up 900 feet in 1.8 miles to the Crater Rim Trail, a long, hot, and dusty trail used primarily by mountain bikers. Go right 1.1 miles to Cinder Hill's peak, with its view to the Cascade Mountains and down to East Lake.

User Groups: Hikers and dogs. No horses allowed. Mountain bikes allowed only on the Crater Rim Trail. No wheelchair facilities.

Permits: Permits are not required. A federal Northwest Forest Pass is required to park here; the cost is $5 a day or $30 for an annual pass. You can buy a day pass at the trailhead, at ranger stations, or through private vendors.

Maps: For a map of the Deschutes National Forest, contact Deschutes National Forest Headquarters, 1001 SW Emkay Drive, Bend, OR, 97702, 541/383-5300. For a topographic map, ask the USGS for East Lake.

Directions: From Bend, drive 22 miles south on U.S. 97 and turn left on Road 21 toward the Newberry Caldera. Follow Road 21 for 17.4 miles to a junction. To go to The Dome, go right following Road 21 for 2.5 miles, and park on the right at The Dome Trailhead. To go to Cinder Hill, turn left at the junction 1.8 miles to Cinder Hill Campground. Continue 0.3 mile to the trailhead at road's end, or if the gate is closed park there and walk.

Contact: Deschutes National Forest, Bend-Fort Rock Ranger District, 1230 NE 3rd Street, Suite A-262, Bend, OR, 97701, 541/383-4000.

106 PAULINA PEAK

6.0 mi/4.0 hr

in the Newberry National Volcanic Monument

At 7,984 feet, Paulina Peak is not only the highest point on the rim of the Newberry Caldera, but it's pretty much the highest point in the entire area. Thus, views extend from the Fort Rock Valley to the Cascade peaks, with the entire caldera below it, including the pudding-like surface of the Big Obsidian Flow, and the shimmering Paulina and East Lakes. Thing is, the road goes right to the top for this stunning view, so most people drive up. But you can climb it on foot, if you're up for a trail with an 8 percent grade that climbs 1,500 feet in only two miles. You'll feel, if not whipped, victorious at having achieved a view stretching from Mount Adams in Washington State to Mount Shasta in California on your own merits and heels.

Beginning at the Paulina Peak Trailhead, start out on the Crater Rim Trail. At the 2.7-mile mark, continue straight on the main trail. In 0.3 mile past this junction, the trail reaches the peak and overlook.

User Groups: Hikers, dogs, and horses. No mountain bikes allowed. No wheelchair facilities.

Permits: Permits are not required. A federal Northwest Forest Pass is required to park here; the cost is $5 a day or $30 for an annual pass. You can buy a day pass at the trailhead, at ranger stations, or through private vendors.

Maps: For a map of the Deschutes National Forest, contact Deschutes National Forest Headquarters, 1001 SW Emkay Drive, Bend, OR, 97702, 541/383-5300. For a topographic map, ask the USGS for Paulina Peak.

Directions: From Bend, drive 22 miles south on U.S. 97 and turn left on Road 21 toward the Newberry Caldera. Follow Road 21 for 13.2 miles and turn right at the visitors center. The trailhead is 50 feet before the vistors center on the right side of the road.

Contact: Deschutes National Forest, Bend-Fort Rock Ranger District, 1230 NE 3rd Street, Suite A-262, Bend, OR, 97701, 541/383-4000.

107 FAWN LAKE, PRETTY LAKE, AND STAG LAKE

6.8-7.3 mi/3.0-4.0 hr 2 7

north of Crescent Lake in Diamond Peak Wilderness

Many of the stretches in the Diamond Peak Wilderness are dominated by dry, lodgepole pine forests, but there are points of beauty. In view of the nearly 7,000-foot Redtop Mountain, and slightly higher Lakeview Mountain, Fawn Lake is a jewel in this wilderness, though its popularity shows on the dusty, well-trodden path. For more seclusion, continue on the Pretty Lake, or take any number of side trails on your map to nearby Saddle and Stag Lakes, or even to big Odell Lake.

Start on the Fawn Lake Trail, crossing Road 60 and a horse trail, continuing straight 3.4 miles to Fawn Lake. At the lake, go left along the shore and continue 0.6 mile to Pretty Lake on the left. From here, the trail is not maintained; it descends into confusing woods 2.5 miles back to the Fawn Lake Trail. To visit Stag Lake, go back to Fawn Lake then continue around the lake, staying left past the Fawn Lake Trail, then left again 0.2 mile beyond that. Climb gradually for one mile, then go right 0.4 mile to this trail's end at Stag Lake beneath Lakeview Mountain.

User Groups: Hikers, dogs, and horses. No mountain bikes allowed. No wheelchair facilities.

Permits: A free self-issue Wilderness Permit is required and is available at the trailhead. Parking and access are free.

Maps: For a map of the Deschutes National Forest, contact Deschutes National Forest Headquarters, 1001 SW Emkay Drive, Bend, OR, 97702, 541/383-5300. For a topographic map, ask the USGS for Odell Lake.

Directions: From Crescent Junction on OR 58, go west on Road 60 for 2.2 miles, then turn right toward the campgrounds for 0.3 mile to Crescent Lake Campground. Turn left into the campground and then right into a lot at the Fawn Lake Trailhead.

Contact: Deschutes National Forest, Crescent Ranger District, 136471 Highway 97 North, P.O. Box 208, Crescent, OR, 97733, 541/433-3200.

108 MILLER AND MAIDU LAKES

5.1-8.4 mi/1.5-4.0 hr 

at Miller Lake and in the Mount Thielsen Wilderness

Two lakes are the goal of this hike, one inside and one outside the Mount Thielsen Wilderness. The Pacific Crest Trail intersects the trail and opens up routes farther into the wilderness area and also along the beginning of the North Umpqua Trail. Broad Miller Lake is a world apart from little Maidu Lake, where the Forest Service removed a shelter to help protect the area.

From Digit Point Campground, you can circle Miller Lake in either direction, a total of 5.1 miles. At the western end of the lake, by Evening Creek, a side trail launches up a cliff 2.1 miles to the PCT junction, continuing on as the North Umpqua Trail 0.8 mile to Maidu Lake, headwaters of the North Umpqua, at which point there is a one-mile loop around the lake.

If you feel like going farther, continue on the North Umpqua Trail another 1.2 miles to a junction. Take the trail to the left, a 0.7-mile loop around Lucile Lake.

User Groups: Hikers, dogs, and horses. Mountain bikes allowed around Miller Lake only. No wheelchair facilities.

Permits: A free self-issue Wilderness Permit is required and is available at the trailhead. Parking and access are free.

Maps: For a map of the Umpqua National Forest and Mount Thielsen Wilderness, contact Umpqua National Forest, 2900 NW Stewart Parkway, Roseburg, OR, 97470, 541/672-6601. For a topographic map, ask the USGS for Worden and Burn Butte.

Directions: From Bend, drive 65 miles south on U.S. 97 to the town of Chemult. Between mileposts 202 and 203, go west on Road 9772, following signs for Chemult Recreation Site. Go 12.5 miles to road's end at Digit Point Campground and park at the picnic loop.

Contact: Umpqua National Forest, Diamond Lake Ranger District, 2020 Toketee Ranger Station Road, Idleyld Park, OR, 97477, 541/498-2531.

109 WOLF CREEK PARK

3.8 mi/2.0 hr

northwest of Grants Pass

If you've driven the long stretch of I-5 through southern Oregon, you'll know that breaks are few and far between. If you *really* want to get out and move, Josephine County's Wolf Creek Park is located so close to the interstate you'll be amazed you never knew it was there. By stretching your legs, I mean stretching them up Jack London Peak to a 2,800-foot viewpoint. You've got to hand it to those who name things: West Coast writer Jack London would have appreciated this rugged climb above the little stagecoach town of Wolf Creek, where he once spent the night.

After walking across the dam, start climbing steadily up 1.9 miles to the highest viewpoint. From there, you could walk the rest of the trail as desired 0.6 mile to its end at a dirt road.

User Groups: Hikers and dogs. No horses or mountain bikes allowed. No wheelchair facilities.

Permits: Permits are not required. A $2-per-car day-use pass is required, or you can purchase a $25 annual pass.

Maps: For a topographic map, ask the USGS for Glendale.

Directions: From I-5, 18 miles north of Grants Pass, take Wolf Creek Exit 76 and drive 0.9 mile to the park at the end of Main Street.

Contact: Josephine County Parks, 125 Ringuette Street, Grants Pass, OR, 97527, 541/474-5285.

110 OREGON CAVES NATIONAL MONUMENT

1.0–9.3 mi/1.0–3.5 hr

east of Cave Junction in the Siskiyou National Forest

Established as a National Monument in 1909, the Oregon Caves are certainly one of the state's treasures. A one-mile tour of the caves (fee required) visits what was originally an island reef scraped up from the ocean floor by the advancing North American Plate. What is left is a series of marble rooms and calcite drippings forming stalagmites and stalactites. Just outside, a 3.8-mile loop trail heads through a Siskiyou Mountains forest to one of Oregon's largest Douglas fir trees. Other trails head out to No Name Creek and along Cave Creek, adding a total of 5.5 miles to the hikes you can do here in a day.

User Groups: Hikers only. Dogs are not allowed. No wheelchair facilities.

Permits: Permits are not required. There is a fee to enter the caves. Parking and access are otherwise free.

Maps: For a topographic map, ask the USGS for Oregon Caves.

Directions: From Grants Pass, drive U.S. 199 south 29 miles to Cave Junction and follow Oregon Caves signs east on Highway 46 for 20 miles to the turnaround lot.

Contact: Oregon Caves National Monument, 19000 Caves Highway, Cave Junction, OR, 97523, 541/592-2100, ext. 262.

111 STURGIS FORK/ BOUNDARY TRAIL

4.8 mi/3.5 hr 2 7

east of Oregon Caves in the Rogue River National Forest

This simple but beautiful hike offers access to a number of backpacking areas: Grayback Mountain, the Oregon Caves National Monument, and the Red Buttes Wilderness. The trail passes through groves of Grand fir and meadows of blooming corn lily, rising to a 6,420-foot viewpoint over the Siskiyou Mountains. From here, the Boundary Trail continues on three miles to Grayback Mountain. From the Sturgis Fork Trail, you could also head 5.7 miles to Sucker Creek Gap.

From the trailhead go in 0.7 mile along the Sturgis Fork, keeping right at a junction and going 0.3 mile on the Boundary Trail to the next junction, again staying right on the Boundary Trail and climbing 0.8 mile through a lush meadow to a pass. From here, it's a 500-foot climb up 0.6 mile to a viewpoint, the turnaround point for this hike. The trail continues three miles to Grayback Mountain (see next listing). Head back to the Sturgis Fork Trail junction to return; from here, the Boundary Trail continues 5.7 miles to Sucker Creek Gap (see *Sucker Creek and Swan Mountain* listing in this chapter).

User Groups: Hikers, dogs, horses, and mountain bikes. No wheelchair facilities.

Permits: Permits are not required. A federal Northwest Forest Pass is required to park here; the cost is $5 a day or $30 for an annual pass. You can buy a day pass at the trailhead, at ranger stations, or through private vendors.

Maps: For a map of the Rogue River National Forest, contact the Rogue River-Siskiyou National Forest, 3040 Biddle Road, Medford, OR, 97504, 541/618-2200. For a topographic map, ask the USGS for Carberry Creek.

Directions: From Grants Pass follow signs to Murphy south for 6.5 miles, continuing on Highway 238 for 11.5 miles to milepost 18. At the Applegate Bridge, go south on Thompson Creek Road for 11.9 miles. Turn right on Road 1020 for 3.7 miles, then fork right on rocky Road 600 for 0.6 mile, then fork left and uphill for 0.1 mile to the trailhead at road's end.

Contact: Rogue River-Siskiyou National Forest, Applegate Ranger District, 6941 Upper Applegate Road, Jacksonville, OR, 97530, 541/899-3800.

112 GRAYBACK MOUNTAIN

4.8 mi/3.0 hr 2 8

east of Oregon Caves in the Rogue River National Forest

Like the nearby Sturgis Fork hike (see previous listing), the Boundary Trail passes right through this region of meadows and mountains. Hovering above these tree-edged meadows is the 7,048-foot peak of Grayback Mountain, with its panoramic view from the Pacific Ocean to Mount Shasta, and from Mount McLoughlin to the Illinois River Valley. At the base of the mountain, a historic cabin and a rustic snow shelter sit in the meadows at the head of O'Brien Creek. The trail is easy enough, and the meadows make for good camping, but for a real adventure you can go cross-country and scramble your way to the top.

From the Upper O'Brien Creek Trailhead, climb nearly 1,000 feet in only one mile, following O'Brien Creek. At the first junction, you can go in two directions: 0.3 mile to the left is the Grayback Snow Shelter and the Krause Log Cabin, and above them the Grayback Meadows; to the right, the trail climbs another mile to the Boundary Trail. Both routes can get you to Grayback Mountain: from the Krause Cabin, head cross-country through the meadows 0.4 mile to the Boundary Trail, then head up the mountain for 0.7 mile; from the junction of the O'Brien Trail and the Boundary Trail, jog a bit to the left then head up the mountain on an unofficial path.

User Groups: Hikers, dogs, horses, and mountain bikes. No wheelchair facilities.

Permits: Permits are not required. Parking and access are free.

Maps: For a map of the Rogue River National Forest, contact the Rogue River-Siskiyou National Forest, 3040 Biddle Road, Medford, OR, 97504, 541/618-2200. For a topographic map, ask the USGS for Grayback Mountain.

Directions: From Grants Pass, follow signs to Murphy south for 6.5 miles and continue on Highway 238 another 11.5 miles to the bridge at Applegate. Turn south on Thompson Creek Road for 11.9 miles, and at a pass turn right at a sign for O'Brien Creek Trail onto Road 1005, following this road 2.3 miles to road's end at the trailhead.

Contact: Rogue River-Siskiyou National Forest, Applegate Ranger District, 6941 Upper Applegate Road, Jacksonville, OR, 97530, 541/899-3800.

113 BOLAN MOUNTAIN

3.4 mi/2.0 hr 2 7

south of Oregon Caves in the Siskiyou National Forest

A perfect place for a lookout, Bolan Mountain has a view of the surrounding Siskiyou Mountains and Mount Shasta, as well as a view down to the Illinois Valley and even the Pacific Ocean. Starting from a campground on Bolan Lake, the trail climbs over 800 feet to the rentable Bolan Mountain Lookout.

From the campground, climb 500 feet in one mile on the Bolan Lake Trail to a junction. Go left an easy 0.5 mile to the lookout road, heading left up the final 0.2 mile.

User Groups: Hikers, dogs, and horses. No wheelchair facilities.

Permits: Permits are not required. Parking and access are free.

Maps: For a map of the Rogue River National Forest, contact the Rogue River-Siskiyou National Forest, 3040 Biddle Road, Medford, OR, 97504, 541/618-2200. For a topographic map, ask the USGS for Oregon Caves.

Directions: Drive 35.5 miles south of Grants Pass on U.S. 199. Between mileposts 35 and 36 turn east on Waldo Road, going five miles then straight onto Happy Camp Road for 12.5 miles to a pass, turning left at a sign for Bolan Lake. At the next two junctions fork uphill, and at the 1.8-mile mark fork downhill to the right. After another 2.4 miles go left onto Road 040 and down 1.8 miles to the campground. Park at the trailhead message board.

Contact: Rogue River-Siskiyou National Forest, Wild Rivers Ranger District, 2164 NE Spalding Avenue, Grants Pass, OR, 97526, 541/471-6500.

114 TANNEN LAKES AND TANNEN MOUNTAIN

2.6–8.3 mi/1.0–4.5 hr 3 8

south of Oregon Caves in Red Buttes Wilderness

Two lakes lie in cliff-rimmed cirques beneath Tannen Mountain and the beginning of the Boundary Trail, all of it in the Red Buttes Wilderness. It's so easy to get to Tannen Lake, you'll want to keep going to East Tannen Lake. From there the wilderness opens up, and the possibilities await. The forest you'll pass through gives rise to Douglas fir, tanoak native to these southern mountains, and incense cedar.

From the Tannen Lake Trailhead hike in 0.4 mile to Tannen Lake. Go left another 0.9 mile to East Tannen Lake, a good turnaround point. Or continue 0.6 mile, passing a left-hand trail to another trailhead, and continue 1.5 miles to the Boundary Trail (and passing the left-hand trail to Sucker Creek). Go to the right on the Boundary Trail 1.1 miles, climbing steeply to the meadows of Tannen Mountain. Head right up to the summit and its amazing views over the Klamath Mountains and ocean, and all the way to Mount Shasta. To make this a loop using roads and a compass, continue 0.5 mile to trail's end at Road 570. Go right 0.9 mile to the Sundown Gap pullout and follow an abandoned road into the meadows, then head due east through both meadows and woods to Tannen Lake and the return trail.

User Groups: Hikers, dogs, and horses. No mountain bikes allowed. No wheelchair facilities.

Permits: A free self-issue Wilderness Permit is required and is available at the trailhead. Parking and access are free.

Maps: For a map of the Rogue River National Forest and the Red Buttes Wilderness, contact the Rogue River-Siskiyou National Forest, 3040 Biddle Road, Medford, OR, 97504, 541/618-2200. For a topographic map, ask the USGS for Oregon Caves.

Directions: Drive 35.5 miles south of Grants Pass on U.S. 199. Between mileposts 35 and 36 turn east on Waldo Road, going five miles then straight onto Happy Camp Road for 12.5 miles to a pass, and turn left at a sign for Tannen Lakes. At the next two junctions fork uphill, and at the 1.8-mile mark fork downhill to the right. After another 2.4 miles go right 3.3 miles to a fork and keep left for 1.4 miles. Watch for the trailhead sign and park 100 yards farther down the road.

Contact: Rogue River-Siskiyou National Forest, Wild Rivers Ranger District, 2164 NE Spalding Avenue, Grants Pass, OR, 97526, 541/471-6500.

115 SUCKER CREEK AND SWAN MOUNTAIN

6.4-9.8 mi/3.0-5.0 hr 3 8

south of Oregon Caves in Red Buttes Wilderness

The Red Buttes Wilderness draws right up to the boundary of California, making this one of the southernmost hikes in Oregon. In fact, from here you could well hike right into the next state. But before you leave, why not backpack into the Sucker Creek Shelter? From here you can visit a little cirque lake and follow the Boundary Trail up to the shoulder of Swan Mountain, making your way up its manzanita-strewn ridge to the 6,272-foot peak.

From the trailhead, follow Sucker Creek up 1.7 miles to a junction, staying to the right another 1.2 miles to a spring and the Sucker Creek Shelter. At the junction with the Boundary Trail, you have two options. You could go straight another 0.2 mile, then right along a faint path to visit Cirque Lake. Or you could go left on the Boundary Trail, climbing 500 feet to a pass, then making your way up the ridge to the left to the peak of Swan Mountain.

User Groups: Hikers, dogs, and horses. No mountain bikes allowed. No wheelchair facilities.

Permits: A free self-issue Wilderness Permit is required and is available at the trailhead. Parking and access are free.

Maps: For a map of the Rogue River National Forest and the Red Buttes Wilderness, contact the Rogue River-Siskiyou National Forest, 3040 Biddle Road, Medford, OR, 97504, 541/618-2200. For a topographic map, ask the USGS for Oregon Caves.

Directions: From Grants Pass, drive U.S. 199 south 29 miles to Cave Junction and follow Oregon Caves signs east on Highway 46 for 13.3 miles. Where the highway switchbacks left, turn right on Road 4612. Follow Road 4612 for 9.9 miles, forking right at the first two forks, then going straight on Road 098. In another 3.6 miles pass a left-hand fork and park 0.1 mile farther at a trail sign on the right.

Contact: Rogue River-Siskiyou National Forest, Wild Rivers Ranger District, 2164 NE Spalding Avenue, Grants Pass, OR, 97526, 541/471-6500.

HIKING

116 MILLER LAKE

3.9 mi/2.0 hr 

east of Oregon Caves in Rogue River National Forest

With Grayback Mountain looming in the distance, this lonely trail runs all by its lonesome over a remote section of the Siskiyous. That being said, there's plenty here to see, including two lakes, a stand of Brewer's weeping spruce, and a view to Mount Shasta from a high pass. You'll also find old-growth Douglas fir, Shasta red fir, and huckleberries.

From the trailhead, follow the new Miller Lake Trail in 0.7 mile to the cliff-rimmed Miller Lake. Go to the right over an earthen dam to follow the trail to the right into the forest, passing the spruce stand and continuing up to Upper Miller Lake and the viewpoint. Then descend 1.1 miles to the shore of Miller Lake, and return as you came.

User Groups: Hikers, dogs, and horses. No mountain bikes allowed. No wheelchair facilities.

Permits: Permits are not required. Parking and access are free.

Maps: For a map of the Rogue River National Forest, contact the Rogue River-Siskiyou National Forest, 3040 Biddle Road, Medford, OR, 97504, 541/618-2200. For a topographic map, ask the USGS for Grayback Mountain.

Directions: From Grants Pass, follow signs to Murphy 6.5 miles and continue on Highway 238 another 11.5 miles to the bridge at Applegate. Turn south on Thompson Creek Road for 11.9 miles, and at a pass turn right at a sign for Miller Lake onto Road 1020 for 4.5 miles. At the next junction, go straight onto Road 400 for 3.5 miles to road's end.

Contact: Rogue River-Siskiyou National Forest, Applegate Ranger District, 6941 Upper Applegate Road, Jacksonville, OR, 97530, 541/899-3800.

117 COLLINGS MOUNTAIN

10.3 mi/5.0 hr 

on Applegate Lake in Rogue River National Forest

If there is one famous resident of Oregon, it must be Bigfoot. He (or she) is such a local icon around the Northwest that it's not uncommon to hear a few jokes passed around here and there, even some serious discussion about where the famed hairy Sasquatch may be. The first sighting in the Siskiyous was reported in 1895, and in 1975 a research group built a Bigfoot Trap here above Applegate Lake. Though the trap is somewhat overgrown in poison oak and the caretaker's cabin worn down by time, the trail to Collings Mountain, passing an old mine, is steady as ever. Looping up and around the mountain's summit and descending down to a run along Applegate Lake, this makes for a fine excursion through woods of scrub oak, madrone, and white pine.

From Hart-Tish Park, head uphill and across the road 0.6 mile on the Collings Mountain Trail to the weird Bigfoot Trap with its steel door and thick cell. The next 3.4 miles passes an old prospector's test prospect shaft and ambles along the mountain before arriving at the 3,625-foot summit at a grassy peak. Then descend 2.9 miles to the Watkins Campground and follow the Da-Ku-Be-Te-De Trail along the shore of Applegate Lake for 3.4 miles back to Hart-Tish.

User Groups: Hikers, dogs, horses, and mountain bikes. No wheelchair facilities.

Permits: Permits are not required. Parking and access are free.

Maps: For a map of the Rogue River National Forest, contact the Rogue River-Siskiyou National Forest, 3040 Biddle Road, Medford, OR, 97504, 541/618-2200. For a topographic map, ask the USGS for Carberry Creek.

Directions: From Jacksonville, head west on Highway 238 for eight miles to Ruch, then turn south following Upper Applegate signs for 15.9 miles. At one mile past the Applegate

Dam, turn right into Hart-Tish Recreation Area and park in the lot on the right.

Contact: Rogue River-Siskiyou National Forest, Applegate Ranger District, 6941 Upper Applegate Road, Jacksonville, OR, 97530, 541/899-3800.

118 APPLEGATE LAKE

17.8 mi/2 days 4 7

west of Ashland in Rogue River National Forest

Though this "lake" is actually a reservoir, its position in the fir, pine, and madrone forests of the Siskiyou Mountains affords it respect. Plus, with the lake being the size it is, you can spend an entire day exploring its shoreline. The trail makes for a good bike ride, too, and some of it follows paved roads. Watch for fish-hunting osprey and three-leafed poison oak. Primitive campsites along the way make this a good backpacking trek.

From French Gulch, head out for a 4.7-mile excursion around a peninsula on the Payette Trail. After jostling along some old mining prospect roads for part of this stretch, continue on the Payette Trail another 4.5 miles along the lake, passing two primitive camps at Harr Point and Tipsu Tyee before arriving at the Manzanita Trailhead. From here, follow a dirt road 1.7 miles to the Seattle Bar picnic area, then continue around the lake on the paved road 1.4 miles to the Watkins Campground. Head into the campground and connect with the Da-Ku-Be-Te-De Trail for 4.3 miles along the shore to the dam. Cross the dam and follow the paved road 1.2 miles back to French Gulch.

User Groups: Hikers, dogs, and mountain bikes. No horses allowed. No wheelchair facilities.

Permits: Permits are not required. Parking and access are free.

Maps: For a map of the Rogue River National Forest or a brochure for Applegate Lake, contact the Rogue River-Siskiyou National Forest, 3040 Biddle Road, Medford, OR, 97504, 541/618-2200. For a topographic map, ask the USGS for Squaw Lakes.

Directions: From Jacksonville, head west on Highway 238 for eight miles to Ruch, then turn south following Upper Applegate signs for 14.9 miles. Turn left over the dam for 1.2 miles and park at the French Gulch Trailhead lot on the right.

Contact: Rogue River-Siskiyou National Forest, Applegate Ranger District, 6941 Upper Applegate Road, Jacksonville, OR, 97530, 541/899-3800.

119 STEIN BUTTE

9.4 mi/5.5 hr 4 8

east of Applegate Lake in Rogue River National Forest

From this motorcycle trail, which climbs steadily, even relentlessly, toward a lookout site on Stein Butte, you will see over the border and into California. By the time you've come this far south into Oregon, you're practically in another kind of region matching California anyway: the Oregon state tree of Douglas fir begins to blend in with California natives black oak, canyon live oak, madrone, knobcone pine, and Jeffrey pine. The lookout that the Civilian Conservation Corps built in 1936 is gone, but despite the towering manzanita bushes on the ridge, the view to Mount Shasta and Mount McLoughlin is unimpeded.

From the Seattle Bar Trailhead, you will climb the Stein Butte Trail 2,400 feet in 4.7 miles to the 4,400-foot peak of Stein Butte. Take in the views of Applegate Lake, then return as you came.

User Groups: Hikers, dogs, horses, and mountain bikes. No wheelchair facilities.

Permits: Permits are not required. Parking and access are free.

Maps: For a map of the Rogue River National Forest, contact the Rogue River-Siskiyou National Forest, 3040 Biddle Road, Medford,

OR, 97504, 541/618-2200. For a topographic map, ask the USGS for Squaw Lakes.
Directions: From Jacksonville, head west on Highway 238 for eight miles to Ruch, then turn south following Upper Applegate signs for 18.8 miles. At a junction past the Watkins Campground, go left 0.9 mile to the Seattle Bar Trailhead parking area.
Contact: Rogue River-Siskiyou National Forest, Applegate Ranger District, 6941 Upper Applegate Road, Jacksonville, OR, 97530, 541/899-3800.

120 HERSHBERGER MOUNTAIN AND CRIPPLE CAMP

5.8-13.4 mi/3.0 hr-2 days 2 7

in the Rogue-Umpqua Divide Wilderness

From Pup Prairie in the Rogue-Umpqua Divide Wilderness, the backpacker and day tripper both can find their way into the marshes and mountains, with trails leading out in all directions. In the distance, Highrock Mountain rises into the thin air, and atop Hershberger Mountain an old fire watchtower, listed on the National Register of Historic Places, looks out as far as the snow-topped Cascade peaks, and nearby the towering spires of the Rabbit Ears. For a start, you can visit the lookout one of two ways: by driving or hiking 0.5 mile to the end of Road 530. From there, a metal staircase and trail lead to the cupola-style lookout.

To hike into the wilderness, start from the road's switchback following the Acker Divide Trail to the left, descending through woods to the meadows of columbine, larkspur, coneflower, paintbrush, and bluebells. After 1.6 miles the trail meets up with the Rogue-Umpqua Divide Trail. Go right another 0.8 mile into aptly named Toad Marsh to the Cripple Camp and the 1937 shelter amidst incense cedars and tiger lilies. From here, it is possible to backpack farther to Buckeye Lake, Fish Lake, and the Highrock Meadows for a 13.4-mile loop that returns to the Hershberger Mountain Trailhead.
User Groups: Hikers, dogs, and horses. No mountain bikes allowed. No wheelchair facilities.
Permits: A free self-issue Wilderness Permit is required and is available at the trailhead. Parking and access are free.
Maps: For a map of the Rogue River National Forest and the Rogue-Umpqua Divide Wilderness, contact the Rogue River-Siskiyou National Forest, 3040 Biddle Road, Medford, OR, 97504, 541/618-2200. For a topographic map, ask the USGS for Fish Mountain.
Directions: From Medford, drive 57 miles east on OR 62, going left onto Highway 230 for 0.9 mile, then turning left across the Rogue River onto Road 6510 for 6.2 miles. Next, turn right on Road 6515 for 9.2 miles, then turn left on Road 530 for 1.8 miles and park at a switchback.
Contact: Rogue River National Forest, Prospect Ranger District, 47201 Highway 62, Prospect, OR, 97536, 541/560-3400.

121 NATIONAL CREEK FALLS

0.8 mi/0.5 hr 1 7

west of Crater Lake in Rogue River National Forest

Traveling through the mountains between Medford and Crater Lake? Why not stop and see an impressive waterfall that drops in two 80-foot drops over a basalt ledge in a deep green forest? People have been stopping here for years—as far back as the 1860s, when the gold miners dropped in for a rest. From the trailhead, it's an easy 0.4-mile walk through grand fir, white pine, and hemlock to the base of the falls on National Creek.
User Groups: Hikers and dogs only. No wheelchair facilities.
Permits: Permits are not required. Parking and access are free.

Maps: For a map of the Rogue River National Forest, contact the Rogue River-Siskiyou National Forest, 3040 Biddle Road, Medford, OR, 97504, 541/618-2200. For a topographic map, ask the USGS for Hamaker Butte.
Directions: From Medford, drive 57 miles east on OR 62 and then go left on Highway 230. After six miles, go right on Road 6530 for 3.7 miles, then right on Road 300 to road's end.
Contact: Rogue River National Forest, Prospect Ranger District, 47201 Highway 62, Prospect, OR, 97536, 541/560-3400.

122 ABBOTT BUTTE

7.2 mi/4.0 hr

in the Rogue-Umpqua Divide Wilderness

From this entry into the Rogue-Umpqua Divide Wilderness, the backpacking choices seem unlimited. Start by exploring the abandoned lookout on Abbott Butte and the enormous rock formation of the Elephant Head, a good destination for that first backpacking camp. In summer, expect to see plumes of beargrass lilies, balsamroot, and monkeyflower.

The Rogue Umpqua Divide Trail sets out around Quartz Mountain, paralleling the abandoned road to the lookout. In 1.4 miles, it reaches Windy Gap, and in 1.3 miles crosses the service road to Abbott Butte. At this point and to the right, up one mile and a little over 300 feet, is the lookout, whose tower shelters its little cabin. Continue 0.3 mile on the Rogue Umpqua Divide Trail and go 1.6 miles to Elephant Head Pond, bypassing a Cougar Butte Trail junction, and the towering Elephant Head. Just 0.3 mile beyond the pond is Saddle Camp, a good place to pitch a tent. From there, the Divide Trail continues into the wilderness area.
User Groups: Hikers, dogs, and horses. No mountain bikes allowed. No wheelchair facilities.
Permits: A free self-issue Wilderness Permit is required and is available at the trailhead. Parking and access are free.
Maps: For a map of the Rogue River National Forest and the Rogue-Umpqua Divide Wilderness, contact the Rogue River-Siskiyou National Forest, 3040 Biddle Road, Medford, OR, 97504, 541/618-2200. For a topographic map, ask the USGS for Abbott Butte.
Directions: From Medford, drive east on OR 62, and between mileposts 51 and 52 turn left on Woodruff Meadows Road 68, staying on this road at all junctions for 4.9 miles of pavement and 7.4 miles of gravel. At the pass by a large national forest sign, park on the right for the Rogue-Umpqua Divide Trail.
Contact: Umpqua National Forest, Tiller Ranger District, 27812 Tiller Trail Highway, Tiller, OR, 97484, 541/825-3201.

123 NATURAL BRIDGE AND THE ROGUE GORGE

2.4-8.2 mi/1.0-3.0 hr 2 8

on the Rogue River in Rogue River National Forest

BEST

As the Rogue River plunges through its canyon, it sometimes squeezes itself into some pretty tight spaces. The Rogue Gorge is one such place, with deep, fern-draped cliffs dropping 100 feet to the river. Even stranger is the Natural Bridge, where the river goes underground, or more precisely, beneath an ancient lava flow for a distance of 200 feet, with the water spouting out of blowholes along the way. You can easily see both sights from near the parking area, but why not make a longer hike out of it? This is, after all, the Upper Rogue River Trail, and it's worth exploring at length.

From the Natural Bridge viewpoint, head on the left-hand trail to a crossing. Follow this trail to a viewpoint of the Natural Bridge—you can even walk out on the sturdy flow itself. From here, you can continue on the trail to a second footbridge, crossing it and going right back to the car to make a 2.4-mile loop. But if you are ready for a longer hike, go left after the footbridge instead, reaching the Union Creek Campground in 1.7 miles and the Gorge viewpoint in 1.2 miles. The trail continues another 0.4 mile to a campground and ends. Return as you came.

User Groups: Hikers and dogs. No horses or mountain bikes allowed. Paved viewpoints are wheelchair accessible.

Permits: Permits are not required. Parking and access are free.

Maps: For a map of the Rogue River National Forest, contact the Rogue River-Siskiyou National Forest, 3040 Biddle Road, Medford, OR, 97504, 541/618-2200. For a topographic map, ask the USGS for Union Creek.

Directions: Drive OR 62 east of Medford 55 miles and turn left at a sign for Natural Bridge Campground. Keep left for 0.7 mile to the parking area.

Contact: Rogue River National Forest, Prospect Ranger District, 47201 Highway 62, Prospect, OR, 97536, 541/560-3400.

124 UNION CREEK

8.2 mi/3.5 hr 2 7

west of Crater Lake in Rogue River National Forest

Near the Union Creek Resort, which was used in the past by Jack London and Herbert Hoover, this woodsy trail of old-growth fir and Pacific yew heads up nearby Union Creek to a pair of small waterfalls. Start out east on the Union Creek Trail for 3.3 miles to reach the first waterfall, an eight-foot drop, then continue 0.8 mile to 10-foot Union Creek Falls.

User Groups: Hikers and dogs. No horses or mountain bikes allowed. No wheelchair facilities.

Permits: Permits are not required. Parking and access are free.

Maps: For a map of the Rogue River National Forest, contact the Rogue River-Siskiyou National Forest, 3040 Biddle Road, Medford, OR, 97504, 541/618-2200. For a topographic map, ask the USGS for Hamaker Butte.

Directions: From Medford, drive OR 62 east 56 miles to Union Creek and park on the right at a pullout by the trailhead.

Contact: Rogue River National Forest, Prospect Ranger District, 47201 Highway 62, Prospect, OR, 97536, 541/560-3400.

125 THE WATCHMAN AND THE DEVIL'S BACKBONE

5.6 mi/2.0 hr 1 9

in Crater Lake National Park

Two hikes fan out along the Crater Lake rim to two distinctive viewpoints. One climbs to the Watchman Lookout with its views over the caldera, and the other circles Hillman Peak to viewpoints of the Devil's Backbone, a volcanic dike left when magma seeped into a crack in ancient Mount Mazama.

From the pullout, go right to climb to The Watchman. Take the trail 0.4 mile to a junction, then to the left and up 0.4 mile to the 8,013-foot peak. For the Devil's Backbone viewpoint, go left from the trailhead and circle Hillman Peak following a two-mile trail to two viewpoints over sparkling Crater Lake below.

User Groups: Hikers only. No dogs, horses, or mountain bikes allowed. No wheelchair facilities.

Permits: Permits are not required unless backcountry camping. A $10 fee, good for seven days, is collected at the entrance stations.

Maps: For a map of Crater Lake National Park, contact Crater Lake National Park, P.O. Box 7, Crater Lake, OR, 97604, 541/594-3000, or for a free downloadable map go to www.nps.gov/crla. For a topographic map, ask the USGS for Crater Lake West.

Directions: Drive four miles north on Rim Drive from Rim Village, or 2.2 miles south of the junction with the north entrance road to the pullout parking area.

Contact: Crater Lake National Park, P.O. Box 7, Crater Lake, OR, 97604, 541/594-3000.

126 CLEETWOOD COVE/ WIZARD ISLAND

4.7 mi/2.0-4.0 hr 2 9

in Crater Lake National Park

Welcome to Crater Lake, one of the most incredible places in the country. This is Oregon's sole National Park, and a stunning one at that. The remnant of a massive volcanic blast, this collapsed caldera slowly filled with abundant snowfall and rain to form this 1,943-foot-deep shimmering lake that casts a ghostly blue hue into the deep. The Cleetwood Cove Trail is the only trail to access the lake itself, but from here you can take a private boat on a 45-minute tour out to Wizard Island to continue your hike; you'll pay $26 for adults and $15.50 for kids to get there, and more if you're dropped off.

From the rim, hike down the switchbacking 1.1-mile trail to Cleetwood Cove and catch the boat to Wizard Island. On Wizard Island, two trails explore this cinder cone: a 0.4-mile trail heads to the left to a lava flow and Fumarole Bay, and a 1.1-mile trail climbs to the crater, with a 0.3-mile loop around the peak.

User Groups: Hikers only. No dogs, horses, or mountain bikes allowed. No wheelchair facilities.

Permits: Permits are not required unless backcountry camping. A $10 fee, good for seven days, is collected at the entrance stations.

Maps: For a map of Crater Lake National Park, contact Crater Lake National Park, P.O. Box 7, Crater Lake, OR, 97604, 541/594-3000, or for a free downloadable map go to www.nps.gov/crla. For a topographic map, ask the USGS for Crater Lake East and West.

Directions: From Rim Village, drive clockwise on Rim Drive 10.6 miles to the trailhead. From the north entrance, go left at Rim Drive 4.6 miles.

Contact: Crater Lake National Park, P.O. Box 7, Crater Lake, OR, 97604, 541/594-3000.

127 MOUNT SCOTT

5.0 mi/3.5 hr 2 9

in Crater Lake National Park

When Mount Mazama blew its top 7,700 years ago, it decimated the surrounding landscape and left the massive crater that is Crater Lake. The highest point remaining is Mount Scott, Oregon's 10th-tallest mountain. The hike to this peak is actually quite easy. The goal is a fire watchtower that overlooks the whole panoramic scope of the National Park and beyond.

From the trailhead, this well-graded trail sets out 2.5 miles up Mount Scott, climbing 1,000 feet to the peak. From the peak, look for Klamath Lake, Mount Shasta, Mount McLoughlin, Mount Thielsen, and the Three Sisters.

User Groups: Hikers only. No dogs, horses, or mountain bikes allowed. No wheelchair facilities.

Permits: Permits are not required unless backcountry camping. A $10 fee, good for seven days, is collected at the entrance stations.

Maps: For a map of Crater Lake National Park, contact Crater Lake National Park, P.O. Box 7, Crater Lake, OR, 97604, 541/594-3000, or for a free downloadable map go to www.nps.gov/crla. For a topographic map, ask the USGS for Crater Lake East.

Directions: From Rim Village, drive counterclockwise on Rim Drive 11 miles to a parking pullout. From the north entrance, go left on East Rim Drive 13 miles to the trailhead.

Contact: Crater Lake National Park, P.O. Box 7, Crater Lake, OR, 97604, 541/594-3000.

128 LIGHTNING SPRING/ DISCOVERY POINT/ DUTTON CREEK LOOP

13.1 mi/7.0 hr

in Crater Lake National Park

Though the Pacific Crest Trail has some of the most scenic views in the Cascade Mountains, its path through Crater Lake National Park is quite hidden. It passes a few miles away from the rim, thus missing Discovery Point, where it is believed that the Hillman prospecting party first saw the lake in 1853. This strenuous hike goes from the rim to the PCT, connecting with a few campsites at Lightning Spring and along Dutton Creek, passing Discovery Point on the very lip of the volcano itself.

From Rim Village, set out north along the rim for 1.3 miles to Discovery Point and continue 1.2 miles to the third pullout. Cross the road and head to the Lightning Springs Trailhead. In 0.8 mile, you'll reach a series of backcountry campsites. Continue 3.2 miles to the PCT and go left 4.2 miles through a lodgepole forest to a junction on Dutton Creek. Turn left to go 2.4 miles back to the Rim Village.

User Groups: Hikers only. Horses allowed on the PCT only. No dogs or mountain bikes allowed. No wheelchair facilities.

Permits: Permits are not required unless backcountry camping. A $10 fee, good for seven days, is collected at the entrance stations.

Maps: For a map of Crater Lake National Park, contact Crater Lake National Park, P.O. Box 7, Crater Lake, OR, 97604, 541/594-3000, or for a free downloadable map go to www.nps.gov/crla. For a topographic map, ask the USGS for Crater Lake West.

Directions: The trail begins in the large parking lot in Rim Village.

Contact: Crater Lake National Park, P.O. Box 7, Crater Lake, OR, 97604, 541/594-3000.

129 GARFIELD PEAK

3.4 mi/1.5 hr

in Crater Lake National Park

Named for Teddy Roosevelt's Secretary of the Interior, who created this National Park in 1902, this 8,054-foot peak set high on Castle Crest overlooks a series of pretty meadows and the Phantom Ship, a rock formation forever adrift in Crater Lake. From the visitors center, set out east toward Crater Lake Lodge for 0.2 mile, then continue up Castle Crest for 1.5 miles to the peak.

User Groups: Hikers only. No dogs, horses, or mountain bikes allowed. No wheelchair facilities.

Permits: Permits are not required unless backcountry camping. A $10 fee, good for seven days, is collected at the entrance stations.

Maps: For a map of Crater Lake National Park, contact Crater Lake National Park, P.O. Box 7, Crater Lake, OR, 97604, 541/594-3000, or for a free downloadable map go to www.nps.gov/crla. For a topographic map, ask the USGS for Crater Lake East and West.

Directions: The trail begins in the large parking lot in Rim Village.

Contact: Crater Lake National Park, P.O. Box 7, Crater Lake, OR, 97604, 541/594-3000.

130 ANNIE CREEK AND GODFREY GLEN

2.7 mi/1.0 hr

in Crater Lake National Park

Two easy hikes explore canyons carved out of the flank of Crater Lake's massive volcano. Since they're located close to one another, it's worth it to hike both. Annie Creek's 1.7-mile loop follows a glacier-carved canyon with a series of ash pinnacles left over from the 7,700-year-old eruption. Godfrey Glen's one-mile loop looks over Munson Creek's canyon and its haunting pillars of solidified ash.

User Groups: Hikers only. No dogs, horses, or mountain bikes allowed. No wheelchair facilities.
Permits: Permits are not required unless backcountry camping. A $10 fee, good for seven days, is collected at the entrance stations.
Maps: For a map of Crater Lake National Park, contact Crater Lake National Park, P.O. Box 7, Crater Lake, OR, 97604, 541/594-3000, or for a free downloadable map go to www.nps.gov/crla. For a topographic map, ask the USGS for Union Peak.
Directions: To see Annie Creek, start from the park entrance on OR 62, driving 0.3 mile toward Rim Village and turning right at a sign for Mazama Campground. Park at the store and walk to camping area C; the trailhead begins behind site C-11. To see the Godfrey Glen, go past the Mazama Campground and drive toward Rim Village an additional 2.1 miles, turning right at a sign for Godfrey Glen Nature Loop.
Contact: Crater Lake National Park, P.O. Box 7, Crater Lake, OR, 97604, 541/594-3000.

131 UNION PEAK

11.0 mi/6.0 hr

in Crater Lake National Park

This trail heads to 7,709-foot Union Peak, making this the most challenging hike in Crater Lake National Park. Union Peak is the oldest mountain in the park; it's a heavily eroded volcanic plug rising above forests of lodgepole pine and mountain hemlock growing from deep layers of pumice. This hike is bit off the beaten path, and it makes use of the Pacific Crest Trail. Note that there is no water on this trail, so bring plenty to cover this long trip.

Set out on the PCT for 2.9 miles along an old fire road. In a pumice plain, go right on the Union Peak Trail 2.6 miles to the peak, switchbacking steeply at the end.

User Groups: Hikers only. Horses allowed on the PCT only. No dogs or mountain bikes allowed. No wheelchair facilities.
Permits: Permits are not required unless backcountry camping. A $10 fee, good for seven days, is collected at the entrance stations.
Maps: For a map of Crater Lake National Park, contact Crater Lake National Park, P.O. Box 7, Crater Lake, OR, 97604, 541/594-3000, or for a free downloadable map go to www.nps.gov/crla. For a topographic map, ask the USGS for Union Peak.
Directions: Drive 72 miles east of Medford on OR 62 to a summit about one mile west of Mazama Village. Park at a Pacific Crest Trail side road on the right.
Contact: Crater Lake National Park, P.O. Box 7, Crater Lake, OR, 97604, 541/594-3000.

132 CRATER PEAK

6.2 mi/3.0 hr

3 9

in Crater Lake National Park

High above the Sun Notch, and with views extending to a host of Cascade peaks and Klamath Lake, Crater Peak is host to high meadows of summer lupine where elk browse in summer. Atop the peak is a volcanic crater filled in with the pumice and ash left from Mazama's violent explosion. From the Vidae Falls Picnic Area, the trail climbs 1,000 feet up 3.1 miles to the crater atop this overlook peak. Once atop the volcanic crater, you can loop 0.4 mile to inspect this long-dead peak.
User Groups: Hikers only. No dogs, horses, or mountain bikes allowed. No wheelchair facilities.
Permits: Permits are not required unless backcountry camping. A $10 fee, good for seven days, is collected at the entrance stations.
Maps: For a map of Crater Lake National Park, contact Crater Lake National Park, P.O. Box 7, Crater Lake, OR, 97604, 541/594-3000, or for a free downloadable map go to www.nps.gov/crla. For a topographic map, ask the USGS for Crater Lake East and Maklaks Crater.

Directions: From Rim Village, follow Rim Drive East 2.9 miles to the Vidae Falls Picnic Area on the right.
Contact: Crater Lake National Park, P.O. Box 7, Crater Lake, OR, 97604, 541/594-3000.

133 TAKELMA GORGE

5.2 mi/2.0 hr 1 8

on the Rogue River in Rogue River National Forest

If you don't have the time to hike large stretches of the Upper Rogue River, but prefer something shorter, a walk where a fanny pack would be enough for an outing, try the Takelma Gorge. This mile-long surge through a 150-foot-deep lava slot comes close to the final stretch of this long trail, and provides an exciting series of views into the Rogue's chasm.

From the Woodruff Bridge picnic area, go downstream 1.6 miles to the beginning of the chasm, then continue one mile farther along the stunning viewpoints to a switchback down to a beach on a much calmer section. This makes a good turnaround point, but beyond that, the river trail continues about 8.5 miles to its end at North Fork Park.

User Groups: Hikers and dogs. No horses or mountain bikes allowed. No wheelchair facilities.
Permits: Permits are not required. Parking and access are free.
Maps: For a map of the Rogue River National Forest, contact the Rogue River-Siskiyou National Forest, 3040 Biddle Road, Medford, OR, 97504, 541/618-2200. For a topographic map, ask the USGS for Hamaker Butte.
Directions: Drive east of Medford on OR 62 and between mileposts 51 and 52 turn left on Woodruff Meadows Road for 1.7 miles. Turn left into the Woodruff Bridge picnic area.
Contact: Rogue River National Forest, Prospect Ranger District, 47201 Highway 62, Prospect, OR, 97536, 541/560-3400.

134 RED BLANKET FALLS AND STUART FALLS

10.0 mi/4.5 hr 3 7

south of Crater Lake in Sky Lakes Wilderness

At the southern border of Crater Lake National Park lies the Sky Lakes Wilderness, with three major basins of lakes and the peak of Mount McLoughlin to claim as its territory. At the northwestern corner, this trail enters in so close to the national park that you'll pass a 1902 corner marker; after that, you'll follow Red Blanket Creek into its canyon, reaching two waterfalls and a lush huckleberry meadow. From there, the trail heads in two directions to the Pacific Crest Trail, with access to Crater Lake and the Sky Lakes.

The first 2.9 miles of the trail follows Red Blanket Creek to Red Blanket Falls and a junction. To head to Stuart Falls, go left up one mile to another junction, then left again another 0.4 mile. From this point, it is 2.8 miles to the PCT. Return 0.4 mile to the junction and this time go left 0.8 mile on the Stuart Falls Trail to the next junction. Staying to the left heads 2.7 miles to the PCT; go right for a 1.6-mile loop through Lucky Meadow. This Lucky Camp Trail returns to Red Blanket Falls.

User Groups: Hikers, dogs, and horses. No mountain bikes allowed. No wheelchair facilities.
Permits: A free self-issue Wilderness Permit is required and is available at the trailhead. Parking and access are free.
Maps: For a map of the Rogue River National Forest and Sky Lakes Wilderness, contact the Rogue River-Siskiyou National Forest, 3040 Biddle Road, Medford, OR, 97504, 541/618-2200. For a topographic map, ask the USGS for Union Peak.
Directions: Drive east of Medford 45 miles on OR 62 and turn right toward Prospect for 0.7 mile. In town, turn left on Butte Falls Road for one mile, then left on Red Blanket Road for 0.4 mile. At a fork, go left on Road 6205 for 11.4 miles to road's end at a parking area.

Contact: Rogue River National Forest, Prospect Ranger District, 47201 Highway 62, Prospect, OR, 97536, 541/560-3400.

135 LOST CREEK LAKE

5.0-18.7 mi/2.0 hr-2 days 3 7

on the Rogue River in Stewart State Park

Stewart State Park is a busy park with lots of visitors and lots of things to do: biking, camping, swimming, boating, you name it. It so happens that the majority of the nearby Lost Creek Lake Reservoir is not only quieter, but provides opportunities for backpacking, making use of three remote camping spots. The Grotto makes an easy destination from Lewis Road, and is actually quite a sight: This box canyon of basalt and green ash left over from the volcanic explosion of Crater Lake is an easy side excursion.

To begin, set out from Lewis Road on the trail. In 0.9 mile you'll reach the first primitive camp, Fire Glen Camp. Another 1.5 miles leads to a right-hand side trail up 0.1 mile to the Grotto overlook. The next 3.4 miles heads to a crossing of Lost Creek, passing Sugar Pine Camp along the way. The next 3.8 miles starts around the opposite shore, passing Four Corners Camp and arriving at a boat ramp at Takelma Park. Here the trail continues 1.4 miles, crossing the dam. The next 2.8 miles heads to the state park, passing through it for 3.6 miles. The final stretch is all on paved roads, following Highway 62 to the left over Peyton Bridge 0.3 mile, then going left on Lewis Road for the last mile.

User Groups: Hikers and dogs. No horses allowed. Trails in Stewart State Park are wheelchair accessible and suitable for mountain biking.

Permits: Permits are not required. Parking and access are free.

Maps: For a topographic map, ask the USGS for McLeod and Cascade Gorge.

Directions: Drive east of Medford 35.5 miles on OR 62. After crossing a bridge over Lost Creek Lake turn left on Lewis Road for one mile to the Lewis Road Trailhead on the left.

Contact: Oregon Parks and Recreation Department, 1115 Commercial Street Northeast, Salem, OR, 97301, 800/551-6949, www.oregonstateparks.org.

136 UPPER SOUTH FORK ROGUE RIVER

12.0 mi/6.0 hr

southeast of Prospect in Rogue River National Forest

The South Fork of the Rogue River is a young river, not as wide as you might suspect, but this section of trail follows it through some substantial trees and large logs along the shore, plus a few gravel bars thrown in for good measure. You'll also find Pacific yew, which Native Americans used for bows because of its flexibility. Along this trail you'll cross several creeks, as well.

From the trailhead, start out upriver on the South Fork Trail, a primitive and seldom-maintained trail. In 0.7 mile you'll cross Big Ben Creek; avoid the side trail on the left leading to a campground. Continue on 4.4 miles, crossing Sam Creek, Wickiup Creek, and Little Billie Creek to a crossing of Road 800. The last 0.9 mile of trail continues to an upper trailhead on Road 37. From here, backpackers can follow nearby Road 720 southeast one mile to the trailhead for the Blue Lake Trail and the Sky Lakes Wilderness.

User Groups: Hikers and dogs. No horses or mountain bikes allowed. No wheelchair facilities.

Permits: Permits are not required. Parking and access are free.

Maps: For a map of the Rogue River National Forest and Sky Lakes Wilderness, contact the Rogue River-Siskiyou National Forest, 3040 Biddle Road, Medford, OR, 97504,

541/618-2200. For a topographic map, ask the USGS for Cascade Gorge.
Directions: From Medford, drive 14.5 miles east on OR 62 and turn right on the Butte Falls Highway for 15 miles to the town of Butte Falls. Go straight one mile then left at a sign for Prospect for nine miles. Turn right on Lodgepole Road for 8.5 miles. Go past South Fork Campground 0.5 mile to a parking area on the right.
Contact: Rogue River National Forest, Butte Falls Ranger District, 47201 Highway 62, Prospect, OR, 97536, 541/865-2700.

137 LOWER SOUTH FORK ROGUE RIVER

13.6-14.0 mi/6.0-7.0 hr  3 7

southeast of Prospect in Rogue River National Forest

The lower stretch of trail on the South Fork of the Rogue River is accessible to mountain bikes. It also provides a glimpse of many sugar pine trees, including one particularly large one on a short side trail. This section of trail ambles over creeks and through woods down to its end at a diversion dam.

Cross the road from the parking area and take the South Fork Trail along the river 1.6 miles to the left-hand side trail; a short 0.2-mile walk crosses Road 3775 and visits the giant sugar pine. The remaining 5.2 miles follows the river down to the dam.

User Groups: Hikers, dogs, and mountain bikes. No horses allowed. No wheelchair facilities.
Permits: Permits are not required. Parking and access are free.
Maps: For a map of the Rogue River National Forest and Sky Lakes Wilderness, contact the Rogue River-Siskiyou National Forest, 3040 Biddle Road, Medford, OR, 97504, 541/618-2200. For a topographic map, ask the USGS for Cascade Gorge.
Directions: From Medford, drive 14.5 miles east on OR 62 and turn right on the Butte Falls Highway for 15 miles to the town of Butte Falls. go straight one mile then left at a sign for Prospect for nine miles. Turn right on Lodgepole Road for 8.5 miles. Go past South Fork Campground 0.5 mile to a parking area on the right.
Contact: Rogue River National Forest, Butte Falls Ranger District, 47201 Highway 62, Prospect, OR, 97536, 541/865-2700.

138 SEVEN LAKES TRAIL

8.4-10.4 mi/3.5-5.0 hr  4  9

east of Prospect in Sky Lakes Wilderness

The Sky Lakes Wilderness is heaven for backpackers and horses, with many opportunities to camp throughout the area. The Seven Lakes Basin, one of the more popular spots, has camps aplenty—just as long as you camp where the USFS asks you to, which means paying attention to posted camp spots. Horses are required to camp at designated areas, are banned from grazing, and are not allowed within 200 feet of lakeshores, unless on trails or near designated watering spots. If this sounds like a lot of information, don't let it dissuade you. It's only to keep the area as pristine as possible. To enter from the west, the Seven Lakes Trail climbs over a pass into a water-dotted landscape that is best viewed from nearby Devils Peak, accessible from the Pacific Crest Trail.

The Seven Lakes Trail sets out from behind a guardrail into the wilderness. At 0.7 mile, go right and continue 2.8 miles, passing Frog Lake, to a pass. Here the trail splits: Take the left trail down 0.2 mile to the basin. At the next junction, going left on the Alta Lake Trail leads to half-mile-long Alta Lake with its campsites. Going straight passes South Lake and Cliff Lake in 1.5 miles; another left-hand trail connects to three more lakes. Continue 0.4 mile to the PCT. For a climb up Devils Peak, turn right on the PCT for 2.5 miles, then heading right up the peak. Head back down and continue on the PCT another 0.6 mile to a junction. Go right on a 1.3-mile spur trail to return to the pass over Seven Lakes.

User Groups: Hikers, dogs, and horses. No mountain bikes allowed. No wheelchair facilities.

Permits: A free self-issue Wilderness Permit is required and is available at the trailhead. Parking and access are free.

Maps: For a map of the Rogue River National Forest and Sky Lakes Wilderness, contact the Rogue River-Siskiyou National Forest, 3040 Biddle Road, Medford, OR, 97504, 541/618-2200. For a topographic map, ask the USGS for Devil's Peak.

Directions: From Medford, drive 14.5 miles east on OR 62 and turn right on Butte Falls Highway for 15 miles to the town of Butte Falls. Go straight one mile and turn left toward Prospect for nine miles, then right on Lodgepole Road 34 for 8.5 miles. Continue straight on Road 37 for 0.4 mile, then go right on Road 3780 for 4.1 miles to a parking area on the left.

Contact: Rogue River National Forest, Butte Falls Ranger District, 47201 Highway 62, Prospect, OR, 97536, 541/865-2700.

139 SEVEN LAKES BASIN VIA SEVENMILE/PCT

11.4–17.3 mi/6.0–9.0 hr 4 9

east of Prospect in Sky Lakes Wilderness

The eastern entrance to this mythic landscape of lakes visits the same area as the Seven Lakes Trail (see previous listing) but is both longer and easier. For one, you won't have the elevation gain. Plus, you'll be in the headwaters of the Middle Fork Rogue River, including Sevenmile Marsh. From here, you can also walk the shore of Cliff Lake with its views to Devils Peak, and you can climb Devils Peak for a world-class view of the lake country.

Start on the Sevenmile Trail for 1.8 miles, and go right on the Pacific Crest Trail for 2.7 miles. At the next junction, you can create a 2.4-mile loop past Grass Lake, Middle Lake, and Cliff Lake by going right then staying left for the next three junctions. To climb Devils Peak stay on the PCT another 3.2 miles up to a high pass, climbing the peak to the right. If you want to expand this loop to a 17-plus-mile hike, continue on the PCT 0.6 mile to a junction and go right 1.3 miles on a spur trail to a second pass, connecting with the Seven Lakes Trail. Then go right and stay on this trail for 1.7 miles back to the PCT.

User Groups: Hikers, dogs, and horses. No mountain bikes allowed. No wheelchair facilities.

Permits: A free self-issue Wilderness Permit is required and is available at the trailhead. Parking and access are free.

Maps: For a map of the Rogue River National Forest and Sky Lakes Wilderness, contact the Fremont-Winema National Forest, 1301 South G Street, Lakeview, OR, 97630, 541/947-2151. For a topographic map, ask the USGS for Devils Peak.

Directions: Drive north from Klamath Falls on OR 62 to Fort Klamath, near milepost 90. Turn west on Nicholson Road and go straight 3.9 miles. Go left on Road 3300 at a sign for Sevenmile Trailhead for 0.4 mile, then go right on Road 3334 to road's end.

Contact: Winema National Forest, Klamath Falls Ranger District, 2819 Dahlia Street, Klamath Falls, OR, 97601, 541/883-6714.

140 SKY LAKES FROM NANNIE CREEK TRAIL

12.8–16.7 mi/6.0–8.0 hr 

west of Klamath Lake in Sky Lakes Wilderness

The Sky Lakes Basin has a challenging side, and this trail is it. This section of lakes huddles around imposing Luther Mountain like jewels flung across the forest. The Nannie Creek Trail will get you there, but once you're there it's up to you to wander around and lose yourself in the landscape. Here are a couple of hikes, both rigorous, to get you warmed up.

The Nannie Creek Trail heads out on a ridge for 2.4 miles to Puck Lakes on the right, and another 1.9 miles to a junction with the Snow Lakes Trail. To hit the main course, go left 1.4 miles passing numerous ponds to a junction. Here you can go 0.5 mile to the right to Margurette Lake, then form a loop: go left 0.2 mile to Trapper Lake, then left at the junction of the Cherry Creek Trail 0.7 mile to Donna and Deep lakes to complete the loop.

For a climb around Luther Mountain, instead go right at Margurette Lake, climbing heartily up 2.8 miles to the PCT. Go right on the PCT for 1.1 miles, then right on the Snow Lakes Trail 2.3 miles back to the Nannie Creek Trail, passing little tarns along the way. Return on the Nannie Creek Trail.

User Groups: Hikers, dogs, and horses. No mountain bikes allowed. No wheelchair facilities.

Permits: A free self-issue Wilderness Permit is required and is available at the trailhead. Parking and access are free.

Maps: For a map of the Rogue River National Forest and Sky Lakes Wilderness, contact the Fremont-Winema National Forest, 1301 South G Street, Lakeview, OR, 97630, 541/947-2151. For a topographic map, ask the USGS for for Pelican Butte.

Directions: From Klamath Falls, go west on Highway 140 for 25 miles. Between mileposts 43 and 44, go north on Westside Road for 12.2 miles, then left on Road 3484 for 5.2 miles to road's end.

Contact: Winema National Forest, Klamath Falls Ranger District, 2819 Dahlia Street, Klamath Falls, OR, 97601, 541/883-6714.

141 SKY LAKES FROM COLD SPRINGS TRAILHEAD

6.9 mi/3.0 hr

west of Klamath Lake in Sky Lakes Wilderness

The Sky Lakes Basin is a picture-perfect mesh of ponds and lakes. For an easy entrance into its wonders—visiting Heavenly Twin Lakes, with its view of Luther Mountain, and Isherwood Lake, as well as Lakes Florence, Liza, Elizabeth, and Notasha—try this easy loop.

From the Cold Springs Trailhead, head in 0.6 mile to a junction. For the quickest walk through the lodgepole and hemlock woods, go right on the South Rock Creek Trail for 1.8 miles to the next junction. To the left, a 0.3-mile spur connects to a shorter loop with the cold Springs Trail and runs between the heavenly Twin Lakes. For a longer loop among far more lakes, go right 0.4 mile along the lakeshore to the Sky Lakes Trail, then left at the next junction 0.8 mile past the rest of the lovely lakes. At the next junction, go right 0.3 mile, then left on the Cold Springs Trail 2.4 miles back to the car.

User Groups: Hikers, dogs, and horses. No mountain bikes allowed. No wheelchair facilities.

Permits: A free self-issue Wilderness Permit is required and is available at the trailhead. Parking and access are free.

Maps: For a map of the Rogue River National Forest and Sky Lakes Wilderness, contact the Fremont-Winema National Forest, 1301 South G Street, Lakeview, OR, 97630, 541/947-2151. For a topographic map, ask the USGS for for Pelican Butte.

Directions: From Medford, drive east 6 miles on OR 62, then right on Highway 140 to milepost 41, and turn north on Road 3651; watch for Cold Springs Trailhead sign. Go 10.1 miles to its end at the Cold Springs Trailhead.

Contact: Winema National Forest, Klamath Falls Ranger District, 2819 Dahlia Street, Klamath Falls, OR, 97601, 541/883-6714.

142 BLUE LAKE BASIN

7.4-11.0 miles/3.0-6.0 hr 3 8

north of Mount McLoughlin in Sky Lakes Wilderness

Sky Lakes seems a fitting name for a wilderness that hosts lakes so pure they seem to hold their own sky. From some of the shores of these lakes, the true sky seems magnificently large, endless, spanning from one horizon to another. Perhaps this is what Judge John Waldo thought as he passed through here with a horse party in 1888. He left his mark carved into a large Shasta red fir on the shore of Island Lake, a spot you can visit on this fabulous hike.

Take the Blue Canyon Trail 2.3 miles, passing Round Lake, to Blue Lake. Go right at the junction with the South Fork Trail and continue 0.3 mile to the next junction (with a horse camp on the left). Go left and continue 2.9 miles on the Blue Canyon Trail, passing access points to large Horseshoe Lake and Pear Lake, then watching for an unmarked side trail to the left, leading to Waldo's signature and the shore of Island Lake. Another 0.4 mile beyond this trail is the junction with the Badger Lake Trail, and a right turn there leads 0.2 mile to the Pacific Crest Trail.

User Groups: Hikers, dogs, and horses. No mountain bikes allowed. No wheelchair facilities.

Permits: A free self-issue Wilderness Permit is required and is available at the trailhead. Parking and access are free.

Maps: For a map of the Rogue River National Forest and Sky Lakes Wilderness, contact the Rogue River-Siskiyou National Forest, 3040 Biddle Road, Medford, OR, 97504, 541/618-2200. For a topographic map, ask the USGS for Pelican Butte.

Directions: From Medford, drive 14.5 miles east on OR 62 and turn right on Butte Falls Highway for 15 miles to the town of Butte Falls. Go straight one mile and turn left toward Prospect for nine miles, then right on Lodgepole Road 34 for 8.5 miles. Continue straight on Road 37 for 7.4 miles, then turn left on Road 3770 for 5.3 miles to a pullout on the right.

Contact: Rogue River National Forest, Butte Falls Ranger District, 47201 Highway 62, Prospect, OR, 97536, 541/865-2700.

143 MOUNT MCLOUGHLIN

10.6 mi/6.0 hr 5 10

west of Klamath Lake in Sky Lakes Wilderness

BEST

After years of having hikers climb helter-skelter to this 9,495-foot peak, the Forest Service finally laid out a trail. Bring plenty of water and sunscreen and prepare for a rugged, demanding climb, but also a view of half the state of Oregon, and far into California. Named for the Hudson Bay Company leader at Fort Vancouver, this mountain is one of the best non-technical climbs in the state. Just be sure to stay on the trail—even with such a view of the surrounding area, it's easy to get lost.

Cross the Cascade Canal and climb one mile to the Pacific Crest Trail. Follow the PCT uphill and to the right for 0.4 mile, passing a right-hand side trail to Freye Lake, then leaving the PCT on the climber's route to the left. For 1.5 miles the trail is steady before it hurtles upwards the remaining 2.4 miles, heading above tree line, with the final half gaining 1,300 feet.

User Groups: Hikers, dogs, and horses. No mountain bikes allowed. No wheelchair facilities.

Permits: A free self-issue Wilderness Permit is required and is available at the trailhead. A federal Northwest Forest Pass is required to park at the Trout Creek Trailhead; the cost is $5 a day or $30 for an annual pass. You can buy a day pass at the trailhead, at ranger stations, or through private vendors.

Maps: For a map of the Rogue River National Forest and Sky Lakes Wilderness, contact the Fremont-Winema National Forest, 1301 South G Street, Lakeview, OR, 97630, 541/947-2151.

For a topographic map, ask the USGS for Mount McLoughlin.

Directions: From Klamath Falls, go west on Highway 140 to milepost 36, and just beyond it turn right on Road 3661 for 2.9 miles, then left on Road 3650 for 0.2 mile to a parking lot.

Contact: Winema National Forest, Klamath Falls Ranger District, 2819 Dahlia Street, Klamath Falls, OR, 97601, 541/883-6714.

144 FOURMILE LAKE TO LONG LAKE

9.0–14.0 mi/4.0–7.0 hr 3 7

west of Klamath Lake in Sky Lakes Wilderness

Fourmile Lake is bordered on nearly every side by the Sky Lakes Wilderness, through which the Pacific Crest Trail glides by on a relatively level trail. This large lake, with its view of the pyramid-like Mount McLoughlin, offers access to a number of lakes in the Wilderness Area. The route can be extended to a 14-mile loop, though much of it passes through viewless woods and leaves the lakes behind for quite a while.

From the Fourmile Trailhead, head left for 0.8 mile, crossing Road 3661, then left on the Badger Lake Trail, which crosses the Cascade Canal. Now the trail heads into the Wilderness Area, arriving at Badger Lake in 1.8 miles and Long Lake in another 1.9 miles, passing Horse Creek Meadow along the way. This is the last of the lakes this trail sees, but to continue on a wide loop, head farther down the trail 1.6 miles to the PCT, going left. Follow the PCT 5.4 miles, then turn left on the Twin Ponds Trail for 2.5 miles, passing one last lake, and arriving back at the Fourmile Trailhead.

User Groups: Hikers, dogs, and horses. No mountain bikes allowed. No wheelchair facilities.

Permits: A free self-issue Wilderness Permit is required and is available at the trailhead. Parking and access are free.

Maps: For a map of the Rogue River National Forest and Sky Lakes Wilderness, contact the Fremont-Winema National Forest, 1301 South G Street, Lakeview, OR, 97630, 541/947-2151. For a topographic map, ask the USGS for Lake of the Woods North.

Directions: From Klamath Falls, go west on Highway 140 to milepost 36, and just beyond it turn right on Road 3661 for 5.7 miles to Fourmile Campground. Follow signs for the trailhead.

Contact: Winema National Forest, Klamath Falls Ranger District, 2819 Dahlia Street, Klamath Falls, OR, 97601, 541/883-6714.

145 TABLE ROCKS

2.8–5.4 mi/1.0–2.5 hr 

north of Medford

The two formations known as the Table Rocks, rising like fortresses above the Rogue River, seem out of place in this valley. They were, in fact, used as fortresses by the Takelma tribe against the U.S. Army, which came for them when they attacked settlers and gold miners in 1853. These mesas are the remnants of a 9.6-million-year-old lava flow, standing 800-feet-high and capped with tough andesite. Atop the plateaus you'll find scrub oak grasslands and a profusion of wildflowers, which is why The Nature Conservancy built the trail on Lower Table Rock, now a nature preserve. In fact, a rare fairy shrimp—federally listed as threatened—is found in the vernal pools atop the mesa.

To climb Upper Table Rock, you need ascend only 720 feet up a 1.1-mile trail to the viewpoints. The trail to Lower Table Rock is longer; it sets off 1.6 miles across the valley floor, then goes up cliffs studded with black oak and madrone to the mesa. From there, you can hike out to two viewpoints: one just 0.4 mile to the left, and the other 1.1 miles down an old airstrip to a viewpoint. You'll catch views of the Crater Lake rim, Mount McLoughlin, and the Rogue River.

User Groups: Hikers. Dogs not allowed on Lower Table Rock. No horses or mountain bikes allowed. No wheelchair facilities.

Permits: Permits are not required. Parking and access are free.

Maps: For a topographic map, ask the USGS for Sams Valley.

Directions: For Lower Table Rock, return to Table Rock Road and turn right, continuing to milepost 10. Turn left on Wheeler Road 0.8 mile to a parking spur on the left. For Upper Table Rock, take the I-5 north of Medford to Exit 33 for Central Point, driving east on Biddle Road for one mile. Turn left on Table Rock Road for 5.2 miles and turn right on Modoc Road for 1.5 miles to the trailhead lot on the left.

Contact: Bureau of Land Management, Medford Office, 3040 Biddle Road, Medford, OR, 97504, 541/618-2200.

146 FISH LAKE AND THE HIGH LAKES TRAIL

12.7 mi one-way/7.0 hr 3 7

south of Mount McLoughlin in Rogue River National Forest

This fairly new trail makes for a great bike ride or an extended hike. Of course, it can be broken up into segments starting from either Fish Lake or Lake of the Woods. The trail crosses the Cascade Crest and largely follows a massive lava flow erupted from Brown Mountain, which occupies the horizon here like a sentry. An easy 6.6-mile round-trip hike follows the shore of Fish Lake and joins the High Lakes Trail at its far end, and it's here that this description begins.

From the Fish Lake Trailhead, walk in 0.6 mile to a junction near the Fish Lake Dam. Go left and follow the main trail 3.7 miles through an old clear-cut, crossing a road and passing the Fish Lake Resort, and following the Fish Lake shore to the Fish Lake Campground and the start of the High Lakes Trail. In one mile the trail crosses the Pacific Crest Trail. From here, it's 4.8 miles to Lake of the Woods, following the edge of the Brown Mountain Lava Flow (see next listing) to a visitors center. The trail continues along the edge of the lake for 0.8 mile to the Aspen Point Picnic Area, and continues across a big meadow 1.8 miles to the upper trailhead at the Great Meadow Recreation Site.

User Groups: Hikers, dogs, and bicycles. No horses allowed. No wheelchair facilities.

Permits: Permits are not required. Parking and access are free.

Maps: For a map of the Rogue River National Forest and Sky Lakes Wilderness, contact the Rogue River-Siskiyou National Forest, 3040 Biddle Road, Medford, OR, 97504, 541/618-2200. For a topographic map, ask the USGS for Mount McLoughlin.

Directions: To access the Fish Lake Trailhead, drive east of Medford 35 miles on Highway 140. Between mileposts 28 and 29, turn south on Road 37. In 0.5 mile turn left at the trailhead parking. To access the Lake of the Woods Trailhead, park in a lot on Highway 140 between mileposts 37 and 38.

Contact: Rogue River-Siskiyou National Forest, Ashland Ranger District, 645 Washington Street, Ashland, OR, 97520, 541/552-2900.

147 BROWN MOUNTAIN

5.8 mi/2.0 hr 2 7

south of Mount McLoughlin in Rogue River National Forest

The Brown Mountain Lava Flow spilled quite a mess here, and the builders of the Pacific Crest Trail, which crosses it, had to dynamite their way through. Now the rugged landscape is being pioneered by chinkapin oak and a variety of lichens. Bring water, as summer sun can make a lava field a simmering experience.

From the trailhead, hike in 0.2 mile and go left on the Pacific Crest Trail. In 0.4 mile cross Highway 140 and continue 0.2 mile to a junction with the High Lakes Trail, going straight. Within the next two miles, you will cross the largest part of the flow and arrive at a high point, with views to Mount McLoughlin along the way. If you continue on, you can travel 5.8 miles to the Brown Mountain Trail, which does not climb the mountain but rather goes around it.

User Groups: Hikers, dogs, and horses. No mountain bikes allowed. No wheelchair facilities.

Permits: Permits are not required. Parking and access are free.

Maps: For a map of the Rogue River National Forest and Sky Lakes Wilderness, contact the Rogue River-Siskiyou National Forest, 3040 Biddle Road, Medford, OR, 97504, 541/618-2200. For a topographic map, ask the USGS for Brown Mountain.

Directions: From Medford, drive Highway 140 to a pullout on the left between mileposts 32 and 33, at a sign for Summit Sno-Park. The trail starts at this parking area.

Contact: Rogue River-Siskiyou National Forest, Ashland Ranger District, 645 Washington Street, Ashland, OR, 97520, 541/552-2900.

148 MOUNTAIN LAKES WILDERNESS LOOP

17.1 mi/1-2 days 4 9

west of Klamath Lake in the Mountain Lakes Wilderness

At only six square miles, the exact size of a township, this is surely one of the smallest wilderness areas there is. This pocket remains as it was since 1964: a stunning terrain of mountainous country hovering over Upper Klamath Lake. Glaciers have carved this area, a collapsed volcano not unlike that of Crater Lake, into towering cliffs, lake basins, and eroded volcanic cones. Piercing a lateral moraine, the grit swept to the sides by glaciers, the trail follows a path of ponderosa pine, Shasta red fir, and white fir into an alpine landscape that just begs for a backpacker or two—but no more than 10 at a time, according to regulations. Even though this is one of the first designated Wilderness Areas in the country, it remains quite a secret to the public.

Follow the Varney Creek Trail 4.4 miles, with views of Mount Harriman, to a fork at the beginning of the loop. If you're backpacking, go left on the Mountain Lakes Loop Trail to the lakes. You'll reach Lake Como in 0.7 mile, and larger Lake Harriette 1.2 miles beyond that; both are suitable for camping. From Lake Harriette, continue 1.5 miles up to a high pass and go right (the left trail dead-ends at South Pass Lake). In 0.4 mile you'll pass a side route up Aspen Butte, a one-mile cross-country climb to an old lookout site at 8,208 feet. Continuing on the loop, stay straight on the main trail for 2.7 miles to a pass on Whiteface Peak, passing both an unmaintained trail and the Clover Creek Trail on the left. At the peak, go right (the other path leads to Road 3660 on the Mountain Lakes Trail, descending 2,000 feet and past Lake Waban) to finish the loop, heading 1.4 miles down to Zeb and Eb Lakes. In another 0.4 mile, you'll meet with the Varney Creek Trail; go left to return to the trailhead.

User Groups: Hikers, dogs, and horses. No mountain bikes allowed. No wheelchair facilities.

Permits: A free self-issue Wilderness Permit is required and is available at the trailhead. Parking and access are free.

Maps: For a map of the Rogue River National Forest and Sky Lakes Wilderness, contact the Fremont-Winema National Forest, 1301 South G Street, Lakeview, OR, 97630, 541/947-2151. For a topographic map, ask the USGS for Lake of the Woods North.

Directions: From Klamath Falls, drive 21 miles west on Highway 140. Between mileposts 46 and 47, turn south on Road 3637 at a Varney Creek Trailhead sign, following this road 1.8 miles. Turn left on Road 3664 for 1.9 miles to its end.

Contact: Winema National Forest, Klamath

Falls Ranger District, 2819 Dahlia Street, Klamath Falls, OR, 97601, 541/883-6714.

149 JACKSONVILLE WOODLANDS

1.0-8.0 mi/1.0-2.5 hr 2 7

in Jacksonville

The little city of Jacksonville is designated a National Historic Landmark, a true distinction here in Oregon. This former mining town at the foot of the Siskiyous is charming in its own right, and retains much of its 1886 allure, a leftover from when the railroad abandoned this area and the gold ran out. The woodlands that lie just outside it add to the ambiance. In 1989, citizens of this little red-brick town rallied to preserve the area, and the result is this 20-parcel forest intersected by eight miles of trail, following Jackson Creek, touring old mining ruins, and climbing to a 1,900-foot summit over the town.

From the lot set out 0.8 mile along Jackson Creek on the Zigler Trail. To climb to the summit of Panorama Point, head up 0.7 mile on the Jackson Forks and Rich Gulch Trails. After the viewpoint, the Rich Gulch Trail heads to Rich Gulch, where gold was discovered in 1852, passing some old mining tailings and a side trail to the Chinese Diggings, where the Chinese teams did some of the most extensive diggings. The trail ends at Oregon Street and heads 0.6 mile back to town. From here you can even tour the historic town itself, well worth the trip, then return along C Street to the lot.

User Groups: Hikers, dogs, and mountain bikes. No horses allowed. No wheelchair facilities.

Permits: Permits are not required. Parking and access are free.

Maps: Maps are available at the trailhead and online at www.jvwoodlands.org. For a topographic map, ask the USGS for Medford West.

Directions: From I-5, take the Medford exit (Exit 30) and follow signs seven miles west to Jacksonville on Highway 238. Turn right on C Street and go to its end at a visitors center lot.

Contact: Jacksonville Woodlands Association, P.O. Box 1210, Jacksonville, OR, 97530, info@jvwoodlands.org.

150 STERLING MINE DITCH

4.7 mi /2.0 hr 1 7

south of Jacksonville

In 1854, just three years after gold was discovered at Jacksonville, miners struck it big at Sterling Creek. After panning gold from the creek, they went after the gold in the surrounding gravel slopes. To achieve this, Chinese laborers built a nearly 27-mile ditch to carry water from the Little Applegate River to these hills. The ditch remained in use from 1877 well into the 1930s. Now that the gold is gone, only the oak and pine forests and open grasslands are left, and a large segment of the ditch has been converted into a trail. Five trailheads—Little Applegate, Tunnel Ridge, Bear Gulch, Wolf Gap, and Deming Gulch—access the ditch trail, but Tunnel Ridge Trailhead offers the middle access with a short loop, and springtime offers a wildflower show to accompany the history. Of course, this trail can be taken for much longer journeys as well.

There are many entry points along Little Applegate Road, so why not start out easy? For an initial 4.7-mile loop, start at the Tunnel Ridge Trailhead and hike in one mile to the junction with the Sterling Mine Tunnel. From here, you could go right one-way for 5.1 miles to the Little Applegate Trailhead, another option. But head left, where you'll pass an old tunnel and continue 2.1 miles on the Sterling Ditch to a junction. Here you could go left 1.0 mile to the Bear Gulch Trailhead, then left along the road 0.6 mile to Tunnel Ridge Trailhead, completing the short 4.7-mile loop. To continue on the Ditch however, go right at this junction as far as you'd like. Another 1.6 miles leads to a junction, where going right leads 1.5 miles to the Wolf Gap Trailhead, and left heads the remaining 7.8 miles to the Deming Gulch Trailhead and the end of the trail.

User Groups: Hikers, dogs, horses, and mountain bikes. No wheelchair facilities.

Permits: Permits are not required. Parking and access are free.

Maps: For a topographic map, ask the USGS for Sterling Creek.

Directions: From Medford, follow Highway 238 through Jacksonville to the town of Ruch. Turn south at a sign for Upper Applegate and continue 2.9 miles and turn left on Little Applegate Road for 9.7 miles to the Tunnel Ridge Trailhead parking on the right.

Contact: Bureau of Land Management, Medford Office, 3040 Biddle Road, Medford, OR, 97504, 541/618-2200.

151 LITHIA PARK

2.8 mi/1.0 hr 1 7

in Ashland

Ashland's idyllic Lithia Park certainly ranks high among city parks. Once the site of a water-powered sawmill, this parkland now stretches along Ashland Creek through some fairly wild territory—just watch out for poison oak. There are spots to pause and reflect on stone beaches or footbridges, flowers to admire, and a sense of peace that radiates from this little town, home to the Oregon Shakespeare Festival, whose stages are nearby. If you dare, you can even take a drink from the fountains of bubbly Lithia Springs water, which is the other thing Ashland is famous for. The 2.8-mile loop follows both sides of the creek, intersecting along a series of footbridges, so you can go as far as you like. Along the way, you can circle little Meyer Lake and Black Swan Lake and follow the creek up as far as Reservoir Park.

User Groups: Hikers and dogs. No horses or mountain bikes allowed. Paved portions of the park are wheelchair accessible.

Permits: Permits are not required. Parking and access are free.

Maps: For a topographic map, ask the USGS for Ashland.

Directions: From I-5, take either Ashland exit (Exit 14 or 19) and follow signs for City Center and Lithia Park.

Contact: Ashland Parks and Recreation, 340 South Pioneer Street, Ashland, OR, 97520, 541/488-5340.

152 GRIZZLY PEAK

5.4 mi/2.0 hr

east of Ashland

Grizzly Peak broods over the town of Ashland and I-5 with views to the snowy cap of Mount Ashland from what was once a forested plateau until a 2002 fire swept over the western face. If anything, it opened up the view even more, and the Grizzly Peak Trail is still a fine walk along the edge to three excellent viewpoints of Mount Shasta, Pilot Rock, and Emigrant Lake.

Climb 1.2 miles to the junction, the beginning of the loop. Go left 0.3 mile to a side spur to the viewless summit and continue 0.8 mile out onto the burn to two viewpoints. Continue along the western face 0.7 mile to a view of Ashland, then return 1.2 miles to the first junction.

User Groups: Hikers, dogs, horses, and mountain bikes. No wheelchair facilities.

Permits: Permits are not required. Parking and access are free.

Maps: For a topographic map, ask the USGS for Grizzly Peak and Rio Canyon.

Directions: From I-5, take the southern Ashland exit (Exit 14) and go east on Highway 66 for 0.7 mile, then turn left on Dead Indian Memorial Highway for 6.7 miles. Turn left again on Shale City Road for three miles, then left on Road 38-2E-9.2 and after 0.8 mile go straight through a three-way junction, continuing 0.9 mile to road's end.

Contact: Bureau of Land Management, Medford Office, 3040 Biddle Road, Medford, OR, 97504, 541/618-2200.

153 WAGNER BUTTE

10.4 mi/6.0 hr 3 8

south of Ashland in Rogue River National Forest

For panoramic views of the Rogue and Little Applegate Valleys and the mountains that surround them, try this mountain named for early settler Jacob Wagner, who operated a flour mill in nearby Ashland—which you'll get a view of, too. A few pieces remain of an old lookout tower on the 7,140-foot peak, which was intentionally burned down by smokejumpers in 1972. The trail passes the Sheep Creek Slide, where 400,000 tons of soil went crashing down four miles to the Little Applegate River in a 1983 thunderstorm. Now a wealth of wildflowers are pioneering the slopes.

The Wagner Butte Trail begins steep, then gets easier for the first 2.4 miles, crossing the slide along Sheep Creek. Then the trail climbs steeply through sagebrush, gaining nearly 500 feet in 0.9 mile to the Wagner Glade Gap. The final 1.9 miles passes through quaking aspen stands and mountain mahogany, and by a piped spring before its pitch over boulders to the summit.

User Groups: Hikers and dogs only. No horses or mountain bikes. No wheelchair facilities.

Permits: Permits are not required. Parking and access are free.

Maps: For a map of the Rogue River National Forest, contact the Rogue River-Siskiyou National Forest, 3040 Biddle Road, Medford, OR, 97504, 541/618-2200. For a topographic map, ask the USGS for Siskiyou Peak and Talent.

Directions: From I-5 take exit 21 for Talent and go 0.4 mile west on Valley View Drive and turn left on Old Highway 99 for another 0.4 mile. Turn right on Rapp Road and go 1.1 miles to a stop sign, continuing straight on Wagner Creek Road for 6.5 miles, going from paved road to gravel. Go left on Road 22, heading 2 miles to the trailhead parking on the right.

Contact: Rogue River-Siskiyou National Forest, Ashland Ranger District, 645 Washington Street, Ashland, OR, 97520, 541/552-2900.

154 MOUNT ASHLAND MEADOWS AND GROUSE GAP

6.8 mi/3.0 hr

south of Ashland in Rogue River National Forest

The tallest peak in the Siskiyou Range is also the most popular. Mount Ashland is the sole ski area in this part of the state, and winter finds Mount Ashland Meadows a destination for the downhill crowd. In summer, it's another story: The meadows are dominated by bursts of lupine, larkspur, sneezeweed, aster, yarrow, and paintbrush. Granite rock formations, stands of grand fir and Shasta red fir, and views to Mount Shasta itself on the California horizon make this stretch of the Pacific Crest Trail worth exploring. It's also part of the final stretch of the PCT before it enters California at the Siskiyou Gap. You can even climb Mount Ashland itself, but it's an easy and short hike up a dirt road.

At the trailhead, cross the road and head on the PCT into the forest for 0.5 mile to the beginning of the meadows. In another 1.1 miles the trail crosses a road and continues 1.8 miles to Grouse Gap and another road leading to a picnic shelter. Here you'll end this hike with a stunning view of Mount Shasta.

User Groups: Hikers, dogs, and horses. No mountain bikes allowed. No wheelchair facilities.

Permits: Permits are not required. Parking and access are free.

Maps: For a map of the Rogue River National Forest, contact the Rogue River-Siskiyou National Forest, 3040 Biddle Road, Medford, OR, 97504, 541/618-2200. For a topographic map, ask the USGS for Mount Ashland.
Directions: From I-5, take Ashland Exit 6 and follow Mount Ashland Ski Area signs. After 0.7 mile, go right on Mount Ashland Road 20 for 7.2 miles and park at a pullout on the right.
Contact: Rogue River-Siskiyou National Forest, Ashland Ranger District, 645 Washington Street, Ashland, OR, 97520, 541/552-2900.

155 PILOT ROCK

1.2 mi/1.0 hr 

south of Ashland in Cascade Siskiyou National Monument

BEST

Pilot Rock is aptly named, as it's what pioneers steered by to cross the Siskiyou Pass between California and Oregon. This basalt remnant of a 30-million-year-old lava flow formed of weird, geometric pillars and columns is a destination for serious rock climbers. With the Pacific Crest Trail running just below it, hikers can get close to the rock as well—though climbing it is not recommended. Stay away from that tempting ledge, too—it ends at a cliff.

From the lot, cross the road and head east on the PCT 0.2 mile to a side trail, following this up 0.4 mile to Pilot Rock. For a longer hike, consider continuing on the PCT another 6.5 miles to Soda Mountain (see next listing).
User Groups: Hikers and dogs only. No horses or mountain bikes allowed. No wheelchair facilities.
Permits: Permits are not required. Parking and access are free.
Maps: For a topographic map, ask the USGS for Siskiyou Pass.
Directions: From I-5, take the Ashland Exit 6 and follow Mount Ashland signs along Highway 99, and in 0.7 mile go under the freeway and follow Highway 99 for 1.2 more miles. Turn left on Pilot Rock Road 40-2E-33 and go 2.8 miles to a parking area on the right.
Contact: Bureau of Land Management, Medford Office, 3040 Biddle Road, Medford, OR, 97504, 541/618-2200.

156 SODA MOUNTAIN

4.2 mi/2.5 hr 

south of Ashland in Cascade Siskiyou National Monument

The Cascade-Siskiyou National Monument is a biologically diverse area that creates a kind of bridge between its two namesake mountain ranges. The trees create a strange mix of white oak, cedar, and grand fir, and the big sunflower-like arrowleaf balsamroots thrive the slopes. Atop 6,089-foot Soda Mountain a staffed watchtower looks over Mount Shasta, the Klamath River Canyon, and the Trinity Alps.

Take the Pacific Crest Trail to the right toward Soda Mountain for 1.1 miles to a left-hand junction. Follow this spur 0.2 mile to a road, and go right 0.8 mile to the peak.
User Groups: Hikers, dogs, and horses. No mountain bikes allowed. No wheelchair facilities.
Permits: Permits are not required. Parking and access are free.
Maps: For a topographic map, ask the USGS for Soda Mountain.
Directions: From I-5, take the Ashland Exit 14 and go east on Highway 66 for 15 miles. Turn right on Soda Mountain Road 39-3E-32.3 and go 3.7 miles to a trailhead by power lines.
Contact: Bureau of Land Management, Medford Office, 3040 Biddle Road, Medford, OR, 97504, 541/618-2200.

157 LINK RIVER NATURE TRAIL

4.8 mi/2.0 hr 1 6

in Klamath Falls

Odd thing about Klamath Falls is that there aren't actually any waterfalls, at least not since the dam on the Link River silenced them. These falls once fell from the outlet of Upper Klamath Lake, the stupendously large inland lake where thousands of birds pass through on their migrations. Though the Link River is now itself a kind of lake, cormorants and pelicans still frequent the water, and this nature trail strides its length between Upper Klamath Lake and Lake Ewauna.

From the trailhead, follow the river through a canyon, crossing a canal and passing a steel staircase to a gauging station and the shore for 1.7 miles. Pass the power station and Favell Museum, go left on Main Street, then continue 0.4 mile to a 0.6-mile loop on the Wingwatchers Trail.

User Groups: Hikers and dogs on leash only. No horses or mountain bikes. The Wingwatchers Trail is wheelchair accessible.

Permits: Permits are not required. Parking and access are free.

Maps: For a topographic map, ask the USGS for Klamath Falls.

Directions: Drive U.S. 97 for one mile north of downtown Klamath Falls and take the Lakeshore Drive exit, following Nevada Avenue onto lakeshore Drive for 0.8 mile. Cross the Link River and turn left into a parking area for the Nature Trail.

Contact: Klamath County Department of Tourism, 1451 Main Street, Klamath Falls, OR, 97601, 541/884-0666.

158 OC&E WOODS LINE LINEAR STATE PARK

6.6–82.0 mi/2.0 hr–5 days 2 7

east of Klamath Falls on Highway 140

BEST

In the great "Rails to Trails" movement, the OC&E Woods Line State Trail is a triumph. A full 82 miles long, this old logging railroad of the Oregon, California, and Eastern Line has been transformed into a linear park that has something for everybody. The first 7.1 miles are paved, and the rest lies a bit more rugged, passing the Sprague River, little towns, and ending at the Sycan Marsh, an avid spot for bird-watchers.

An easy introduction to the trail is the first 3.3-mile segment, which begins in Klamath Falls and ends at Highway 39. Because it is in town, this section is busy with bikers, joggers, and walkers. If you want a longer day on the paved portion, continue to the town of Olene 3.8 miles away, passing through countryside with views of Mount Shasta along the way.

Beyond Olene, the trail is less improved but enters the southern Oregon landscape in full force. The next 24.2 miles passes through old farming communities and juniper and sagebrush country. The end of this stretch reaches the Switchbacks Trailhead, where restrooms and camping are available. In the next 5.5 miles the trail reaches the Sprague River, following it 12.5 miles to the Sycan Siding Trailhead.

Here the trail splits. To the right, one path continues along the Sprague River 14 miles to the town of Bly, the official end of the trail. The left-hand trail crosses the river and heads out for 18.7 miles, following Five Mile Creek for a stretch, before arriving at the Horse Glade Trailhead, another spot to camp. The trail continues 14.2 miles, passing the 400-foot-long Merritt Creek Trestle to its end at Sycan Marsh, a spot renowned for waterfowl and wildlife.

User Groups: Hikers, dogs, horses, and mountain bikes. The eight-mile stretch from Klamath Falls to the town of Olene is paved and wheelchair accessible.

Permits: Permits are not required. Parking and access are free.

Maps: For a free park brochure, call Oregon Parks and Recreation, 800/551-6949, or download a free map at www.oregonstateparks.org. For a topographic map, ask the USGS for Klamath Falls, Altamont, Bonanza, Sprague River East, Beatty, Bly, Sycan Marsh, and Ferguson Mountain.

Directions: To get to the Klamath Falls paved trailhead, begin on Main Street in downtown Klamath Falls and go east on South 5th Street/OR 39, continuing onto South 6th Street, for 1.6 miles. Turn right on Washburne Way for 0.4 mile, then left on Crosby Avenue 0.2 mile to the trailhead.

For the Switchbacks Trailhead, drive north of Olene 12.5 miles to Bliss Road and go north 12.3 miles to the trailhead in the National Forest, to the left on Road 22. For the Sprague River Trailhead, continue 4.1 miles on Bliss Road to the town of Sprague River, then go left on Main Street less than a mile to the trailhead. For trail's end, drive 44.3 miles east on Highway 140 to the town of Bly. Go right 1.1 miles on Edler Street, left 0.5 mile on Gerber Ranch Road, and left 0.8 mile toward the OC&E State Trail.

Contact: Oregon Parks and Recreation Department, 1115 Commercial Street Northeast, Salem, OR, 97301, 800/551-6949, www.oregonstateparks.org.

Index

E

F

G

H

IJK

L

www.moon.com

DESTINATIONS | ACTIVITIES | BLOGS | MAPS | BOOKS

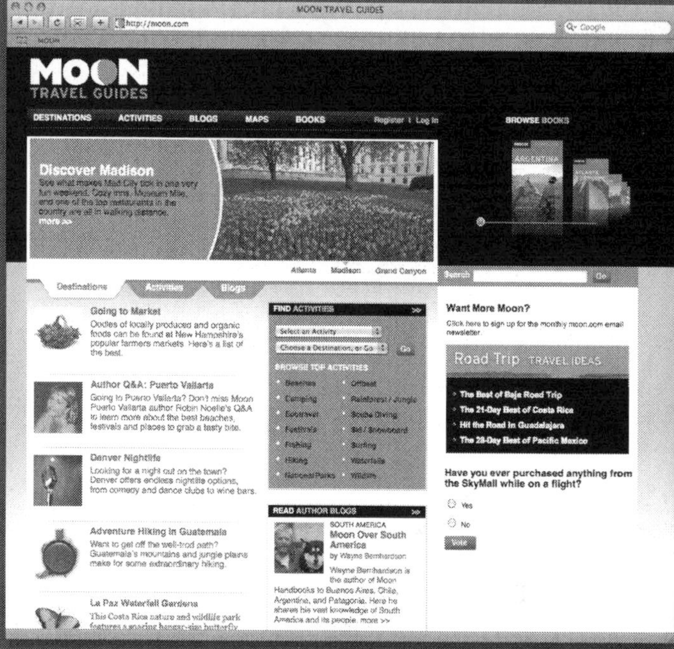

MOON.COM is ready to help plan your next trip! Filled with fresh trip ideas and strategies, author interviews, informative travel blogs, a detailed map library, and descriptions of all the Moon guidebooks, Moon.com is all you need to get out and explore the world—or even places in your own backyard. While at Moon.com, sign up for our monthly e-newsletter for updates on new releases, travel tips, and expert advice from our on-the-go Moon authors. As always, when you travel with Moon, expect an experience that is uncommon and truly unique.

MOON IS ON FACEBOOK—BECOME A FAN!

JOIN THE MOON PHOTO GROUP ON FLICKR

MOON OREGON'S SOUTHERN CASCADES CAMPING & HIKING

Avalon Travel
a member of the Perseus Books Group
1700 Fourth Street
Berkeley, CA 94710, USA
www.moon.com

Editors: Elizabeth Hollis Hansen, Sabrina Young
Series Manager: Sabrina Young
Senior Research Editor: Kathie Morgan
Research Editor: Glenn Mayeda
Copy Editor: Valerie Sellers Blanton
Graphics Coordinators: Elizabeth Jang, Domini Dragoone
Production Coordinators: Elizabeth Jang, Domini Dragoone
Cover Designer: Kathryn Osgood
Interior Designer: Darren Alessi
Map Editor: Mike Morgenfeld
Cartographers: Michelle Trame, Brice Ticen, Kat Bennett
Illustrations: Bob Race

ISBN-13: 978-1-59880-575-8

Front cover photo: Snow capped mountain reflects off a stream in the Oregon Cascades © Weldon Schloneger | Dreamstime.com
Title page photo: Trail marker in the Oregon Cascades © Joe Klune | Dreamstime.com

Printed in the United States of America

ABOUT THE AUTHORS

© JOHN BEATH

Tom Stienstra

For 30 years, Tom Stienstra's full-time job has been to capture and communicate the outdoor experience. Tom writes a weekly outdoors column that is distributed across America. He has won more than 100 national and regional writing awards, and has twice been named National Outdoors Writer of the Year. His television show, *The Great Outdoors,* is broadcast weekly on CBS/CW. His first edition of *Pacific Northwest Camping* was acclaimed by the *Portland Oregonian.*

Tom takes part in all facets of the outdoors, and as a pilot and airplane owner, can cover great distances quickly in the pursuit of adventure. He lives with his wife Stephani at their ranch in the "State of Jefferson," near the Oregon border.

You can contact Tom directly via his website at www.tomstienstra.com. His guidebooks include:

Moon Oregon Camping
Moon Washington Camping
Moon Pacific Northwest Camping
Moon West Coast RV Camping
Moon California Camping
Moon California Hiking (with Ann Marie Brown)
Moon California Fishing
Moon California Recreational Lakes & Rivers
California Wildlife
Moon Northern California Cabins & Cottages
Tom Stienstra's Bay Area Recreation

© ANDY BUDOR

Sean Patrick Hill

Sean Patrick Hill is a freelance writer, poet, and teacher who has spent many weekends and summers exploring the best of Oregon's mountains, deserts, and coastlines. Born and raised in upstate New York, Hill moved to Oregon after graduating from the University of Buffalo. He lived in Eugene, Bend, and then Portland, graduating with a masters in writing from Portland State University. For two summers he worked with the Oregon Youth Conservation Corps, leading teenage crews into the Cascade Mountains to do everything from maintaining trails to building bridges to counting frogs. Later, as an AmeriCorps volunteer, he organized tree plantings in local parks, clean-ups of riverside environments, and field trips into the wilderness for high school students.

Hill has written outdoor travel articles for *The Oregonian, The Source Weekly, Columbia Gorge Magazine,* and *Oregon Coast.* His poetry appears widely in online and print journals, and his first book of poems, *The Imagined Fields,* will be published this year.

Made in the USA
Lexington, KY
03 June 2011